MIDNIGHT RUGBY

Also by Stephen Jones

Endless Winter

MIDNIGHT RUGBY

Triumph and shambles
in the professional era

Stephen Jones

HEADLINE

First published in 2000
by HEADLINE BOOK PUBLISHING

10 9 8 7 6 5 4 3 2 1

British Library Cataloguing in Publication Data

Jones, Stephen, 1953–
Midnight rugby: triumph and shambles in the professional era
1. Rugby football 2. Professionalism in sports
I. Title
796.3'33

ISBN 0 7472 7230 1

Typeset by Avon Dataset Ltd, Bidford-on-Avon, Warks

Printed and bound in Great Britain by
Mackays of Chatham PLC, Chatham, Kent

HEADLINE BOOK PUBLISHING
A division of Hodder Headline
338 Euston Road
London NW1 3BH

www.headline.co.uk
www.hodderheadline.com

Contents

To Andrew, Rosanna and Duncan

*(No, Rosie. Of course I can't dedicate a book
to your guinea pigs)*

Acknowledgements

It is both an inevitable accident and a happy outcome of life on the sports writing circuit that your esteemed colleagues also become your close friends. Sincere thanks are due to three people in this joint category, and especially to Steve Bale, of the *Daily Express*. Even with his other commitments he found time to make a whole series of entirely indispensable suggestions and corrections at every stage of production. I incorporated them all. He also made other suggestions under the banner of his 'personal pedantry'. I incorporated those, too.

Nick Cain of the *Sunday Times* is the finest work colleague anyone could wish for; his good sense and rock-solid grasp of rugby and its trends were invaluable. David Walsh, also of the *Sunday Times*, helped in a different way. We were both going through the hellish book-writing process at the same time, David with his life story of Richard Dunwoody, so we were able to compare notes on progress. David, loyally, never made me feel bad by making any progress.

I would also like to thank Caroline North, my outstanding agent, for her guidance and friendship and for tearing herself away from the competing attractions of Barbara Windsor; John Griffiths, still rugby's No 1 statistician; Ian Marshall, Juliana 'Adolf' Lessa of Headline, and Monica McDonald for their patience and professionalism.

Finally, warm thanks for various important services rendered to Frankie 'Mr Rugby' Deges in Buenos Aires; Nicky Goodwin, the fine media manager at Worcester and also of the England women's teams; Mickey Steele-Bodger, of the Barbarians; Chris Thau of the Welsh Rugby Union for help with World Cup qualifying stories; Tony Hallett, former Commander, RN, for ensuring that I made no naval errors; Liz Jones and Phil Davies of Newport RFC; Paulo Ricci Bitti from Italy; John Inverdale of the BBC.

Also to Karen and my family for coping so well with me while I was 'away' with the book.

CHAPTER ONE

Wye

**Five years have past; five summers, with the length
Of five long winters.**

Fear not, the philistines among you, and I know there are a few of you who'd rather chat about sport over a curry than about fine literature like the rest of us. I won't be quoting William Wordsworth, English literary giant, too liberally. It'll be mostly people like Pat Lam, Samoan rugby giant, from 200 years later. I know that my school contemporary Stuart Barnes once wrote a rugby book carrying enough literary references to sink the *Bismarck*, but he was obviously paying attention in English lessons. And at least I didn't buzz off and suddenly become English, Barnesy . . .

Wordsworth wrote these lines upon his return, near the end of the 18th century, to a beautiful spot on the banks of the Wye near Tintern Abbey in my native Gwent. In the five years since he'd first sat there in contemplation, the memories and sensuousness of the scene had often sustained him, 'a worshipper of nature', in bad times and good, lifting his spirits to high planes. He said of his memories of the Wye Valley:

> But oft, in lonely rooms, and mid the din
> Of towns and cities, I have owed to them
> In hours of weariness, sensations sweet,
> Felt in the blood, and felt along the heart;
> And passing even into my purer mind,
> With tranquil restoration.

After five years he found it largely unchanged, still marvellous and serene, and if anything more vividly evocative. It gave him a profound sense of life's natural stability.

It is five years since rugby union went open – professional, in other words.

Five long winters. I too have been on high planes, usually travelling to the next international rugby match billed as the most important ever played (we always say that, till the next one a week later). Had any of today's international coaches visited Wordsworth's sylvan Wye, their only consideration would have been far removed from the contemplation of nature as a vehicle for healing and serenity: they would have wanted to raze it to create a training pitch, the new high altar of rugby.

I've also been in some lonely rooms over the past five years, trying to resist eating the chocolate the chambermaid has placed on my pillow, and to unravel the seventeen different electric leads and chargers and adapters without which the modern-day journalist cannot function. And briefly sitting down and wondering why I have lost, at least in some part, the vast enthusiasm and joy with which I used to contemplate my own vista – the soaring, exuberant, usually frustrating and yet spiritually uplifting vista of the world of rugby. At times it has seemed as if it's become just another game.

What I have never felt in these years is serenity. Wordsworth found the Wye unaltered five years on. The view in rugby is now profoundly different, wherever you look. Serenity? It's been a furious scramble. Stability? About as stable as living on the summit of a volcano emitting rather disturbing loud rumblings.

Why? To make rugby professional was a gigantic step, because amateurism was the rock on which rugby was built and so many people had insisted for so long that terrible fates would befall the game were that rock to be removed. I remember Peter Yarranton, a former Rugby Football Union president and a chrome-domed true-blue, pronouncing that rugby *was* amateurism, that rugby being amateur was a kind of truism, that if it wasn't, then it wasn't rugby – or anything. I remember that as he propounded his philosophy those of us in his audience grunted a low, communal and rather un-Wordsworthian 'Bollocks!' But his reverence was shared by many. In some eyes, amateurism was viewed as a shield to the outside world. Now, that shield is gone and the modern world attacks, as they see it, with its greed and drugs and violence and vicissitudes.

I haven't needed five years of contemplation to conclude that amateurism as a concept was inherently worthless, an elongated con trick and an excuse for people who had made their money elsewhere to hang on to privileges of rank in rugby officialdom. (Though there were, of course, millions of selfless amateur heroes too, at all admin levels.) I believe that amateurism also did the sport the grave disservice of conveying to the outside world an image of rugby as a cliquish, middle-class pastime, an image which stuck fast and yet was almost entirely erroneous. I was delighted to hear recently the author of the sublime 1960s book *The Art of Coarse Rugby* and former colleague Michael Green dismissing rugby's middle-class image with alacrity.

I believe that very little of rugby's greatness – and an awful lot of its paranoia and underachievement – was due to amateurism, and that discarding the worthless concept enabled the game to grow and flourish. I also believe that most of the problems in all our unquiet lives since amateurism was removed have been caused not by its loss but by the fact that it took so long to root out. It took rugby more than 125 years to realise that it had enslaved itself to a pointless dogma.

But if rugby survived the end of amateurism, then something has made it less appealing and more severe. If not, then why was it that when I asked twenty of my colleagues on England's recent rugby tour of South Africa – twenty good rugby men and true – if they were as in love with the sport and its surroundings as ever, not one gave an unequivocal yes? Twenty votes that the sport has at least in some ways declined.

Are we all just more tired? I do not, of course, expect a swelling collection of violins to accompany my contention that the commitment of time and anxiety in covering top rugby these days has probably trebled inside five years, and that some of my colleagues, probably myself included, look fifteen years older in five. Admittedly it could be true that much of rugby's magnificent old feeling survives outside our frantic circle.

Are we just getting older? Bruce Springsteen (still waiting for the call, Boss) used to sing in his youth about hiding on the backstreets and riding the mansions of glory on a suicide machine. I didn't go in for that riding mansions and suicide stuff a lot myself, but being youthful I knew what his underlying message was. Now he's older, too, and dedicates songs to 'your kids and my kids'. Wordsworth also warned that time passes and youthful exuberance fades.

> That time is past,
> And all its aching joys are now no more,
> And all its dizzy raptures. Not for this
> Faint I, nor mourn nor murmur, other gifts
> Have followed; for such loss, I would believe,
> Abundant recompense.

Recompense? Maybe. We do have a game that is bigger than ever. We have a sport which can stand square, can take the discredited true blues with their predictions of mayhem and calamity, look them in the eye and point them to, say, Pat Lam – as an individual but also, I am sure, as a representative of the modern-day rugby player. Lam's role in and around the glorious Heineken European Cup final in May 2000, the stupendous way in which he reveals the enduring goodness of rugby, was a boost to flagging morale. And not the only one.

And yes, there are still high old times, heroic afternoons of sporting wonder. When Scotland thrashed England in an emotional day of storms; when England thrashed South Africa on a cool highveld evening; when I sat on the wall and watched Newport, revived and roared on by 10,000 people, and saw the happiness in the faces of the old gang I'd watched with twenty years ago and who'd hardly seen them win since; the day my previously diffident eldest son took off with the ball and ran through the defence as his team won the Easter tournament; or any number of evenings, humble and uplifting at the same time, when I sat down over pizza or peri-peri or potatoes with no intent other than to feed myself and found rugby's conversation and warmth taking over, so much so that afterwards I'd forgotten how the food was and shyly thanked people for their company.

It is seven years since the publication of *Endless Winter*, my book dealing with the sport as it was driven along, almost out of control, by the pace of modern life and commercial realities. Eventually it was those realities, not any kind of coherent decision by the sport, that swept away the old doctrine. Five years is long enough in which to reach a conclusion, especially as the fifth of those years brought a World Cup, a recon-stituted Six Nations tournament, a gleaming new European competition – and yet also anxiety, financial loss, bickering, a decline in the number of people who play the game and, therefore, the suggestion that rugby's wonderful global family affair is in danger of ending. Rugby's essential universal spirit set it way, way apart. Does it still? There are times to suggest otherwise, times now when you come across sharks and greed, endless wrangling by officials, when you find that the sport out on the field has been changed to worship false gods, when the menu is dust.

In some parts, the Wye is still beautiful. In others, all you have to contemplate is the hissing tarmac of the M4, the new housing estates, the bustle and strife of the two Severn Bridges and their charging vehicles, and a vista changed so radically from the older, calmer days that the sense of loss is almost an agony.

And in rugby, too?

CHAPTER TWO

Chipping Norton

Dereliction and panic on the menu at the last supper of the
amateur code ♦ The middle-class sport that never was ♦
Mickey's new world Barbarians cash in

It's a strange thing, this. In the years (well, more than a hundred of
them) when baleful rugby officials were preaching the amateur doctrine
and insisting, on pain of lifetime excommunication, that it be maintained;
in all the years when they predicted dire calumny, greed, violence,
imbalance and (often) the end of rugby if professionalism ever arrived,
there was one question they never answered: Why?

Why did they see a causal chain between amateurism and the main-
tenance of the core values? Why did it *have* to be that dire things would
happen to the dear old game if it stopped being amateur? So many
sermons, so many threats from them. Yet they never explained precisely
the logic behind the idea that you and your team would behave badly if
you were paid to play. If you were a nice guy, liked your rugby, why
would that change? Your character is your character, surely. And there
were plenty of examples of activities where payment had not driven
things into the gutter. Golf, for one. Banking, mining, factory work,
farming . . .

The question that was never answered by rugby's grandees in all the
decades after decades that they worked so hard and blustered so long to
keep the code of amateurism.

Why?

In 1986 the International Rugby Board, governing body of the game,
marked their centenary with a congress held at Heythrop Hall in an
agreeable part of Oxfordshire near Chipping Norton. Delegates were
invited from many rugby-playing countries (even though the IRB then
comprised only the old eight nations which, largely, it had always
comprised). They flexed their jaw muscles – the muscles which, with the

exception of those in their right arms, they reckoned to use most in the week ahead – and sat down. (Right arms for drinking, readers. What did you think I meant?)

The drinking was well blended into the itinerary for the week. The agenda began briskly, with two days of sessions. It tailed off with a big lunch and trip to a centenary match at Cardiff on the Wednesday, and disintegrated entirely with a lunch in London on Thursday and dinner with the Lord Mayor of London in Mansion House, lunch in Twickenham's Rose Room on Friday, the same on Saturday, and then dinner in the Guildhall on the Saturday evening. In these new millennium days of professional play and dedicated abstinence, it is probably only the honourable callings of rugby officialdom and journalism that do not betray the game's finest tradition of gluttony and liquid intake, so I am told.

No prizes for guessing the lead item on the agenda back in the dim days of 1986. Not the promulgating of the game, not its technical advancement (why should the governing body of the sport concern itself with frippery?), but its amateurism. The pressure of the encroaching commercial world outside was already at fever pitch. It was just one year before the sport, bowing to the looming external realities and to its own bubbling good health, played the first World Cup.

Harry McKibbin, CBE, an Ulsterman who had followed the proud tradition of all Irish Rugby Union grandees in sitting on every single rugby committee and then forming a few more (it's known as the Tom Kiernan Principle these days), gave the keynote address on amateurism. He began with a plodding historical trawl, and then gave his estimation of what was at stake in a game which was by then making cruel demands on its amateur players. He pressed on grimly, claiming in his closing remarks that he had adopted 'a detached position' through most of his address although by its general tone he was clearly as detached on the subject of amateurism as a demagogue of Victoriana. At this time, you were still regarded as a long-haired left-winger if you suggested that transgressors of the amateur principle should not be flogged. Even if you were bald.

But McKibbin admitted that something must be done. Progress was essential. He wished rugby to travel the road between 'co-existence and economic reality'. The tension must have risen, beads of sweat must have appeared on the delegates' brows as he prepared to set out his proposed new agenda. He tried to lessen the shock by apologising in advance for upsetting any traditionalists; he stressed that he was only expressing a personal view.

Then he dropped the bombshell. One of the regulations of the game banned players from receiving money from 'certain types of sporting activity, generally referred to as *Superstars* competitions'. McKibbin put forward that this sub-section could be erased. Most of the other regulations he wished to be enforced with their usual severity. But he was suggesting, begging your pardon, delegates, and feel free to blackball me from the conference, rogue devil that I am, that rugby players who competed in the ludicrous *Superstars* programmes – those gems involving Joe Frazier sinking in the swimming race, Gerd Müller failing to complete the 100 metres because it was too long for him, John Dawes failing to clear the opening height in the hurdles and Kevin Keegan crashing on his bike – could keep the money. It was probably as much as £20 a time. Phew. The revolution is here.

Nonetheless, there was indeed fear in the air. We were already, in an era where the old, assured urbanity of the defence of amateurism in the IRB, the Rugby Football Union and other senior bodies had been replaced by an anxious stridency, which was in turn about to be replaced by notes of sheer panic and terror.

In all there were fifty-five countries represented in the congress. Don't forget that this was marking 100 years of existence of an organisation which, you might have thought, should have made its *raison d'être* the expansion of the game and the encouragement of all nations who wished to share in rugby's joys. This is what Albert Agar, a former RFU president and long-serving IRB delegate, said in his opening remarks: 'The problem comes down to this. We don't necessarily know much about the men who run the game in other countries throughout the world.'

It was a stunning reflection of 100 years of frightened indolence. Why frightened? Because the preservation of the principle of amateurism was allowed to override all other considerations in rugby, even those palpably for the good of the game. The IRB had never gone out and promoted the game, never donated just a few pounds from the vast income from packed international stadiums to buy a ball or two for the underprivileged, because to promote the game was, they felt, to establish potential rivals. They sought always to control the game, they wanted eight voters only, and eight votes they could control inside the portals of what was the most cosy and smug gentlemen's club in sport. To allow any other advancing countries a vote would have been to accept votes from those not steeped in the tradition – possibly even from people who did not grasp (the fallacy) that amateurism meant everything. Lepers.

The supreme unctuousness with which the delegates from the lesser-known rugby countries were treated then was a vivid example of the patrician and haughty way in which the grandees of the game always looked down on players as well as on supposedly fellow officials. At the congress it was revealed that the IRB were considering creating a new category of member – an associate member. Providing all the forms were filled in delegates could go back home and tell their rugby mates that they could now join the IRB. The IRB revealed that associate members could put up motions for changing laws, even regulations relating to amateurism. Marvellous.

'What you won't have,' a grave IRB man told his audience, 'are voting powers.' Delegates could raise motions, but would not be allowed to vote on them. But would the associates be able to attend meetings and speak from the floor? No, said Mr Grave: 'We are not expecting associate members to attend meetings, even as observers.' What the IRB were proposing was that the farmer could send in a motion to ask the turkeys to vote for Christmas. According to the official record of the congress, no delegate summoned the nerve to tell the IRB to stuff it.

It is a tribute to the IRB of today that they are presently planning to welcome their 100th country to membership and are fiercely promoting the game worldwide (although strictly speaking the old eight can still summon a majority, they are now fragmented, no longer a block-vote). But how big would rugby be now had they started this expansion when they should have, fifty or more years earlier? It is at least arguable that there would now be fifteen serious contenders for every World Cup instead of the usual three.

The sad truth about the IRB when they celebrated their centenary in 1986 was that it had taken them 100 years to reach it.

There is no doubt that had the IRB's appetite for amateurism ever waned in those years (it didn't, but if it had) the zeal of the Rugby Football Union at Twickenham would have gingered them up and had them guarding the borders with a passion. The RFU were always the game's core union; for many years, their insistence on being called *The* Rugby Football Union did not even infuriate people as it does today. For such a huge body, in 2000 their influence on the rest of the world is preposterously small. It is a matter of opinion whether they will ever regain their former status, although the current administration is showing better signs.

Why they lost it is surely *not* a matter of opinion. It happened because when the world was clearly slipping from under their feet, when the ground was collapsing beneath those things they held sacred, the RFU maintained a stance that was pig-headed and myopic, neither of which is a grievous offence, but also jealous, which is. And it set the RFU against the rest of the world, particularly the southern hemisphere, because there was a grasp of reality to be found elsewhere. There was a grasp of the fact that, while to maintain principles is very fine, there comes a time when to hold on doggedly to the principle demolishes that which the principle was established to protect. The King Union of the game became its King Canute and a desperate amount of grief was caused because of it, both within and outside the RFU.

From time immemorial till well into the 1990s, the great, rolling succession of RFU presidents who address their subjects at the annual general meeting every July would thank the deposed president and his charming wife and then launch into the expected diatribe. E. Watts Moses, president during 1949–50, thundered marvellously in his cancer-of-professionalism blast: 'We have in our keeping a game which meets the modern longing for adventure and comradeship, forms an imperishable link with our kinsmen and friends across the home seas, and also the distant oceans.' Bless him.

By 1968 something was arriving which many people believed to be another creeping cancer: coaching. It was mistrusted not as a practice in itself but because a drive towards improvement meant a drive towards . . . well, you've guessed it – begins with P. President Tom Berry, therefore, had a 'word of warning' at the 1968 AGM: 'It is imperative that a club coach should never undermine the authority of the captain.' He'd hate it today, when the authority of the coach makes that of the World War Two Axis dictators appear as some kind of benevolent democracy. In Berry's era a coach would be referred to as the less threatening 'adviser to the captain'.

There was a further major scare at that 1968 AGM. It was something that the Lions of that year returned with from South Africa. A new venereal disease? Demands to be paid? Condemnation of apartheid? None of these. It was a word. 'No one realised that the word "competition" which the Lions bought back with them from South Africa would make such a turning-point in rugby circles,' said a minuted speaker. Good God, not *that*. What had happened was that the Lions had yet again been beaten by a team honed in their domestic game in decent competitive events, and some mad fool in the beaten ranks had suggested that if they were ever going to win then maybe British rugby had better have some events as well instead of months and months of glorified friendlies in which the performance of clubs, national teams and individual players did not have to be maximised. Competition, however, was another P-word.

Perhaps the most truly frightening speech came from Dr T. A. Kemp. His presidential address was in 1971, just weeks after the end of the glorious British Lions tour of New Zealand during which the Lions had given British rugby the biggest fillip and the biggest upsurge in interest ever. They had done so because the brilliant coach Carwyn James had ended years of happy-go-lucky losing Lions tours with wonderful coaching and organisation which reaped an historic reward. Listen to Kemp just afterwards: 'The amateur ethos that [rugby] reflects is the most important concern that our coaches have to get over to their players. Unless we are prepared to sacrifice everything to the spirit of the game, sooner or later it will perish.' So coaches were not supposed to improve their teams so that they beat the All Blacks, nor work for the advancement of rugby on the field to make it a better game and a spectacle. They had to rant about amateurism. Surely that could be left to the ludicrous old buffers of the RFU?

That same meeting, meanwhile, 'condemned pornography as a social disease which had no place in our game, as we recognise the responsibility to youth and virile players'. Shame, that, as all the youths and virile players had to then chuck all their dodgy magazines into the dustbin. Amazingly, given Kemp's (fatuous) comments, rugby continues to this day. To be so far off the pace prewar was one thing. To hold these opinions when rugby's modern era was in full swing was nothing less than terrifying, and yet typical.

In 1981 John Kendall-Carpenter faced the annual meeting and delivered the usual true-blue blather. He also made a point about low crowds. 'I have a suspicion that the stagnation of the game as a spectacle since the late 1960s may have links with the falling off of gates,' he said. Novel theory, that. People don't like crap rugby. Who'd have thought it? Kendall-Carpenter actually chaired the committee which organised the 1987 World Cup, proving that some people can't bear to be out of the limelight even when a cherished principle is at stake, and proving it again with an horrendously badly-timed and badly-worded speech as the Kiwi captain David Kirk hung around waiting for Kendall-Carpenter to hand over the cup itself.

The problem was that the RFU themselves spent well over 100 years utterly failing to effect even a basic improvement in the English rugby scene – not encouraging coaching (which is, after all, simply the betterment of a rugby team), not encouraging the game to spread, not encouraging genuine competition – and all because they felt inherently that to improve the game, to install an ethos of achievement instead of a culture of what might be called honest and sweated under-achievement, would shake amateurism. The whole scene was stultified by the worship of one item.

For me, there is no causal chain proven here, never even hinted at. But all these things were seen as the advance guard of a new and horrible era. Proper replacements for injured players; proper television deals; allowing out-of-season tours; refusing to allow players who had gone to rugby league to play any active part in union clubs bar paying their subscription; asking the ref to actually pull his ruddy finger out instead of smarmingly thanking him for giving up his afternoon (short-sighted old goat though he was); organising a World Cup, even organising an English Cup; allowing players to write books and take the money once they had retired, without being excommunicated . . . All these things potentially meant the end of that which they held most dear. So rugby was always held back, until well into the 1990s. It is true that the new freedoms to aspire and maximise have led rugby far in the opposite direction on several fronts. But sudden explosions are always impossible to control. The other home unions were as bad, but never so pious. It was just that the RFU was in the best position to lead a move towards change, and this they never did.

It led to a sub-culture of snobbish stories with which anyone in any era could recall his glorious part in upholding amateurism. If I hear one more story about good old Catchy or good old Wakers or good old someone else having a penny docked from their expenses-claim of three shillings and then re-submitting it with a claim of one penny to go to the loo on the train; or the one about someone being selected for Scotland after the war, and after the six-year absence of international rugby, asking for his jersey and being told he'd been given one for the last match. The likes of Cliff Morgan, the kind of man who makes rugby life worth living, would tell of catching the bus down to a Welsh international, but that was because he couldn't afford a more grandiose means, not because he was making a smug point from a position of riches. Fill in your own story-bore; there are enough of them. I repeat: they spent ages telling successive generations what was good for them but without ever explaining why, linking doom with professionalism without evidence. The RFU's history as the major governing body of world rugby is, therefore, the history of a body which failed rugby. Utterly.

The retreat from the absolute was also a sorry mess. Harry McKibbin may have set the ball rolling with his show-stopping suggestion that you could keep your cheque from *Superstars*. Thus emboldened, at that same IRB congress he suggested that players might even keep proceeds for books they had written. 'Writing a book for publication entails a skill and discipline well beyond the ability of most people,' he told the delegates. Obviously true. But what of the riches beckoning author/ players? They could keep the money, Harry suggested, if they had 'irrevocably and publicly announced their intention to retire from the game . . . with safeguards against disclosing any privileged information obtained through their connections in the game, or which might tend to bring the game into disrepute'. In other words, ask them to sell to a publisher a book in which they could say nothing juicy or interesting whatsoever. (Not that it's ever stopped some publishers, to be fair.)

However, consider the contortions which the IRB and others have always had to perform. One of the supreme ironies of the Chipping Norton conference in 1986 is that at the exact moments when the delegates were jaw-jawing a group of All Blacks, led by Andy Haden (who was in Britain playing in the IRB centenary celebration matches), were just finalising their plans to make a rebel tour of South Africa. Indeed, it would start almost as soon as the congress broke up and, by the testimony in later years of everyone involved, brought huge financial rewards for the touring rebels.

It is utterly inconceivable that the tour's recruiting and other arrangements could have been concluded without the active connivance of at least some of the South African delegation who attended the conference, listened so politely and without demur to the hard line on amateurism. Dr Danie Craven, the South African president, declared that he could never support a rebel tour, something not sanctioned by the IRB and which violated all the precepts of his brother union, the NZRU. A few days later Craven sat happily in the stand as his beloved Springboks played the Cavaliers.

At last. After all the unproven accusations of dodgy deals, here was the most flagrant violation of behavioural norms and the precious amateurism. Surely this was the day the keepers of rugby's conscience had prayed for. What happened? What swingeing action was taken? Nothing. Having raped the rugby world's ideals, South Africa promised not to do it again. Faithfully.

A year later, a rebel South Seas Barbarians team played South Africa. The tourists even refused to play one match until the money was raised, instead sitting in the dressing room in sulky mood. South Africa had been warned once. They had again abused the sacred principle. They were again let off scot-free. They did ban for life from rugby Arthur Jennings, manager of the South Seas team. Jennings was a liability but the idea that he could have arranged a tour by himself was beneath contempt. It was easily the most unhappy and pathetic episode in IRB history. Naturally, no one on the IRB would ever condemn players for touring a country ruled by an apartheid regime. But the supreme cowardice the IRB showed in not expelling South Africa brutally exposed most of the rhetoric on amateurism as a complete sham. As they twisted this way and that, what explanation did the IRB come up with to justify themselves? That if South Africa were expelled on the grounds that they had organised rebel tours, they would become a loose cannon and organise rebel tours. It was all revolting and, in some ways, grimly hilarious.

But if these incidents marked a retreat then it has to be said that the remainder of the surrender was equally disastrous. In 1990 the notorious bylaw 4, 3, 2 was passed, which enabled players to cash in on ancillary activities provided that they were not 'rugby-related'. The RFU then declared almost every activity rugby-related – even banned, disgracefully, an advertisement from appearing in a Twickenham match programme, showing players dressed in Timberland gear, not rugby jerseys, and fulfilling all the criteria. They said it was rugby-related because it was in a rugby programme. Even the Scottish Rugby Union allowed the advertisement to run in their programme.

Brian Moore, the England hooker, at this stage engaged in a pitched battle with the RFU, remembers the time with a shudder. It was obvious that full-scale betrayals all of the amateur rules were being perpetrated all over the world; it was also obvious that the RFU were refusing to bow to reality and were being spiteful in their refusal. 'They preferred to believe that all the abuses were not happening and they never admitted that they were retreating all the time because they were forced to by the speed of outside events and the outside world. They fooled themselves into believing that there was still something left that was worth defending.'

I wonder if their faithful defenders ever stopped to consider how they just might have bought themselves time at least to organise an orderly retreat instead of causing shambolic flight. Here are a few humble suggestions. In almost every one of the RFU AGMs from the 1950s onwards someone brought up the subject of the increasing demands made on players. These demands grew and grew, pulverising the chances of many to hold down a decent job in which they could advance and thus keep a family life together. Every year rugby admin said that commitments really must be cut down. Given a little more free time, the players may just have been more amenable. Those demands were never, ever cut. Commitments were loaded on by the lorryful.

The RFU used to hold media briefings in which technical administrator Don Rutherford would announce that players not meeting fitness standards would be 'ruthlessly eliminated' from the England squad. He'd then hand over to RFU secretary Dudley Wood for a ringing denunciation of amateurism.

What if the RFU and other unions had met the players head on? For years, committee members were given four times more tickets for internationals than were the players. Still a preposterous thought. Why not even up the score, ensure that players were properly looked after, were able to distribute more tickets to their friends rather than see themselves as some adjunct to the business-entertaining lives of the massed ranks of the RFU committee?

Why not, when loopholes did allow a certain amount of commercial activity for players, work to let them maximise it? Instead, at the very point in history when good relations between players and officials were vital, the officials utterly lost the ear and sympathy of players all around the world. For God's sake, at least if you give a player a professional contract he has to do as you say. By the 1980s and 1990s no one was listening to what Will Carling was to describe inelegantly as the 'old farts'. Inelegant, but inaccurate?

Anger must be directed at the RFU because they were, for so long, the prime force. It is important to remember that the IRB was only formed in the first place because the Irish, Scottish and Welsh unions were cheesed off that England called all the shots. The IRB at least gave them a formal vote. For years, until long after the war, the Down Under unions were known as the dominions unions, adjuncts.

But, as well as being hard on the RFU, it is important to be clear about the contribution of the Scottish Rugby Union, the Irish Rugby Union and the Welsh Rugby Union to the process of modernising rugby in the post-war years. It is also easy to be clear about their contribution. They never made one. The Welsh Rugby Union briefly gave a technical lead in the late 1960s and 1970s, due to the efforts of Ray Williams, a visionary coaching organiser whose methods were aped by Australia. Apart from that, the WRU have been as tame and ineffective as a pet mouse on amateurism and other issues, and still are. The Irish Rugby Union, presiding over perhaps the one place on rugby's planet where the description of rugby as a middle-class sport does have a ring of authenticity, have been the slowest-moving and most smug union, and still are. The Scottish Rugby Union, in many ways, were always the head prefect to the RFU's Quelch-like amateur lessons.

Take what I then and still find a staggering contribution to the debate on amateurism from Bill Hogg, formerly chief executive of the SRU. He made it in a long article in a programme for a Scotland–Wales match. It typifies for me, in two laborious, self-satisfied and myopic pages, all the failings and utter lack of foresight of rugby's rulers, all their blind allegiance to a dogma which was found to be a waste of time.

'The position of the SRU committee is that it strongly feels that the game must remain amateur,' he wrote. He then went on (as they all did, the predictable old dears) to emphasise the good things in rugby – no drugs, happy social scene, community spirit, great amateur game, agreeable bonhomie. As ever, he gave no evidence whatsoever that these good things sprang from amateurism. He only guessed that they did.

He went on to predict various calamities which would befall the game and he was to be proved wrong on every prediction. He did not seem to see the irony that there was no more or less justification for him to be paid than the players. If he was to carry through his views on not paying players, then there was not the slightest reason to pay the chief executive, either, so why not stop his own salary and take a another job alongside his rugby activities, as all the players had to do?

He made an awful lot of the kudos which, he thought, accrued to employers who have international rugby players in their ranks. He forgot that the kudos meant nothing to most employers in a hard-hitting commercial age and that even if the old family-of-rugby theory meant a damn in the post-war years, then it had ceased to mean anything in the latter part of the century. By then, players were normally treated just the same as normal employees; they had to play a full part or have money docked or move on. Or be sacked.

And when did Hogg contribute his lamentable article? In the 1960s, when the game was gradually flexing its muscles? In the 1970s, when two winning Lions tours boosted the sport and changed the stakes? In the 1980s, when the World Cup and rampaging commercialism arrived? No, he wrote it for a match which took place on 4 March 1995, just before a massive World Cup, at the very time when there was nothing left for amateurism to cling to. He wrote it less than six months before the game was thrown open.

And yet, far from doing what he should have been doing, and planning for the arrival of the inevitable (or resigning if the thought offended his principles), he did not even appear to be well-informed or savvy enough to believe that anything had changed in 100 years. On he went, paragraph after paragraph, beautifully illustrating the core failure of generations of rugby's leaders.

Hogg is still with the SRU. I wonder if he, or other officers of the Union, ever ask themselves, if they had planned for a pro game, whether they would have avoided the shambles of the past five years when they have come close to killing their domestic rugby and have lost, perhaps for all time, their paying public with the Super District shambles. I wonder.

The humiliation was complete in 1995. Ever since the Heythrop conference, the true blues had been looking for a bolt-hole, somewhere they could retreat, draw breath and hide from encroaching reality. But every time they retreated and dug a defensive trench they found that the enemy had already passed their position and moved on. IRB chairman Vernon Pugh was sharp enough to realise that there was nowhere left to run, and he shoved the 1995 IRB meeting in Paris bodily towards accepting the inevitable.

An open game, there and then, on a Parisian pavement. The Tri-Nations agreement with Rupert Murdoch was already signed. The game was growing massively in both size and power. The players were being ravaged by the competing demands of sport and work. There was no other decision to make. Following the vote one true-blue newspaper reported the reservations of some unreconstructed RFU grandees that the vote in the IRB meeting had not been properly conducted. After over a century of taking refuge in the procedural labyrinth of its hidebound committee structure, old habits were hard to break.

Now, the moment of truth. Brian Moore, like myself, had always been fascinated to see how many of the fifty-odd people on the RFU committee, the men who sat on their principle for so long, would resign now that what they saw as the core of rugby had been removed against their will. 'I have kept a close watch on the list of resignations; to date, there have been none,' Moore reiterated after the burial of the old doctrine.

I myself may have missed some. People may have drifted away without making a fuss in the media. Sorry if I've overlooked anyone. But apart from hearing that Leicester's secretary, John Allen, had resigned on principle (happily, he soon came back to the club), I can't remember one resignation either on or outside the RFU because the game has gone professional. Some who had been ferocious in their denunciations and in their warnings of doom carried on and even became presidents. It seems a shoddy and embarrassing end to what they all portrayed as a matter of high principle.

They have a lot to answer for in rugby's image, too. From time immemorial rugby's rulers have been drawn from the upper middle classes, from high ranks of the services, and their spokesmen for rugby's entire first century were almost always Englishmen of a kind of hectoring gravitas. The driving forces were the two great universities. I suppose that it is no wonder that rugby soon gained its image as an exclusive, almost excluding, amusement for toffs and semi-toffs.

This image was resoundingly reinforced when the Northern Union broke off to form rugby league, as the working classes who wished to be reimbursed for the time they spent away from their jobs split from representatives of the class who didn't much need to have their money made up because they had enough anyway. As justification for rugby's image, this did not work either. Some of the fiercest defenders of amateurism were petty bureaucrat beaky-nosed Welsh working-class rugby club secretaries, poring over documents and investigating alleged transgressions with all the zeal of South Africa's police testing the temperature of bed-sheets in the days of the Immorality Act.

I think that rugby's image has always been complete baloney, something for hard-up sporting historians to be unctuous about. I've never managed to plough all the way through any of the many treatises and scholarly works about rugby's so-called middle-class ethos and all the blah-blah and snobbery and inverted snobbery. It is not only that I come from a background where social class in rugby means nothing. It is that I've seen a few places in rugby, experienced a few cultures, and found all the exhaustive and earnest works painting rugby into a class corner not only tiresome but profoundly mistaken.

The BBC produced a throughly decent series called *The Union Game* last year; along with it, a historian called Dai Smith (he's Welsh, you know) produced an enormous tract reinforcing history's stereotypes of rugby. But not the truth of rugby, then or now. 'The English middle class found in rugby football a sport that gave them a collective definition,' Smith spouts. 'To challenge this was to lose the deeper purpose of the game.' Piffle. If the only way in which the English middle class could think of to define themselves was through rugby then what a sorry lot they must always have been anyway. And next time I stand in The Shed at Gloucester I'll congratulate them all for being middle-class. History's perspective is frozen, deaf to reality, complacent. Wrong.

Rugby's problem was that its movers and shakers were always of a kind, its officialdom and spokesmen were drawn from (trapped in) a certain social class and calling. I agree with Michael Green, whose *The Art of Coarse Rugby* was a social history as well as a revelatory funny book, that rugby has never been remotely so class-bound as its image. It is just that whenever the general public heard someone spouting about rugby, sermonising on amateurism, he was always from some character of the rank of field-marshal or above, without common touch or sympathy

17

for his audience and representing a class, not a sport.

The real rugby people, the people who played it and loved it, were always elsewhere. In fact, they were everywhere, unrestricted. High-calling servicemen; Tigers' family outings to Welford Road; unemployed steelworkers at Stradey Park; woodsmen in the Forest of Dean; Cornish-men at Hell Fire Corner; raging Tucumános in Tucumán, pullovered punters shivering in Carisbrook, Dunedin, or Hawick, Scottish Borders, or Thomond Park, Limerick; Stade Toulousain striped hordes in the South of France; Northampton Saints roaring on their cosmopolitan men; millionaires sprung from working-class families, investing in rugby clubs; redneck farmers in Potchefstroom . . . What do labels of class mean to them, any of them? What have they ever meant?

The labels were applied by others and did not represent rugby, only small parts of it – those who were in charge of it. The reality was always far different. Now they've gone, even the image is crumbling. Good riddance.

The final president of the official amateur era had been Ian Beer, former headmaster of Harrow. Beer had made an England B team cringe on a New Zealand tour by insisting on running out with them on tour training sessions, then delighted them by pulling a fetlock and collapsing while running in a grid. 'The most hilarious thing I've seen in rugby', said a colleague who was present. He was the founder of the charity SPIRE which helped players who had suffered spinal injuries, and therefore quite properly illuminated rugby's secret dark area. His presidential address to the 1993 AGM was one of some force. He mentioned alleged abuses of amateurism in South Africa (well, he didn't mention them all; he'd have been there all week). He promised that he was going to tackle the South African RFU's president, Louis Luyt, about it all, and also demand that the IRB stop shilly-shallying. If they were going pro, get on with it. If not, police things properly. His promise to buttonhole Luyt reminded me forcibly of the nerdish figure in *Fawlty Towers* who beards Basil Fawlty about the hotel's insultingly bad service: 'Look, you're getting my dander up, you grotty little man.'

At that time Beer seemed to have realised that the game had gone, and was going to go pro. He obviously never realised that there could be a life afterwards. 'I can see an amateur team of England players playing an amateur team of Welsh players before the professionals take the pitch, and I know which game I would prefer to watch.' Me too, Ian. Me too. Want a bet on which would draw the bigger crowd? But, to be fair, he did try to mount a case in his presidential speech, tried bravely to explain *why* it would all assume the shape of a pear. It was the first time in my experience that somone had actually tried to take the debate beyond a blind 'no'. Off he went, sketching scenarios under professional rugby.

'We lose players who do not want to be paid employees; the professionals go – doctors, teachers, serving officers, barristers.' I don't think he was intending to emphasise the hoary old rubbish about a better class of chap, so in essence he was correct. Players since 1995 have had to hack out part-time jobs or forsake the professions altogether.

It is absolutely amazing how few have actually declared their rugby careers over, though. I felt that around one in four top players would leave the game. It is more like one in a thousand, because they want to be paid to play and maximise the talents they can exhibit only in their younger years. Rugby has also become more egalitarian. Less blues, more bruise. Fine, inevitable.

Former RFU secretary Dudley Wood used to hold up as an ideal the fine full-back Dr Jon Webb. Here was a man who could hold down a senior professional job and also give time to play top rugby. However, Webb was actually the example who disproved Wood's theory that the best life was to earn a living and play rugby as a relaxation. When Webb was eventually forced to retire under the weight of swingeing demands, he looked thin as a rake and white as a sheet. We do not as yet know whether the first generation of rugby professionals will end up battered and drifting and jobless in their mid-thirties, because the first generation is still active.

Perhaps Beer, if he is still counting, will make something of the announcement from the Saracens and England A hooker George Chuter in July 2000 that he was giving up the game in England and moving to Australia. 'I didn't want to play on . . . when my heart was not in it,' he said. A casualty in the professional era, but nowhere does Chuter declare that he was a casualty *of* the professional era. People have always chucked it in, had a bellyful.

Beer's next prediction was that 'players who may be on a bonus to win and devoid of the spirit of the game may resort to violence'. Wrong. What happened when money arrived was that players retained their respect for each other but decided that they would now stop throwing the game away by punching and kicking and conceding penalties. Case utterly disproved, thrown out of court.

Next. 'In this scenario, players move based on inducements of cash and you lose loyalty to clubs. Matches are then won and lost according to the bank balance.' It is worth nothing that in any form of business riches usually mean power and influence. That said, case partly proved. It is probably my chief regret concerning the new era that rugby clubs are now ranked, at least in part, according to their access to financial benefactors rather than in terms of the qualities that make a real rugby club – warmth, a community base, kids raised in rugby. Having a heartbeat.

Orrell were always one of my favourite clubs, a wonderful institution with few natural resources but who fought their way up through the leagues on heart and soul and grit and twice came within an ace of winning Division One. They used to play for their jerseys. Now they are merely in the middle of Division Two and, for my money, sadly missed at the top. It should also be pointed out that more than one Orrell player from the club's great days sees the decline as not only a by-product of the professional era and lack of a sugar-daddy but also of some near-sighted officialdom. It is germane to point out as well that easily the best new trend in the second half of season 1999–2000 was that of the moneyed clubs returning to their own communities and becoming less austere, more of a social hub again. Yet I cannot say that Beer's words were not perceptive.

Beer's final warning on what he saw as the eve of destruction was that professionalism would 'undermine voluntary committee-men and the type of person who will administrate the game-changes'. Given the history of the RFU and other bodies, only the heartless would suggest that there is a lot to be said for it. My impression is that this case is not yet proven, though there is circumstantial evidence in Beer's favour. Committees and great old secretary-doyens have indeed been replaced by chief executives and decision-makers (the first crop in European rugby were not remotely of the required standard, incidentally). But many of the great amateur admin heroes plough on, some because they like their little bit of glory, some because they dole out the international tickets, and far more because they love the game, because their own part of it is still recognisable, so why be jealous of people in other parts? Let's give Beer a retrospective star for 1993, though, for at least taking on the debate. Not everything he felt would be lost has been lost. Not by any stretch.

I'll tell you something that was lost. Great men. Yes, some of that lot who'd defended the indefensible. Great men. If you have grown up with something ingrained in your soul – be it communism, socialism, fascism, amateurism – it is always the Devil's own job to shake yourself free of it, even if you want to. There is no doubt that a large number of committee-men in England, and also in Wales, Ireland and Scotland, fought because they could see their free foreign trips and their business-entertainment tickets fading away. They're still around, feasting away. But others, many of whom had given a lifetime of service at lower levels before arriving at Twickers, made the stand for genuine reasons.

Some of them are among the best people I've met in rugby, some of the most gracious, engaging, most frightening when taking me to task. During a post-international dinner in Wales some years ago the Wales captain, Paul Thorburn, understandably goaded by a crass headline one of our dear sub-editors had stuck on an article I had written, asked me to leave the room because he considered me to be 'the scum of the earth'. It was my Warholian fifteen minutes of fame. My colleagues took delight in pointing out to anyone who would listen that as I was still eating my sweet, and as I was one of the leading trenchermen, I was unlikely to go.

But, one after another, unorchestrated as far as I know, four former RFU presidents came up and shook my hand. I had attacked at least three of them in the paper over the years, from pillar to post. They expressed the opinion that it was not right for a guest at any table to be abused, and that had the same thing happened at an RFU dinner they would have taken action. The whole incident rather washed over me, but I was tickled by their support and more so by Dudley Wood, who came over when the last of the presidents had moved away. 'It's bad enough being insulted by the Welsh captain but now you've been supported by the RFU presidents,' he said. 'You must feel terrible.'

Wood may have been the bane of the players. He was also easily the most inspired rugby official there has ever been. He puts to shame some of the pettiness and shallowness of top officials around the world. He had an unsurpassed, blissful facility for marketing the game and for communicating with its media and public. He was and is far too clever not to have known the way the wind was blowing years ago. Though it would not be breaking private confidence, I hope, to say that Wood believes a great deal of rugby's goodness departed with professionalism.

I would argue that some of the goodness has gone but that professionalism was inevitable; that some goodness remains and that that which was lost may not have been lost purely because of the transition. It was a sad thing that Wood was a die-hard amateur, because it meant that he left the sport just when it had urgent need of his talents, his sharpness and his humour. It would not have taken Dudley Wood five years to thrash out a structure for pro rugby, always providing his heart was in it. He was also an unmerciful pricker of petty pomposity. One media briefing at Twickenham was attended by none other than Sir Peter Yarranton, then president of the RFU and a major figure on the Sports Council. Sir Peter had just attended a match during which he'd sat next to Prince Edward. 'Sir Peter's asked me to tell you that Edward is one of the nicest princes he's ever sat beside,' Wood said. I can think of drastically few people who are regarded with such reverence by the media corps.

Happily, others did not live or die on the basis of whether or not amateurism stayed. The RFU have had some fine presidents since its death. Peter Trunkfield was president for season 1998–99, and told me that in that time, in the cause of promoting the game and trying to spread a message of reconciliation from the RFU, he had attended a staggering 350 functions, usually as the guest speaker. Trunkfield is a pillar of Marlow Rugby Club, of rugby officialdom at all levels in Buckinghamshire and elsewhere. He is also one of the most popular liaison officers in history, having cared for umpteen incoming tour-parties. He may have endured a sticky term of office with its various disputes, but he proved, perhaps even to himself, that it was no time to hark back, just to make the best of what was ahead and to rediscover some old bonds into the bargain. Long may your bonds hold, Trunkers.

The first speech at the Congress in 1986 was given by Mickey Steele-Bodger. If there was ever a name to put up the backs of those who saw rugby as sport dominated by the English middle classes, then it is probably that of the hyphenated Bodger. If ever there was a background (Rugby School, Cambridge University, long-time president of the Barbarians) to have the same effect, then it is his. He even followed other RFU presidents by having a delightful wife (Muff) . . . apparently named after leaders of sixties rock bands, joining Elvis (Burgess) and Roxane (Simpson). During a long spell on the IRB he was often seen as the chief of the amateurism police. He is reputed to have said, on encountering Andy Haden after one of Haden's numerous escapes from charges that he had accepted money: 'I'll get you one day, Haden.' The epitome of a discredited era?

Not entirely. He can be infuriating, but this is arguably rugby's most rumbustious character. It is true that you will have had to move in exalted committee circles – or, like me, on their outer limits – to have caught him in full flow; and he has been, and still is, a pain in the nether regions when it comes to certain issues. Nonetheless he is a delightfully challenging, warm and entertaining man. He has also been a marvellous man of rugby – a top-class player with Edinburgh University, Cambridge University, Harlequins, Moseley, Barbarians and England; an IRB grandee; an RFU president; an England selector; and a member of hordes of other high committees. He was a practising vet, making him the only man who could preserve amateurism and doctor a tomcat at the same time.

He was always a defender of amateurism, and the defence rang authentically in his hands (although it wobbled just a fraction when my colleague Nick Cain found the Barbarians treasurer's notebook lying around at a sevens tournament in Portugal one year). Yet it struck me that he put the game and his legion of friends above dogma. Maybe he did, maybe he didn't; whatever, he has been in rugby for years and still appears to be going strong.

In season 1999–2000 he bravely decided to renovate his beloved Barbarians. The great old team had fallen into near-disuse with its old Easter tour gone (the Easter Tuesday Newport–Barbarians match was the shining light of the season of my youth). The traditional Christmas holiday fixture with Leicester, for which tickets were once gold-dust, had gone; other fixtures from the grand old amateur Barbarian days had become – whisper it gently – devalued.

I could no longer see why, in this day and age, when home-followers want their teams to train up properly and bloody well beat the major incoming touring sides, tours should end with a fixture against a team like the Barbarians – who made a point of not preparing well enough and also a point of choosing an uncapped player. It was a tradition with an absolutely magnificent past but not, I feel, a future.

Mickey never wavered. At the end of the season, with the help of Scottish Amicable, the Barbarians assembled an absolutely splendid squad of players, including Jonah Lomu, Zinzan Brooke, Lawrence Dallaglio, Neil Jenkins, Thomas Castaignède, Joeli Vidiri, Os du Randt and a host of other giants. With a keen eye on current trends they also invited the great Fijian centre Viliame Satala. Anything more removed from the traditional pat-a-cake festival matches was difficult to imagine and the Barbarians, playing with fire, beat Ireland (31–30 with five Irishmen taken off injured); Scotland by 45–42; and then absolutely devastated Leicester, the Allied Dunbar champions, by 85–10 at Twickenham and, festival day or not, played brilliantly. More than 100,000 people saw the games, which were richly enjoyable and instructive and hard-fought. There was hardly a Barbarians player who did not say out loud and in public that he found the experience of mixing with peers at the top of rugby a wondrous experience.

Mickey would say that the Barbarians magic had pulled through again. Those of a more realistic, perhaps even cynical, bent would say that these days there is no way a massive raft of the game's superstars would drain themselves even further and put themselves under even more severe risk of injury (most had major tours and matches coming up) unless they were splendidly well paid. Mickey claimed that they came unpaid but spoke, a little vaguely, of them having commercial opportunities once they arrived. I did not have the heart to investigate. If someone bunged the lads by the back door then good luck to them because we saw great rugby – I hope the bung resurfaces every year, Barbarians ethos or not.

Steele-Bodger must grasp that even the Barbarians are dragged along with the times. In the modern game, you have to fight for your place, not have it handed down to you. Yes, there were Satala and Os du Randt and Waisale Serevi and Zinzan Brooke and Jonah and the others happy enough to wear the jersey and count their proceeds. But I doubt they all sat around and bawled the Baa-Baas song. 'It's the way we have in the Baa-Baas, and a jolly good way too.' I don't think it would be appropriate for these modern-day denizens to raise their voices for the line: 'For the rugby game we do not train but we play it with a will.' Sing up, Os!

How does Steele-Bodger view it all now that the era he knew and loved and fought for is over? 'The game has changed greatly and for the players, it's lucky for them to get the money. But unless they are careful they will be asked to play too often.' Sorry, but that was the truth of the amateur era too. 'I think the spirit of the game is still alive, but people are being pulled in many different ways. One example is that fixture lists are being issued so close to the start of every season.

'Some of the fears of the professional game have been justified. It was always a hard game but it is much more physical now and you cannot avoid thinking that many players will not be playing top-class rugby into their thirties. Lawrence Dallaglio had forty games last seasons yet he was talking to Australian players who had twenty-five.

'And do the players have Saturday nights like we had? I just wonder if they are having as much fun as we did. At least they come on time. In the old days, if you set a time for training they'd come along within half an hour of the appointed time. Now, they are used to reacting and they will all be there on time.'

The great man's ploughing on. He doesn't like everything, by any means. He's worried about his Barbarians. He thinks the players might burn out. But he isn't talking end of the world. He isn't saying that the old game's gone to pot. I'm sure the players don't have so much fun as did Mickey's generation. These days, they're a funny old lot, Mickey. They measure their enjoyment in different ways. They have a drink some Saturdays, some of them. Other days, probably not. Rumbustious they are not, like you, rampaging around berating people with a badly hidden twinkle in your eye, revelling in some friendship you've just resumed precisely where you left off two minutes or thirty years ago. They're dedicated and proud blokes good enough that you'd have them in the Baa-Baas without staining the club's reputation. They're fine, just different.

You fought for amateurism for a long time, but it seems you've accepted that rugby is bigger than a doomed-principle-becoming-dogma. Rugby has had magnificent characters in all its eras, and it would have been disastrous if they had all left in a rush. Significantly, you also feel that the goodness of the game is still with us. That's certainly good enough for me, Mickey.

Rugby was the last great amateur sport to succumb, the last to find the key to unlock the door to its own future. Back at the start of season 1999–2000 there were still some wounded trying to recover, still various shambles to be sorted and still many questions to answer. There were, quite obviously, aspects of the game that had changed and not for the better. Even people who knew that professional rugby was inevitable were not substantially happy, were unsure whether or not to blame all these things on the fact that a small percentage of players, the best ones, now get paid for doing it.

As I set off to investigate, the background was that in so many ways rugby had been badly served by its leaders, who spent such a nonsensical amount of time trying to protect their first principle that they neglected the progress of the game itself. It was hard for rugby to realise, quite suddenly, that it had wasted so much of its 100 years and more of existence and was badly under-developed. Amateurism cost rugby catastrophically dear. What a waste.

CHAPTER THREE

Isle of Man

Wrong men at the wrong time – the disaster of the advent of professionalism in England ♦ Cliff Brittle's columns of pain ♦ The screaming journey

Here's the southern hemisphere approach to sorting out a format for top rugby for a professional season. Get a tiny group of power-brokers together. Serve coffee. Sort it. Leave. Here's the northern approach. Flap around helplessly for five years in a cesspool of ill-feeling, self-aggrandisement, self-interest and incompetence, wasting priceless opportunities. And still fail.

The three Big South sorters met at a corner table of the Gazebo bar in the Sandton Sun hotel, in Johannesburg's northern suburbs, in 1995. (I recently pointed out the very table to some colleagues on a subsequent visit.) They were Louis Luyt, the heavy-jowled then president of the South African Rugby Football Union, Richie Guy of New Zealand, whose sharp-suited and rather slight frame belied his past as an All Black prop, and Leo Williams of Australia, whose wider frame did not belie his status as a leading rugby union official. It was just a few days before that year's Rugby World Cup final at Ellis Park and the sport remained electrified by the semi-final in which a New Zealand team, inspired by the unstoppable Jonah Lomu, had smashed England's aspirations to smithereens.

The three presidents already had in their pockets an agreement, its ink still running, under which Rupert Murdoch's News Corporation would give them $555 million for the rights to televise major southern hemisphere rugby for ten years. A few days earlier Murdoch had apparently watched the semi-final on television, marvelled at the thundering Lomu. 'This is amazing. We've got to have that guy,' he said to Sam Chisholm, at that time a lieutenant.

It was still almost exactly two months before the IRB officially declared the game open in Paris. When the News Corporation deal was announced

Louis Luyt, with the ghostly knowing smile characteristic of most of his public utterances and which one might suspect did not reach nearly as deep as his skin, kept up a pretence of amateurism, saying that the proceeds would go to the 'development of the game'.

Perhaps surprisingly, it was Tony Hallett, then RFU secretary-designate, who was most realistic. Immediately after the press conference announcing the SANZAR deal at Ellis Park, he said: 'Amateurism is in a state of rigor mortis. The pressure on players is such that they can't hold down full-time employment, and some of this money will inevitably have to support them in a professional sense.' That pressure, and the sheer size of the deal and the evidence of what rugby could then command, ensured that amateurism was shuddering in its death throes, and the three grandees worked on the premise that it would soon be six feet under, where it bloody well belonged.

The deal had been driven from rugby's side because Murdoch's company had already signed up English rugby league, lock, stock and whippet, creating the Super League, and also invested massively in Australian rugby league, detonating the first explosions in a mighty battle between Murdoch's organisation and Kerry Packer. For a game which remained defenceless in that it could not offer contracts to its leading players, there was briefly the prospect of Jonah leading rafts of union stars over to play run-and-bash without flankers.

Initially, people were panicked. Guy especially. I sat in his room in the week before the 1995 final as he explained his belief that all of the All Blacks (not just the stragglers, not just the superannuated, but *all* of the All Blacks) would have signed for the newly moneyed rugby league unless the NZRU gave them a reason (coloured green, with noughts on) to stay. The former Wallaby and Kangaroo Michael O'Connor was already in South Africa trying to recruit league players as we spoke.

Essentially, however, the three presidents were indeed confronted with the impending end of amateurism. The massive amount of Murdoch money conveyed to them a heavy responsibility to create a professional structured season in their countries. Murdoch may not have gone public on the issue, but it was known that he would not want to pay $555 million for a re-heated Currie Cup or a dull Southland–Nelson Bays match in a dripping Invercargill and an ad hoc series of international matches. The trio had to produce final details of some compelling events.

Right. Here we go, mates. They sat down, ordered coffee and began to talk. I know, because I was on the next table trying to eavesdrop. We checked the trio now and again that morning but after three hours maximum they'd hacked it out, signed for their biscuits and gone their separate ways.

They'd fixed a new name for a joint operation between their three unions: SANZAR. Better than ARSANZ. They'd fixed an annual, home-and-away Tri-Nations event, at last giving them the means with which to emulate some of the rampaging success of the Five Nations in Europe. They'd quickly ditched any other teams likely to compete, such as the Pacific Islands and Argentina (ushering in an era in which no major union gives a damn about another).

They'd also hacked out a brand new concept, the Super-12, which involved the augmentation of provincial teams in an event which changed domestic landscapes in their respective countries for ever. There. A new, appealing and commercially whizzing structured season was in place within three hours, with barely a raised voice. Pay the bill, Louis.

How long did the same process take – the job of setting up structures for a pro game at the top level – in Europe? Can't say, because it hasn't finished yet. Raised voices? No more than a few thousand. Yes, and threats, bickering, bankruptcies, character assassinations, blundering unions, blundering new club organisations. And jumped-up mini-Napoleons, almost terminal anger and stupefaction from the general public, a complete waste of potential. Rugby had a wave to catch. It missed and almost sank.

Costs to rugby in Britain? Millions of pounds and even more in terms of goodwill and feel-good factor. Cost to rugby in the southern hemi-sphere? Three coffees and three toasted sandwiches. Say, thirty rand. Or three pounds.

My car phone rang, somewhere on the clockwise M25. 'He's in again. He's in this morning!' I did not have to ask who was in, or what he was in. I was driving to a match at Saracens, and by the time I arrived in the press room at Vicarage Road, Watford, the newspaper was laid out on the table and the lads were eagerly scanning it, reading out the best bits and ladling dollops of withering sarcasm on to the mind-numbing tedium of the whole exercise. They hadn't even paused to wolf the sandwiches.

'Means f**k all in the back streets of Barnsley.' One my colleagues is apt to dismiss thus any articles on sporting grandees outside the sphere of interest of real sporting fans. I cannot think of a finer litmus test as to whether an article on sport really works for rank-and-file sports followers than the Barnsley test. This particular series of articles, as far as I can make out, fascinated one household on the Isle of Man, none in the back streets of Barnsley, and none anywhere else. Except by default.

So, nothing proved quite such an excruciatingly funny-by-default diversion to the grind of season 1999–2000 as this series in the *Daily Telegraph* in which Cliff Brittle, a businessman based in the Isle of Man and, for two years – until deposed summarily in July 1998 – chairman of the RFU's management board, conducted interviews with a series of Top Suits from various British sports. Brittle's stuff was so painfully boring, so utterly devoid of colour or fascination or humour or form, that it was hilarious. One of my colleagues has saved them all, keeps bursting out with his own highlights on trains and planes in the same way that other people recite bits from *The Goon Show* or *Fawlty Towers*.

Brittle had emerged in 1996 from almost complete rugby obscurity to lead a host of grass-roots and in some cases paranoid backwoodsmen who had convinced themselves – or had been convinced by others – that professional rugby would entail the top English clubs descending on every small club in the land, robbing them of all their money and players, raping their cattle and stampeding their women, then carrying the spoils back to Twickers to take over international rugby. This has been one of the core misapprehensions in the sorry tale of English rugby over the past five years: there are still people who believe that the top English rugby clubs are trying to take over the whole game. They aren't.

In the dread days after 1995 when all was doubt and chaos in English rugby this was a scenario all too easy to paint, and at the very time when rugby should have been investing in its major clubs (and demanding an awful lot in return), the clubs were portrayed as angels of death. It was a perspective encouraged by Brittle, in order to boost his populist support as he challenged John Jeavons-Fellows, the official RFU committee nominee, for the post of chairman. The public-relations agency he enlisted – which dutifully kept pro-Brittle stuff chuntering away on my fax machine, often long into the night – also represented ERCA (English Rugby Counties Association), such a prehistoric body it was a wonder that they didn't claim their future wives by hitting them on the head with wooden clubs.

Brittle was anxious to portray himself later as a champion of the new rugby revolution, and who am I to say that his motives were not genuine? But it was to these grass-roots legions that he owed his election. This he realised, and fought hard for elections for the post of chairman to be conducted among every club in membership – the equivalent, some felt, of having the chairman of Sainsbury's main board elected by the check-out chaps and shelf-fillers.

In January 1996, on the shoulders of the hordes, Brittle defeated Jeavons-Fellows and became chairman of the board. He was chairman during what was categorically the most sorry period in the history of the RFU – say what you like about the dear old union (and I have), they have always carried out their function with a certain grace and style, never descending to petty backbiting and factions and self-interest. Read the minutes of every decade's committee meetings and annual general meetings and all you will see is grace and manners. Read the minutes of such meetings in the Brittle era, 1996–98, and you will read about secret faxes and media manipulation, face-to-face fury and mistrust, and abuse from all sides.

For God's sake, these were the years when we wanted definitive action, not Brittle's intransigence – not his utter failure, as an eminent judge later pointed out, to entertain the belief that he could ever be wrong about anything. Still less to grasp that he was wrong in my view about almost everything. He produced a paper called 'Vision 2000' on proposed restructurings of the game which would, in my opinion, have killed rugby's professional arm stone-dead, having driven the paying public away from rugby grounds after creating needless layers of bureaucracy. Apart from that, it was hopeless.

I first met him when he was on a meet-the-subjects tour of the realm at Twickenham on an international match-day, just after his election. It is unheard of for Twickers grandees to enter the media centre. He popped in, had a look around. He popped out. After his visit, he reported to two different people that I was 'the rudest man he'd ever met'. After some moments of stunned thought, I realised he was referring to the fact that, after we had exchanged an initial handshake, and after I had expressed my congratulations on his election to office, I had walked away to get on with what I was doing. He apparently expected a long chin-wag.

I seem to recall that I was tapping anxiously at my laptop when he came in, was festooned with various electric and modern leads and other bits and pieces and trying to make them all fit. I was trying to follow up a news story; trying to ascertain who was ghosting Bob Dwyer's columns while he was doing the quotes at the press conference; trying to make sure that all three of us reporting for the same paper would not write the same article; hunting for that elusive BT engineer to check if our three phone lines were working; apologising for the decade of abuse I'd given the poor chap . . . and if my manners to our incoming chairman were poor then I'm very sorry, but so was Brittle's grasp of the requirements of working for a Sunday newspaper on a Twickenham international Saturday.

Back to his interviews. If he blames a hostile media for part of his eventual downfall – and if he doesn't, he should do, because no other figure in the history of my twenty-four years in rugby reporting evoked such hostility in my colleagues, both in private and in their columns – then, perhaps he'd decided to have his revenge by taking over acres of column inches for his interviews with the sporting gaffers.

He obviously arrived for his interviews with a formal list of questions through which he then ploughed, doggedly and in order, and to which he appeared to stick even if the subject – by some staggering stroke of luck – actually said something interesting and deserving of further investigation. The format was straight Q and A, no colour or comment or embellishment or gilding, just the question and the text of the answer. It was an excruciating read.

But on went Cliff, regardless. The articles came at regular intervals. One was with Michael Bonallack, retiring secretary of the Royal & Ancient Golf Club. The piece was illustrated by a picture of our roving newshound, Brittle, with Bonallack, seated awkwardly on the bridge over the Swilcan Burn on the 18th of the Old Course and looking as if the photographer was pointing an AK47 rather than a Nikon and they couldn't think of a last request. No doubt the two men are bosom pals, though it might be that the wan smile on Bonallack's face covered his bafflement as to what on earth was going on.

Cliff was merciless with Bonallack. 'Tell me about the finances of the R & A?' he said, for the benefit of all those still awake.

Dave Moorcroft of UK Athletics was next under the microscope (albeit that Brittle was peering down the wrong end). Moorcroft seems a decent chap, and in my personal opinion is the most thunderously boring inter-round summariser in the history of British sports television, able to share with us such dazzling insights as his estimate that a runner must be 'very disappointed' at being lapped three times when in line for the gold – and that in the 800 metres. Brittle really got stuck into Moorcroft with the question about UK athletics the whole world was asking from its clubs and armchairs: 'How much autonomy exists in Wales, Scotland, Northern Ireland and the three regions of England, and who funds it?' That night in my local, people were aghast. 'I see Northern Ireland has little autonomy,' they all said, shaking their heads.

Brittle then upped the pace of the series to a stumble and gave a grilling – well, more of a slow de-icing – to Rodney Walker, Big Suit of the UK Sports Council and therefore (not his fault) ostensibly the most important man in British sport about whom rank-and-file sports fans care least.

Brittle asked Lord MacLaurin, head of the ECB: 'Where would you like to see your finances in five years' time?' In the back streets of

Barnsley, they were agog. (Well, I didn't check. But I'm sure they were.) We have also had Geoff Thompson, chairman of the Football Association – yes, you can imagine the fans in the pubs of Manchester chewing over their favourite subjects: Beckham, Fergie, Giggsy . . . *Thommo*?

Cliff was obviously going to use his new platform to hark back to his pet themes of his two years of office in rugby. Brittle did not agree with the RFU's decision to sell rights to Sky Television. So he asked every single grandee if they'd sell their rights to Sky, whether it was an issue relevant to that sport or not. Moorcroft – and this is a strange one – plumped for the BBC, who have employed him as summariser for years. Brittle asked Thompson if the Premiership football clubs had too much influence over the national game (because Brittle had been terrified in his own rugby reign that the big clubs would win the authority they deserved).

'Since rugby union went professional, the top clubs have tried to steal the family silver built up since the late 1800s. Has professional golf tried to take over the Open?' Brittle asked Bonallack, instead of another question to which Bonallack's answer would have been interesting. 'No,' Bonallack replied. Bonallack was not to know, of course, that the top clubs in rugby had not done any such thing – never seriously considered the possibility.

More prejudices. Brittle would never have been elected chairman if the usual principle of allowing the management board to choose its own had been followed. He was elected because the vote was thrown over to the four winds and everyone voted, even those so drastically removed from the actual issues at stake that they had no idea what they were voting for. So, vividly obvious as ever, he asked MacLaurin: 'There was a move within the RFU for the chairman to be elected by the council, therefore disenfranchising their membership. Who elected you and your management board?' Amazingly, and I am sure Cliff did not realise this already – of course not – the answer was: 'The membership of the ECB.'

Brittle was a conservative BBC man when it came to television rights, so was able to smugly and tacitly agree with Bonallack when he asked the poor man why the Open was on good old BBC, whereas the Twickers rotters had sold out to Sky.

Q. 'Why do the R & A choose the BBC to televise the Open Championship?' Brittle knew that Bonallack would deliver the perfect reply about not selling the family silver, good old Auntie, agreeable Peter Alliss, dinner-jacketed linkmen, etc. Brittle did not ask Bonallack why the BBC are given rights to the Open and next to nothing else on the whole European tour, including the Ryder Cup – but then Cliff's penetrating questions never penetrated more than epidermis-deep. So it went on, leading question after leading question. I asked one of the interviewees what he thought of the Brittle interrogation. 'Well, I didn't mind going along with it. Wouldn't call it a racy read, though, would you?'

At least one interview had the merit of a tremendous riposte. Cliff's final effort to date was a return to his stamping ground to question Francis Baron, the chief executive of the Rugby Football Union. If Brittle took any stance in any of his interviews then it was to try to get his subjects to confirm his own beliefs by asking them leading questions. When Baron told Brittle that he was a firm believer in a strong English national league, Brittle said: 'I'm delighted to hear that.'

'You're just an interviewer, you shouldn't be delighted one way or the other,' Baron said. It was a response which saw through the whole exercise. Not even the *Telegraph*'s own men could explain why it was that Brittle was given enough newsprint to wallpaper your lounge. This is, after all, the paper which employs Michael Henderson as its cricket correspondent and Paul Hayward as its chief sports writer. It might not have taken their sports coverage to the same stratospheric heights as our humble efforts in the *Sunday Times*, but if I had to deliver a blueprint for a thrusting hack on what a senior correspondent in a major sport is supposed to do, then I would simply refer people to the millimetre-perfect demonstration provided daily by Henderson – ferociously angry, sad, joyful and vivid in turn, often annoying as hell, but deliberately refusing to sit on any fence or to do anything bar plump down heavily on one side of the argument, report entertainingly and tilt at every sacred cow. If I did the job description for what a general sportswriter should be, then Hayward's splendid mixture of authority and colour would also do the job, for consistency alone. Why on God's earth they lumbered themselves with Brittle, who can say? Still, it was fun while it lasted. Good old *Telegraph*.

There was one further moment of interest in the interminable slog of the Brittle interviews. It was when he asked Baron the following question. 'Why is rugby union in England still in a mess after five years of professionalism?' There is no way of knowing how long Baron pondered his answer. Eventually, he gave some long-winded reply. What he might have said, of course, is obvious. 'Cliff, you tell me.' The truth about the transition to professionalism and all its accompanying disasters is that at precisely the point when the game in England needed sympathy, pragmatism and flair, and needed officials of pace, charm, intent and genuine talent, along came none. And Cliff.

✻   ✻   ✻

To be fair to Brittle, those who had to pick up the gauntlet (well, the sheepskin muff, hipflask and fawn overcoat) of the previous RFU administrations had not exactly been handed down a manual for the pro game. Instead, they fought till the bitter end, and while our chums Louis, Richie and Leo sipped their coffee and concluded their business in Johannesburg, no one in England had the foggiest where to start. Cappuccino or espresso? Prosperity or bankruptcy?

But wait. What was the problem? I felt that in one sense they had precious few strategic decisions to make. Obviously they had to pay England's international squad the going rate as international athletes. This would have the happy result, too, of allowing them to offer the players proper contracts and would, therefore, keep them behaving well and promoting the sport. Second, the full-scale promotion of the top echelon of the club game was now an overwhelming priority. Television and sponsors were keen on the product of international rugby, wanted to put together rugby crews, rugby staffs. But for around thirty weeks of any season there were no internationals, and in those thirty weeks the image of the game, its appeal and its prosperity were in the hands of the major rugby clubs. They generated their own new income. While no one was suggesting they rob the poorer clubs, time was short; the other lot down South were already scuttling happily along.

So what was the first reaction when the news came from Paris that the IRB had abandoned amateurism? High-level Twickers executive emergency meeting? Five Nations in standing session until it was all sorted? Calls to draft in business people for their expertise? Ask the players? None of these. They called a moratorium. A pesky, flipping moratorium. The RFU announced that their national team could be paid, but that for one year, 1995–96, the domestic game in England would remain amateur.

I could see the point, I suppose. At best, it was an understandable if ludicrously damaging attempt to buy the new-look RFU some time to react. Tony Hallett, a prime mover in the moratorium, had been given around two months to create an entirely professional arm in the English game from a standing start – standing in a bucket of manure. He carried the bucket for all the years of myopia and lack of forward planning. At worst, the moratorium was seized upon by the rearguard of amateurism as another precious twelve months of tweet-tweeting in cloud-cuckoo land.

If the RFU had set the process in motion a few years before, or if the RFU had had the powder to act decisively there and then, then so much anguish would have been avoided. As it was, in that moratorium year other people were going to work. They were going to work in a market place which did not observe moratoriums. Multi-millionaire Newcastle businessman Sir John Hall bought the ailing Newcastle Gosforth club, employed Rob Andrew as director of rugby (an inspired choice) and set about signing players for the first professional rugby season.

If the RFU had set a wage-cap for their domestic rugby – as they were later forced to do in conjunction with the clubs for season 1999–2000 – then they could have controlled the situation. They did not, so what controlled the situation was the size of Sir John Hall's purse – 'more capacious', as Blackadder once said of a relative's riches, 'than an elephant's scrotum'. Newcastle, and then Richmond and the other clubs who had attracted benefactors, were quickly offering contracts of up to £100,000 per year. Zero to six figures overnight. The top players, and even a few without noticeable talent who were heavily bunged, were thrilled. Hall, paying lip-service to the moratorium, at first employed the new signings as 'development officers'.

But rugby salaries were immediately inflated and costs rocketed, and with a depressing irony they rocketed at the very moment when moves to raise income drastically were stillborn. The result was five years of pressure and anxiety. Those people who berate the top clubs never seem to grasp that it was not the clubs who voted for pro-fessionalism to begin. They should remember Peter Wheeler's words. Wheeler, chief executive of Leicester and one of the few men presently at the top of the game whom you would back to run the sport on his own, said: 'I have every sympathy with clubs at all levels of the game, but there are ninety families directly affected by the prosperity or otherwise of Leicester, and perhaps as many at other clubs. Hundreds of other people are indirectly affected.'

It is easy to blame Hall for the initial mad rush. The likes of Brittle and Fran Cotton – the former Lion who formed an alliance with Brittle, baffling all those who had revered Cotton's judgement for so long – attacked him unmercifully. They didn't even attempt to tap into the expertise of this genuinely charismatic man who had made a success of a professional sport while the rest of us were passing ludicrous motions about 'rugby-related activities' and all that bilge. The reaction to Hall in some parts was also rugby's odious snobbery towards people who had not come up in the game and were therefore not to be trusted. The snobs never explained how rugby was ever going to meet the challenges of the new era were it to rely on the same limited talent at its disposal and without new investment.

Of course, Hall was misguided. He and other club grandees have wrested control of Premiership football from the Football Association, kept the proceeds of television and other commercial deals, made the Premier League wonderfully colourful and profitable and made the FA pay a heavy price for their decades of inertia. Hall reckoned that he and other club owners could do the same in rugby, and they were proved wrong. He was too extreme and too confrontational.

I have not the slightest doubt, however, that in essence he was correct. The current Rugby Football Union should have, on their committee or council, not one single representative of the old county scene; their senior members should be representatives of the senior rugby clubs and of Club England, the national team's overseeing committee and representatives of the lower leagues. Because it is still set up to run rugby as it was in the days of the Raj, because the clubs are represented only on joint bodies, the wheels grind exceedingly slowly. As they did in 1995, when the dear old RFU came up with their moratorium.

What has followed in the five years since has been appalling. It has turned off thousands of potential customers, corporate or individual, and in many instances made rugby appear to be a dodgy and riven investment. The transition to professional rugby in England has been by far the worst story I have ever had to cover. It has often made my colleagues and myself furious and disbelieving, as the rumours and the factions proliferate, and as threats fly. More so than usual, it has made Saturday the great, joyous day of any week. For it is on this blessed day that you can actually go out and watch a live rugby match, forget the bickering and the off-the-record briefings and see the game as it was meant to be seen. It is particularly nauseating that so many of the people who credit the onset on professionalism with the difficulties were those who failed to prepare a proper path for it by hanging on to amateurism for so long. It is not professionalism from which the game has suffered since 1995. It is amateurism.

The battle lines have been easy to spot. The RFU have been at loggerheads with their partner unions on the Five Nations ever since the news broke in March 1996 that the RFU had departed from previous tradition that domestic television contracts be signed after a joint approach, and had instead for £87.5 million sold the rights to Twickenham internationals and other big rugby to Sky. On two occasions the RFU have been threatened with expulsion from the Five Nations Championship. The poisonous state of relationships with the other unions – a poison not entirely drawn to this day – affected not only television but also anything in the nature of cross-border domestic rugby competition along the lines of the Super-12, which the southern unions had sorted in a tick. It also affected the chances of establishing a structured season.

The best solution would have been a holistic one. All five unions, plus Italy, the club bodies representing the professional arms in England and Wales, plus sponsors, should have sat down together. And allocated certain Saturdays for internationals, others for Cup and League and European Cup games, and acted in concert, so that the poor paying punter knows where on the planet he is. Since for much of the past five years these participants would have been unable to sit down together without wearing an armour breastplate reversed to cover their backs, the hunt for the structured season has met with the same success as those for Jack the Ripper and the Loch Ness Monster. (At least some people have seen the latter, so they say. Admit to having spotted a structured season in European rugby and people will call you a nutter.) England's influence in the world of rugby, its influence in Europe and especially its relations with the southern hemisphere have waned faster than the light in a dark gloaming. But the RFU is easily the biggest and most powerful union. The RFU had to provide a counter-balance to the power of the south, and whatever the jealousy which existed between the five major European unions (and that jealousy in 1996 was nothing compared to what it was to become), rugby in England was the commercial powerhouse of the European game. England was the place where commercial interest was at a high, the place where the professional revolution would be driven. Shame, therefore, that the means of moving forward in this powerhouse country turned out to have all the force of a sodden firework.

Internally, it has also been nightmarish. As I've said, the paranoia within smaller clubs around England that the major clubs were coming to get them, and, frankly, their small-town jealousy of the city slickers, was enormous. At the very time when the Premiership clubs in England were trying to claim what was rightfully theirs in the way of new authority and new financial streams (relating to events they were playing in), various administrations blocked them. The clubs originally banded together as English Professional Rugby Union Clubs and were buoyed by new investment and hope. They appointed as their chief executive a member of the Harlequins club, Donald Kerr, a decent man with as much experience in professional rugby as the rest of us: none.

It was Kerr's job to liaise with Brittle at the height of Brittle's suspicion that the major clubs wanted to take over. Progress was not so much slow as non-existent. After one meeting Kerr admitted that he had emerged in tears: 'The man is totally intransigent,' he said of Brittle. On two occasions, in September 1996 and September 1997, the clubs threatened to pull their players out of the national squad. They had the perfect contractual right since they employed the players and had primacy. As a public-relations move it was a disaster, because it meant that Brittle and Cotton could portray the clubs as a bunch trying to demean and disgrace the land of hope and glory. To me, it was a cry for help from the clubs, directed towards the rest of the game. The clubs also withdrew from the European Cup in January 1998, incensed that European Rugby Cup, the organisers, shared the paranoia about their intentions. They had new investors but without proper agreements, income streams or properly organised competitions, and with the threat that Brittle and Cotton would bring in divisional or provincial rugby they were running scared, being slowly squeezed. On two occasions they threatened to break away from the RFU.

'The dispute between the First Division clubs and the RFU is not a petty wrangle between obdurate personalities,' Brittle once wrote. 'It is a struggle for the soul of English rugby.' He was correct in part. It was not a wrangle between obdurate personalities. It was a wrangle between one obdurate personality and a game desperately trying to pick up the pace of the pro era. Nothing to do with personalities? In February 1998 Peter Brook, then the RFU president, wielded some of the remaining authority of his office. The union and the clubs decided that the whole debate was being bogged down by personalities, which it clearly was. The clubs sidelined their hawks; Brook sidelined Brittle. If Brittle's suggestion that the good of the game came before personalities was serious, he would have welcomed the move. He clearly wasn't happy; Cotton resigned – something he did, or threatened to do, more than once when things went against him. Within weeks the Mayfair Agreement was signed. It was imperfect and rushed, but genuinely bought time for the two sides to thrive and co-exist. It was a real achievement for Graham Smith, the RFU man who drove it through.

Brittle's days were numbered. Colleagues and I remember with sincere regret one Cotton/Brittle special when they held a stunted press conference in a hotel in Richmond to make what they declared was a disastrous revelation for the game: the text of a submission by the clubs to the European Commission asking for clarification of their trading and commercial rights. The bitterness, mock-horror and abuse of RFU committee-men with which they ran their media briefing was astonishing. They had also dragged in Clive Woodward, the England coach. Unforgivably. It was only recently, in South Africa in 2000, that Woodward was able to distance himself from the exercise and reveal his optimism for an era of cooperation with the clubs.

At that meeting Brittle and Cotton revealed only open hostility to the clubs – no encouragement. English clubs bearing great old names, still producing great players, trying their best to attract the public and still realising that a fine England team was the priority. Cotton berated me for not having attended a previous press conference before which I had sent my apologies because my daughter was ill. I had always revered Cotton, as a player, man and official. I did not recognise him on the top table that day, and it was far more to the liking of those who held him in esteem when he and Brittle went their separate ways; when Big Fran entered the future with all guns blazing by sketching out a professional model for his beloved Lions and thereby saved the concept.

I, along with all my colleagues who eagerly scanned the pages for the latest Cliffisms (including some who cut them out and pasted them in a special book), would willingly have defended Brittle's right to maintain any opinion he held. Perhaps I want it both ways. I was critical of the ostrich stance of the RFU for so long but also admired their civility. Was the price of professional rugby and a new realism the end of civility and rugby's ambience, in favour of barking and shouting and furious faces in media briefings? It would also be preposterous to blame Brittle for all of the problems. There was just a yawning gap between what we needed from English officialdom, and what we got.

Brittle was vindicated in a sense after he was voted out of the chairmanship, in that the pace of progress remained funereal, so he could not be blamed. He was succeeded by Brian Baister, formerly a high-ranking police officer, who immediately impressed me and still does. Baister realised that the time to stand on doomed principles and individual ego had long gone. His period of chairmanship has seen the slow rebuilding of bridges between the RFU and other unions, though suspicion remains. It has seen the re-building of trust between the RFU and the clubs, now represented by a body called English First Division Rugby with a chairman in Tom Walkinshaw, owner of Gloucester and of the Arrows racing team, who has occasionally attracted the same sort of criticism as Brittle. EFDR, too, have been too slow to find their stride – and, five years after Paris, there is no longer any excuse. They have been pitifully poor, with a lack of PR, and a lack of unity, flair and statesmanship.

The anxious search has continued for a structured season, for something which includes domestic, European and international competitions, which suits all parties in terms of timing, available prize money, the destination of the proceeds, the number of qualifiers and the urgent need for marketers to get their teeth into something. The desperate truth for rugby in England, Wales, Scotland and Ireland is that in five years of professionalism the people charged with marketing the RFU or individual clubs or the clubs as a body have not once been able to set out their season long in advance, to start marketing the matches to spectators, season-ticket holders, sponsors, ball sponsors, kids, local radio and television, the lot. Not once. How can they, when no one knows the fixture list until a few weeks before the first game?

There have been various blueprints, a host of working parties, more bickering and so little real negotiation. It is truly amazing how few clubs have folded, and amazing that we have lost only the professional arms of Richmond and London Scottish – and then only because Ashley Levett, the Richmond benefactor, pulled out in peremptory fashion in the middle of season 1998–99, provoking EFDR to abandon the large crowd-base Richmond had established in lightning-quick time in the splendid Madejski Stadium in Reading, all in the cause of dividing the central pot fewer ways. It was a PR disaster for Walkinshaw, and I would estimate that in the eyes of the sport he has never recovered.

Eventually, the RFU asked Rob Andrew to draw up a structure for the season. He did so, majoring in domestic terms with an English-only Premiership, originally with franchised teams. While he was doing so, Walkinshaw did roughly the same, although his domestic event was a cross-border British League. The two parallel universes existed side by side for some time; there was briefly the prospect of further strife as Walkinshaw realised that support was ebbing.

It was ebbing because the RFU voted for the Andrew Plan. It was also ebbing because while funding for Walkinshaw's plan remained a secret between Walkinshaw, his maker and a select few others, the RFU offered the major clubs the sum of £1.8 million each per year, rising gradually, as reward for staying under Rob's umbrella. The clubs also looked around with a new sense of optimism. A new breed of rugby-loving business brains was moving in, in particular David Thomson at Newcastle Falcons and Brian Kennedy at Sale. The 1999–2000 Heineken European Cup was a stratospheric success and gave the clubs a kind of separate existence now that they had a product of their own that television – in this case the BBC – lapped up. The Allied Dunbar Premiership attendances held up well, considering the feel-bad factor and lack of real marketing and confidence-building which had pervaded English rugby for five dreadful years.

It was not quite the signal for Peter Wheeler's ninety families to breathe easy. There were still creases to be ironed, notably that provided by the Andrew plan which stated that automatic promotion to the top flight and automatic relegation from it was not part of the scheme. This, quite rightly, offended anyone in rugby whose club wished to aspire to dream even an impossible dream, and the final peace was still not won by September 2000. But the penny seemed to have dropped somewhere, and people throughout English rugby were at last beginning to realise that if the top of the game was shown to be in rude health and not simply to be rude, then the benefits cascaded.

The earliest indications as 2001 approached were that the RFU were now presiding over a great escape, had bungled the transition with a spectacular awfulness, had reduced rugby's committee rooms to a graceless shambles and should really have sent the game into bankruptcy, aided by the clubs' own bungling. But they were recovering, still living and breathing. Andrew wants the clubs to have stadiums which take 10,000 people. My belief is that the game will need them, soon.

Optimism is too strong a word for those who have lived throughout the fall, not so much of civilisation as of civility. There is still a way to go for the RFU to recover their position of influence. They must recover. They are too big and too important. At least when they do begin to fork-lightning again the old smugness and arrogance will be long gone.

It is important to remember that there are enough trip-wires to set off more ruinous explosions. And also that the true measure of the final triumph of professional rugby in England will come only when we hear nothing more of committees and plans and chairmen of the board and votes and structures because the whole lot of them have receded into the deep background, where they belong.

England is still a magnificent rugby country in almost every respect. The affection for the game among its disciples it still vast. And so too, perhaps astonishingly, is its capacity to drag in outsiders and welcome recruits – though it has also turned many away along the endless passage from amateurism to professional and from chaos to order. Often when rugby people have sat down together there has been nothing to say and nothing to do except shake their heads at the shambles. Sports editors have complained: 'Not that same old story again this week.' People from outside have come up and wondered aloud: 'What is happening in that sport you used to brag about?' Steve Bale of the *Express* put it perfectly: 'For most of that time, all you wanted to do was scream.'

It has been, by any standards, a horrible journey.

CHAPTER FOUR

Buenos Aires

The final bastion of the amateur faith ◆ Wales fight for respect ◆ The lost Pumas re-discovered ◆ The Devil's stadium ◆ New momentum dying

Diego Maradona, hand of God, boots of fire, brain of sponge, was in trouble. He was being arraigned in preliminary trial for shooting at a journalist who was bothering him; the latest chapter in his drug-addled and pot-bellied decline. The Argentine public were incensed at Maradona's behaviour. Why, oh why, they said angrily, had he used only a small gun?

It was a sunny winter Sunday in June 1999, in the week of Maradona's brush with authority, and yet even on the day of rest the traffic streamed around Buenos Aires. They paint white lines on Argentine roads – pointless. BA cars merely weave through gaps, scenting chances and accelerating on like metal Phil Bennetts, undertaking and overtaking in a hair-raising shambles of cars stampeding along up to seven abreast on three-lane roads.

We drove for nearly an hour, out from the elegance of the centre to the faded elegance of the outer, to the never-elegant of the suburbs and then to the clatter of the shanty bits. And suddenly we came upon . . . England? A vast expanse of green and pleasant rugby fields where the hubbub was drowned out by the gentility. And out in the club's hinterland, hordes of mini-teams and youth teams of all age-groups from U9 to U22 – a heroic effort by unpaid volunteers. All purposeful and ordered. Teeming like wasps, or Wasps.

Two decent-sized stands lined the main pitch, where groundsmen were planting the flags for that afternoon's match against La Plata, fifty kilometres south of Buenos Aires. (A few days previously the ground had staged the Buenos Aires provincial team's defeat of Wales, who were on their tour a few months before the 1999 World Cup opened in Cardiff.) There was a large clubhouse, not palatial but laid-back and roomy and friendly, with a restaurant facility for Sunday dinners, steaks and fighting Argentine red wines. Our decision to join the diners was subliminally influenced by the fact that one of the dark-haired waitresses had a skirt of such brevity that it was nothing much more than a belt. We had nine courses.

The Buenos Aires Cricket and Rugby Club. It is the oldest sports club in South America, founded officially in 1864. It is the club where almost every major sport ever to have arrived in Argentina, football included, was first played. The rugby section was one of the founders of the Argentina Rugby Union, along with the Belgrano, Lomas and Rosario clubs. In the early 1950s Mr Evita, President Juan Perón, allegedly sent gangs to burn down the club at its former site nearer to the city centre. The populist Perónists were not partial to anything which rang with oligarchical and British tones. The present-day Perónists under recently, deposed President Carlos Menem are less fiery, but the old feelings are bubbling away underneath all right. I don't know how to make a Maltese cross, but when in Argentina we did find out how to make an Argentine furious. You'd slip into the conversation: 'Cor, wasn't that Madonna good in *Evita*. Bloody good piece of casting, didn't you think?'

Now the club thrives tolerably. Frankie Deges, long-time member, globetrotting journalist, was our host on that Sunday during the Wales tour. All rugby nations have their Frankies, inveterate universal rugby men chiselling away in rugby's global media, popping up wherever they can find outlets, prepared to take net losses on trips just to get close to the action and, hopefully, to record rugby's warmth as a fact, not as a bygone relic. Bless them. Poor old Frankie. He took us to his flat and showed us a picture of himself and a stunning woman. He claimed that she, Vali, was his fiancée, and just to keep up the cover story in the face of our disbelief that such beauty could be associated with such a lived-in shape, he married her and they had a child, Matias, in the Argentine spring.

The BACRC is, above all things, amateur. So is the rest of Argentine rugby. When the Paris Bombshell of 1995 removed all restrictions on payment of players, some unions, notably the southern hemisphere giants, merely bolted down smoothly the plans they had long ago laid, and were immediately ready. Others still, notably the major European unions and particularly England, flapped around, did no more than accept the decision and then tried to think up ways not to implement it, they are still trying to catch up.

One union, and one alone, decided to do nothing. The Bombshell did not compel anyone to go pro. The Argentina Rugby Union announced with a kind of heroic unctuousness that rugby in Argentina would remain amateur. To tour Argentina in 1999 was therefore to live in a throw-back to that elapsed age of 1995 and before. You wouldn't have been surprised had you came across enclaves of old English amateur buffers hiding out there, with their old doctrine swept away and nothing for them back in the old country. I looked up 'Steele-Bodger' in the Buenos Aires phone book but the irrepressible Mickey's obviously there on false papers.

Good old amateurism. The fine Puma back-row forward Pablo Camerlinckx was to miss the second Test of the series against the touring Welsh because he had to go for a job interview. Such was life under unions who always demanded that you trained and played like an international athlete, saddled up their income-streams and even their personal business associations on your broad back and then treated you like a dog.

Yet the image of the BACRC as a fossilised relic of old Argentina and old England is misleading. As evidence of the Anglo-Latin society which Argentina became after it imported English goods, customs and invest-ment when the English came to build the railways early in the twentieth century, you can still read in the genteel *BA Herald* about tea dances and cake decorating and whist drives. (The *Herald* featured a gem of a football report during our stay; its subject was an Argentine Division One football match, and only in the last paragraph bar two did you learn that three players had been sent off.) But the rugby club we encountered was most definitely Argentine. After all the lesser matches had ended, and after BA had beaten La Plata in the main event with a late penalty try in a match which probably hovered somewhere in class around the Jewson Two level in England, the clubhouse filled with a mighty throng, the players and their friends and girlfriends. Hernan Vidou, the coach whose five penalties gave Argentina victory over England in 1992, held court. 'Sometimes it gets wild here,' Frankie Deges said approvingly.

It was a middle-class gathering. Few of these revellers would have been present at the Boca Juniors football match in the giant and gaunt Bombanero Stadium a few days earlier. Different sports, different social groups. This party was big and colourful and tactile and glamorous, entirely South American in flavour. And youthful. In a faithful echo of old England and amateurism, there was a separate gathering for com-mittee grandees in an adjacent pavilion. What's Spanish for alickadoo?

Here there was vivid if more measured chat, ranging from sport to politics. There was also the traditional rugby welcome unfailingly extended to rugby visitors, even visiting British hacks, by rugby people throughout the world. Juan Gerlach, owner of one of the biggest building companies in Argentina, was in the chair. On his right, an empty space – soon to be filled by the referee who had just handed the match to Juan's team with the penalty try, though the hospitality was coincidental, I'm sure. Gerlach's generosity of spirit and wallet is one of the club's engines.

There was Englishness in the menu, with sticky buns and tea; in a rather odd reversed sequence, the buns were followed by sandwiches and finally, at the end, by a hot meal and beer. Those visiting trenchermen who'd gone too early on the sticky buns bravely munched on. There was conservatism, both sporting and political, in the group of businessmen and club grandees. Some scoffed at the professionalism of rugby in the outside world.

Others scoffed about politics. We'd already witnessed the weekly vigil of Las Madres de Plaza de Mayo. The mothers of some of the 30,000 people who disappeared without trace in the years of the Videla dictatorship still pace the square in downtown BA next to the Casa Rosada, the office of President Menem. The mothers hold pictures of the sons they lost without trace; if they are buried at all then it is in communal graves hastily dug by the death-squads of the dictators.

'People talk about the disappeared ones,' said one rugby club grandee. 'Most of them just went abroad.' We did not quite have the bottle to wonder aloud why, if Los Desaparecidos had indeed decided on mass emigration, they didn't take the time to drop their families a postcard, give them a quick ring. Argentine history is apparently packed full of real and alleged shady gangs materialising to do dirty work in the middle of the night. Sounds like Newport town centre at the weekend.

But in any parallel gathering in a southern England club's committee room during the amateur years you would have found precisely the same suspicion of professionalism, radicals and protesters. It was in some part a relief, in these days when rugby has become more serious, touring savagely curtailed, to find that you can still find the spirit of the sport alive and burnished. Even if you had to step back an hour or two on history's clock to find it.

I love stadiums. Each of the major arenas where top rugby is played is emphatically different; each has its own appearance, atmosphere and facilities, its own concept of design, whether uniform, even bowl-like, or piecemeal, bunged together bit by bit as each wedge of cash has become available. Their greatness or otherwise lies in something other than the identity of the team that plays in them, lies even in something other than the atmosphere created by the crowd there. The Millennium is my favourite, of course, and not because it is in Cardiff. The old Arms Park was a pit and I hated it, and that was in Cardiff too.

The Ferro Carril Oeste (West Railway Stadium) in the Caballito neighbourhood of Buenos Aires is spectacular in a way that is all its own. Buenos Aires is a magnificent city, and those parts of it which have faded have done so so elegantly that the disintegration adds to the charm. The Ferro Carril is more than faded. It's practically cremated, standing there dark and old and gaunt, surrounded by languishing high buildings and by the Meccano-like skeletons of half-built structures which were going up well till the cash ran out. If it was in some newish city it would stand out like Martin Bayfield in a mini-rugby match. In BA, it's perfect.

It has dungeon-like changing rooms, odd nooks and crannies, bare fenced terraces, and stands pretty well unadorned with creature comforts. Once the match is over you return to the ground floor from the high media eyrie, a concrete platform sprouting from the edge of the stand like a jug ear, by one of two unappealing routes – either a narrow, steep and dark spiral staircase which bores down and down into the earth, never opening out into lower floors until, disorientated, you briefly wonder if you are simply rotating into the bowels of hell; or a clanging, lurching four-person lift, undiscovered by Mr Otis and his men and therefore bearing no safety plaque that you can see, and manned by a gloomy character who once, you would swear, played a lead role in a Hammer film you saw late one Saturday night after *Match of the Day.*

The atmosphere, provided Argentina are playing well, resembles that found in a bear-pit. There are no offices or permanent installations there, no souvenir shops or fast-food outlets. When the match is over, after a few cursory beers the thousands exit, seeking civilisation; you scurry along with the nightmarish thought that unless you get out now someone will lock you in, no one will hear your cries and you will be prey to the dark forces, to whatever malevolence fills the deserted Ferro Carril Oeste when the floodlights switch off and sport moves away. Great place. Great place.

In that summer of 1999, after the Wales tour ended, we travelled from Buenos Aires to Sydney to catch England's pre-World Cup Test against Australia. They took us around the Olympic stadium, Stadium Australia, with its soaring and pristine stands and dark-suited PR men vaunting it up; its security men and safety precautions and wide thoroughfares and bing-bong public announcements and agreeable restaurants and hissing lifts. What a tip . . .

※　　※　　※

The potential nightmare for Wales at the Ferro Carril Oeste lay in something evil on the field. When they reached Argentina they had won four of the seven matches they had played under Graham Henry, three of these victories being the last three matches – against France in Paris, against Italy in Treviso and against England at Wembley. They toured with a genuine optimism, spurred on by the pressure of being World Cup hosts. At the time, however, they were still assumed to be weak in the scrum, the lair of the Argentina Puma; the phase of the game where Argentina produces professors, the game within a game so beloved that Puma props have often been accused of ignoring the game outside the game within a game. Wales had hardly produced a tight forward of true class for more than a decade, had been playing off a base of powder for years. Moreover, the Pumas had pushed Wales all over Llanelli in a Test match there in autumn 1998.

I was convinced, however, that Wales were well on the way to developing an outstanding front five. So, I was in a minority of one. Who cares? In the 1999 Five Nations, Wales had begun to scrummage with renewed authority, so much so that they convincingly had the better of the argument against the England front row at Wembley. They had recruited from South African rugby the formidable Peter Rogers, who was educated in Wales and quickly became the most feared scrummager in Europe. They finally got David Young, he of the growling calf muscles, fighting fit and near his extraordinary best on the tight head, and were also developing the young Swansea giant Ben Evans to compete on the tight-head side as well. But as Wales prepared for the first Test at the Ferro Carril Oeste, they still had it all to prove.

They proved it. In the first Test, they convincingly had the better of the argument in the tight phases. Rogers, Garin Jenkins and Evans were up against an illustrious three from the proud lineage in Roberto Grau, Fréderico Mendez and Mauricio Reggiardo, and a fourth scrum-professor appeared when Omar Hasan replaced Grau at half-time. Yet Wales were emphatically on top in the scrum. They soon realised how far ahead they had been. The week after the Test was remarkable for almost daily pronouncements from Mendez on how Wales had indulged in sharp scrummaging practice and the like. It was the surest sign that Mendez was taken aback.

During the Test series there was another matter which Wales had initially overlooked as they admired the invigorating power of their own scrum – they forgot to do the other bits. Against Argentina they trailed 23–0 as half-time approached. Gonzalo Quesada and Octavio Bartolucci, the giant wing playing in France, scored the tries. The Welsh retention of the ball had been disastrous and they were lucky to be as close as they were, because Quesada had missed two eminently kickable penalties.

Yet pricelessly, in that strategically vital time just before the interval (at least, I assume it is vital; we all keep harping on about it), Wales scored ten points, featuring a try in the corner from Dafydd James after Allan Bateman had set Scott Quinnell thundering through the middle. The Mighty Quinn had made space and excellent handling gave James the try. A searing lineout peel from Craig Quinnell led to a try for Brett Sinkinson and a few more kicks from Neil Jenkins, a few more big scrums, and a snap drop-goal from the outstanding Shane Howarth . . . and Wales had won 36–26. Statistically it was one of the greatest comebacks in the history of international rugby. The memory of the Argentina lead of 23–0 seemed to have sprung from some match played about twenty years ago.

There was a week to go until Wales returned to the Ferro Carril Oeste for the second Test, and fair play to them, they moved camp in the true spirit of touring – to Rosario, more than an hour by air up country, to play Argentina A. Wales have always been dicey tourists, clique-ridden and homesick, sometimes pissed and often sullen. Under Henry and manager David Pickering this party were sleek, hard-working and committed. They had already played and lost their opening match by 29–31 against Buenos Aires Province at the broad and majestic BACFC, and they then won a high-scoring match against Tucumán.

For lovers of fire and brimstone, for connoisseurs of argy and bargy, Tucumán was a sad disappointment. By the accounts of those who had played there and survived, during the years when Tucumán – the Clockwork Orange – raged around the place, when matches were abandoned because of brawling, when Tucumán were banned from hosting, it has clearly been the most hysterical place to play on earth. Pontypool Park? Sunday school. Welford Road? Butter-soft. Brive? Tepid. House of Pain, Dunedin? Darby and Joan. The Tucumános crowd were banshee wild, and when England played there in 1990, in an era where England made proper tours rather than glorified day-trips, the crowed howled away and burned the Union Jack.

But in 1999, a travesty. Wales won easily by playing badly; the crowd was muted, the game powder-puff. It ended 69–44, one of those absolutely horrendous results reminiscent of the Super-12 early years, when everyone considered a match to be fabulously entertaining because it brought fifteen tries, not realising that tries were cheapened every time another was run in. Maybe the fires are dying in Tucumán, one of world rugby's great furnaces. Or maybe the new and sanitised rubbish that rugby has become has got to them, too.

There was so much to see in Rosario, so much to be gained from the exercise. It was good for the tour party to move *en bloc*, to experience differences, perhaps privations. It was a momentous trip for the travelling media because a long and proud record finally fell. The hotel in which we were billeted in Rosario was the worst in the history of rugby media-touring, and so the celebrated Cherry Court Motor Inn in Dunedin, New Zealand, was finally knocked off its lofty perch after reigning unchallenged for more than sixteen years (ever since the week spent there before the third Test on the 1983 Lions tour, when it hosed down with rain as we cowered in outside toilets and horsehair blankets).

In Rosario the deposed manager, robbed of glory, was unavailable for comment. So was I, owing to the effort needed to consume my room-service ham sandwich, featuring two giant wedges of a most fluffy and tasteless white bread with a vague, brownish discolouration grafted on to a thin layer of butter which I took to be a token effort to qualify under some loose version of the Argentina Trades' Descriptions Act as a ham filling.

More yet. Early arrivals at Rosario's ground were given an absolute treat as Wayne Erickson, the Australian referee, went though his warm-up routine on the touch-line. Schoolchildren in the stand behind the goal-line were entranced as he passed along in front of them. John Cleese's silly walks sketch is now hackneyed, but here was Wayne recreating, or even deconstructing, the whole genre. He would take a little hop, stick one leg out high in front, hop onwards and retract, then repeat with the other leg. He looked like the progeny of a threesome between a member of the Tiller Girls, a Glaswegian meths drinker and an instructor for the Gay Gordons.

It wasn't so funny when he had to stop the game. Most of the installations at the ground were basic temporary structures holding as many as five times their proper capacity, and one scaffold stand to my right collapsed during the first half with a horrendous crunch and shriek of grinding metal and the shouts of those people involved. The first on the scene were the Welsh coaches and medical men, and when the tangle was sorted there was just one minor injury. Lucky. A few visiting hacks had to battle with their disappointment, having briefly imagined that they were on the scene of a major story. 'Come on, some f***er must be a bit injured.'

It brought home in shocking fashion how easily these things can happen, and that no matter how much we complain about it being too nanny-state, the Safety at Sports Grounds Act is better than the alternatives. You feel much safer in British stadiums than you do in those anywhere else, and other parts of the world are going to have their Ibrox or their Hillsborough before they catch up.

Looking at their vast and crumbling stadiums, I fear that Argentine football will be next.

Next day, we flew back from Rosario to the Buenos Aires domestic airport, Jorge Newbury. It was on a 737 of Lineas Areas Privadas Argentinas and to me, an occasionally queasy flyer, the flight never felt right. The plane seemed to change gear, flop around; it circled as if lost and I was not the only one on board to offer a prayer of thanks when it landed safely. A few weeks later, a LAPA 737 flying an internal leg into Jorge Newbury crash-landed, shot through the perimeter into a busy road and around ninety people lost their lives. As in the case of the murky gangs of the night, no proper explanation for the crash has yet been offered. To be part of rugby's Munich was never an ambition.

To be on a proper rugby tour, always.

The second Test reversed all known trends. Wales massacred the Argentine scrum. Rogers was clearly having the time of his life out in the Ferro Carril Oeste. At one scrum, Pichot fed the ball and then watched in amazement as his pack were shunted back, collapsed in a heap and suffered the indignity of having the Welsh scrum march all over them. Rogers stood up and gave the come-on gesture to the opposition, beaming all over his face. Even when both Rogers and Evans were replaced, by Andrew Lewis and David Young, the authority never wavered and Reggiardo in particular looked shattered by the experience. It was a sign of a platform of growing strength. Rugby history had been turned on its head. A bit like Mauricio. It was as if England bowlers had terrorised Australia, or had sledged better than the mouthy Aussies. You know, the kind of thing that never happens.

The match, the final denouement of the *bajadita* ('the low one', the trademark Puma scrum-style), went to Wales by 23–16. Mendez was replaced in the second half when uninjured, an embarrassment for the great Argentina nobleman of the pack. Wales courageously survived the home backlash, calming their nerves with an early try by Garin Jenkins after brilliant approach work by Allan Bateman.

Although Wales' ball-retention was once again poor, Neil Jenkins pushed them onwards with an assortment of kicks and they took the series.

It was their first series win over a major nation in the southern hemisphere; and no British Isles team had even won both Tests of a two-

Test series in Argentina. The basis of their game was strong, and if they played poorly in patches then they went home with the knowledge that there are no bad Test wins down south. They continued to improve rapidly until the big weeks came, in their own Cardiff, when they came out pale and slowed. This was yet another thing that has never been properly explained.

But what of the hosts? Though the crowd tried to keep its spirits up, there was by the end of the second match a sullen air about the whole proceedings from the Argentine point of view. The Pumas had looked resigned before it was over, robbed of their historical platform. There was no verve about the team, no exuberance, little belief. The coach, José Luis Imhoff, a rather grave-looking man, had clearly lost the confidence of captain Pedro Sporleder, his players and Alex Wyllie, the former All Black back row man who was employed as an occasional 'adviser' (how the term rang back to the dread old days). Wyllie spoke very little Spanish, but clearly had a better vision than Imhoff of what was required, clearly moved the players.

It was also a depressed rugby nation as a whole. But what were the upholders of amateurism doing about it? You've guessed it. There was no lead from the Argentina Rugby Union. Nothing. The great thing about opting to remain amateur is that it gives you at least a partial right to be smug and ruddy hopeless, and the ARU were taking full advantage of this fact. There appeared to be no promotion for the national team, no Puma marketing or merchandising to speak of, no vision for the country's domestic rugby, no idea of how to entertain the crowd (apart from with a military band), no attempt to make the old stadium vivid – and apparently no attempt to give the squad a decent preparation for the World Cup. The ARU president, Luís Mariano Gradin, had been a distinguished player and coach; he seemed to be resting on his laurels.

Above all, it seemed that no one on the ARU grasped that if they abandoned their appalling priggishness just for a few months they could send the Pumas away with just a little financial recompense for their time – just something to make up for the lost salaries of those who were travelling unpaid. Grudgingly, they handed out around £60 per day to the squad while they were at the World Cup, describing the handout as expenses. To those of us on the side of the underdogs in world rugby, a great rugby nation in such depression was a sad sight.

Rugby did not seem to impinge much on the consciousness of the average Argentinian, either. It was obviously submerged by football in all the papers (though not by any means totally uncovered), and was shown quite extensively on television. But you could sense that the ARU and Argentine rugby had no idea how to appeal to non-rugby sports fans, to extend its narrow support and move from its middle- and upper-class fan-base to something a little less exclusive and a little more popular. In no country bar Ireland have I found a national rugby union with so few ideas of how to push the game even a degree towards the mass of population, let alone to recruit the odd one or two supporters. Good old amateurism: good neither for the national team nor the greater good of the sport. Good, as ever, for nothing.

Wyllie was in overall control when the team arrived in Cardiff for the Rugby World Cup. There had been a nonsensical interim period when Hector Mendez had taken the coaching reins, but Wyllie was finally appointed and Gonzalo Beccar Varela became coach of the backs (and at one point in 'Grizz' Wyllie's career he would have needed a backs coach to remind him that there were any). It was not a happy prospect for the Pumas: they had been turned over by Wales on their own ground, and now they were travelling to play in the Wales groups against a home team they knew would be snorting with passion. They themselves were snorting with frustration.

Admittedly, Wyllie was precisely what they needed. It is unfair to label him as some kind of forward stomper, because he certainly has a wider vision of the game, but this is a man so grizzled that grizzly bears call him Grizz. It was not time for some British-type theorising coach banging on about long-term plans and the need to re-build. They needed some grim and terse Kiwi to give them an uncomplicated game-plan and boot them in the backside as they went out to try to fulfil it. Grizz to a T.

But Wyllie's men knew that their port in a storm, the scrummage, had been closed to them. They knew much that was negative, and apparently very little about their proud rugby history had stuck in their minds. Whatever those Cambridge blue and white jerseys contained when they ran down the (just completed) tunnel of the Millennium Stadium to open the tournament, with the notes of the opening ceremony, of Shirley Bassey and Cerys Matthews and Grizz Wyllie ringing in their ears, it was not the life-blood of confidence.

But soft. There was a certain progress. Argentina competed extremely well, were comfortably better in the Millennium than they had been in the Ferro Carril Oeste. They lost, but only by 23–18, a better margin than they had accomplished in either of their home Tests three months previously. Gonzalo Quesada kicked six penalties for Argentina and, although Wales scored two tries and had just about enough in hand, it was close. Mendez missed the World Cup through injury, and in the front row at Cardiff came Mario Ledesma, who was to have a wonderful tournament. Reggiardo and Grau shored up the scrum tolerably well, and so the campaign was tolerably well launched.

The Pumas returned to the Millennium a few days later and thumped Japan by 33–12 in front of a huge crowd. Pichot and Diego Albanese scored tries and Eduardo Simone and Lisandro Arbizu, their centres, began to move with a little elan and dash. Quesada kicked seven booming penalties. However, advances were small. Unless they could beat Samoa, who had thrashed Japan by a bigger score and who were short odds to qualify for the knock-out stages along with Wales, the whole thing was for nothing.

Stradey Park, Llanelli, 10 October. I can be even more specific than that. It started just before two in the afternoon. Not the match, but the process. Argentina had endured a miserable first half against the flying Samoans in a match which kicked off at 1.00 p.m. They could bring none of their forward power to bear, were tactically confused and were trailing 16–3, almost gone, mentally back in Buenos Aires.

It was difficult to spot the ringleaders because it was a collective, but I suppose it started around Alejandro Allub, the big lock. Then, suddenly, something clicked. Something harked back, and then rolled forward. They found that if they simply drove the ball down the middle, set it back in the tackle for the next man to pick and drive, they could make headway. Allub made a few bursts; Reggiardo made a few bursts. So did Rolando Martin, the flanker. Momentum grew rapidly. The second half was suddenly seething. Argentina would win possession, thunder down the middle with a confidence which fast became a conviction, then a passion, then almost a hysteria. Doubts, defeats, deceits, the fools in charge – all were quickly banished. It was as if someone had thrown a fast-forward switch.

The Samoans, shocked to their studs, had to infringe desperately, had to find any means – usually foul – to stop the tide. Quesada, with a mixture of penalties and drop-kicks, began to pick them off. Samoa fielded some vastly experienced warriors – Pat Lam, George Leaupepe, Junior Paramore, Trevor Leota, Inga Tuigamala – but they had no answer. 'It was like a battering ram versus a cocktail stick,' said one report.

The Pumas scored twenty-nine unanswered points after half-time, and sealed the victory when Allub drove over for a try and he and his locking partner, Ignacio Fernandez-Lobbe, ran joyfully back to halfway, arm in brawny arm, beaming all over their faces. It would have been a shock to the facial muscles involved in the formation of a smile; they had lain unused for too long. It was the Pumas' first Rugby World Cup finals victory since they beat Italy in 1987 in New Zealand. Reflecting the Argentine media's coverage of the match, the papers in Britain two days later reported a major stirring of interest, a few pictures of happy Pumas jockeying with the footballers on the sports pages.

Argentina's victory put them into the quarter-final play-offs as the best third-placed team from the five pools, and they travelled to Lens in northern France to meet Ireland. It was to be the match when Argentine rugby knocked thunderously loud on the door of its country's perceptions. It was a wonderful battle, with the Irish, limited in rugby ideas, in direction at half-back but never in terms of heart, trying to swarm all over Argentina with multi-phased play. Yet by this time Argentina's morale, their willpower, had come flooding back. Whereas only months previously a single penalty for the opposition would have troubled them, the team now demonstrated soul and resistance. With the superb Agustin Pichot now organising the defence, and with Martin and his back-row colleagues, Santiago Phelan and Gonzalo Longo, performing similar heroics, they were transformed.

Ireland did take a handy lead in the first half, but in the second half Argentina scored a stunning set-piece try, probably their best one-phase movement of the tournament. Quesada began it with a long miss pass; one line of Argentina attacks moved up as a decoy while the real targets came gliding up behind; Ignacio Corletto came up from full-back and Diego Albanese made a stunning finishing burst. Genius. Clinical genius from these men who had forgotten how to express themselves on the field. Fantastic.

The score was 28–24 to Argentina into injury time, and it was here that the maddened Irish launched what was arguably the most vigorous and desperate series of attacks the game has seen. They projected Keith Wood and Malcolm O'Kelly from their front five, the powerful Kevin Maggs and Justin Bishop from the backs. They pushed fifteen-man drives from line-out takes, with the backs piling in and driving on in a frantic, crabbing mass. In the tingling excitement as the whole thing inched towards the Argentine line, one onlooker observed that Ireland might be in a little trouble if the Pumas won the ball.

Eventually a final Ireland attack was stopped by the pale-blue wall. The whistle went. Argentina now resembled the Irish at one of their line-out drives – but celebrating wildly. It was one of the great sights and great celebrations. And mirrored at home. Next day, Argentina's media went rugby mad. 'I've never seen so much rugby in the papers here,' Frankie Deges said.

People back in the United Kingdom reflected that this was why they have World Cups.

By now the Pumas were playing with verve and belief. They marched on to Dublin, the venue of their quarter-final match against France. There were no patronising pats on the head for them now. Argentine television began dogging their footsteps, and suddenly players of this fringe sport became household names. Typically, Lansdowne Road took them to its heart. It was still way less than a week since the Llanelli revival, just before two in the West Walian afternoon.

The match was marvellous, it was stunning in its movement and twists and turns; in the way that Argentina, who had played a fierce night-match against the Irish less than three days before – while France were given eight days off – stuck to the task. It was stunning in the way that Argentina had thrown off their history of forward power, a history which sometimes helped them and sometimes throttled them, and were almost joyously taking on France out wide, with the brilliant Pichot prompting. It was powerful testimony to the rejuvenating properties of a little self-belief, and to the theory that anyone who says that rugby is ninety-nine per cent a mind game may have been under-estimating the deal.

Argentina lost, by 47–26. It was one of those results which became something of a speciality of RWC '99, because it gave the impression of an entirely different match from the one that had actually been played. 'If ever a scoreline failed to represent the heroic efforts of the losers, it was this. Out on their feet after their extraordinary win over Ireland in mid-week and 17–0 down after only ten minutes, Argentina responded with an hour of the bravest and most physically committed rugby you will ever see.' So read Brendan Gallagher's introduction in a London daily the next day. Argentina had to absorb the blow of conceding tries to two charged-down kicks and were savaged by the sharp edge of the whistle of Derek Bevan, who appeared to make harsh decisions at key moments.

But there were periods when they were likely winners. At one stage the Pumas had reduced that 17–0 lead to 30–26, scoring tries from Pichot and Lisandro Arbizu in a riot of running rugby. Indeed, some of their better movements ended just when the line beckoned, notably when Bevan gave a harsh penalty against them when to recycle the ball once more would surely have brought them a try – and the lead. Yet France too were super-charged in patches, playing their best rugby and finally killing off the Pumas with two tries in a heady finale.

Adventure over. But a great performance by a team that was in tiny pieces in its administration, its selection, its direction and its mind, not only in the months before the World Cup but when it began and for some time during it. Before, Argentina's away Test victories could be counted on one finger. The Puma effect was remarkable. Channel 9 Azul in Argentina recorded one of their largest television audiences of the whole year for this, a mere rugby match. More than 5.4 million people had picked up the Puma trail and watched the French match. The coverage was blanket.

When the team returned home they were received as if they had won the tournament. (The final rankings actually placed them at a splendid fifth in the world.) The adulation was an outward and visible sign that rugby in the country was popular after all, but that its popularity, just like the confidence of its players, was hidden below the surface. It was a rugby country, and it had a rugby team.

Politicians did as politicians do. The day after the France match saw the Argentine national elections. The newly elected president, Fernando de la Rua, had delayed an appointment in order to watch the end of the game, and when the team arrived home the next day he invited them to a reception at 4 p.m. But outgoing president Carlos Menem had a final shot in his locker. Menem was a friend of scrum-half hero Pichot, so rang him and organised a group of Pumas for a midday reception. He had handed over the reins, but had beaten de la Rua by four hours.

For at least a week there was no TV show, whatever its theme, which did not have the Pumas as guests. The team's jersey sponsor, Visa, even came up with a bung of £600 a head if the players agreed to appear in various programmes in official Visa gear. The logistics turned out to be too onerous. Having spent so long in a vain battle for recognition in their country, the team members soon realised that things were getting out of hand and agreed to restrict their appearances. Ironic, or what? Visa ordered 35,000 replica Puma jerseys and launched a special programme to market the kit, the company and the Pumas. These programmes were duly sold out, practically overnight. And Pichot, not a footballer, became the nation's sportsman of the year.

And now, the final tragedy of the rugby nation that lost itself, found itself and then lost itself again. If there was anything about Argentine rugby administration which was not in the Dark Ages (and delighted to be there), here was a brilliant opportunity to secure the future of the country's game, to cash in on the sudden and dazzling glare of publicity and to capture the attention of the nation while everyone was looking their way. To ride the wave which had risen in Llanelli.

And also to stop being so ridiculously smug about professional rugby and form a professional national squad with proper back-up. Not necessarily the full-time pro, £150,000 per annum lot with massed back-room blokes, as fielded by certain other countries. Just something to show the players that they were regarded as athletes rather than pawns. And obviously, after the job he'd done, the overwhelming priority was to re-sign Wyllie (at the price he set, if necessary) and make him full-time coach on a proper contract, with *carte blanche* to name his back-up squad.

Fair enough, the ARU does not have access to huge income-streams, but a couple of reciprocal agreements to play big Test matches at home and abroad and, with relatively small overheads, you are almost there. To harness the adulation, it was naturally imperative to get the team back on the home field – at Ferro Carril Oeste, or even at a bigger BA stadium such as Velez Sarsfield. Any opposition would have been fine – a South American select, Uruguay, Argentina A, even bring America down the continent for a game. Anything, any excuse to put the Pumas on the field, get the TV cameras in, throw the biggest lunch for potential major new sponsors, bring the people down to see their new heroes in the flesh.

What happened? The Pumas returned home on 27 October 1999 and, bar a few games of beach rugby, the next time they played as a team was in June 2000. They played and beat Ireland, who were on tour, and 25,000 came to Ferro Carril Oeste to watch. The World Cup factor still existed but had dissipated, or had been allowed to wane. Wyllie, the architect of the great revival, was long gone, signed to coach Clontarf, a fine and friendly club in the Dublin suburbs but not one where crowd noise or a rarefied atmosphere causes a problem. It was back to the coaching merry-go-round. Your turn, Mr Buggins.

The players disappeared quickly, too. With nothing to keep them in their own country and in their country's domestic rugby, more than half the squad went to play abroad, where they could earn a living. At least the ARU, enlightened devils, did not ban them for it. Previously, the simple act of going overseas to play had been greeted with a lifetime ban, whether or not it could be proved that a player had transgressed the precious bylaws relating to amateurism. As a result Argentina had for years played matches with their second XV. But in this modern era, how fine the implications for Argentine domestic rugby had the squad been rewarded, if the 1999 Pumas had stayed at home, fired up an elite club set-up and dragged up the rest by example and aura. If they had traded on their fame and promoted the sport, even gone and knocked on doors outside the usual restricted catchment areas. A few decent sponsorship deals were done, but for the rest, as the World Cup factor ticked by, the

Argentina Rugby Union re-entered the torpor of the decades.

The export trade was brisk. Martin Scelzo, Roberto Grau, Omar Hasan, Mauricio Reggiardo, Ignacio Fernandez-Lobbe, Fréderico Mendez, Agustin Pichot, Gonzalo Quesada, Gonzalo Camardon, Eduardo Simone, Lisandro Arbizu and Diego Albanese were all playing abroad in 2000.

Roberto Grau is one of the most worldly of the Pumas. He was regarded highly at Saracens, until recently his English base. He is an outstanding prop and a wonderful character. Roberto lost his brother Martin, a fine forward in his own right, in a freak medical accident during a routine operation following an injury to his arm on the field. I once asked him if this had turned his parents and family against rugby. 'Of course not. It was the opposite, because it was the sport that Martin loved.'

Like his mates, Grau is also inordinately proud of being a Puma. He is anxious for there to be a small professional elite. He thinks that it could have a dramatic effect: 'If changes are made then we will continue to improve. If not, we will lose what we built up during the World Cup. A lot of the boys made big sacrifices when they were preparing. They had to set aside their work and their studies. A World Cup makes it all worthwhile; but you also have to consider your life in financial and career terms. The elite of Argentine rugby should be professional. Otherwise we will never complete on level terms as a nation and as individuals – it will be the players who carry the burden.'

As 2000 wore on, the Argentina Rugby Union had not even instituted a formal debate on the subject of the professional elite, still less gone about the process of setting one up and funding it. So the likes of Pablo Camerlinckx would still miss Test matches because they had to go for job interviews. Students would still miss crucial studies, and the rest would lose out financially as they missed work. Players would still disappear abroad, and even though there are regulations meant to ensure that national teams always have first call, Argentina had to make their 2000 tour – to Australia, the champions of the world – without Quesada, who had finished as RWC 99 leading scorer, and Reggiardo, the soul of the pack. Both were required by their French clubs. Annexed might be a better word. The clout of the Argentine RU to bring the French into line had the power of a wet lettuce. In the circumstances, for the Pumas to have held Australia to 32–15 in the second Test, a match they could have won, spoke well for their hearts. The first Test was lost by 53–6. Argentina had two training sessions before they took on the Aussie Machine.

What did the ARU think they were preserving when they declared so pompously in 1995 that they would remain amateur? What benefits did that decision bring? How did it improve Argentine rugby? The splendid Buenos Aires Cricket and Football Club would have continued their happy operation either way; nothing else would have changed. Had they set themselves up to take advantage of the new possibilities available to them, then their marketing could have come out of the Stone Age; they might have attracted a few kids who did not come from rich families; the Pumas would never have dipped in the affections of the country; and the national squad, properly looked after, would have retained its players, pride and passions. 'It's OK if they want to be amateur,' Pichot told me. 'But then don't arrange matches against the big teams.'

The Argentine players rejuvenated their country's passion for rugby, brought the hidden but bursting national pride to the fore and entranced their country once more, giving hope to all those who want the smug international rugby elite to be smashed to bits. The story of how they did so is a tribute to them, and one of the most vivid aspects of the 1999 World Cup.

The lesson to be learned from the only country to retain amateurism is that, intrinsically, amateurism meant nothing. It meant under-achievement, almost a deliberate under-achievement – almost a revelling in under-achievement. It meant that the natural pride of top rugby players was brutalised, used against them; that they were competing with the great teams of the rugby world from a disadvantaged standpoint. Amateurism was, and is, a silly concept inherently empty of merit. Perfectly useless.

CHAPTER FIVE

Pan-Europe

World Cup 1: scrabble on a global scale ◆ How they failed to organise the tournament ◆ Directors call for inaction

The last day of a bright October, 1999. Vapour trails in the air above Twickenham, that normally staid old stade. 'There'll always be an England . . '. Not in this tournament, there wouldn't be. The rose had been pruned by South Africa in Paris seven days before, and yet even in England's absence, the arena was going bonkers. 'An absurdly exciting match,' one of the finest sports scribblers, Paul Hayward, scribbled the next day under the heading 'WAS THIS THE GREATEST GAME EVER PLAYED?', as if the question were rhetorical.

Could well have been, Paul. It's all subjective but many people agreed at the time. The media room after the Twickenham game was alive with something different from the normal world-weariness, the muted clackings of laptops and the retching responses to the catering. It was alive with heady excitement and head-shaking joy. The action had been marvellous, the sense of occasion hair-raising, the feeling of shock equivalent to that which you'd experience were your late grandmother to suddenly sprint past the window.

The only point at issue in Hayward's vivid account of the staggering events of the second Rugby World Cup semi-final – in which France scored a dizzy thirty-three points in twenty-seven minutes against New Zealand, dumping them out of the event in sensational style by 43–21 – was that his reigning rugby best was the Barbarians–New Zealand game in 1973. I could not grant that match such status because it had the elements of a festival and was not, looked at in its entirety, a full classic. It tapered off. It is also now a sacred cow, and I'm not fond of untouchable beef.

But Hayward was correct with his new No. 1. It superseded my personal favourites, my own pet sensations: the Battle of Nantes, when France crushed New Zealand in 1986; the Australia–France World Cup semi-final in 1987; the first and second Tests of the New Zealand tour of South Africa in 1996; the first and second Tests of the British Lions tour of South Africa in 1997. So the 1999 World Cup, based in Cardiff but played also in England, Scotland, Ireland and France (Timbuktu's rugby stadium was double-booked, so the TRFU turned down the chance of hosting a pool), gave rugby its greatest afternoon. Not a bad start, that, when you are assessing the 1999 tournament's legacy.

What else? Lots. The tournament made a massive profit of well over £40 million, £35 million of which was earmarked for the International Rugby Board's genuine efforts towards the global development of the game, with bungs to buy boots in Bolivia and to introduce the game to nippers in Nigeria and to fund starter-packs and coaching systems and development all over Planet Earth. It is the thing that the IRB does best of all these days, admittedly after eighty years during which, to its eternal disgrace, it sent abroad not funds and encouragement, but only its own committee members to drink foreign gin. The resulting undeniable lift given to the local economy was still no substitute for new direct funding into rugby.

Masses of people came to RWC '99, boosting the Welsh economy marvellously. On the night of the final a group of French officials were trying to find accommodation as near to Cardiff as possible and were offered rooms in Basingstoke. The average attendance at the forty-one matches was over 40,000 – would have been higher had the Scottish Rugby Union had the first clue as to how to market the tournament of which they had angrily insisted on a share. (Turn up at Scotland's grounds and you panicked you'd got the day wrong.) At the knock-out stages of the tournament the average attendance was 66,830, exceeding the average attendance at the knock-out stages of the football World Cup, which was 61,000.

People tuned in. Independent figures revealed that 3.10 billion people in 209 countries watched the event on television. God knows how they know that, but they do. (One graph compared the income generated from television and sponsorship for the event to that for the 1987 World Cup. The graph was in the form of a Manhattan-skyline graphic, each item represented by a tall – or otherwise – building. The 1987 event's overall income appeared as a dog kennel for a poodle; the income from 1999 as one of the World Trade Towers.) Australia won the Cup, and John Eales, their captain and an avowed Republican, was presented with the Webb Ellis Trophy by Her suitably sour-faced and disinterested Majesty. All fine and dandy, and momentous.

A World Cup, self-evidently, will always show us with total clarity the current state of the sport at top level – its standards of play and style of play, of entertainment value, of behaviour, refereeing and officialdom, of commercial appeal and pulling-power. Here, in 1999, we had the greatest match, the greatest wedge, the most goggle-eyed TV world, King John, Queen Elizabeth.

We had as a backdrop the Millennium Stadium in Cardiff, and across Europe some of the greatest sporting stadiums of the day. Even today I cannot enter that soaringly intimate bowl of the Millennium without experiencing the kind of reverential wonder you would feel if you entered one of the most spectacular cathedrals and then not so much felt the presence of God as saw him up in the pulpit, bashing the bible.

Therefore the answer is quick and simple as to whether or not Rugby World Cup 1999 measured up, showed modern-day rugby in a glorious light.

It did not.

It isn't quite fair to lay it in context alongside its predecessor, South Africa's World Cup in 1995. The location in itself lent that momentous event inbuilt advantages which neither Wales nor any other World Cup hosts could ever enjoy. Like being one of the most history-dappled and stupendous countries on earth. At the time, South Africa as the Rainbow Nation was carrying a hopeful optimism that it could emerge intact from the apartheid years and subsequent interim period and from the possibilities of vicious extremism tearing it apart. There was symbolism around every corner. Sport – our little old rugby, our game, our love – played a central role in re-drawing that political landscape.

More yet. World Cup 1995 had a home-nation victory; it had the express train in ballet shoes in Jonah Lomu; it had, for a short period at least, the sight of rugby healing some of the self-inflicted wounds in South Africa's non-white community. It had Nelson Mandela dancing with François Pienaar at the presentation of the trophy, and I remembered realising that however marvellous Wales '99 would be, to see Robert Howley dancing with Vernon Pugh would simply not have the same symbolic value. Vernon's a bit short, and he is not, as is Mandela, the most vivid and famous example of humanity on earth, the epitome of forgiveness and the salvation of a whole country and a whole continent. At least, the IRFB have never put out a release to that effect. Not that they would if he was.

But 1999 was still a World Cup. For the Welsh, it was *our* World Cup. We wanted to see our country sitting easily on the world stage, wanted others to realise that we hold it so dear to our hearts because of what it is and what it does to our senses, not just because we were born there and are therefore stuck with it. I prayed for my country for months beforehand, for the perceptions of us and our own fierce pride to be boosted.

The World Cup is, you see, a mighty deal – by any standards of any sport. To host it is the opportunity of a lifetime. And yet what is the key to a World Cup's success, wherever it is played? In rugby, the key is different from that in soccer or cricket. It lies in the ability or otherwise to create a marvellous atmosphere around the whole thing, a friendly buzz which revitalises the palates of any rugby-lover, enhances the game's reputation and shows the sport in a light so wondrous that even aficionados are surprised. That is precisely what had happened for my colleagues and myself at all three previous World Cups. But it also creates an ambience which drags thousands and millions more people into its orbit. It shows off.

Great rugby on the field? Yes, fine. But you can have a great Rugby World Cup without really vintage playing standards, while a football tournament lives and dies on the field. Big wedge? Yes, very nice, too. But feel-good factor? Utterly indispensable. That was where the whole edifice of RWC '99 began to unravel.

And from way back. It is now well documented that the Welsh Rugby Union bid for the tournament against a combined bid from Australia and Japan. (We really keep these things compact, don't we? 'Let's just pop over from Brisbane to Osaka for this morning's match; we'll be back in the local for last orders.') The WRU naturally assumed that they would receive the support of the other unions in Europe for their bid. They were already prepared to grant the other three home unions some of the games, a decent chunk of pool and knock-out action. They had to. Wales is finely off for hotels but not so for stadiums. Drop down from the Millennium and you're in shabby Ninian Park.

There was no intention to involve France in the tournament because the five-union fudge had been tried in 1991 and every sporting, technical and commercial conclusion from the experts was that this scattered the thing too far and too thinly and made it phenomenally complicated and unfocused.

What happened? Soon, the greedy started blackmailing. At least one and possibly two of the home nations – supposedly Wales's allies in the attempt to regain some authority in world rugby from the southern hemisphere unions who'd ruled the game themselves for a decade – threatened to vote for the unwieldy Australia/Japan bid if they were not given a larger slice of the cake. The height of jealous bitterness. In order to win the votes, Wales eventually had to hand out an assortment of pools and knock-out matches to all and sundry; had to give both semi-finals to Twickenham, for God's sake, the least atmospheric of all the major rugby stadiums in the world. One pound for every visitor to RWC '99 who asked me, 'Why the effing hell are both semi-finals at Twickenham?' and I'd retire tomorrow.

Worst of all, the spineless French finally scuppered any possibility of a focused World Cup. The French Federation refused to vote unless they could host one of the groups in its entirety as well as a couple of knock-out matches. France lost the final in 1987 and therefore had a perfect right to bid for the sole hosting in 1991; they chickened out. They had the right to bid for the sole hosting for 1999; they chickened out. And, lacking the courage and vision to host their own event, they then tried to scupper and diminish the union that did have that courage and vision.

One of the latter-day sporting equivalents to General de Gaulle and his famous big-nosed 'Non' to British entry into the Common Market was Marcel Martin, formerly an official of the French Rugby Federation. By 1999 Martin held no post on the Federation, but was still a director of Rugby World Cup – even though he was essentially without portfolio, constituency and validity and, therefore, had no representative right to be there, speaking as he was for no one but himself.

Martin used to give a knowing shake of the head whenever I asked him why France did not bid alone. 'We cannot. We don't have the infrastructure in this country, or the quality of officials,' he would always say, chuckling as if in exasperation at these silly, uninformed questions. When France staged a brilliant football World Cup in 1998 Martin must have banged his head on the floor, the rug was yanked from under his feet so fast. So France cannot stage a big event, M. Martin? Compared to soccer's lion, rugby's still a kitten. If soccer can . . .

In any case, anyone who has ever watched more than one big rugby match held anywhere in France, and tapped into even a smidgen of the country's riotous, colourful, brutal, vivid and splendid rugby scene – all enacted in splendid stadiums – knows perfectly well that the first French-based World Cup will be the greatest ever played. Sorry, world. M. Martin and his *amis* have called it off.

Vernon Pugh was chairman of the Welsh Rugby Union when the bid for the World Cup was made. Though he never publicly admitted it, privately he felt shockingly let down by the hard-faced lack of sympathy for the bid and the lack of concern for rugby's image as he battled his way through a series of blackmailing committee rooms. Every time he emerged from a meeting Wales had lost a chunk of RWC '99. Apart from the opening day of the event and the final three days, there was ultimately no particular focus on Cardiff at all. No chance for communities to 'adopt' teams, to give outposts any more than a token kick.

The multi-hosted World Cup is a joke. The fact that none of the five nations would drop their demands for a pool meant that there had to be five pools, and therefore a *repêchage* quarter-final play-off stage to find eight teams for the quarter-final.

That was the practical drawback, but consider the ethics of the whole thing. They have Olympic Games centred in one city; they have football World Cups held in one country only. The blindingly obvious structure for European World Cups is for each of the four home countries to host a pool, and for the major bulk of the knock-out stages to take place in the one country which is the official host – or for the French to host the tournament on their own. By 1999 Pugh had left the WRU and was both chairman of the International Rugby Board and a director of Rugby World Cup. He had to sing from a different song-sheet and it was now his job to defend the five-centre effort. He spoke about the five unions being a natural grouping stemming from the Five Nations tournament (not relevant). He spoke about the relatively short distances in air-time between the various capitals (so what?). 'Er, that's it,' he really should have concluded.

Pugh has many critics in rugby, as befitting the leading official in the sport. I tend to think that whatever chaos the game has descended into would have been a sight worse without him. Whether or not that is true, and whatever he said after the tournament had ended, Pugh is far too savvy and sharp not to conclude in his heart that RWC '99 was hijacked by greedy, jealous officials. As for his own words upholding the five-host structure, I personally didn't believe he agreed with them for a moment.

Once stuck with all the hosts, of course, I suppose the only thing to do was make the best of it, hide the joins as much as possible and especially mount a massive PR and marketing blitz. What better way to begin to spread the feel-good factor than with some major pre-publicity to set the stage? At last, RWC Ltd could start to earn their corn.

So what did they do for Rugby World Cup 1999? They tried to keep it a secret. It at first surprised me, then increasingly annoyed me, then caused me to seethe with a mixture of disbelief and incredulity and anger that whenever I arrived at Cardiff Station in 1999 as the tournament approached there was not one solitary banner or advert to indicate that I was entering the home city of the 1999 World Cup. Eventually, one day before the tournament, they stuck up a big banner on one of the nearby buildings. And a blow-up dragon.

Are we asking for marketing rocket-science here? Was it too much for RWC to contemplate one massive poster at Cardiff Station, just for a start? You can always get a bloke to design it and another bloke to print it up and another bloke to come along with his ladder and bucket of glue. Three man-hours for the third-biggest sporting event in the world. Another poster at Cardiff Airport's arrivals hall, maybe (the three blokes could get the bus down there, to save costs). Another at or near each of the two Severn Bridges and another at Paddington Station and you've captured everyone arriving in Wales as a visitor or any Welsh man or woman – commuter or housewife or whatever – making any journey of any significance. Who knows? They might even tell their friends. It might not be considered particularly outlandish and wasteful, either, to suggest that, since the tournament was split into five hosting countries, each of those countries might just stick up a few posters at their main points of entry. You know, just to build some sense of anticipation.

Better still, keep the same sites hired for the duration but change the wording on the posters, reflect a growing sense of anticipation as the tournament approached. South Africa in 1995 was supposed to be a Third World country when it came to sports marketing, but proved to be drastically more advanced then than the First World represented by the home countries four years later. Advertising World Cup 1995 was a stunning poster campaign featuring the charismatic coloured wing Chester Williams. New posters were displayed the closer the tournament aproached, upon which the message changed gradually while the theme and style and logos remained the same. When the teams arrived, the latest in the series bore the message: 'THE WAITING'S ALMOST OVER'. It charged the air with static just to stare at it, and the series was plastered all over Africa.

For ages before the tournament and throughout its duration, overhead banners were hung about every 200 metres along the dark and dusty main highway between Pretoria and Johannesburg. When the world of rugby flew out home, the big South African cities and airports were covered with the same type of poster, now bearing a farewell message. It was superbly effective. Feel good about South Africa? You bet we did, mugged or not.

And for RWC '99, nothing. Bits and pieces by individual tourist boards and hoteliers and individual sponsors and a window display by your local butcher. Nothing coordinated. It was a disgraceful failure. RWC whined that ITV, the tournament broadcaster, whose heart was elsewhere, were running a few trailers, and pointed out that some of the main sponsors, notably Guinness – the purveyors of the old black nectar had a fine tournament – were running campaigns, so there was no need for the media to complain about lack of build-up. Rubbish. It was RWC's job to run their own high-profile, high-cost campaign, not to leave it, piecemeal, to other people. So they made £40 million. So what? They made money to sell rugby *outside* the five nations, but they ignored rugby *in* the five nations – and they ignored people in the five nations. The benefits of hosting are supposed to accrue to the hosts.

What has the official RWC Ltd report to say on the lack of promotion that cost the image of the game so dear? The report popped up on the IRB website shortly after the *Sunday Times* and other papers wondered loudly if the accounts were to be hidden again. In what had a profoundly and depressingly familiar ring, the report took random pot-shots at television and sponsors, even at companies that had no direct responsibility.

What else? 'No marketing or public-awareness-building was undertaken by RWC Ltd/IRB. A feel-good factor was lacking.' God! Honesty! Albeit tucked away in a paragraph near the end, it was honesty nonetheless. Whatever next? The report recommends that major steps be taken next time for a promotional campaign. It is all as if the need to promote the tournament is some kind of public-relations revolution instead of something you'd do automatically if you were running your local village-green bowls tournament.

There was plenty of opportunity to get even more sick to the back teeth of the administration of rugby at the top level, especially the buck-passing bunch, the endless horde of initials who organised the 1999 tournament. The administration of the tournament was a ghastly amalgam of Scrabble and Snakes and Ladders, with a series of bungling and bickering bodies all supposed to be under the same roof and working towards the same end, some setting out with the sole and slithering intention of evading blame for any of the significant number of cock-ups. Some tended to place that goal ahead of any intent to run a tournament for the advancement of rugby.

The weaknesses in the event sprang directly from the weaknesses in RWC. The RWC organisation is itself hopeless, unwieldy and unnecessary. For the 1999 event they were a polyglot bunch of chiefly ageing administrators, some retired, others in part-time work, others in full-time work, from different parts of the globe under the chairmanship of Leo Williams of Australia. Their talents clashed when they should have dovetailed. The body included, and still includes, Tom Kiernan, who is an official (usually a paid official) on the Irish Rugby Union, the International Rugby Board, RWC Ltd, European Rugby Cup and the Six Nations. Sorry if I've forgotten your other committees, Tom.

Maybe he's brilliant. Maybe not. Maybe excellence as a committee-man is subjective. Maybe I can't grasp his brilliance because (thank the good Lord) I don't have to spend hours in committee. However, my researches have not provided me with a firm testimony to his talents. I do not attack Kiernan specifically; rather the point is that no one man should hold that number of offices for so long. Kiernan was a strong supporter of amateurism and is from a union who are grinding slowly towards making a fist of professional rugby (it is far easier to do in Ireland than anywhere else in the world) but have no idea how to be populist or accessible or how to market the sport. No matter how good his intentions, someone like him should not continue to hang around in the modern game.

It is high time for the well-meaning Kiernans of the rugby world to move aside in favour of freshness and modernity, and that was one of the resounding lessons to be learned from RWC '99. Pugh apart, the only director who really impressed anyone I came across during the tournament was Rob Fisher, a thoroughly decent Kiwi. On the subject of the excellence of the remainder of RWC – either individually or corporately – those many people to whom I spoke maintained the silence of the grave.

It was the weakness of RWC which brought about the giant Scrabble. Also involved in the tournament and forming the triple-word-scoring 'blunderers' were the WRU, the hosting union; the RFU; the SRU; the IRFU; and the sub-host, the French Rugby Federation. There was also IMG, the commercial partners – and Lord knows what this successful commercial company really makes of RWC (well, maybe the Lord doesn't, but I do). And RSL (Rugby Solutions Limited), a small group appointed to liaise with anyone who wanted to be liaised with (Tom Kiernan, unstaggeringly, was a director), and since there were so many people on so many fronts with whom to liaise, RSL was entirely overstretched and collapsed in a heap. Then there was the IRB, under whose auspices the tournament is run, and their tournaments directorate. Phew.

All this was impossibly tangled and gave everyone the excuse to blame everyone else. It was made more frantic than it might have been because Pugh's hitherto firm friendship with Glanmor Griffiths had been lost. Griffiths was the chairman of the WRU who drove the Millennium project, and had, it seemed, drained himself of clarity of action and flair in the process. The situation was desperate, with the organisers and the hosting union at loggerheads before, during and after the event. And, of course, there's the fact that the Welsh Rugby Union were and are spectacularly inadequate, and accelerated not one bit for the event itself. The union is constructed along the same lines as it was when Welsh rugby was a cottage industry; manifestation of the fact that only a pitiful few class people in Wales are responsible for the administration of the national sport.

Yes, the Welsh Rugby Union built the Millennium Stadium; yes, they had the vision and the size of bung to bring over Graham Henry, one of the top coaches in the world. Otherwise, and certainly in terms of RWC '99, pathetic. In June 2000 the bunglers sought refuge in that age-old Welsh hiding-place of calling a talking-shop committee to discuss things. The bunglers appointed a body to discuss the future shape of the WRU – and therefore, one might hope, the best way of ditching the bunglers. With a sharp eye on their self-preservation and their divine freedom to harvest the salaries and other perks of rugby high office, who did the bunglers appoint to sit on the committee? Themselves.

The situation was no better elsewhere as the tournament approached. The RFU had fallen out with everyone long before the event, and were positively desperate for the Millennium Stadium not to be finished in time so that they could a) gloat and b) ride to the rescue with Twickers. RSL also fell out with all sides, and were swamped by workload; the WRU ticket office blundered spectacularly – grandees arrived for matches, even the final, to find great hordes of the unwashed in their seats. No one organisation had a good word to say about another.

The brutal effects of all this mess were made even worse by the fact that the Millennium Stadium was a project of such size and complexity that it became a desperate race against time to have it finished. Matters such as ticketing, hospitality and safety certification were put back months. Add to this the bitter in-fighting and back-stabbing and you have an appalling shambles.

The contractors employed in the various fields for media facilities, accreditation, travel, marketing, sponsorship and licensing all found it the worst experience of their lives. 'I have never worked in such a poisonous atmosphere. If rugby people only realised what is happening behind the scenes of this thing they'd be sick,' one of their number told me as we watched the France–Argentina quarter-final in a Parisian bar. On the day before the final I asked another leading RWC contractor if he was going to the Big One. 'I'm not going because I don't want to be anywhere near that lot,' he said, sweeping his arm towards a metaphorical grouping of the Scrabble. 'I do not even want to be in the same room as that bunch of wankers. I am going to go home and go for a walk with my family.'

When Pugh was speaking at one official dinner, another top official cupped his hands together and shouted 'Bullshit!' Each body timed dinners and functions to scupper concurrent events thrown by other bodies, thus giving the innocent the wicked choice as to who to patronise. Both official and unofficial PR men representing the various bodies whispered into media ears for the whole month. Had we heard, they asked, about this or that cock-up, or what X had done to Y, or how many tickets were unaccounted for, or who'd been seen travelling in an RWC-hired limo, or who'd demanded a bigger room, or what A had said about B, or that this top official had told another top official to f**k off? Off the record, of course; don't quote me, old boy.

The buck-passing was shocking. Hardly a single body took responsibility for their failure, each blaming another for the various teething problems which arose – matters such as lack of marketing of Scotland matches; lack of atmosphere at Twickenham; lateness of tickets for travelling fans; hiring of vast fleets of big cars to convey top officials; payment for expensive suites for the same bunch; complaints from sponsors (notably British Telecom) that their sponsorship investment had been partly wasted; the miserably poor merchandising operation, which could have been bettered by someone flogging World Cup shirts out of the back of a van. The hair-raising nature of the media operation so incensed Nigel Rushman, chief executive of the company which erected the media centres, that on his arrival one morning he told his men to turn off the power and to start to dismantle. Rushman and his team ultimately did a splendid job under ridiculous pressure; at this point, making a stand was the only way he could bring the inertia of the whole thing to someone's attention.

Marcel Martin was asked to defend the ticketing policy. 'It's nothing to do with us,' he said. He said nothing on the subject of collective responsibility. Nothing of the fact that, because every one of the rugby bodies involved was part of the IRB, the buck stopped with them all. Rugby World Cup never had a motto. If it had considered one in 1999, then 'It's nothing to do with us' would have been apt.

Who cares about media arrangements? Probably only the media, where there were in fact further horrors. There was a nonsensically complicated communications policy for telephone hire. This reached its stunning epitome when Clinton van der Berg, a very fine South African journalist, was trying to file his story from the France–Fiji match to his paper.

70

We had all been given BT phone-cards which required us to input an access number, a PIN-code and an eight-digit account code before we could even begin to dial our newspapers' numbers. Poor Clinton, sitting in his hotel room in Toulouse, had to dial for an outside line from the hotel, then dial the code for England to access his Telecom World Cup account, bung in all the PIN-codes and account numbers, dial the international access number for South Africa and finally his own paper's number for modem copy. If memory serves, had Clinton wanted to file his story over his laptop and modem, he would have had to dial thirty-two digits – in order – waiting for contact to be made between at least three of the various groups of digits before he could continue. For that reason, he could not simply hit 'last-number redial' if the line was engaged. He joined us for dinner that night. We were on the coffee.

Catering for the media is never high on the rugby public's list of musts – although were the food poisonous it might get a ripple of enthusiasm out there. You rotters. But the truth is that the food was so horrendous during RWC '99 that one poor waitress at Twickenham confessed to us that she was ashamed to serve it. And what does the RWC report say about media? That too much was spent on us. It states blithely how much money could be saved next time by cutting expend-iture on us. It also indicates that in future the media will be asked to stump up towards the cost of the facilities provided.

Fine. Send the invoice well in advance, RWC. But be warned. It might pass in the post an invoice addressed to you, if that's how you want to play it. We at the *Sunday Times*, like our Sunday rivals, will be charging you for the space and cost of running eight pages of a broadsheet newspaper – up to fifteen if you take in regional-edition changes – for every week of a six-week event. The daily papers will obviously be invoicing you for even more of the hitherto free space.

Bear in mind that for much of the pre-tournament and for months beforehand, the press was the only place in which the tournament was being promoted, or even mentioned. The enthusiasm of my rugby-writing colleagues and our sports editors was a marvel. Rugby was, in my opinion, over-covered. But this at least meant that had you wanted to read about the tournament you could buy a paper at Cardiff Station, or Edinburgh Airport, or Dublin Station, or Paris Charles de Gaulle. You couldn't see a poster promoting your event at any of those places, RWC. Nor, without us, would you have been able to suck so much into your sponsorship budget.

So fine. We'll pay for your facilities, poor though they are, and even though by charging us you'd be breaking all the ethics of the media. And you pay us for the space we devote to your event. Deduct the lower figure from the higher, and then send us your cheque for around £10 million. And the balance later.

Officialdom at RWC '99 was appalling. All the good things that happened happened either in spite of it or because parts of the event are so easy to organise that a bunch of bunglers could do it. They did. Rugby World Cup Ltd at RWC '99 were very poor. So were the WRU and almost every other body which helped to disorganise it. The proper companies, run by the proper directors, were aghast.

In official places, the inquest, the wash-up, was minimal.

On the final day of the event John O'Neill, chief executive officer of the Australian Rugby Union, spoke out. Australia had already been named as hosts for 2003 (with New Zealand). O'Neill called for RWC to be disbanded. 'The days are gone when you can have a tournament of this size – which we continually pat ourselves on the back for being the third-largest in the world – run by a group of part-timers,' he said. 'We just do not need the RWC structure. There need to be far clearer lines of communication than exist at present. The way we would prefer it is they leave it to us. We are dead against setting up separate structures and vehicles for RWC.'

Easy. The two hosting unions appoint a small group of real professionals, bring in IMG to run the commercial side, and the IRB hand them a World Cup charter which they must follow. Pugh, as IRB chairman, can be the point of liaison. Australia's stadiums are already prepared; they will have all the experience of the World Cup; they will have blunt Aussie expertise. Why on earth, as O'Neill wondered aloud, would you need a bunch of semi-retired, often pensionable men, some from the wrong era, who have already failed? They would just be in the way.

The manoeuvring started soon after O'Neill spoke. At the time of writing, RWC remains in place (and in the way), almost intact. O'Neill, I guarantee, will tear all his hair out by the time RWC 2003 starts, unless his union can mobilise the IRB to act against its own problem child. It looks as though Williams will be jettisoned, and, as he holds no official position on his own union, why should he remain? One director, sensing the way the wind was blowing, was trying for a post as paid adviser to another part of the labyrinthine organisation.

Loose cannons? 'From a distance,' says John Jeavons-Fellows, a former England IRB representative, 'RWC appears to operate as if there is accountability. However, it makes its decisions in private then presents them to the IRB, which only meets twice a year, as a *fait accompli*.' RWC directors earn around £20,000 from that post alone, to add to any remuneration from their other committees. In Cardiff, many stayed in suites at a cost of up to £650 per night.

What of the most vexed question surrounding the operation of the World Cup since it began in 1987 – the question of hosting, and the urgent need to focus the tournament? And, especially, to end the nonsensical five-country hosting in Europe? On the day before the 1999 final, with the stock of French rugby at a high (though an artificial one, admittedly) after their superlative victory over New Zealand, I asked Bernard Lapasset, president of the French Rugby Federation, if he would bid for the 2007 World Cup. It was, and is, his perfect right.

'There is great support for rugby in France, from our public, from the French government and from our national Olympic committee,' he said. 'We would like France to bid for the position of premier organisers in 2007.' Then the knife in the stomach. 'We have agreements with the other European nations that we would not act alone; and we would look to act in concert with our partners in the Five Nations.' (He did later announce a French-only bid.) I would be fully in favour of England bidding to host the 2007 tournament if the French are to be so lily-livered. And midway through 2000 there was talk of an RFU bid which would base much of the tournament in England – why not all of it? There is Twickenham and a re-built Wembley; there is the splendid McAlpine Stadium in Huddersfield and St James' Park in Newcastle to give the good old Geordies a slice; you'd have at least two matches at Ashton Gate, a great success when the West Country turned out to see New Zealand–Tonga in 1999; you'd want to go further west to give Redruth and the rugby Mecca of Cornwall a pool match. You'd go anywhere and everywhere, but everywhere you went in England you'd feel the fever.

But forget it. I guarantee you – I bet my house – that as soon as England moot a bid, four other unions instantly decided that there is no way the arrogant English can be allowed the stage, decided how best to filch away pools and knock-out matches. Decide how best to act in their own, not rugby's, interests.

So there we have it. The Rugby World Cup, wherever it is played in the northern hemisphere, will be a ridiculous pan-European fudge because no one union has the bottle to bid for it and no one union has the grace and far-sightedness to trade their support for an application against a promise of support for a later event. The notion of a France-only World Cup is dead.

So, apparently, is any notion of staging a World Cup in a new location, although a possible shortfall in profits would be offset by the mighty boost a particular country – America, Argentina, Italy, to name just three – might get to their rugby economy if they were given their head and allowed to have a go. That would, however, infringe the jealously guarded right of the top gang of leading European rugby officials to swill around in the same circuit, with the same privileges, the same lack of real accountability, the same lack of real inquest into their efforts. On they go, robbing world rugby of a good deal of its potential.

The true power of Rugby World Cup will never be unleashed.

I am perfectly aware that those of us more privy to the behind-the-scenes bickering had more opportunity to become jaundiced and to complain about matters which meant little to the paying and watching public outside. I am perfectly aware that out at the games – especially those in Wales and France, the only venues where there was a real sense of occasion – there was a helluva party going on; that some of the rugby was decent, if not spectacular. I know that many people were infected by World Cup fever.

Of course, I realise that the outside world was neither present at the opening press conference nor cared a fig about it. RWC chairman Leo Williams tried to announce that everything was ready for the off. He was drowned out about five times by loudspeaker announcements calling various tradesmen to various bits of the stadium that were hanging off. Then a power saw starting up in the adjoining room interrupted his speech.

He was also set back by a world-class question (at least in terms of sheer length) asked by me. 'Leo,' I said. 'This is the fourth World Cup. There is still massive controversy surrounding its operation and RWC itself, in the fields of PR and promotion and the stadium and the scheduling and the bickering . . .' I carried on bravely in this vein for several minutes, undeterred by loud snoring noises from my colleagues behind. I presented to Williams the whole litany of failures as I saw them, and the fact that, twelve years after the first tournament, there we were with no sign that the sport could organise a piss in the toilet, let alone a piss-up in a brewery. Williams was honest. Either that or he'd forgotten the first sixteen parts of the question. 'I can't disagree with anything you've just said,' he said. They themselves knew that they were partly a shambles.

And, of course, rugby followers were not present in person when we held the post-event press conference. Even if they had been invited they wouldn't have made it. There was a wonderfully funny and farcical scene in the Millennium Stadium bowels because no one really knew which room the conference was supposed to be in – and, if they did know, had no idea where the room was. This led to a merry procession, lasting around half an hour, of a combination of laughing hacks and furious RWC directors tramping up and down the stairs in a modern-day version of the 'Grand Old Duke of York'. At one stage, after the thirty-fourth wrong turning, a director of Rugby Solutions rested his head gently against a wall and cursed softly to himself in desperation.

But when it began, the conference at least demonstrated the first shred of PR flair for months. Obviously the directors realised that their performance might come under attack (it wouldn't have, actually – I think the media by that stage were simply numb from it all, and had live rugby to cover the next day). Williams set off with a blistering digression – a fierce assault on ITV's coverage of the tournament. It was a splendid diversion, well carried off.

The World Cup concluded the following day. Australia won. Cardiff emptied of its visitors, and the high officials left for Heathrow in their luxurious hire-cars, obviously not trusting one of the best rail services in the country, which could also have taken them there in a number of different ways.

However much rugby's public enjoyed it all, I also know beyond a shadow of a doubt that the tournament never came remotely close – as a party, an ambience, a celebration – to any of the previous three World Cups. In 1991 an infectious tide rose and engulfed people from inside and outside rugby borders. In 1995 the tournament cascaded into the wider world. This time, the party was curtailed by lack of promotion, by the scattered nature of the event robbing it all of focus, by silly fixture-scheduling, by bungling. And most of all by the pervading atmosphere.

Feel-good factor? Yes, the event made millions. But without the feel-good factor, any World Cup partially collapses. If you could have been there in the pioneer years in Australia and New Zealand you would know about feel-good factor, the shy and yet awesome realisation that our old cottage industry was about to explode. There was a feel-good factor in South Africa in 1995, where sport and politics mixed, and mixed so gloriously. And also in the 1991 World Cup, where the winners, Australia, charmed the pants off the sport; where the sense of the gladiatorial and of rugby's goodness spread so that non-rugby people discussed it in the street or on Radio 1 and Radio 4, in house-music raves and chamber-music intervals; when to be a rugby follower was to be the centre of attention with your mates.

I love being out on rugby's road. I have four pictures in my mind, from four World Cups. On the evening after the 1987 final, a gang of around 200 people – players, public, media, officials, Kiwis, Brits, Japs – formed a huge circle around a large reception/function area in the Sheraton Hotel, Auckland. The first World Cup was over; we had a marvellous multi-nation and multi-cultural sing-song. On the last night of the second World Cup, still overflowing with that tournament's glories, I remember breakfasting at dawn somewhere in London after another fantastic night. And following Mandela's final I spent hours in quieter contemplation of the explosive impact of what we had seen.

The grand closing dinner in 1999 was perfectly in keeping with previous RWC organisation. It was badly organised by all accounts, wasted thousands of pounds, and they had to bring all the speeches forward because people started walking out of the two-thirds-empty hall almost immediately. At least they maintained the proper protocol by inviting as their guest Steve Bale, chairman of the Rugby Union Writers' Club. They invited him at 7.15 p.m. on the evening of the function, for a 7 p.m. start.

Work finished after the 1999 final, I went with two colleagues to the Tredegar Arms in Bassaleg. We were shattered, from wallpapering rugby across all those pages for six weeks in three separate editions. But mostly we were brought down in mood because there was little to feel up for. I had two pints of Ansells Bitter and drove home, tired of rugby.

It is, admittedly, impossible to measure and quantify a feel-good factor. It is a personal matter. That said, it can be vastly fuelled in the proper ways. If, rugby being the type of sport it is, no World Cup can be a success without that feel-good factor, then RWC '99 was a failure. It let down rugby and it let down Wales. I can forgive and forget on neither count.

CHAPTER SIX

Trinidad and Llanelli

**World Cup II: Mina and the march of the deserving ♦ World
united in mediocrity ♦ The pool stages of RWC '99**

Now here's a thing. In the months and years before the opening of
Rugby World Cup 1999, most of the twenty teams – and especially the
moneyed top ten – spent a mind-altering amount of time and the
equivalent of the gross national product of a middle-sized African nation
in building up for the tournament. All the squad sessions and tours and
warm-up matches and state-of-the-art conditioning and video analysis
and diet and psychological theories and back-up backroom-boy legions
are what this whole process now entails.

What happened? How many teams from the top ten actually played
better than expected? One. Argentina. Yes, the good old Argies did
better than the game thought they would. The rest? Australia, surely,
because they won it? Nope. The Aussies were fine, defended well, but
they did not have to be anything special and good job, too, because they
weren't. New Zealand? Collapsed in a heap. England? Never threatened, leaving a colossal gap between the way the team talked and the
way it played. Wales? Came off a rampaging run of form and when the
destiny days dawned were sluggish and drained. France? One performance away from utter humiliation. South Africa? Brave, but by their
standards, poor. Scotland? Awful. Ireland? Draw the curtains, Grandma.
Italy, disappointing.

Argentina, as I described earlier, played with growing resolution.
They reached the quarter-finals, played splendidly in defeat against
France. And went home to a hero's welcome. Consider their farcical
preparation. Only three months prior to the tournament they had a
dishevelled coaching structure led by an Argentinian who had lost the
respect of his players, a Kiwi who had that respect but didn't speak their
language, no budget from supinely amateurish Argentine RU, no
momentum and a sketchy back-up. They lost at home to Wales, chiefly

because in the scrummage, their area of supreme historical strength, they were massacred. They appointed another coach, and sacked him immediately.

And they came to Cardiff and played with verve and freshness. Any lessons there, lads? Far be it from me ever to suggest that obsessive and over-heating national-team managements are thrashing the life and soul and vibrancy from the bodies and minds of their national teams, are bringing them to the major events tired in the leg and arm and jaded in the heart, and that if they all slashed their preparation time by around sixty per cent they would produce better sides. Far be it from me ever to suggest that.

The teams gathered in the home countries and France towards the end of September. Spain and Uruguay, the two nations who had never played in the finals before, departed to Scotland. To most rugby followers who believed in the game's global family, and who wished all parts of that family to be in rude health, Spain and Uruguay were the best news. We all said a prayer for the tyro little devils.

Yet by others, they were cursed. The South African camp expressed dismay that they were lumped into such meaningless pool games; the Scotland marketers gave up on them without firing a shot; one leading Australian rugby figure launched a long, private tirade one night just before the tournament started, in which he said that Spain and Uruguay devalued the event, should have been banished to some little boys' group well out of the way of the serious players. 'At this level people want to watch their heroes, the best playing the best,' he said.

Hmmm. Uruguay undeserving of their place in the finals? People wanting to watch their heroes, the best against the best? Garbage. Pitiless, pompous, narrow-minded garbage. I'll tell you about my World Cup heroes. One of them was R. Mina of Brazil. I never saw him play, I admit, and wasn't entirely sure of his Christian name, though I did my best to establish it. But his contribution meant a lot to me. He hooked for Brazil in their first and only match in the 1999 World Cup. Brazil were playing Trinidad & Tobago in their first match in Americas Zone, Pool One, Round A, in Port-of-Spain. To give some idea of the size and scope and lung-bursting nature of the qualifying competition, to give some idea of what you had to go through if you were not Australia or one of the others in the smug elite, the Trinidad–Brazil match took place on 11 November 1996: three years before the final at the Millennium Stadium on 6 November 1999. The first match of RWC '99 actually took place on 26 September 1996, between Latvia and Norway in Riga.

I doubt if Mina was dreaming of the Millennium Stadium then. With good reason. It hadn't been built or even mooted. A few of us who realised what a ghastly tip the old Arms Park had become may have dreamed about something a little better. But even had the new stadium been there, gleaming, Mina's aspirations would not have been too elevated. I wondered how he felt as he prepared for the match in Port-of-Spain – part of a great adventure and global brotherhood, or that this was just something he did for the weekend trip? I wondered if he felt part of the front-row union, if his friends from work took the piss because he played such an odd game, a tiny game, whereas they worshipped the samba-writhing god called football. I doubted if in his build-up he'd been able to pore endlessly over videos of the Trinidad front row in action.

Mina didn't get very far. In conditions described in one account as 'extreme heat' Brazil lost 41–0, with Durtis Nero of Trinidad scoring a great individual try. Mina never again appeared in the tournament because Guyana, the only other team in Americas Zone, Pool One, Round A, withdrew – creditably: they were the only one of the seventy-one countries who entered the tournament, some of whom must have been catastrophically short of funds and infrastructure, to default. But Mina had a footnote. He was the only Brazilian player mentioned in the one report of the match I could uncover. 'He played with great courage and never gave up.'

Durtis Nero and his Trinidadians proudly advanced. They were now through to Americans Zone, Pool One, Round B. The other contenders were Chile and Bermuda, the latter having qualified through another pre-group by beating Bahamas in the Bahamas, and Barbados at home. Against the visiting Chileans not even Durtis could inspire his men. They played heroically at Port-of-Spain and lost only by 6–35 in conditions of high humidity and 30°C. 'Both teams received a rousing round of applause as they left the field at the conclusion of a very competitive match played in extremely adverse weather conditions.'

The Trinidad–Chile game typified the colour splashed on rugby's canvas away from its normal gallery. Brian Lara, the great batsman, was there to support his countrymen at the Queen's Park Oval. After the match, the team repaired to a traditional watering hole, the Pelican Inn in St Ann's.

The only absentee was Mark Hamilton, the team's young back. He had to go straight back to a youth detention centre, where he was serving a three-year sentence for armed robbery. He and a gang had robbed a bread van of its receipts, had been shot at by police and were eventually caught hiding out in a forest. The youth training centre prison facility where Hamilton was incarcerated had begun a rugby programme, the previously wild Hamilton had taken to it. He had made the U19 national team and was released for the day to wear the red, white and black of the full Trinidad side for the Chile match. Wayne Albert, the YTC rugby coach, said before the match: 'I'm trying to help the fellas renew their lives through rugby. I am not a psychologist but I know from my own experience that rugby is a road to a better life.' Hamilton himself believed that his sport had saved him. 'I won't have to look over my shoulder for no police car again.' What did Trinidad's defeat matter set against that?

Trinidad also went down to Bermuda in Hamilton, Bermuda, in front of a crowd 'estimated at two per cent of the Island's population' – that would mean, by my maths, a splendid 1300. Ross Webber was by all accounts outstanding at fly-half for the Bermudans. However, Bermuda lost to Chile in the Prince of Wales Stadium, Santiago by 65–8. Three things were notable about the match. There was a punch-up, but order was quickly restored. The pitch was 'sparsely grassed'. And the Chileans fielded, incredibly, just three players who were over twenty-one.

Chile, fresh-faced, progressed to Americas Zone, Pool One, Round C, and their next challenge was to try to win a round-robin pool of three, with Uruguay and Paraguay. The Condors (Chile) beat the Yacares (Paraguay) by 54–6 in Santiago even though Nicolas Caceres of Paraguay 'tackled his heart out'. Their big clash of the group came in Montevideo against Uruguay, and it was probably only home advantage that allowed the Teros (Uruguay) to squeeze through. They won by 20–14, the match having turned towards the end when the Canadian referee David Steele reversed a penalty he had originally awarded to Chile. The defeated captain, Alfonso Escobar, said, 'We are very disappointed. As never before have the Chilean team prepared for this game. But we will be back.'

So it was Uruguay, making light of bruises and feeding on new experiences, who progressed to Americas Zone, Pool One, Round D. Argentina, Canada and the United States, the big guns of the Americas, joined them for a tournament in Buenos Aires, with the top three to enter the tournament proper in Cardiff. Uruguay found it tough, lost to Canada 38–15, to Argentina 55–0 and then, in the decider for the third-placed position and a passage to Cardiff as of right, they played a superb match against the United States and lost by only 16–21. Diego Ormaechea, a vet with three children, their No. 8 and captain, who had been thirty-eight when Uruguay's qualifying matches began, scored a try. It came in his twentieth year of international rugby and as his caps total reached the sixties.

But now it was at least permissible for Ormaechea's men to dream of Cardiff and, if not of the Millennium Stadium itself, then of the artist's impression of what it would be if it was finished in time (it was, as it turned out, finished in good time – about nine minutes before the opening ceremony). They faced a preliminary *repêchage* in a two-leg match against Portugal, who had risen via one of the European qualifying routes. They hammered Portugal by 46–9 in Montevideo – watched by Said Zniber, Morocco's rugby president. The Moroccans had heroically battled along their own path, coached by Daniel Dubroca, a former hooker, captain and coach of France. They now faced Uruguay, who had beaten Portugal 33–24 in the second leg, in a marvellously culture-clashing two-leg 'final', the end of the whole ball-breaking, globe-travelling process. It was a close thing. Morocco played courageously and lost by only 18–3 in Montevideo; then in the return, in Casablanca, the powerful Uruguay forwards kept a grip and despite raucous support for the home team and two splendid tries by the talented Moroccan back Karin El Oula, Uruguay lost by only 21–18.

I wonder if my Australian friend – and all those who shared his views as to the presence of Uruguay and Spain in RWC '99 – would have had the guts to go up to Diego Ormaechea on the final whistle in Casablanca, prise him out of the collective embrace of his squad and tell him to his face that he had no right to go to Wales for the finals. Sorry, son, two years of high water and hell and self-discovery. Now get lost.

No right? No one had more right. Not only had Ormaechea and his men grafted their way heroically through any number of obstacles; not only had they probably stayed in hotels in which some of the leading rugby coaches would have disdainfully refused to board their dogs, trained on some fields on which the same sniffy coaches would not have walked their dogs; not only had the entire squad lost out on work time and home life, but they had also done it for free. For nothing. They had, almost to a man, paid dearly for their place of honour.

It was more than that, though. It was something intrinsic in the essential greatness of RWC '99's vast qualifying set-up. Uruguay had effectively been a snowball (not the best analogy, given the heat in which their particular qualifying thread had been played): as they went rolling along they had picked up all the aspirations, the courage, the dreams and hopes of the smaller rugby nations who had been in on the start of the thread, all the teams they had beaten and all the teams those defeated teams had beaten.

To me, Uruguay in the finals represented Brazil and Trinidad & Tobago, Bermuda, Chile and Paraguay, Portugal and Morocco. To me, their arrival had catapulted Ormaechea to the ranks of all-time RWC heroes; but also up there with him, with a stripe from their own national colours metaphorically borne in Ormaechea's powder-blue Uruguay kit, were Durtis Nero and Ross Webber, Nicolas Caceres, Alfonso Escobar and Karin El Oula. Up there was any other selfless, perhaps even penniless, hero who had given the lot for his rugby nation, be that nation fledgling or tiny or impossible to spot through a telescope. Up there, too, was R. Mina, who 'never gave up' on a field in Port-of-Spain three years before the opening ceremony. In one sense Tim Horan, the official Player of the Tournament, stood only level with R. Mina.

Diego Ormaechea led Uruguay out at Galashiels on the first Saturday of the tournament. Against Spain. The Spanish were, of course, themselves representatives of a wonderfully vivid and hard qualifying thread; they had their own seasoned hero in the red-haired, rumbustious forward Albert Malo. This was obviously the only chance either side had to win a World Cup match – neither had an earthly against South Africa or Scotland, although Uruguay competed brilliantly in both games. In a match of verve and charm and excitement, Uruguay beat Spain by 27–15. Their first try was scored by Diego Ormaechea, others by Jean Menchaca and Alfonso Cardossa. Ormaechea was then forty, the oldest man in the tournament. He led a team that some thought should not have been there. Strange, then, that he looked so like a man in his element.

It was by no means a special World Cup in terms of standards and style of play. Yes, of course, there was dedication, courage and fair play and everyone, to borrow one of Bob Dwyer's splendid Ozisms, was as fit as a trout. There was honour among the competitors, too. Only one positive drugs-test out of hundreds, and that unwittingly caused when Anton Oliver took a prescribed substance for an ear infection as he boarded an aircraft. As sportsmen, the top echelon of world rugby players were shown in an excellent light.

But the framework the game had given them let them down. The efforts of the lawmakers and law-benders and referee grandees, and the way the efforts of all these parties had mutated to create the era's rugby style, were badly flawed. They revealed an unbalanced sport in which defence was dictator, in which the true contest between two packs of forwards, rugby's authentic crunch, had been reduced in some cases to the equivalent of the Gay Gordons. In which, in pursuit of the laudable notion of a fifteen-man game, it had become too easy for forwards to enter back play (and slow it up) and too many backs got involved in the bish-bash, multi-phased head-down style which so reminded everyone –

perish the thought – of rugby league. Another casualty was the skill to move sideways, to shift off line as opposed to straight up and down. Prior to the World Cup you could still hear people braying about the need for endless continuity and the southern hemisphere way. What they meant was that the ball is in play in straight lines in the endless bish-bash, and yet nothing is happening to it.

The video era obviously hampered the action too. These days, if you pull off some surprise play, or if one of your team units shows a particular world-class strength, you will find it neutralised the very next time you step on the field by the opposition video-moles. If wars were won on the playing fields of Eton, then World Cups can be won in the coaches' lounges.

Only eight of the forty-one matches played were vintage. What is my definition of 'vintage' in this context? Top rugby can exist on several levels; it is not necessary to provide classic rugby to make a great match or occasion, because sometimes a 3–0 can almost stop the heart. My criterion is that a match should have in high measure at least one or more of the following elements: superb play, the highest drama, a reverberating shock or a brutal intensity. (Or a spectacular post-match piss-up for the media after which the waiter, under no pressure whatsoever from the diners, accidentally and without you even noticing adds a nought on to the end of the receipt. However, this latter requirement for greatness is not one widely held by players or the general public.)

So here they are. My eight sexiest autumn '99 afternoon stunners, in no particular order outside the first:

1) France–New Zealand. The amazing semi-final in which France climbed from a pit of crawling ineptitude and when, for a day, British rugby supporters enlisted on the French side of the Beef War. New Zealand were lacerated.

2) England–New Zealand. The pool match won by the Kiwis through a blasting Lomu try, easily the high point for both teams (something we did not suspect at the time), and with the authentic feel of a titanic, atmospheric battle.

3) France–Fiji. The deciding pool match in Toulouse, theatrical and colourful, in which the electric Fijians were robbed of glory by poor officials and ill-luck.

4) Ireland–Argentina. No stratospheric rugby in Lens, but almost painfully gripping, and after a dynamic climax lovers of the so-called lesser teams celebrated as joyfully as the dancing Pumas. Goodnight, sweet Erin.

5) South Africa–Australia. The first semi. Again, no flowing classic but two monsters charging, an oppressive, edgy match sent into edgy injury-time by a late Bok penalty; and Australia escaped.
6) New Zealand–Tonga. In the end, a big Black win in Bristol, but not before heroic Tongan resistance and leg-gnashing passions. Epitome of the *faka Tonga*, the Tongan way.
7) France–Argentina. A deliciously fast and daredevil match, sweeping movements electrifying a Dublin quarter-final crowd as Argentina exited with heads held skywards.
8) South Africa–England. Momentous, not just for de Beer's bursts of drop-goals but also for the creeping, chilling realisation as the match developed that there was a raft of England inadequacies.

Er, that's it, folks. There was, admittedly, an honourable second division. A further seven matches could be said to have provided a reasonably rich level of entertainment for one reason or another: the loose and lively victory by Samoa over Wales; the contests between Scotland and South Africa, and Scotland and New Zealand, when at least the Scots were competitive and at least Murrayfield was more than half full; the Italy–Tonga game won by Tonga with a stunning last-kick drop-goal; the USA–Romania match, charming and close and with a Romania win striking a blow for the underdogs; Fiji's play-off defeat against England in which they scored three sparkling tries against what was supposed to be a ruthless defensive machine. Other matches, such as USA–Romania and Uruguay–Spain, were entertaining because for the teams involved they were mini-World Cup finals.

But there was raw disappointment as well; too much that was drab, pathetically one-sided or lacking in passion. The New Zealand–South Africa play-off was lamentable, remarkable only for what it represented (a low-grade *corrida* for wounded old bulls). There were some numbingly poor games – among them, strangely, that between Ireland and Australia, in which Irish passion and Australian excellence might have been taken for granted except that neither was seen in this match of unrelieved tedium. And this on a weekend when the tournament was poised on the launchpad. Eight truly fine matches from forty-one played. Not much to show for all that preparation, really.

It was Pool A that was the most desultory. 'Gerron with it,' we all wanted to shout from the sidelines as events ground on in Scotland. The Scottish Rugby Union had been one of the most vociferous hard-bargainers when it came to carving off a slice of the action from the Welsh joint, but had apparently put so much energy into bringing a pool home that it never occurred to them that the job was not finished. They forgot the add-ons like marketing and promotion, proper staging and scheduling of matches. The truth is that television and newspaper pictures of massed ranks of empty seats at Murrayfield did untold public-relations damage, because the event became known as the no-show World Cup when attendances were in fact very healthy. It surely ruled out Scotland's chances of taking any significant part in the hosting of a future World Cup – unless in the role of stand-in to the third spear-carrier.

And it may be a small point, and I'm generally in favour of the vividness of new-style jersey designs and the dosh they bring to the game from percentages of replica sales, the extra colour they lend the scene. How well I remember Treorchy Rhondda Zebras unveiling their new kit some time ago. It was black but with dazzling streaks of white and red, a sponsor's logo on the front underneath a giant Zebra logo, and on the back, in tribute to the Rhondda's past, a graphic representation of a colliery winding-engine. Then they unveiled an alternative kit in purple. We asked the marketing manager if this was for use in the event of Treorchy meeting another team with the same jersey.

And how well I remember the reaction of the great David Watkins when he saw Newport, his team, run out in a kit that looked as if the embroiderer's son had tipped his ice-cream down it. 'I don't mind too much, myself, but Bill Everson [great Newport official of the amateur past] came round my house last night to complain about it, and he's been dead for twenty-five years.'

All good fun. But did the Scots really, *really* have to play World Cup matches in bright orange? They looked like they'd been Tangoed.

The brave squads of Spain and Uruguay battled on. Uruguay lost by honourable margins of thirty-one and thirty-five to Scotland and South Africa respectively; and Spain by margins of forty-eight and forty-four. The spread-bet firms who had been talking in terms of 120-point margins found all their clients who'd 'bought' taking an ice-cold bath. The IG Index company, one of the big boys, were uneasy about the World Cup after what is still regarded by the spread-betting firms, poor loves, as their biggest disaster – when, in the 1995 World Cup, they set the spread in the seventies for the New Zealand–Japan game and the flying Kiwis won by 145–17.

Yet if they ruined the punters by failing to subside by the expected century, Uruguay impinged on the tournament in a major way against South Africa in a game thoughtlessly staged in the cavernous Hampden Park and which attracted only 3500 people. No thought, then, of taking the match to a club ground in the Borders or Edinburgh, where people would have created an atmosphere, where there would have been a full ground, some excitement. 'More club grounds should have been used,' as Bill McLaren wrote later. The SRU even played canned applause over the tannoy, an admission of failure which escaped Graham Law, the SRU spokesman who lamely tried to defend it.

South Africa were frustrated by the Uruguayans, ill at ease with this strange team that did not react as they'd expected. Uruguay were like some kind of inferior boxer who won't stand still to be laid out, and South Africa lost their rags. Brendan Venter was sent off for the crudest stamp on Martin Panizza's head. 'I went for the ball, not the guy's head, but Joost van der Westhuizen took it away at the last moment.' Blimey. A worthy entrant in the Lame Excuse of the Year, Dr Venter.

The pool had rested on the match between South Africa and Scotland, and South Africa's 46–29 victory stacks up as one of the more predictable results. Yet it was all in the balance in a third quarter which Scotland ended leading by 19–18, when Scotland lost their Kiwi-born centre John Leslie with an ankle injury. Leslie is one of the world's great backs, and overwhelmingly Scotland's key man; the injury caused him to miss the rest of the match, the rest of the World Cup, most of the Six Nations after he had been made captain of, er, his country by Ian McGeechan, and what would have been the advent of his career with the Newcastle Falcons.

So one man doesn't make a team? As one of Scotland's finest rugby writers says, 'When Leslie's playing we're nae bad, when he isn't, we're shite.' With the powerful, all-seeing Leslie installed as their core figure, Scotland had won the 1999 Five Nations. And now, in the World Cup, they were holding the Springboks to a point at Murrayfield. Leslie departed and Scotland collapsed. They conceded four tries in a loose final quarter and six in all. The match turned when Townsend, who is an entirely different player with Leslie alongside him, helped give Ollie le Roux a try with a poor kick and then helped give Deon Kayser a try with a poor pass. Scotland limped badly though the rest of the season with Townsend again faded without his strong man. Newcastle, another Leslie-free zone, also ended their season weakly.

Leslie had been stretching for the line for a possible try when he hurt his ankle in a tackle by Kayser. And individuals don't change history? If only he had made it and scored, and not torn his ankle in the process, how different would rugby history have been? Here's a few possibilities. The Falcons would have finished strongly and would have beaten Northampton in the match the Saints needed to win to qualify for Europe.

Therefore, with the pressure of Euro qualification still hanging heavy around their sainted shoulders, the Saints would have tensed up and lost the Heineken final to Munster (whom they in fact eventually beat by only two points).

England would have won the Grand Slam. Why? Easy. Because with a properly fit Leslie on board Scotland would have won at least two of their first three matches in the Six Nations; that would have meant that when the time came for them to play England at Murrayfield the Scottish hunger and sense of desperation would have been less and thus the English over-confidence less pronounced. So England's slam.

And England would have won the World Cup, beating Scotland in the quarter-final in Paris (assuming Scotland would have beaten South Africa in their pool had Leslie scored as he dived). Then, England would been presented with a tough semi-final against Australia but with the match at home at Twickenham and (Australia being nothing special) they would have won that in a rare old squeeze, then hammered France in the final at Cardiff. That's the trouble with history. Give it two inches and it takes a mile. And after the England victory the mad rush on behalf of the rest of the civilised world to not have to listen to the English harping about it for four years would have made multi-millionaires of anyone manufacturing ear-plugs.

As it was, South Africa, never really convincing, ploughed onwards to the quarter-finals, firing neither behind the scrum – where the ponderous Jannie de Beer was installed at fly-half in the absence through injury of Henry Honiball – nor, indeed, anywhere else. There was continual talk of moans and cliques, and it was blindingly obvious that coach Nick Mallett had mishandled the removal from the captaincy and squad of Gary Teichmann, the No. 8 who had led the Boks on their world record-equalling run of seventeen matches.

Teichmann had his supporters but it always seemed to me that, when you considered the hard-nosed band of Bok back-row brawn available, he was not quite as effective or powerful as you would want your No. 8 to be. It was only when Teichmann signed for Newport for the 1999–2000 season that I first began to appreciate the full effect of this magnificent, all-powerful and good-looking athlete. Mallett is as diplomatically skilled a coach as there has ever been – with all the shades of skin and opinion and race to appease in South Africa, he has to be. But he knows as well as anyone that his loyal and (joking apart) much-admired captain deserved more than a summary dismissal without proper explanation. It caused a fissure in the South African squad, and much was made during the World Cup of the fact that a large contingent of the

Springboks travelled from their training base to Glasgow to watch Teichmann's Newport play a Welsh–Scottish League match against Glasgow Caledonians. The rotter attacked me in his autobiography. As if I'd ever write something nasty about someone in a book.

It had already been established by this stage that one of the World Cup's potential wonderboys, Bobby Skinstad, would not be favouring us with the presence of his true self. Skinstad had lost months of rugby after being injured in a mysterious car accident.

Pool B had the crunch combination of England and New Zealand and although on paper it was much more competitive than Pool A, there were two centuries run up: one by England against Tonga and one by New Zealand against a dispirited Italy, who played hunch-shouldered and lamely, causing acute pangs of anxiety for those of us who had championed their richly merited inclusion in the new Six Nations Championship. The century was reached when Jim Fleming and his touch-judge gave Glen Osborne a try even though the New Zealand full-back was so far in touch that he actually passed outside the touch-line, the first six rows of spectators and a hot-dog van before he grounded the ball. He re-entered the stadium by a side gate to be told his touchdown had been awarded. As a testimony to the need for rugby to introduce the video referee, this was an eloquent incident. It was the last thing the Italians wanted. They had already gone down by 67–7 to a sharp and bristling England when nothing whatsoever went right for them.

The Tongans were a delight, at least until the fatigue of the competition and their thin resources caught up with them. The bursting national pride of their team and the excellence of David Waterston, their voluble Kiwi-born and South African-domiciled coach, forged an impressive team spirit. To have his side so together in the head and on the field was a staggering feat, considering that his men were playing their rugby in Japan, New Zealand, Australia, Wales and England as well as in Tonga.

By some deft manipulation of finite resources, Tonga even scraped together £90 a week payment for each of the squad. Riches indeed. Other squads would have spent more than that in a week on aftershave, but it was a start. They worked hard at their team bonding, gained sustenance from the scores of faxes and messages of support received from passionate fans in their tiny island group, where they had 2500 rugby players to tilt at countries like England, who had 541,000. It was a reminder, once again, of the glorious richness the three main Pacific Island teams have brought to our rugby, and of what a dull old place the game would be without them. It was also a reminder of how feeble-minded we have been over the years in allowing Australia and New

Zealand to filch away so much talent for their own use when they really should have allowed all players who qualified for the islands teams to play for those sides. Still, when was the last time a major rugby union did something for the good of rugby in general? Pre-war. (Crimean.)

Tonga had never been granted a full Test match against New Zealand, and so there was a bite and menace around Ashton Gate, home of Bristol City, as the scarlet-clad Tongans performed the *sipi tau*, the war cry, directly opposite the All Blacks' *haka*. It was theatrical; the ground was packed and raucous and expectant (though those in the press box were anxiously awaiting the arrival of the *Sun*'s estimable David Facey, who'd rung from the Memorial Ground, home of Bristol RFC, puzzled at the lack of atmosphere – or teams, refs, spectators, or anything at all, really).

For the first half it was mighty, and mighty close. New Zealand's Christian Cullen, recently converted from full-back to centre by coach John Hart, laid down few markers as an international centre; Taine Randell, the busy but inadequate captain, looked the way he has always looked: like a decent, medium-grade provincial player struggling to come to terms with the extra class of Tests. But the All Blacks pounded away relentlessly in the second half, and gathered for the kill by putting down six attacking scrums in close succession in the Tongan right-hand corner.

On the loose-head for the All Blacks was Craig Dowd, the forty-nine-times capped veteran and the only surviving member of the Dowd/Fitzpatrick/Brown triumvirate from hell. Against this experienced grizzled giant was a giant young policeman from Nuku'alofa, Ta'u Fainga'alofa, an amateur till the tournament began and till he received his first ninety quid; a tyro, because he was one of the minority of the Tonga squad who had not played overseas. 'It wasn't so much the welding of the different styles of players who were playing in different countries that was my problem,' Waterston said. 'It was the difference in approach between the lads who'd come straight from the island to the tournament and those who knew what it was to be a pro player.'

But six times the scrums crunched down. Six times, our man Ta'u held on grimly. 'He did a wonderful job,' said Waterston. 'We had more experienced props, but along comes this big brute and does it for us. We held out superbly.' I spoke to Ta'u afterwards. 'Ah, mate, it was satisfying, you know. It's great to play against these guys because you learn so much. Who knows, though – maybe today they learned something from us.' For one day, the Ashton Gate Eight meant the Tongan pack, not Chris Garland and the victims of one of Bristol City's financial crises of the 1970s.

And yet callowness shone through after all. The scrummage siege was raised, the Tonga contingent in the crowd celebrated and there was still that last, lovely hope of a staggering victory. 'That was when we should have slowed it all down, feigned an injury to re-group. Anything,' Waterston said. Instead, New Zealand attacked from deep, set loose the awesome Lomu for a score and the floodgates opened. The Tongans went down, eventually, by 45–9. It was the least representative scoreline of a tournament in which there were many such misleading results, and Tonga did amazingly well to re-group afterwards – retreating to their team room and Tongan customs and bonding evenings and re-emerging again with the heart-stopping win at Leicester against Italy.

Only against England, when Ngalu Tafuo'ou was sent off, did Tonga crumble in morale, and they conceded a century to ten. The only consolation being that it is now profoundly easier to concede the really vast score than it ever was – these days, with the way the game is played and the way it is so unfairly weighted in favour of the team with the ball, even a reasonable side can concede forty or fifty points in a short period of play without ever seeing the ball, except when they are kicking the damn thing off.

It seemed the only issue to be resolved in Pool C was whether it would be Fiji or Canada that would finish as runner-up to France. However, France began taking a series of body-blows as key players were lost to injury and suspension. And it was not as if they had much of a body to absorb the blows. It was clear to me that while the combination of Jean-Claude Skrela and Pierre Villepreux may have brought together two of the great players in rugby's history, as coaches they made great former players. They were two dreamers with no real relevance to the forging of a Test team in the furnace of the current era.

Villepreux had come out with some romantic rubbish over the years – in my opinion because he set too much store by the abstract called French flair – and it seemed to me that he was always more comfortable in the days of the various coaching regimes which set him as a outsider, championed by his Toulouse faction, than when actually brought under the official umbrella. It is always easier to heckle in Parliament than to set policy. It is also true that when a team is losing matches, your stock as a coach rises rapidly if you are the coach-in-waiting.

He and Skrela had made some selections of awesome nonsensicality, such as sending out a midfield pairing of Emile Ntamack and Thomas Castaignède against the All Blacks in Wellington in 1999. On paper it was the worst defensive pairing ever sent out in a Test match, considering that the opposition were the straight-line All Blacks and that Ntamack is one of the most moody players around. Leave him out on his wing and

The great Pat Lam, with the assistance of Tim Rodber, lifting high the Heineken European Cup after the emotional victory over Munster (*Dave Rogers/Allsport*)

So rugby is not all about internationals after all. On a day that was later to bring the brilliant Heineken final at Twickenham, George Smith rejuvenates the Brumbies' challenge with a try against the Crusaders in an exciting but controversial Super-12 final at Bruce Stadium, Canberra. Crusaders won by 20-19 (*Adam Pretty /Allsport*)

Still the most awesome sight in rugby: Jonah Lomu on the rampage during the Australia–New Zealand Tri-Nations game in July 2000, because of its scoring twists arguably the greatest match ever (*Rob Cianflone/Allsport*)

Mickey Steele-Bodger – Barbarians tie neatly knotted (*Dave Rogers/Allsport*)

Fran Cotton, resignations rescinded and still wielding the old influence (*Dave Rogers/Allsport*)

Cliff Brittle – tortuous entry into journalism after tortuous exit from the world of rugby officialdom (*Dave Rogers/Allsport*)

Scott Quinnell drags the reputation of Welsh forward play back to the heights en route to a series victory in the Ferro Carril Oeste Stadium, Buenos Aires, 1999 (*Jamie McDonald/Allsport*)

Another stop on the endless and heroic road towards attempted qualification for the Rugby World Cup finals. Here, Aziz Andoh of Morocco tries to make progress towards Cardiff and towards victory against the Ivory Coast in Casablanca (*Dave Rogers/Allsport*)

The oldest man in the tournament, and one of the most heroic. Diego Ormaechea (Uruguay) in his fifth decade, takes on the Spanish defence at Galashiels (*Alex Livesey/Allsport*)

The picture that the Scottish Rugby Union's marketing department really should have tried to ban. Not even the presence of South Africa, the reigning world champions, could inspire the marketeers to drag more than a handful of people to an eerie Murrayfield (*Colorsport*)

They had entered the World Cup playing like pussycats. They ended it by playing like, well, Pumas. Argentina celebrate the glory of victory over Ireland in Lens
(*Alex Livesey/Allsport*)

Some wanted to retain the crumbling old Arms Park. By the time this inspirational and soaring cathedral had appeared on Cardiff's skyline, they'd all gone distinctly quiet
(*Shaun Botterill/Allsport*)

One of the juddering collisions between Scott Gibbs and George Leaupepe in the Samoan defeat of Wales in the World Cup pool. An early and powerful indication that potential would not be fulfilled (*Dave Rogers/Allsport*)

Fabien Pelous risks aggravating the Beef War by flourishing the Tricolour in celebration after the rout of New Zealand in the semi-final at Twickenham (*Colorsport*)

French brothers in arms, as Christophe Dominici and Abdel Benazzi celebrate on the plateau of world class the French arrival in the final (*Dave Rogers/Allsport*)

Forced smiles all round as Her Majesty presents John Eales with the Webb Ellis trophy shortly after Eales voted Republican in the Australian referendum. Behind them, Keith Rowlands contemplates life without the hassle of organising a World Cup (*Colorsport*)

he's passable and, when in the mood, undeniably a great; in the centre, though, useless. He needs notice in writing in triplicate to react. And whatever the considerable talents of Thomas Castaignède, front-on defence isn't one of them. The Black midfield motored through gigantic holes in the French midfield all but unchallenged. If it looked weak on paper, on the field it looked *like* paper.

Villepreux and Skrela appointed the wrong World Cup captain in Raphael Ibanez, keeping the teak-tough Marc dal Maso on the bench. Ibanez was personable, upright, dignified. See what I mean? Absolutely hopeless. Dal Maso was more grizzled, wild-eyed. That's more like it. They mucked around the great lock Adbel Benazzi. They shattered morale; the team played with no purpose or direction in the 1999 Five Nations, their summer tour, their World Cup warm-ups and the early World Cup matches.

Judging by Villepreux's reaction when we ran into each other in Toulouse during the tournament (he kept a large crowd of onlookers entertained with a gesticulating diatribe in excellent English), I think it's fair to say that he didn't share my view of his contribution. I didn't mind Pierre taking me to task; what I wasn't going to do was hang around to see if Gerard Cholley was his close friend who'd do anything for him. I did have Paul Ackford with me, but Big Ackers' fighting days are a little way behind him. Not as far away as mine, however. It was a ticklish problem when France annihilated the All Blacks in the semi-final. Should I ignore the result as if it had never happened, or write an article explaining that I'd always known Pierre would pull the boys through in the end? I climbed down as far as a note of heartfelt congratulation, and it is not being wise after the event to say that even in the glory of that great Twickers afternoon, the victory had all the air of a one-off.

France did manage to beat Canada in the pool opener, 33–20 in Béziers. By this time, the sheer pressure of impending doom had concentrated the minds of Jean-Claude and Pierre and they were playing tackling centres in the centre; Abdel was back and they were, just, good enough.

But Fiji had given notice, by way of an easy win over Namibia, 67–18 in the second match of the tournament in Béziers, that something of a miracle was afoot. Watching the Fijians on television in that match, Brad Johnstone, their coach and a fringe All Black prop, one of a minor horde of New Zealanders on the coaching staffs of the competing nations, looked like he might just be achieving an unlikely blend. A mix of natural talent (with which Fiji are overflowing) and the hard-headed demands of modern Test rugby (with which they have usually only a nodding acquaintance). And though you rarely find a field anywhere in Fiji without swarms of people playing rugby on it, none of those fields has a scrummaging machine.

Yet here were the scudding, glorious full-back Alfred Uluinayau and Viliame Satala, the cutting centre, reviving the grand tradition. Uluinayau was my full-back of the tournament by so far that no one else was in the frame as he raced past the post; Satala was one of the outstanding figures in a galaxy of Barbarians talent that the old wandering club brought to see out the season with a short tour in the spring of 2000. And here, also, was a team prepared to scrummage, anchored around the bear-like figure of Joeli Veitayaki on the tight-head (in the culture-shock transfer of the century, big Joeli signed for Ulster after the World Cup, which meant that the country was then split into three divides: Protestants, Catholics and Veitayakis). And a fine locking partnership of Simon Raiwalui – the shaven-headed grafter then from Sale without a dishonest bone in his body when it came to selflessness – and Emori Katalau, a tall athlete who had the priceless ability to get a set of long Fijian fingers ahead of the opposition line-out ball and claw it back. Fiji ploughed on, showed devil and organisation in holy tandem against Canada, winning this key match 38–22 in Bordeaux with two tries from Satala.

Ah, Canada! The marvellous Canadians deduced that they had a poor World Cup, especially compared to their epic and forward-driving run to the quarter-finals in 1991. But the truth was that they had once again proved their dedication and excellence, and proved to my satisfaction at least that, given a level playing field of proper salaries and preparation, they would be among the world elite. But in 1999 they had Brad Johnstone's miracle working against them. Gareth Rees, the Canadian captain and the only man to have played in all four World Cups, played in all three of their group matches, carried lightly the usual number of serious injuries and went out of the tournament in grand style by kicking twelve from twelve against Namibia. People like Gareth Rees perform such an incredible service to world rugby, to its play and to its image and amiability, that it could not be properly rewarded with all £35 million of the tournament profit. Great man. I've written it before, but when the time comes for Earth to appoint a rugby ambassador to the other planets, then only Reesie will be interviewed.

So France and Fiji clashed in that great rugby city Toulouse, where the mighty Stade Toulousain can draw more than 35,000 for a club match. The winners would proceed to a quarter-final against Argentina and the loser to a midweek play-off at Twickenham against England. In Toulouse, at least, you could tell there was a World Cup on, because on the morning of the match there was music, side-shows, stalls, verve in the centre of the city, banners and logos. As we walked around in the morning, taking it all in, we even noticed what was for RWC '99 a revolutionary move – a poster advertising the game.

There were also three blokes still in their hotel who would spoil it all. The officials. Rugby still reminds me, occasionally, of Denis Norden's *It'll be Alright on the Night*. You know, lots of fun apart from that dreadful old bloke in charge. Yet Paddy O'Brien, the New Zealand referee for that day, has always been one of my favourites; so has Col Hawke, his fellow Kiwi and, that day, his touch-judge. There is a certain grace and class about them, and now that the Super-12 had been brought back under central control after an initial period when they were running a separate code, the two Kiwis had hit a decent reffing wavelength. They lost that wavelength entirely in Toulouse. Because of it, Fiji lost a match they deserved to win, were robbed of the greatest day in their history and, conceivably, a World Cup semi-final. We were to discover later, after Hawke had made a spectacular mess of refereeing the Wales–Australia quarter-final, that in terms of cock-ups, in Toulouse he was only warming up.

There had already been a number of bewildering decisions in the first half, when the three officials ran around shrugging and looking balefully at each other for guidance as if their talking-flags communications system was playing old Status Quo hits rather than their own mini-network of advice. But just before half-time, at what would have been a psychologically killing moment, Ugo Mola, the disastrous French full-back, ran out of deep defence – disastrously. The gliding Satala came up and scythed Mola down, the ball jerked loose from his grasp without any Fijian touching it, rolled back towards the French line, and Setereki Tawake, the Fijian back-row man, touched it down. The three pairs of eyes available to the officials found a totally non-existent knock-on to blow for, and O'Brien blew for it, recalling Tawake for a French scrum. No offence had taken place. It was not even close. Tell me that a seven-point swing at that stage of a tight match would not have mattered either way. On second thoughts, don't even bother to try.

The officiating was on the point of total collapse soon afterwards when O'Brien, desperately searching for advice from Hawke, from the Lord, anyone, allowed play to proceed after a French player had chipped the ball forward about ten metres up the field to a colleague who caught it and took off with it. Australian Rules football scouts were beginning to circle when O'Brien smelled a rat and finally called the play back.

The seminal moments of a marvellous, gripping occasion came in a sequence of nine consecutive scrums on the Fijian line. Goal-line stands. Rugby's sex. You go and applaud your flowing tries and leave me to my long and agonised minutes in which the ball moves only by inches. This goal-line stand came with Fiji leading by 19–13 (even after being robbed of their other seven) and after a third-quarter performance when they were absolutely dominant, when the French crowd were loud in their derision of French efforts and when French shape had ceased to exist. The major component of the lead was a set-piece try to savour. Waisake Sotutu threw a flat pass across the Fijian midfield and the dazzling Uluinayau came up, cut a jagging, devastating path through the heart of the French cover and scored. France, knowing true flair, stopped jeering their men for a few seconds and put their hands together for Alfred's run.

Back to the sex. The scrums went down with French pride hanging by a thread. For a race to which affection for scrummaging has never come easy, the Fijians held on brilliantly. Each time, a Fijian would concede an initial foot or so but then would dig in. On four occasions the scrum had to be re-set; on another four Fijians were penalised, usually for standing up – a hard call, as both front rows often seemed to pop up together. Fiji were actually appearing more comfortable as the succession of scrums passed by, and by the ninth they hardly budged when the weight came on. It looked like Dal Maso's head which popped up first but O'Brien was already scuttling to the posts to award a penalty try. It was seen by an overwhelming majority of observers as a harsh decision. It showed that these days the requirement that a try would probably have been scored had it not been for a penalty offence has gone by the board. You only have to keep a team pinned back for a few minutes and the ref will eventually go to the posts. I had sympathy for O'Brien. I felt that he was wrong in fact and possibly in law, but that he was in this instance a victim of the ridiculous policies imposed on him from above rather than a victim of his own bad day at the office.

That was not the case at the end, however. The mistakes and the penalty try had given France life; they now led, and they sealed their shaky win with a try from Christophe Dominici. The key parts of the move were level with my seat in the press box and contained two passes that were garishly forward, both of which John Elway would have slobbered over had he thrown them for the Denver Broncos. The final score was a preposterous 28–19 to France.

Afterwards, in a display of honour which became them exceedingly well, the Fijians took it on the chin. The hooker and captain Greg Smith contented himself with pointing out that his scrum had not felt on the point of caving in during the extended sequence and that he was disappointed with the penalty try. 'I play in the front row and I'd back myself to know more about what's happening in there than the referee,' said the splendid Smith. I'll have a tenner on that too, Greg. And if it really was as easy as the score suggests, then how would you account for the knees-knocking departure from the field of the feeble French? Up in the ITV commentary box Steve Smith, the former England scrum-half working as summariser, earned a letter of rebuke from the Broadcasting Standards lot for describing one of the frustrated French as a 'stroppy Frog'. This underlined once more that the rest of the civilised world have *carte blanche* to take the piss out of the English, using any kind of derogatory expression they can think of, but whenever the English try to strike back there is always some politically correct new puritan to slap his wrists. Long may it continue.

With the dire disadvantage of a day less to prepare than England, who had played on the Friday, Fiji went to Twickenham for the quarter-final play-off. The French experience had been played in heat and humidity, and yet Fiji's injury-hit team were once again a delight, going down 24–45 but lifting everyone present on a cold and windy day with three tries and splendid running from Uluinayau. It suggested that Johnstone was a great man for soothing the inner Fijian and re-firing his morale, as well as for the technical bits.

After the tournament he stood down from the post he had held for three years. On his departure the affable, straight-shooting, shiny-bonced Johnstone was fêted at club functions and church services (one lasted three hours) and sent on his way with an extraordinary display of affection. He was made an honorary officer of the Order of Fiji at Government House, and this bull of a man later confessed that his battle to keep back the tears had been a notable failure. 'They are very special people,' Johnstone said of his former charges, both players and public. 'I left part of my heart behind when I left.' He looked back a little ruefully to the old days. 'When I first arrived three of our squad couldn't even do a chin-up. And when I asked about their defensive systems there was something of a long silence.'

Johnstone got his men to apply themselves; he ended the silly and wounding over-reliance upon sevens play which had put Fiji on the sevens map and wiped them entirely off the real rugby scene. Yet while he was pragmatic enough to force Fijian noses to the grindstone he was also free enough in spirit to choose Waisale Serevi, the sevens genius, as his starting fly-half at Twickenham and to allow Alfred and his friends the opportunity to run. When I named Johnstone as coach of the World

Cup in the *Sunday Times* after the tournament, some people were surprised. I was surprised myself – that anyone could possibly be considered to have come anywhere near him. I was less surprised when Johnstone, culture-shockingly installed as Italy's coach for the Six Nations, repaired morale so quickly that Italy (famously) greeted their own arrival by levelling Scotland in Rome. Not bad for a fringe All Black prop. And good old Fiji. Extraordinary rugby heaven. During the shambolic coup in May 2000 there was a temporary break in hostilities in Suva as the conflicting parties broke off to wave at the Fiji team bus as it went by taking the squad to their training for the Pacific Rim tournament.

At least Pool D was guaranteed a buzz, because it was where the Welsh World Cup became, well, Welsh. The atmosphere at the Millennium Stadium was always marvellous, and the Welsh public joyously supported the team but also the tournament. More than 43,000 people went to the Millennium to watch Argentina play Japan, after RWC had budgeted for less than 20,000. It was a princely gate indicative that rugby, not necessarily parochialism, is in the hearts of Welsh people. There were also fine attendances at Llanelli and Wrexham, where the match between Samoa and Japan had been sold out for weeks.

Wales were able to qualify despite losing to Samoa. Before that match there appeared to be a breakdown in communication between Graham Henry and his team. Either that or one of his lieutenants chalked up the 'dos' and the 'don'ts' on the wrong blackboards. Henry's game-plan would have included such 'do not at any price' or even 'do this and you're dropped' elements as coughing up the ball loosely in the tackle, spinning the ball wide away from the forwards (where Wales were thumpingly superior) and kicking the ball badly down Samoan throats. Yet Wales apparently believed that this was the game-plan rather than the shortest route to suicide, and five superb Samoa tries, usually long-range counter-attacks feeding on Welsh errors, put paid to Wales by 38–31. When the match was over the stadium rose in unison to applaud the Samoans. To have turned out a team of such craft with limited resources was a feat accomplished by coach Bryan Williams which almost matched that of Johnstone with the Fijians.

The other key match was Argentina's win over Samoa at Llanelli. Here, for all to see, was the way to play Samoa – and the way that Wales had shunned. Having fooled around in a Puma Limboland for more than a half of play, Argentina suddenly realised that they had a forward pedigree, and after trailing they simply thundered down the middle with the ball, hammered away for the whole second half and cut Samoa off at the ankles. They scored a driving forward try touched down by Alejandro Allub, and won by 33–16.

It was stirring stuff and it rejuvenated the whole Argentina rugby scene in one afternoon. It evoked an inspirational feeling which pervaded the usually doubtful arena of Argentina rugby for months. The victory meant that Argentina would proceed to the quarter-final play-offs as the best-placed third team, another indication that the Wales group was the toughest in the competition. To finish third was nothing to cheese you off, either. Samoa had to go to Murrayfield to play Scotland in their play-off as the reward for finishing second, but Argentina had to go to Lens, to play the misfiring Irish. There are Irish communities in so many parts of the world, but Lens is hardly some French equivalent of Boston.

Ireland's Pool E had been characterised by the dreadful Ireland–Australia match and indeed it was the other nations, Romania and the United States, who added much of the colour. There was something remarkable in the Ireland–USA game when the Irish hooker Keith Wood scored four tries. Wood is a remarkable figure, one of those compelling men who drags you to the edge of your seat; one of those big-hearted men whom it is impossible to subdue.

When the two minnows of the pool, USA and Romania, played their match we saw a hair-raising, thrilling affair which Romania won, on the back of two tries from Gheorge Solomie. Tudor Constantin was inspirational in the second row for Romania, but victory was only assured after Kevin Dalzell, the American scrum-half, missed a late conversion from the touch-line after Kurt Shuman had dived across near the left-hand corner flag. Romania's celebrations were ecstatic afterwards.

Once again, a near-tragedy in the world of rugby's undercard was exposed. At heart, rugby in Romania is extremely powerful. Yet the country's privations, both political and economic, have crippled the game, robbed it of morale and resources. Worse still, of course, they make it extremely difficult for players to gain exposure to top-level international competition. The leading coaches from other countries wouldn't dream of going to Bucharest if they could help it, since the configuration of the country's bus fleet, the taste of its isotonic drinks, the texture of Romanian grasses, the unpadded nature of their physio tables, and the inconvenient flight time (two hours) to get there would be so unfamiliar that they could not seriously be expected to properly prepare an international rugby team under such awful conditions. Leading administrators could hardly be expected to arrange fixtures for their teams in this difficult location. How could they function properly? Bucharest hotels simply do not have the required size of suite (to wit, the capacity of a small aircraft hangar).

Sometimes, you see Romania go out and lie down and die. You see matches where the privations are such that they subside meekly, where the top French clubs for whom their elite play have refused to release them. Morale shot to pieces, body-language sullen. On other days, not. Call me an old softie, call me a dreamer, but one of the worst and greatest games of rugby involved Romania. It was played against France in Auch in 1990, less than five months after the Romanian revolution (that strange affair which we greeted as a stirring, popular uprising against oppression but which later turned out to have been the clinical removal of one nutcase dictator by the existing power-brokers). With their country experiencing a new freedom the Romanian people were able to watch their team on television. Previously, the TV service had beamed out hours of programming lauding the achievements of Nicolae Caeuşescu. Foreign travel was now easier, and the crowd in Auch was augmented by two busloads of supporters who had chugged heroically through Hungary, Austria and Switzerland and pitched up at Auch waving the ad hoc new Romanian flag (the old one, with the logo cut out). The buses were of the same vintage as the wheezing van from the film *Ice Cold in Alex*, and whether the passengers ever made it back has never been recorded.

It was a dire rugby spectacle and a glorious thing to witness. Romania won 12–6; the scores came from kicks. They were battling heroically in the teeth of a French team of superior talent and conditioning. It made you realise that, deep down, the traditional Romanian rugby player is a proud beast. It is a country of tactical and technical sophistication. How powerfully all we neutrals were willing Romania to victory that day; how we applauded inside as Gelu Ignat put over his kicks. I can still see the Romanian captain, Haralambie Dumitras, beaming massively as he disappeared down the tunnel to an ovation from a crowd who had been calling for every Frenchman's resignation. I still see the French-domiciled Hari around the place now and again. We both point at each other. 'Auch!' we exclaim. 'Wonder who that was,' he probably asks himself after we part. It is a crying shame that – the RFU efforts on the Fund for Romania apart – the rugby world outside cares nothing for Romanian rugby.

With their liveliness in Ireland, Constantin's men at least showed that the modern game is impinging on their country. The United States had scored tries through Brian Hightower and Dan Lyle but, as usual, their athleticism and their sheer, effervescent commitment were let down by lack of technical ability and they probably would have been lucky had Dalzell's kick gone over.

The States have been on the threshold for so long. There has been talk of a major professional league in their country, financed by one of Rupert Murdoch's television companies. There has been talk since time immemorial of harnessing the athleticism in the country by dipping into the pool of people unwanted by the National Football League. And also of harnessing the vast numbers of people who participate in the sport in the USA, both men and women. American rugby still stands, expectant, on the launchpad, waiting for someone to count down to ignition. Mission was aborted again in Ireland in 1999. I wonder if Rugby World Cup would ever demonstrate the initiative, the ability and, above all, the courage to award a World Cup to America and thus try to blast the game off from within. Better, surely, than bouncing between scattered and confused northern hemisphere locations and scattered and confused southern hemisphere locations. Better than awarding the tournament on the scientific principle of Buggins' Turn.

We saw another reason for the failure of the nations outside the top echelon to cause real damage to their more illustrious brethren when the USA took on Australia in Limerick. (Typically, the people of Limerick gave a tremendous atmosphere to proceedings, reminding us yet again that had the French not greedily insisted on mucking up the home nations World Cup then another match could have been staged in Limerick, and one in Cork, perhaps, thereby celebrating a true and gloriously passionate rugby area instead of giving the locals a one-match sop.)

Australia won by 55–19, easy enough. But, as ever, the Americans played with tremendous heart, scoring a try by Juan Grobler, the centre. In the final quarter America's blood was up and the team really found itself. The forwards began to drive with an almost fanatical urgency and there was what amounted to a siege to the Australia line as the USA went in search of greater respectability. I watched that whole passage of play on the video the day after the event. On the one hand, you have a heroic, if callow effort. On the other, the most cynical bunch of Australian offences you can imagine – all sorts of black tricks and offsides, and lurking forwards just happening to appear in an offside position between two Americans, putting up hands in mock surprise, and the move ends as the ball 'accidentally' strikes them. You can identify at least five occasions when a yellow card should have been shown; at least two when a penalty try could have been awarded.

And if the play had been down at the other end, of course, then

enough cards would have appeared to keep Maverick in business for a
year. But in the minds of top referees (we'll be understanding and say
their subconscious minds) it's the dodgy and inept lesser teams who kill
the ball and kill the play. How could the superbly coached and ramrod-
upright top nations stoop to that sort of level? Observers of the genre
will note that, according to referees, it is always the artful Italians who
cheat against the gleaming English; it is always the ill-disciplined Pacific
Island team who fall offside, never the ever-regimented All Blacks. The
truth is that top nations have become top nations at least partly because
they cheat better, and it is up to leading referees to realise that and not
simply to police one side. The South African André Watson was the
culprit in Limerick, blithely allowing Australia to get away with it. And
look what happened to him. A few weeks later he refereed the World
Cup final. It makes you weep, it really does.

It was in Dublin that you made the comparisons, and kept weeping.
In 1991 it was in Dublin, above all places, that the tournament came
alive. Lansdowne Road staged two Sunday matches in succession. In the
first, a quarter-final, Australia beat Ireland when they came back with a
try by Michael Lynagh at the last gasp, after Gordon Hamilton's famous
surge had put Ireland in the lead and shoved the eventual World
Champions to the very brink. In the second, a semi-final, Australia
hammered New Zealand, and in the process gave a first-half performance
which ranks among the finest chunks of rugby the game has seen, with
David Campese and Tim Horan conjuring tries.

If the rugby was outstanding, there was also a marvellously exhilara-
ting atmosphere generated off the field in the Irish branch of RWC '91.
There was a magnificent spirit abroad, a sense of urgency in the
celebrations, a sense of rugby family, of great sporting theatre, of a city
and a country entirely absorbed. It was so infectious that you didn't even
mind when the taxi driver bringing you in from the airport launched the
traditional 'over-fer-the-match-are-ye' unstoppable sermon about rugby;
you did not even feel like nudging your mate in the back of the cab to
ring your mobile so you could pretend to be talking and make the bloke
shut up.

After Ireland had departed the competition their supporters, as one,
turned to support Australia. The Australian team had been based among
them for some time, and instead of cutting themselves off in their
headquarters they had emerged and drunk Guinness in ordinary bars,
were accessible, glamorous and brilliant ambassadors. Their media and
public relations, fuelled by Greg Campbell, the former journalist who
was their liaison officer, were immaculate. Campbell re-wrote the book

on the subject and it is a crying shame that so few of his counterparts in other countries ever read it. By the time they were out there beating New Zealand, the Awesomes were being supported almost as loudly as any Irish team. It was all emerald-tinged, stout-based, top-quality theatre.

Compared to that, Dublin in 1999 was doornail-dead. No sense of expectation had been evoked, the matches were poor and in the case of the pool keynote, Australia–Ireland, pitifully so. The people, as far as I could see, and with Limerick being the exception, could take it or leave it. Rugby was no longer so exciting a game, the Aussies were no longer so affable. The Australia team of 1999 was never remotely as accessible as its predecessor; after both Australia and Ireland had completed the formality of beating the USA and Romania, the curtains were drawn.

There was just one day in the whole Irish experience to compare with 1991, and that was when Lansdowne Road was well filled and excited for the thrilling quarter-final between France and Argentina, the Pumas having taken the place which the Irish had prayed would be filled by their men. On that day there were just a few echoes. It may have had a little to do with the fact that to watch Ireland had become a numbing and rather painful experience; to watch Australia was to listen to the grinding of a machine, not to a symphony. And people were secretly relieved that neither side was there any more.

The circumstances of Ireland's removal from the event provided a dramatic highlight, something of which the tournament was in heavy need. The Lens match provided regal entertainment, devastated the Irish almost out of their wits, and accelerated the revival of Argentine rugby even more. It was 15–9 to Ireland at half-time but they had never been dominated, and in the second half you could see the confidence flow into the Pumas. They dragged themselves in front with a brilliant one-phase try, created in midfield around Gonzalo Quesada, the donkey-booted fly-half, and finished by Diego Albanese. It was clinical, brutal and brilliant. It threw into the sharpest relief the fervent yet ultimately uninspired Irish attempts to swarm over the Argentines through multi-phased attacks.

And the whole thing starkly illuminated the lack of inspiration at half-back for Ireland, where David Humphreys and Tom Tierney were simply inadequate, and the abject failure of the appointment as Irish captain of Dion O'Cuinneagain, gloriously Irish-named but mostly South African. O'Cuinneagain was never of international class as a back-row man despite a rare turn of foot, and, rather embarrassingly for Warren Gatland, the Irish coach who had made the bewildering appointment, decided to chuck in the Irish Test scene to return to his studies in South Africa at the end of 2000.

The end game was a sensation. (Perhaps we should even have praised the Bunglers, because it was their greed in all claiming a slice of the action which had necessitated that the tournament be played in five pools, and therefore required play-off matches to sort out the final eight.) But as the Irish hammered away – adding their backs to a series of drives from the line-out, steaming at Argentina in midfield with a sheer desperation – the ball was only inches from the Argentina line for long minutes, was still there when the final whistle blew, and the celebrations were something to behold. The electric scrum-half Agustin Pichot reckoned that he had never experienced such a moment. The dray horses of the front row, Mauricio Reggiardo, Mario Ledesma and Omar Hasan, formed a single, bound tableau for their passage from the field.

As a finale to the preliminaries, as a stage-setter for the quarter-finals, it was momentous. At last, someone from outside the old and, in parts, faded elite of world rugby had been throttled – something worth celebrating for everyone who was not Irish. I could still discern a thread down to Pichot which was sent spinning over the years, and through the matches, by R. Mina of Brazil. And, while feeling for the brave and fighting Irish, I was thrilled for rugby and for its nonsensically overblown preparation culture; thrilled that a team whose preparation had been endless had been beaten by a team whose preparations had been a joke.

Finally, I traced my man Mina. Ramiro Mina, Brazil's hooker, was born in Tucumán, Argentina, but is now domiciled in São Pãulo, where he plays for the Bandeirantes club. 'Ramiro is very good and very brave,' Sebastian Arrieti, Brazil's captain, says. As befitting a rugby hero. Mark Hamilton, the Trinidad armed robber, has been released and is now a regular with the Trinidad team.

On 28 September 2000, Norway played Luxembourg in Oslo. It was the first match of the 2003 World Cup.

CHAPTER SEVEN

Cardiff and Catatonia

World Cup III: music and mystery in the air of Wales ♦ Peeved Pierre's final word and the final triumph of Australia's Republicans

Cerys Matthews may sound to certain uneducated ears (ears uneducated enough to require perfect pitch and the right notes) like a chipmunk on helium. Most Welsh males of my acquaintance were in love with her in 1999. And at least she was our chipmunk, at least she was squeaking on our helium, I shouldn't wonder. When Cerys, gloriously catch-throated and charismatic, took the stage at the Millennium Stadium during the opening ceremony of the World Cup with her band Catatonia, then the hottest group on Planet Rock, she threw off a sparkly jacket underneath which she was wearing a red rugby jersey. The crowd roared as loudly as they were to roar later, in a heady afternoon during which Colin Charvis scored the first try of the Welsh World Cup campaign.

It was a telling act by our girl, something more than a crowd-pleasing stunt. It was a communion between rugby and rock music which had been growing stronger in the years and months before the World Cup came to Cardiff. Both rugby and rock became sexy in Wales, and they became sexy with each other. Usually, the rather staid rugby ranks and the raucous rock ranks would keep well apart – that is, if there *was* anyone rocking in Wales. All I can remember from my younger days is the Midnight City Soul Band, whom we deemed sexily well-named and yet realised that the Cat Stranglers would have been more appropriate for their distinctive sound. There was then a bit of a gap until the Icons of Filth in the punk era. It is a true story that the late Kurt Cobain of Nirvana proposed to Courtney Love in TJ's in Clarence Place, Newport. 'Anything,' she is reported to have said. 'Just get me outta here.'

By 1999, in the shapes of Catatonia, the Stereophonics (from Aberaman – who needs Detroit?), the Manic Street Preachers

(Blackwood) and the Super Furry Animals (north Wales), Wales was enjoying a surging rock boom, ridden for all it was worth by Tom Jones, the Grand Swiveller himself, who made records with so many trendy new bands that he once again became cutting-edge, notably with the stunning 'Reload'. The rugby had become almost as bad a joke as Tom in his smug sub-Liberace Las Vegas years, had been weakened and indolent, lost confidence and devil and leadership. Lost matches.

In the 1970s the Welsh ratio of success in international matches was running at seventy-one per cent; in the 1980s it plunged dramatically to forty-seven per cent; and for the greater part of the 1990s was running at a feeble forty-four per cent. And don't forget that in the 1970s all the opposition would have been of top quality whereas afterwards, when Test caps were awarded against all properly constituted national teams, there were easy pickings on offer. Few as easy as Wales, however, who even developed a consistent habit over the last decade of losing at home to Ireland. That, with respect, takes some doing. It means that there is now a generation which has grown up with an assumption of Welsh rugby inferiority.

But as 1999 wore on there came a great, surging Dragon revival, and new headiness in the nation as rugby and rock began to capture youth and imagination once again. Jones had already sung the cheesily anthemic 'Delilah' at Wembley before the Welsh Six Nations victory over England, in which a late and sensational try by Scott Gibbs, jack-knifing madly off his left foot to score, had shattered an arrogant England's aspirations to a Grand Slam. That day ranks with the greatest in the country's rugby history – not because of quality of performance, not just because it was only the third success in a run of ten which reverberated around the world game as evidence of true recovery, but because in the stadium, a home 150 miles from home as the Millennium was being built, there was the electric atmosphere indicative that pride and passion was returning to Welsh rugby.

And that Wales, and the pride involved in the process of being Welsh, was undergoing a major revival. Heads were held high. The vibrant Welsh rugby website, gwl@d, was a fine indicator-board, seething with new national passions and also anti-Englishness. There was derision at the dire, defeated 'Saes', a strange matter because for all that Wales detest losing to Englishmen on the rugby field, there has always been well-founded respect for them. After that Wembley spectacular the twin scions of the country – the team and the rock band – partied together. Raised glasses to Cerys and Scott.

❖   ❖   ❖

There was another element in this new and animated Wales. It was inanimate. Concrete and girders, but formed in shapes that took the breath away, stirred the hearts of men like Sean Fitzpatrick, the seen-it-all and notably unemotional New Zealand rugby captain, who confessed that he was in awe every time he saw them during the World Cup. The Millennium Stadium was in a way un-Welsh. In rugby we had become too used to walking round with resignation and hunched shoulders; the last time something stemming from a wider vision had happened in Wales was lost in time's mists.

But when Vernon Pugh and Glanmor Griffiths, then allies on the Welsh Rugby Union, looked at the Cardiff Arms Park as it stood through the 1980s and 1990s, they realised that it was a pit: crumbling stonework, no lovely lines, no proper catering, no proper shops or bars. It was a mess of concrete and smelly toilets. It held only 52,000, pitifully inadequate. Leading observers and former internationals mounted a 'Save the Arms Park' campaign, attributing all kinds of mystical properties to the stadium and talking as if to tear it down was to kill Welsh rugby, not to save it. Which it did. At least some had the grace to blush when it was completed; they looked around it, and realised.

I remember some years ago Pugh mooting the idea of a 72,500-capacity stadium, and asking me if that capacity would be too much, wondering aloud if there would be empty seats because of the huge uplift. I told him that he'd soon be wondering why they settled only for 72,500, because the extra capacity would bring into the box-office domain all those who never even bothered to try for tickets for Cardiff Arms Park. Those who'd never been able to bring their sons and daughters or brothers and sisters, because it was simply impossible. New bridges create their own traffic. Welsh rugby stadiums create their own public.

Pugh was to depart the WRU for the IRB, leaving Griffiths in charge. Griffiths is a controversial figure – there are many who profoundly doubt whether he is the man who should be in charge of Welsh rugby as it sets out its professional future, and certainly his facility for public relations and speed of action is not high. From the time that Wales were granted the 1999 World Cup, to give birth to the stadium was already proving a mighty battle. There was the onerous process of liaising with the Millennium Commission, who put up half the £120 million needed from National Lottery funds. There was the fight with the neighbouring Cardiff club, who were in dispute with the WRU throughout, stood on their pride to such a ridiculous extent that they passed on the concept of a brand-new stadium out in the reclaimed docklands, all-seater and gleaming, and are therefore entrenched still in the mini-pit, that profoundly unlovely concrete jungle they call home, dwarfed by the Millennium Stadium and to which they are lucky to draw 5,000 people even on a good day. Good old Cardiff. There was also the battle against a sceptical public and media who could be forgiven, considering the Welsh reputation for whining and low horizons, for worrying more about the humiliation of the stadium not being finished in time than craving the potential glory if it was.

As these disputes raged, and all through the time when building began and the team left for Wembley, a baleful spotlight fell on the retiring, white-haired, clipped-toned Griffiths. The spotlight became ever more searching as the project advanced, seemingly at a snail's pace, and the tournament approached, seemingly at a greyhound's pace. The Millennium Commission wanted silly stipulations adhered to; the Cardiff club were not inclined to cooperate with contractors; the contractors lost an awful lot of money on the project, especially when they fell far behind and had to institute twenty-four-hour working which delighted the hard-hats on site and infuriated the local residents.

Scare stories were circulated that contingency plans had been made to move the Wales World Cup to Wembley (at least, those parts of the Wales World Cup which had not been blackmailed away from them already by their so-called partner unions in Europe). Griffiths doggedly soldiered on, doggedly insisted that the stadium would be ready, even though, with so many imponderables, he could not have been certain of this himself. He remained, well, dogged. In the end, as the pre-tournament press conference held a day before the opening ceremony was interrupted by drills and saws and hammering, and even though the ancillary building intended to form part of the complex was still under construction, and even though the pitch, brought in on pallets, was bare and worn and criticised, the Millennium Stadium – just – won its own hair-raising race.

And was it ever worth it. The stadium achieves something priceless. It is marvellous to look at and stirring for the senses, it is vast and imposing. And yet it has a homeliness, it is close to the action. It is cantilevered, so at a certain height leans back inwards. So many new stadia, especially Twickenham, are soulless bowls from which the atmosphere evaporates. Soon, the Millennium factor began to operate. The players felt wonderfully inspired when they came home from Northwest London to their new arena. The first matches, staged for the safety-inspectors when parts of the stadium were as yet unfinished, created a tingling atmosphere, something which touched proceedings with a kind of magic. The sliding roof was installed, said Max Boyce, 'so

God can see us play'. (And so shame on the dullard Australian Rugby Union for demanding that God's view be blocked, that World Cup matches should be played with the roof closed. Rugby is an outdoor game, and must take what the weather-gods throw.)

When more than 40,000 people went to watch what was a rather humdrum World Cup match between Argentina and Japan it was obvious that they saw the stadium itself as an attraction. The Welsh football team, accustomed to playing to 12,000 crowds at Ninian Park, here drew first 63,000 and then the full 72,500 capacity to friendly matches in the spring of 2000. If the crowd held that day's opposition, Brazil, in awe, then there is no doubt that the awe was returned by the Brazilians to their surroundings. Even my mum went to the stadium, when it was again sold out – this time for *Songs of Praise* – and her enjoyment at the stirring new edifice was only partially spoiled when some know-all neighbour passed on the gossip that the stadium wasn't safe and when some fool of a doorman let in Cliff Richard. On the safety front, I tried to explain the rigour of the inspectors these days, but it was too late.

The Millennium Stadium, in my opinion, lifted the whole country. It lifted the team, anyone walking by *en route* to work in Cardiff or who had been born there and saw the pictures. Anyone who thought, as did I, that Welsh people were afraid of vision and grandeur. It showed a lead in rugby, in construction. It became what is, until some new giant overtakes it some time in the future, the greatest sports stadium in the world. In the week that it staged its first rugby match (Wales against South Africa on 26 June 1999) I was in Sydney with the touring England. They showed us around Sydney's Olympic Stadium, which in not one sense – situation, appearance, closeness, removal of breath through sense of wonder – even began to compare. The opening of the Millennium Stadium was part of a process in which the re-nascent rugby team and the rousing rockers united in propounding one message: that our country was alive and rocking.

The opening ceremony of the World Cup was in similar vein. As well as Cerys and Max, there was the world-class baritone Bryn Terfel and – dressed in a glorious red dragon get-up which would have looked ludicrously over the top on anyone else but which on her looked splendidly understated – our Shirley from Tiger Bay. The ceremony was unashamedly Welsh, with Gerald Davies commentating, intoning gravely about a new Wales, about a new-found confidence. On the giant screens they showed Welsh tries. They interrupted the stream of Taffmania only for the ineffably gorgeous Ladysmith Black Mambazo, with Joseph

Shabalala in splendid voice. Then back to Taffmania.

Afterwards, a few little Englanders and others complained about the excessive Welshness, seeing it as some sort of snub to the other competing nations (whose flags and songs were well represented, incidentally). What did they expect at a Welsh opening ceremony? Pan-pipe music from the Andes? Bouzouki music from Greece? Herds of wildebeest sweeping majestically over the plain? The breathtaking opening ceremony at Cape Town in 1995 was entirely and exclusively South African and all the better for it, apart from some pure tokenism in which Wales were represented by a group of people wearing mining helmets. At least they spared us the sheep.

As I say, our country came alive. I believe that the revival continues today, and that although it was in part driven by rugby matters, by the statement made by the new stadium and the improvement in rugby results, it now has an existence separate from such rugby matters. If it was easy to adopt a professional detachment when the team played, then to remain detached and unexcited at the resurgence of my country proved impossible. And I wouldn't have had it otherwise.

But back in the autumn of 1999 there was the prospect of something else. It was a distinctly unfashionable view, but it seemed to me that Wales could win the World Cup.

Graham Henry had arrived in Wales a year before the tournament. His record at all levels up to Super-12 in New Zealand was outstanding and he was obviously a contender to coach the All Blacks at some stage. It was deeply ironic that soon after he left for Heathrow and the M4 down to Cardiff, New Zealand's form collapsed, and the position of John Hart, the coach, was severely under threat. Had Henry still been in Christchurch, his home town, he might easily have arrived at Wales '99 as New Zealand coach. He may have mused, as he settled into his new home, appropriately called the Coach House, in the marshes between Newport and the C-word (that place we Newportonians can say the name of only when spitting at the same time), that had he held on for a week or two he might now be picking up the reins in one of the most focused and successful rugby countries in the world, instead of flogging the dead horse of a nation where rugby had declined dramatically.

Henry rolled up his sleeves. He had the priceless advantage not only of the £250,000 per annum which was both his salary and his insurance against his reputation disappearing completely, but also because, in a land where insularity and village-pump politics are all the rage, he was an outsider and so could brush off parochialism as if he never even noticed it. He did notice it. He told me that he had detected it everywhere since the time when, on the back-of-the-hand say-so of some well-known Welsh figure, he dropped from his squad players he did not know well, only to realise later that the advice had been based on where the players lived, not on how they played. So Henry was to affect a blissful ignorance of every parish-pump politician in the country.

Soon, Wales were looking a little more likely. Henry and David Pickering, a splendid flanker turned influential manager, set up a proper management structure and into it brought Steve Black, a remarkable black-bearded Geordie, who was un-slight of build and gruff in appearance but had been a sprinter and playwright. Black had an outstanding reputation as a fitness coach and also a motivator/father confessor to a raft of different sporting teams and individuals. He came to Henry recommended by the latter's former charge Pat Lam.

Having lost the winning habit so long ago, Wales came out and opened the Henry era at Wembley with a heroic performance in a 20–28 defeat at the hands of South Africa. They beat Argentina at Llanelli and lost to Scotland at Murrayfield in a match which caused deep gloom but in which I discerned the definite signs of a revival in their forward play. They lost to Ireland at Wembley purely because while they had improved, they were still infinitely happier when fighting as underdogs rather than operating in matches they were expected to win.

Suddenly we were out on Thunder Road with Henry's men. It was not as if there had been monumental changes made – apart from the fact that Henry finally got over the message that Welsh rugby players and officials and coaches and club grandees had missed: that professionalism was a state of mind, not a bulge in the trouser pocket. But the strokes that Henry pulled were masterly. He had recruited the former New Zealand full-back Shane Howarth, and although it was later proven that Howarth was not eligible, he played with as much commitment and elan as any Welshman. Henry also based his pack around the two square Quinnells, Scott and Craig, whereas previous administrations had gone to enormous lengths to avoid choosing them and the Quinnells had managed to fall prey to any injury going. Most shrewdly of all, he plucked Chris Wyatt, the tall and athletic Llanelli back-row man, out of his habitat and installed him as the main line-out jumper (though, not so handily, often as the only line-out jumper), where he quickly became one of the most influential forwards in the 1999 Five Nations Championship. The team were expertly marshalled by Neil Jenkins, who was soon the world-record points-scorer in Tests; and the scrum was transformed from the weak and milky units of its recent past to something of authority, all built around the stocky and powerful figure of Peter Rogers, the new loose-head. It took some time before we all realised that the South African prop Wales had imported was not the past-it Heinrich Rodgers, as even the *Playfair Annual* recorded the wrong man. This Rogers was born and raised in Wales, and London Irish coach Dick Best had signed him. Best, faced with the ceiling on holders of overseas passports, had scoured the world for players holding British or EEC passports and finally dredged up Rogers. Good old Bestie, thanks for your commitment to the Welsh cause, Messiah. Rogers quickly became the most powerful and awkward loose-head prop in the world. Phil Vickery, of Gloucester and England, was given a tough time by Rogers in the 2000 Six Nations England–Wales match, and later held me spellbound during an interview in which he explained what Rogers tries to do in a scrum and how hard he had found it to develop counter-measures.

And so off they went, this team that had forgotten how to win. Wales achieved a memorable victory in Paris, their first for twenty-four years, when they finished ahead at 34–33 in the Stade de France after what was by common consent one of the most exciting Five Nations matches ever played. Black's influence on the players was obvious as the delirious Welsh team sought him out for congratulatory hugs when they celebrated at the end. Henry, meanwhile, had identified early on the need to prevent the hopes of the Welsh nation from burgeoning far more quickly than the strength of the team (and has therefore been a relentlessly downbeat figure ever since he arrived). He proclaimed that Wales were nothing like a great side, which was true, but that he was glad that the victory had made a lot of people happy.

Wales beat Italy in Treviso, scoring sixty points; and, with confidence surging, they then beat England at Wembley – although it was Gibbs who provided the final flourish, the authority of the Wales scrum over the vaunted England eight was marked, and telling. Next, they moved on to Argentina, an opportunity for their confidence to be tested and especially for the forward revival to be examined in what has been the graveyard for visiting packs. They won the first Test after trailing by a long way in the first half; and they won the second, thereby becoming the first British Isles team to win both matches of a two-Test series in Argentina, one of the most difficult places to play. Their scrummaging, with Rogers in commanding form, overturned any notion of Pumas supremacy and overturned all known history. The home scrum was reduced to matchwood.

Significantly, too, they won the fight. It was as big a step forward as winning the scrums. A ferocious punch-up started on the half-hour of the second Test in Buenos Aires which involved sixteen players and even spilled down into one of the dug-outs. It appeared to begin when the burly Mauricio Reggiardo threw a punch at Dafydd James, and when it ended the home captain Pedro Sporleder, Reggiardo and Rogers were sent to the sin-bin. Any Welsh follower would have celebrated. Yep. Celebrated. Sanctimonious sermons about dirty play could come later. Welsh forward play was once some of the most frightening in the world. Whether you were playing a Welsh side on their own patch, or entertaining them on their Devon tour, or wherever you met them, you would always find iron-hard men. Not lunatics. Just hard men. Fixers. Characters.

You could write a book on them. From one era alone in Wales, there was Randall Davies, the ferocious Neath flanker; Morrie Evans of Swansea, who once dislocated his shoulder without realising and stood while a physio vigorously rubbed Deep Heat into it; Omri Jones, the crew-cut policeman who hurt people as Aberavon's openside; John Hickey, lanky and dangerous Cardiff flanker; Del Haines, the Newport flanker who once hit the great Springbok Frik du Preez with a tackle so hard that the rhino-like Du Preez collapsed in a heap, and so did the Boks – Newport beat them easily after Del's game-crushing hit. But there were loads of sub-fixers, too. Every Welsh community rugby club would have one, and revere him. It used to be unpleasant to play Welsh rugby teams, and bloody good job, too. With such men around, no liberties could be taken.

Then, the roll-over years. The Other Cheek years. There are many theories. If true physical and spiritual hardness can be gained only from environment and employ, then the decline and disappearance of the coalmining and steelworking industries in Wales was obviously a factor. Sports science is wonderful, can no doubt turn out bodies of exceptional durability and hardness. But there is a deeper dimension to the great Welsh forward traditions which cannot be found in a gym.

The Paul Ringer match, the roughhouse in which England beat Wales at Twickenham in 1980, was another factor. Ringer was sent off for an offence that by any standards, was almost entirely innocuous – a so-called high tackle on John Horton of England. At a time when the pre-match build-up and various bleatings had the referee and the whole world expecting Welsh skulduggery, Ringer's real crime was to have given them anything whatsoever that might have been interpreted as such. He was a victim of outside pressures but also of his own failure to grasp what those pressures were.

With Welsh rugby players labelled as savages, the resulting furore robbed Wales of an edge which it is doubtful they ever re-discovered. Due to the changing nature of Welsh life the traditions of Wales's forward play were already dying, and the Ringer match further crushed them. For the next twenty years, at all levels and in all locations, Welsh forward play became apologetic. After Wales were slaughtered by the All Blacks in the first Test in 1988, their forwards were taunted by the All Black captain Wayne Shelford. In the week before the second Test he was widely quoted as having expressed surprise that not one Welsh forward had reacted as he lay on the floor to kill the Welsh ball, and as he generally made a nuisance of himself. He said how amazed he was that none of them had booted him on the ground, taken the law into their own hands. If such was needed, Shelford making these comments with a Test match still to play in a few days' time was a most eloquent statement about the decline of Welsh play: he knew that even when goaded systematically the Welsh would do nothing. If Buck had been up against Omri, Del, Randall and Morrie he'd have kept his big Black trap firmly shut. They would have kicked the Black shirt off his back.

We're not talking psychosis here, or premeditated violence. We're just talking reality. In 1999 the sight of Wales refusing to be messed around by the Pumas was welcome. And even more so was the fact that after the fight it was the Pumas whose rhythm was upset and the Welsh who gained strength.

And continued to improve at a rattling rate. In late June, marking the opening of the first wonder of the Welsh world, Wales took on and dismantled South Africa, winning 29–19. If the victory over England could be said to have come against the run of the play, and the victory over France to have been something of a lottery, then Wales were now taking on and beating, fair and square and no excuses, some of the best teams around. They had two more World Cup warm-up matches, in which they beat Canada by 33–19 and France by 34–24. Henry marked every victory by pointing out that Wales were still fairly poor, were only just among the top ten nations in the world, would need a miracle to beat anyone in the World Cup, and so on down the long length of the cold-water hosepipe. Yet in the match against France, on a furnace-hot day in an excited and by now almost-finished Millennium, I thought that they had crossed a significant boundary It was by now obvious that they were a horrible team to play against. And what better criterion is there? The French players hated that game, because they were hammered in the scrum by Rogers and David Young and company and because Wales played with a tremendous and stroppy verve and purpose. And if they lacked burning pace, then there was no little speed, either.

✿　✿　✿

Wales ground on through the weeks of final preparation, taking the camp around the country, north, south and west, to allow the people to see their heroes working up in the flesh. As they did so, the fascinating question was this: how good were Wales, and were they capable of winning their own World Cup? Presumably Henry was not in private telling the team how bad they were, how they didn't compare with the top teams.

So now, the mystery that has never been properly explained. Take the state of the Welsh national squad of, say, the horrendous fifty-point defeat by France at Wembley in 1998, when they were butter-soft, some of them had apparently resigned beforehand, and they did not even manage to score a point. Now compare that with the team of not much more than a year later, when Wales were on their ten-match winning run and blasted the French with sheer power and energy. By this time Wales had tight forwards, they had a game-plan, an expert general and brilliant kicker in Neil Jenkins, genuine power-runners in Scott Quinnell and Colin Charvis, and, in Scott Gibbs and Mark Taylor, the best all-purpose pairing in the European game. Above all, they had passion. They seemed to have caught up with the requirements of professionalism, and under Black, seemed happy, motivated and fit.

If you draw a graph recording this level of improvement, and continue that graph through to the World Cup, you have a team that should have been contenders to win the tournament. Henry played it down, but only to ease the pressure. It was obvious that Wales had faults. Their ball-retention was not always good, though you would expect that as a matter of course this would be improved out of sight in the final months of training camp. They lacked pace down the wings, but in Gareth Thomas and Dafydd James they had two players who would prosper in any case. They had a line-out weakness if Wyatt and his throw-in were off the mark, but Wyatt could also go through a match with a perfect line-out score.

But when assessing Wales's chances there was another key factor to consider: the advantage of being host. The momentum conveyed by being the home team in your own World Cup has always proved massive. New Zealand were not a great side in any way as they entered the 1987 World Cup, but they won that tournament at a canter, waxing weekly. England were by no means even a good side when they entered a World Cup that was to climax at Twickenham, but it was only a spectacular tactical blunder with which their captain, Will Carling, must live until his grave that cost them the title. South Africa were borne home on a tidal wave of emotion and political significance in 1995, and found that the holes in their team were filled by the magnitude of their impending achievement.

What happened in 1999? Nothing. In the four matches they played in the World Cup, I doubt if Wales ever got within twenty-five points of the level of performance they had achieved in any of the ten victories on their march towards what they hoped would be glory. In the event they were pale, puffy, slow, wan, halting. For no sustained period of play in any of their four matches did they show the same freshness and excellence of the 1999 run, nor anything remotely resembling it. They were the first team not to train on, not to gather strength in their own tournament. A mystery.

The opening match, Wales against Argentina, kicked off to the fading tones of Bryn and Shirl. The theory with which Wales explained their patchy performance was that they were just overwhelmed by the sheer Welsh passion of the occasion. 'Some of the boys had tears in their eyes just from walking round the pitch before the start,' Gibbs told me later. 'That was when we really felt the pressure and realised that after all the months of hard work, the time had come.' Gibbs himself had to leave the field because of a severe stomach upset which had left him drained, and it is a moot point whether he was affected by some kind of bug or simply by the magnitude of it all and by what he, the talisman, was expected to produce. Charvis seemed to settle the nerves with his early try but Wales won by only 23–18, and this against an Argentine side which had not yet begun their own splendid revival.

They recovered well enough to beat Japan in the next pool match, by 64–15, but this was no real test. When they faced Samoa in the final pool game they really should have hit the straps. Samoa still had some decent players and were led by the extraordinary Pat Lam, but their scrum's front-five operation was weak, and, unlike that marvellous occasion when they ambushed Wales in the 1991 tournament, they no longer had the surprise factor. Nor Frank Bunce.

Wales really should have run up fifty points, and done so with the realisation that to play a wide game and make mistakes would give Samoa their only chance. Led by poor Scott Quinnell, who coughed up the ball like a junior schoolboy confronted by the school bully, Wales made an horrendous number of errors, took Samoa on at precisely those areas of the field where Samoa were comfortable, and duly lost by 38–31. Gibbs, at least, was partly restored and was full value in a juddering contest with the equally powerful George Leaupepe, the Samoan centre. It was the kind of performance that the All Blacks, for example, would never have given. The pressure was apparently still affecting form and judgement; the team were still playing as if drained.

So the dream died as early as the quarter-final, and ended in deeply unsatisfactory circumstances. Australia had played tolerably well, if never explosively, in the scruffy Irish pool, hampered by the lack of fluency, pace and kicking ability of Steve Larkham, their fly-half. The quiet desperation which seemed invariably to tinge the Australian camp's praise of Larkham in the year leading up to the World Cup had always struck me as a wish fathering the thought because they were so short of real class in the position, a fact which their matches played when Larkham was injured showed so brutally. They even made an abortive attempt to convert poor Tim Horan, who played like a fish out of his tank. The tournament had proved that Australia had a decent if not terrifying pack, a hard if not irresistible running game in which Toutai Kefu, the No. 8, was tough but could be tackled. They had the gem, Horan, in the centre and two strong-running wings in Joe Roff and Ben Tune. But all the evidence of the season and the World Cup pool matches suggested that when you added this lot up it amounted to nothing to write home about, Rolf.

Oh, but if you wanted to beat them you had to score. This was tough on two counts. They were splendid at slowing down and killing possession without penalty, just as all top teams are these days. And they had an excellent defence. It was profoundly depressing to read the words of England's defensive guru Phil Larder after the tournament, for he concluded that the winners had won because they had the best defence. Profoundly depressing because, through gritted teeth and with a prayer for the future of a sport which had lost its way on the field, and with the knowledge that Australian ability in attack never much exceeded the power of a wet haddock, you had to agree with him.

There was always the chance that Wales would suddenly switch back on, of course. That the magnitude of the occasion would inspire them instead of stifle them. But in the first quarter-final of the World Cup, at a loyally thunderous Millennium Stadium and in a match that was reverberating in its collisions, Wales lost by 24–9.

A team which had suddenly lost momentum was beaten by a team which was overrated though still superior, but the story was admittedly more complicated than that. Colin Hawke, the New Zealand referee and usually one of the finest, reduced his art on the day to gibberish. To view the video of the match even now is painful, and watching the endemic rear-feet offside of the Australia team, for which Hawke awarded a grand total of one penalty, the cynic might assert that a team comprising his grandmother's select XV could defend from a position two yards upfield from the offside-line. Nor does the video provide any evidence that Hawke was correct to disallow a try by the Wallaby flanker David Wilson.

Hawke gave Australia a priceless opportunity to establish themselves and, crucially, quieten the crowd when he allowed an opening Australian try after a garish accidental offside. Australia won a ruck but a stray Aussie boot hoofed it straight back in. Hawke dithered, Australia won it again and scored. Afterwards, it was perfectly acceptable for observers to point out that Australia would have won anyway, even were you to deduct both their dubious tries. Fine. But my theory of Test rugby has always been that tries cause momentum, not that momentum causes tries. The early score for nothing took the crowd out of the equation and sapped the confidence of a Welsh team desperately seeking hope.

Near to half-time, Wales had battled back to trail by only 10–9 and were having the better of it. There was another fuss just before the whistle when the alarmingly fallible Larkham threw the ball forward, an Australian forward tried to play it from an offside position, Wales knocked on and Hawke gave Australia a scrum. A penalty then and Wales would have disappeared down the tunnel leading by 12–10. Jenkins was furious at Hawke as they left the field. My momentum theory suggests that the match would have been by no means cut and dried.

A splendid chip by Larkham set up a critical try for Ben Tune to make it 17–9 with only fifteen minutes remaining, and this was where we saw that Wales' poor form had pursued them into the quarter-final. Their play was patchy, lacking the new verve. And if there was life where there was hope, then the worst refereeing blunder I have ever seen killed off both. Hawke was actually running alongside Tim Horan as the great centre threw the ball yards forward; George Gregan appeared to check, decided to carry on when there was no whistle, and ran on to score. There is a telling photograph of the scene as five incredulous Welsh players surround Hawke, who is gamely indicating the score. God only knows what his blithering touch-judges, who have an advisory role in knock-ons, were doing.

There is no doubt that in old stadiums and in new the Cardiff crowd are the most gracious in world rugby, the most appreciative of true rugby class. It is difficult to imagine Twickenham singing 'For He's a Jolly Good Fellow' to the visiting captain as did Cardiff to the All Black Wilson Whineray in 1963; or Lansdowne Road rising as one to clap David Campese all the way to half-way after he had scored a try. The uproarious reception given by the Cardiff crowd to the winning Samoans in the earlier pool match was one of the happiest features of the 1999 World Cup and one of Lam's warmest memories.

But the storm of derision which burst around Hawke's head as he left the field was ear-splitting and unedifying. There was a postscript which may well have made the Welsh public even more angry. The Welsh Society of Rugby Union Referees issued an edict through their secretary, Hugh Banfield, deploring the criticism of Hawke and offering him their support. If the Welsh SRUR is a social club committed to the unctuous closing of ranks to mask the errors of their colleagues, then fine. If it is in any way a body committed to high standards of refereeing and which acknowledges that a World Cup quarter-final should demand the very highest standards, then it should have joined the clamour itself. The press item referring to the SRUR's move even portrayed the communication to Hawke as an apology on behalf of the nation. I imagine that the nation would have liked to remind Banfield that if he was apologising then he was doing so on behalf of no one but a group of whistlers in a committee room, the only members of the nation on whose behalf he was qualified to speak. Later in the season one former ref asked me in heated mode, 'Who calls you lot in the media to account? You just have a free hand to get it wrong and no one comes down on you.' I promised to introduce him at the earliest opportunity to Mr Alex Butler, sports editor of the *Sunday Times*, with whom he could discuss the subject of people never coming down on me. Incidentally, the next time I saw Hawke, when he took charge of the South Africa–England first Test in Pretoria in June 2000, he seemed reasonably well restored.

There was a fair old clamour as the Welsh team did a shattered lap of honour at the end of the Australia match. They were clearly distressed that the adventure and the revival should have concluded as it did. The crowd was warm and generous, but there was no man or woman in that gathering, whether on the field or in the towering stands, who did not realise that the listless Wales had not explored the top of their ranges. From the line-out to Jenkins and Rob Howley at half-back to Gibbs in the centre, Wales had fallen dramatically short of the fine potential shown in the months before the tournament, and who had not dreamed or fully expected that improvement to be maintained?

There are many theories. Henry had a few. 'Firstly, we had played too much Test rugby. Thirteen Tests in eleven months leading up to the World Cup was significantly more than any other team. Australia had played nine. Also, the players found the winning of ten Tests on the trot difficult to handle. Winning creates a different pressure which the players had not experienced before at this level. They need to handle success as a positive and not as an Achilles' heel. They still bear the scars of the unsuccessful years.'

Hmmm. So they were knackered, or they were unable to cope with the idea that they might win. It does seem to me that Henry's theories clash – it seems he's saying that Wales played too many matches but were not far enough along the road. It also appears to me that no top-level team could win eight matches on the trot without handling success reasonably well. There is no doubt that the pressure on Wales at the start of the World Cup was vast and, as Gibbs said, almost suffocating: players had, after all, come back into the dressing room in tears after merely walking around the stadium before the match. But surely that should soon have become a positive.

The numbing, dumbing effect of too much time in training camp must also be considered. Wales spent so long in squad session that they must have become almost institutionalised; and by now you may have got the picture: I believe that putting too much effort into trying to improve your team means that your team will consequently decline. Compare again the zip of the Welsh team in the winning run and their drained appearance in the Big One. Henry must take some of the blame for that contrast.

Wales appeared to be very slow and, frankly, to be carrying a few extra pounds. Thus question marks were raised over their fitness and Steve Black's methods. Bob Dwyer, the former Australian coach then at Bristol, went public on the physical appearance of the Quinnells, who were not the only Welsh forwards who looked less than sleek to the untutored naked eye.

Eventually, despite support from Henry and the rest of the management team, Black reflected on a poor Welsh start to the Six Nations programme and heavy defeat at the hands of France, then he resigned, returning to his former post at the Newcastle Falcons. Henry was furious. 'Steve is a proud man and has been put under intolerable pressure,' he said. Rugby commentators who had questioned Black's methods were sent to Coventry by other angry management members.

But Henry could easily have added that the issue was handled badly from his side, too. Wales were sluggish in the tournament – that is surely not in dispute. Black's methods have worked superbly for many sportsmen but do not include formal fitness-testing, a staple of programmes run by more orthodox people in the field. A series of official fitness tests could have established once and for all whether Black's methods had worked. If they had, then he would have been due a pay rise and an apology from Dwyer and everyone else. I have no doubt whatsoever that Steve Black is a boon to any team, a core character. Whenever Howarth took the field for Wales, he and Black would come down the tunnel in each other's embrace; they had been driven together initially because they were both non-Welshman in a tight-knit squad. Black had a massive role to play and need not have left his post, if only some of the freely available testing measures had been employed to back up what he said. Black, for whom I hold a vast admiration, was not too proud a man to undertake them.

Having come down the straight of their final preparatory lap like Michael Schumacher, Wales spluttered to a halt and gave easily the worst performance of any hosting team in a World Cup. Henry, alert as ever to the almost cataclysmic power of Welsh public opinion, nipped any whining in the bud by declaring afterwards that Wales had achieved what he had expected of them. This was also a defensive mechanism for his own position. Only he knows whether he secretly expected more, or if he dreamed of more. I think that he did. I think he knows that had Wales continued improving in the months before RWC '99 at only a fraction of the rate at which they had improved since their revival, they could easily have reached the final of the tournament. Then, with a Wales team in the Cardiff final of a Wales World Cup, who knows? Shame that in the end this is all merely speculation.

Three British teams were standing as Rugby World Cup 1999 entered the weekend of the quarter-finals. One by one their hopes, like three giant chimney stacks in the hands of that ludicrous professional Northerner with the festering flat 'at and the steamroller and his own TV series – you know, Fred something – toppled and became dust. Wales crashed on the Saturday; England were hammered by South Africa, drop-kicked into oblivion by Jannie de Beer, on the Sunday in Paris.

For those who had lived for so long in a kind of proximity to England's World Cup bid and to all their frantic aspirations for their team, it was an odd sensation. Theirs was a devastating defeat and one which revealed in sharp relief the weaknesses they had carried throughout their campaign. Now they were gone, sent packing. It was a dreadfully disappointing experience for the squad, who had worked till they dropped. For others of us it was as if part of our lives had ended, something that had consumed us, professionally speaking, for three years which felt like thirty-three. And we hardly knew what to do next. I wandered round the Stade de France with Nick Cain, my colleague from the *Sunday*

Times, our heads down, discussing this sporting tragedy in hushed tones, trying to make some sense of it. Would things ever feel right again?

Yes, inside about two minutes. Stuff it. We gatecrashed a massive tented village just outside the ground of the Stade, where a series of major companies were entertaining their guests, where they served champagne, foie gras, all kinds of delicious nibbles and thirty-four different kinds of fine wine. We watched the riotous, marvellous France–Argentina quarter-final on a giant screen and commiserated with the Pumas as they unluckily subsided by 47–26; we shared a beer with Keith Barwell, distinguished millionaire owner of Northampton, told him what a fantastic job he was doing (just in case he was the host); we grumbled heartily about the refereeing of Derek Bevan (who'd robbed the Argentines of what might have been a match-winning try with one of those ferociously unfair penalties which refs now give against the team in possession); then we left complaining to the doormen about the large number of gatecrashers they'd let in. We then staggered happily back to our hotel near the Gare du Nord in preparation for the telecast of the Scotland–New Zealand match from Murrayfield; tried to remember if England had won or lost earlier; cleaned out our entire mini-bar, champagne and all, in company with Dick Best, who we had found wandering feebly around gibbering to himself that, now England were out, what were the chances of Scotland beating New Zealand and therefore handing him the nightmare double? And the thrill of the months-long chase we knew lay ahead as we tried to get someone back at the *Sunday Times* to sign our expenses for that weekend was hardly lessened for one moment by the certain knowledge of eventual (and utter) failure. The game goes on. Next day, incidentally, the first of England's post-tournament life, the sun surprised everyone by rising as normal. Birds sang, too.

Our man Best was quickly reassured as we watched the match from Murrayfield. New Zealand cruised into a 25–3 lead with decent but only token resistance from Scotland on a soggy old Murrayfield evening. Tana Umaga, a great player when the going's good (and when the going gets tough, his form tends to get going, in the sense of departing), scored two tries and Jeff Wilson one; and although Jonah Lomu knocked on three times in the wet conditions, his power was again a marvel.

Scotland came back strongly in the second half, and (for connoisseurs of these futile little facts) actually won it by 15–5. Budge Pountney and Cammie Murray scored, although Lomu sealed it for the Blacks with a powerhouse try. Afterwards there was something approaching euphoria in the Scotland ranks. The team did a lap of honour and were loudly acclaimed by what was almost a capacity crowd. Jim Telfer was bowing out as coach and that great grey-haired steely man joined the team of their touchy-feely-wavy lap, though among a squad wearing ludicrous bright orange jerseys he looked like an innocent bystander in an explosion at the Outspan factory.

It was also the last bow at international level for Gary Armstrong, one of the hardest and most indomitable men who ever played. Armstrong is the kind of bloke who gives professional rugby a good name. He was a lorry driver in the Borders, and was able to maximise in his life the talent with which he had been most blessed (the talent to play rugby) by turning pro and playing with such supreme application for Newcastle and Scotland that he was worth every penny they paid him. And yet the priceless thing was that had he been playing for either team in the amateur era for nothing, the effort he put in would not have lessened by a scrap. In his later tribute, Telfer was correct to say that only a couple of inches and a pound or two stood between Armstrong and an alternative career as a world-class flanker, such were his all-round gifts and powers.

However, the post-match atmosphere seemed in many ways bogus. The crowd were raucous in their support; but was it really something to celebrate when the marketing men boasted of 'almost a full house'? Was the fact that some seats had remained unsold for a clash in the Rugby World Cup quarter-finals between Scotland and the mighty All Blacks not more of a story? And I am always suspicious of euphoria surrounding second-half comebacks if such are staged only after the match is over. It is when a game is alive that devil and drive and scores can be acclaimed, not after it is gone and buried. Scottish rugby lost itself during the World Cup, lost its public and its energy and its team. Lost its blue jerseys. We had to wait until a passionate day in April before we once again detected a heartbeat, and then only after an anxious vigil.

By the time the focus of the tournament had moved to Twickenham for the two semi-finals it was blindingly obvious that two semi-finals of supreme moment and drama were required to save what had been a drab old affair, coloured black and white with a few bright streaks shot through at random. Even though the old plodding pace of events was resumed in the play-off and the World Cup final itself, history shows that the semis did elevate the tournament. The first, between Australia and South Africa, did so with a marvellous old-fashioned battle involving extra time; the second, stratosphere-high, with what is now held in popularly perceived wisdom as the greatest match, France–New Zealand. Saved – just. Phew!

The Saturday semi was not of a vintage quality and no tries were scored. Yet there was high drama and a sense of import befitting a semi-final. Twickenham was lashed by rain and high winds and it was a storm-tossed affair. Joost van der Westhuizen was outstanding for South Africa but their pack could never gain an authority. Tim Horan was splendid in the midfield for Australia and there were some decent drives from the No. 8, Toutai Kefu. But the fly-half, Steve Larkham, had a poor match, and in the end these southern hemisphere giants fought out a contest that had all the hallmarks of an old-style northern hemisphere scrap.

Australia led by three points, and when normal time ran out the announcement over the tannoy was that there would be two minutes of injury time. Bewilderingly, then, the match was still battering onwards in its eighty-seventh minute when Owen Finnegan, the Wallaby flanker, gave away a penalty. Jannie de Beer, with only the World Cup final hanging on his success, stepped up to kick for goal from thirty-six metres out and only eight metres in from the right-hand touch-line. De Beer, who had dropped five goals against England in Paris, fell from his drop-kick throne on this day, putting over just one from five attempts. And here, placing the ball as the loneliest man in the sporting world, he was long odds against. He knew it was to be the last kick of the match. And he slotted it. It was a brilliant kick.

The fascinating question then was whether De Beer would even play the extra time. Hero to shower soap-on-a-rope inside a minute. Henry Honiball, who lies yards flatter than the conservative De Beer, had missed the whole event through injury but was now fit and on the bench. Nick Mallett must have been torn between bringing Honiball on – because for all his fine kicking, De Beer never looked remotely like sparking any kind of South African attacking machine – and leaving on De Beer on the basis that on such a day and in such tension the match would be decided by kicks in any case. He left De Beer in place, and the match *was* decided by kicks. Steve Larkham dropped a goal for Australia and Matt Burke kicked a penalty. Advance Australia, rain-swept and thrilled.

Oh me of little faith. That Sunday dawned and the rugby-loving readers of the Sunday newspapers clustered eagerly round their breakfast tables, and they read in every paper the (finely crafted) utter dismissal of any chances the French might have. This was done on the admittedly well-founded grounds that France had been a joke for almost eighteen months, had lost by fifty the last time the teams met and New Zealand had declared at half-time; and also that New Zealand were, for all anyone knew at the time (and despite the fact that they had a visibly weak second row and a midfield of mediocrity), only warming up for the final stages.

Musing on a likely introduction for our feature discussing the semi-final, I was interrupted by an e-mail from my colleague Tom English offering me forty points to back France. I didn't want the bet but I did want the intro, and so made much play in it of ostentatiously turning down the forty points because that was roughly the margin by which I expected New Zealand to be leading at half-time (provided the French defence improved). Ah well, pride comes before a fall – although the only thing worse than taking a strong line on the morning of a match and being brutally exposed is taking no line at all and sitting on the fence. Correct me if I'm wrong, but isn't the biggest bore in newspapers when the writer can't, or won't, make up his mind?

And who cared anyway? The important thing was the sheer, soaring magnificence of what lay before us at Twickenham. I'd promised to take the Jones youngsters. They were therefore able to tell their friends that they'd be present at the Greatest Ever, though in the event their lack of perspective perhaps diminished the impact in that they probably assume it is always like that. In the subsequent summer my son Andrew went to his first ever day of Test cricket – the Lord's match between England and the West Indies. It was the day when at least a part of all four innings (two in their entirety) took place when those magnificent men Courtney Walsh and Curtly Ambrose were seen in glorious action. And when Andy Caddick and company threw it back in the West Indians' faces – and, more to the point, bowled it straight at their throats – we found that, hey presto, they were no more partial to playing the short stuff than anyone. Dominic Cork saw England home the next day, and presumably Andrew now thinks that Test cricket's like that all the time, too.

At first, it went roughly to plan. France were undeniably giving it a thrash, and Abdel Benazzi and Olivier Magne, two of the players who would have found a place in any world XV (Magne, easily, over the celebrated Josh Kronfeld), were marvellous. Christophe Dominici, the wing, made a dazzling run in the first half to set up a try for Christophe Lamaison, running a decent show at fly-half. But Lomu scored a screaming try in the first half, hurtling through six tackles. When he crossed again early in the second half, it was 24–10 to New Zealand. Lomu would have gone straight through a desperate tackle by Xavier Garbajosa, the French full-back, to score. At least, he would have done had Xavier not run up the white flag and almost swallow-dived out of his path. And at that stage all you could see was a rush of New Zealand scoring as French morale collapsed. Well, to be frank, you couldn't see Xavier as a finger-in-the-dyke man.

We did have a rush of scoring. We had thirty-three sensational points in a shattering burst, and all from the same team. The one in blue. We had some driving mauls from France that simply plundered a path straight through the middle of the All Blacks, smashed them to bits, cut off acres of territory. It set looming question marks, if they did not loom there already, over Norm Maxwell and Reuben Thorne and over the unhappy, inadequate Taine Randell, the captain and No. 8. We knew that Benazzi and Magne would lead, and the celebrated pair were monstrously good. But so were the likes of Olivier Brouzet and Fabien Pelous, who'd done little more in their international careers than stand around looking dangerous but who now helped crush the All Blacks' aspirations in a mighty Gallic grip.

Lamaison kicked France back to within a point with two drop-goals and two penalties, and all the kicks came because the All Blacks wilted under pressure. Slowly but steadily, bits were falling off the Black machine. Tana Umaga made the first of what was to become a series of horrendous and nervy errors. Perhaps even more amazingly, a Twickenham crowd who, because of the Beef War raging at the time, had started the match unanimously in the anti-French camp began suddenly to support France in ear-splitting fashion. For the first time in ages Twickenham reacted like a rugby stadium should, and it was an irony that they did so in the absence of their own heroes.

The avalanche continued and France took the lead. Jeff Wilson was hammered in midfield by a manic band of French chasers, Galthié chipped ahead, the All Black cover made a mess and Dominici set off with the ball and ran it in from forty metres. Shortly afterwards Lamaison chipped beautifully into the in-goal area and that strange, talented centre Richard Dourthe leaped high and scored. As the match swept gloriously on heady diagonals, French hope became conviction.

Later, after the ball went loose on the French twenty-two, the super-charged Magne hacked it on, and on and on. Philippe Bernat-Salles, the grey long-hair on the wing, touched down. Wilson scored for the All Blacks just before the end – the end of the match, the end of the New Zealand Cup, of John Hart, of Randell's reign as captain; the end of the ill-feeling of the Beef War, of my career as a World Cup semi-final crystal ball-gazer. And the start of the best French sporting celebration since the football World Cup.

In New Zealand, people mourned, wrote savage letters about how the All Blacks should all be shot; people in Parliament made pointed speeches; industrialists complained that production would now decline. When Wales were knocked out of the tournament the country shrugged, complained over a beer and forgot about it. The reaction in New Zealand, into which I tapped via fax and radio and e-mail and website, confirmed in spades what those of us who had recently toured there strongly suspected – that All Blacks Inc. had become ludicrously too important to the people of the country.

But in the old country, and for the first time, the World Cup was suddenly on everyone's lips. The feel-good factor that had pervaded the entire proceedings in 1991 belatedly made an appearance, and there was a rugby euphoria which infected non-rugby people. Better late, in this last week of the tournament, than never. People in England, just for the day, put their hands on their hearts and said (even if they said it quietly when everyone else was out of the room): 'I am a Frenchman.'

Those for whom the natural self-assurance of the two most successful nations in rugby's history – South Africa and New Zealand – tends to jar slightly (and I couldn't possibly reveal whether I'm included in their number) were sniggering behind their hands that the two giants now had to go to Cardiff for the third-fourth-place match. Everyone complains about the play-off match, but this one drew more than 50,000 to the Millennium. (Well, I suppose the travelling thousands of fans from the two competing countries had booked their passages until the end of the tournament – no doubt they'd also booked the tickets for the final.)

By this time New Zealand were shot to pieces, their management team knew full well that they could never survive, and poor John Hart, whom I respected almost without reservation as a coach and man, spent the whole match staring moodily down at proceedings. South Africa won by 22–18, deservedly so. In what was meant to be a match in which they could let down their hair, New Zealand could manage only six penalties from Andrew Mehrtens. South Africa's victory was sealed with a try from Breyton Paulse, fast advancing his claims as a hand-on-heart merit selection rather than as a non-white who deserved a chance.

The anxiety before the final was precisely the same as in the week of the first World Cup final, when France lost to New Zealand in Auckland in 1987. The French had produced a marvellous effort to demolish Australia in the semi-final at Concord Oval, Sydney, with the signature of Serge Blanco sprinting hell-for-leather for the corner for the winning try. They were never remotely the same team in the final. In 1999 France had to contend with their own tiredness; with the knowledge that stunning performances of the kind they had produced against New

Zealand are not ten-a-penny, and certainly not twice-in-a-week; and with the knowledge that they'd come further than was expected. It would not be true to say that they shouldered arms in the final, but they were fifty points inferior to their true, glorious Twickers selves of the previous Sunday.

Even the run-on was lacking. When French teams are confident, when they fancy the job, they spring on to the field like mad dogs, usually bleeding from cuts inflicted by butting each other. It was a French team which performed the greatest run-on of all time, when the Bègles-Bordeaux team sprinted on to the pitch, shaven-headed and ranting, with such a vengeance for the 1991 French Cup final against Toulouse, that it seemed as if they would carry straight through and demolish the opposite stand at the Parc des Princes. By comparison, Raphael Ibanez and his men arrived apologetically.

It was never a great final, nor anything remotely resembling one – not least because neither of the competitors was a great team. Australia won by 35–12, a canter. Again, they defended superbly. They allowed France only twelve points, from four penalties. They clinched the match when Ben Tune scored down the right; they rubbed it in when Owen Finegan ran down the heart of the French defence, past tackler after tackler, and scored a soft try at the posts. Tim Horan reeled another in a majestic series of displays in the centre, somehow finding time and space where none existed for any other centre in the tournament. Steve Larkham draws wildly different reactions for his gawky efforts, but to me the 1999 World Cup suggested that Australia, while becoming the first team to win the event twice (a genuinely fantastic achievement), had also become the first to win it without a fly-half. At no time in the final, or the tournament, did Australia electrify a rugby field. A year later, they were easily a better team.

The Queen, whose body-language suggested that she had a sizeable bet on France or an understandable aversion to presenting the trophy to a fervent Republican such as John Eales, did her stuff. Eales held the golden trophy high in the Cardiff sky; the principals disappeared for the ten thousandth and last press conference relating to issues surrounding the Rugby World Cup, and in terms of fascinating reaction we heard precisely what we had heard in all the others. Nothing.

At the end of the closing ceremony a laser rather cleverly placed a map of Australia hovering above the centre-circle. Good job the Kiwis didn't win. How can a laser depict a small country divided into three islands? Having messed around, scattered the tournament and lost impact, failed to promote it and bickered throughout it, the organisers ensured that they went out on an appropriate note by making a complete balls-up of the post-match dinner.

Those people who dispersed into the Cardiff evening, some already nostalgic for RWC '99 and others glad it was over, reflected on two matters which caused a certain disquiet when it came to considering rugby's progress since it went professional in 1995. First, although there can never be such a thing as a bad Rugby World Cup, in its staging and impact and feel-good factor, this was as close to one as you'd ever want it to get. Second, whatever goals of freedom and entertainment the game had pursued in changing and tinkering with its laws and style to produce a better game, the ball had finished in its own net. It had lost the balance on the field of play and left itself at the mercy of defence. That, palpably, is a disaster.

On New Year's Eve, 1999, the Manic Street Preachers played a concert at the Millennium Stadium. It was reckoned by those present to have been one of the greatest rock concerts ever. Wales danced happily into the new millennium.

CHAPTER EIGHT

Hell

England I: the Clive Woodward era and how only the fates saved him ◆ The challenge that never grew ◆ How soggy England left Europe unconquered

A pause. An awkward instant, lasting a maximum of two seconds. But in that fleeting time, as one team stopped, you knew that the match was over. South Africa had been attacking England in waves, the crowd noise in the Free State Stadium in Bloemfontein was finally noticeable whereas before it had been eerily quiet. The move rumbled on and on, with Braam van Straaten, the hard-bashing fly-half, bashing forward; one recycle, then André Venter on the flank had a go; another recycle, and it was the promising De Wet Barry's turn. Breyton Paulse came in from the blindside wing, jinked and tried to scuttle through, the ball was moved wide to the tall wing Pieter Rossouw. He was swallowed. André Vos picked up the ball and put his shoulder down. Barry had another lunge.

What was compelling, all this time the Springboks were feverishly trying to cut down England's lead, was the contrast. Bishing and bashing Boks, hurling and hollering. And England, heads up, shouting not so much encouragement as advice; coolly shifting resources this way and that, coming up and choosing the various points of high impact, making heavy tackles on the advantage-line or on the South African side of it; extricating, re-aligning, anticipating, hitting, marshalling.

Eventually, on the umpteenth recycle, with not one England man out of position or drawn in or cowed, the ball came back to Joost van der Westhuizen, the scrum-half. He checked, almost stopped. Looked around with something of a wild surmise. Finally he made a run, and was overwhelmed, and soon after that the move petered out. Joost, you see, had simply run out of ideas. Such was the impenetrable wall ranged against him, he had to stop to think. Have a quick rummage in the conjurer's top-hat of his mind to find another trick. They had run so many plays in the same attack without success, they were far beyond any pre-planned move. Now what the blazes did they try?

England won that Test match, on 24 June 2000, and therefore drew the series. They could easily have won the series by 2–0, and not simply on the basis of a few good old losing English what-ifs. It was a highly significant result, not least because Test victories by European teams in the southern hemisphere come not so much in torrents as in drips. When we left Bloemfontein that night, flying back to base in Johannesburg in cold and clear skies, the high veldt moon was blue all right.

For the first time in years, perhaps ever, it seemed to me that England were genuinely on the point of joining the highest echelon of world nations and that the top three (the three southern hemisphere giants) had become four. It was significant because, for the first time since Clive Woodward had taken over as England coach in the autumn of 1997 (since when the results had been so poor as almost to mock the supposed strength of rugby in England), they were playing the game nearly as well as they talked it. At the end of season 2000, after years of disappointment, England were on the march. It was an exciting sensation.

Woodward must have enjoyed it as much as anyone. When England flew home from the tour he had been in charge for thirty-five matches in all in the thirty-one months since his first, against Australia in November 1997. (Why the game continually attempts to butcher its golden-egg-laying goose by arranging for any international side to play matches at a rate of more than one per month is another story.) In that period Woodward had been given coaching, administrative and financial back-up of which his predecessors can only have dreamed. He was given £8 million to fund his World Cup preparations alone. The Bloemfontein win meant that his record was hovering at around fifty-five per cent, deeply unsatisfactory and drastically lower than the percentages of the records of Richard Best and Jack Rowell, who were up around seventy-six per cent and seventy-four per cent respectively.

In Woodward's record were victories in World Cup qualifiers and warm-up matches so easy it was hardly worth removing your blazer to play them. He was also fortunate in his tenure coinciding with the almost total collapse of France, who veered between moments of high excellence and months of breathtaking ineptitude and so allowed England free rein to try to subjugate Europe. The operative word is still 'try'.

In his three years in the job he has had two major strokes of good luck which have enabled him to keep it: he would otherwise have been well in line for the dreaded vote of confidence from the chairman. The sack. It is a lesson, perhaps, to all sports that he is still there and coming through. It is also a lesson to our Clive to offer a prayer of thanks.

❉   ❉   ❉

England, our England. You have to love them, don't you? Well, don't you? Yes, you do. It is my personal opinion that of all those from the major European rugby nations it is England's players who have best adapted to the possibilities of professionalism. They are the most dedicated, and by comparison the rest are toying with the game. Harsh? Not through my binoculars.

Yet the quest to cash in on this dedication in order that England can actually win anything worth winning has been an agony. Woodward's part has been controversial. Formerly a centre of renown if in a style from a different era, he has coached at Henley, London Irish and Bath and the England U21s with varying degrees of success. He arrived as England supremo as – depending on the strength of your inside info – either third or fourth choice, after Ian McGeechan, Graham Henry and several others had already been approached. Uncle Tom Cobbleigh announced himself unavailable due to the forthcoming Fair at Widecombe. Woodward announced himself in his first match, against Australia at Twickenham, by throwing in the tyro Bath hooker Andy Long at least four years before the young man was ready, and by stationing Will Green alongside him at tight-head prop even though Green was not really fit to play.

This flaky selection affected him for at least the first two years of his tenure. As is ever the case, this essentially decent man admitted his error, although you might have expected your national coach to sort out a front row well enough, inexperienced at Test level or not, fourth choice or not. It was like a concert pianist admitting to his audience that he was really sorry, it would never happen again, he was taking full responsibility but he had forgotten to bring his piano.

For collectors of stupendously ludicrous fixture lists, that first autumn, 1997, of Woodward's reign contained one of the classics of the genre. England had to play New Zealand (twice), Australia and South Africa in four weeks, a fatuous waste of three wonderful touring teams, two of which should have preserved at least some of their old mystique by touring properly, individually and at a greater length in subsequent seasons. Don Rutherford, for decades the technical administrator of the RFU, once said that fixture-making of this kind was an attempt to 'replicate a World Cup, with top matches in quick succession'. Why would you want to replicate it? Why not spare yourself that kind of ordeal until you have to go through it for real, especially as it could quite easily shatter your confidence for two years if it all went horribly wrong? If Lewis was up to fight Holyfield, he wouldn't ask for a warm-up fight against Holyfield. England failed to win any of the devil's own series, but salvaged something from the first autumn of Woodward's tenure with a 27–27 draw against the All Blacks with a performance that was daring and exciting and yet, frankly, freakish.

England crushed the undercard of a 1998 Five Nations that was pathetically weak. They beat Wales by scoring sixty at Twickenham, hammered Scotland at Murrayfield on a passion-free Sunday when their second XV could easily have done the job, and completed a fourth Triple Crown in succession by beating Ireland by 35–17. However, the reality was that they were hammered in Paris, where their vaunted forwards came apart against the dashing Christian Califano and company, and the final scoreline of 24–17 did not represent French superiority.

Conquest of Europe postponed.

Then, a further battering by circumstances. The horrendous consequences of slavishly making barmy inter-hemisphere rugby tours no matter what were yet again proven in 1998, when an England squad shorn of virtually all their first-choice players went deep Down Under to undertake what quickly became known as the Tour to Hell.

What possessed the RFU to arrange such an itinerary, involving all the accompanying time-changes, is impossible to comprehend – even if they had been anticipating taking a full team.

What was the point? Was it worth giving up the delights of the true rugby tour to make such an austere and colourless trip? Was it worth the inevitable humiliation? It was all a grotesque lunacy. In terms of the international rugby schedule, it seemed to have become a goal of the RFU to have an itinerary in which every team played all the others every few weeks. There were even rumblings from within the RFU, from those who'd actually been party to the lunacy, when so many players withdrew.

But not nearly so loud as those from Australia. Dick McGruther, a high official of the ARU (at least, he was then – it would be pushing it to say his achievements are all over the paper these days), and John O'Neill, ARU chief executive, obsessed day and night that the nineteen players who had withdrawn from consideration had done so because their clubs had secretly banned them from touring. This all happened at the sorry height of the RFU's anti-club paranoia, and there was no doubt that the Aussie pair were 'briefed' that the clubs were acting malevolently. It was also the height of the IRB's anti-English paranoia. IRB chairman Vernon Pugh was incensed that the major English clubs had completed a submission to the European Courts concerning their commercial rights. He fulminated away at the primacy of international play. McGruther spouted that the England team represented 'the biggest sell-out since

Gallipoli', which showed a lack of either tact or historical perspective and prompted one of the more sexually attractive English-based rugby writers to label McGruther 'the biggest Dick since Turpin'.

All this was supremely irrelevant to the fact of the matter. Which was that the bodies of the team were simply crying 'enough'. Players who had been hammering away and carrying injuries for years rejected a tour that was stupidly conceived and would merely put their careers at risk. The first country which calls off an international rugby tour because too many of their core players are unavailable will have my fullest support.

The whole thing was a disaster for Woodward, of course. And a stroke of luck. It saved him. At that time England's top squad were simply not good enough to cope with a tour of that sort. Had most of the best players attended – had Martin Johnson, Lawrence Dallaglio, Neil Back, Richard Hill, Paul Grayson and Mike Catt and the others been available – they would still have lost all four Tests and Woodward's record would have stood at three wins from twelve, with the prospect of more disasters when the team met the southern hemisphere cream the following autumn. As it was, Woodward and his tyro England, with a squad comprising players who both before and after the tour were not even to gain regular places in their club teams, could hardly be blamed.

They opened the tour by losing to Australia by 76–0 on a horrendous evening at the Suncorp Stadium, Brisbane. Some of us had watched the State of Origin rugby league game in the same stadium on the previous evening; State of Origin is an acquired taste, and its essential emptiness has never appealed to me. Yet that match was not nearly as empty as the proceedings the night after it, when players like Spencer Brown, Steve Ravenscroft, Scott Benton, Jonny Wilkinson and Ben Sturnham were ripped in untimely fashion out of their true time of at least two years in the future (if it was even then), played bravely but were utterly out of their depth.

McGruther and O'Neill, possibly fed by propaganda from inside Twickenham itself, came scuttling round to the press room. Wasn't this a disgrace, who was going to bring the English clubs to heel, you Pom rotters? We agreed. Those players who had had serious operations at the end of the English season should clearly have travelled straight over as soon as they came round from the anaesthetic. Even if your arm's in a sling you can always hold the ball with the other, as long as you don't need a wee at the same time. Our Aussie chums did not grasp that the real culprits are the idiots who fix endless reciprocal tours and Test matches and damage players, either on the wheels of avarice or because unions cannot revise their income-streams well enough to avoid having a financial independence from the imperative of fixing even more matches.

On the day after that defeat, as the team licked their wounds in Brisbane, there was a public disagreement between Woodward and his forward coach, John Mitchell. Woodward had prescribed a day off for his beleaguered men; Mitchell's Kiwi work-ethic wanted them all out training. Woodward was correct, on the grounds that you cannot make a racehorse from a carthorse, even if you flog it all week.

England were beaten by New Zealand A at Hamilton; conceded fifty to a mediocre New Zealand Academy at Invercargill, the edge of the rugby world; and then made only a show of contending a match against the New Zealand Maori at Rotorua, the smelliest end of the rugby world. They did play with courage, at least, in subsiding by 64–22 to New Zealand in Dunedin and by 40–10 in Auckland, in a match where the sheer footballing ability and indomitable will of Matt Dawson, the tour captain, shone through. They lost by only 18–0 to South Africa in Cape Town, though admittedly on a filthy day of lashing rain and mud which, besides keeping Table Mountain obscured for the week as if it never even existed, also helped keep the score down. It was a shocking experience which literally dragged the good name of English rugby through the mud.

The first All Black Test in Carisbrook, that genteel and even apologetic stadium with the atmosphere of a cucumber-sandwich cricket match rather than of rugby, threw up major controversy. The referee, Australia's Wayne Erickson, sent off Danny Grewcock, the England lock, for stamping. Whether the decision was justified, we never knew. But what, you might ask, about the replays? Well, New Zealand TV had no angle on the incident, even though it occurred in what amounted to open play.

Those Brit fans used to the coverage of Sky TV in the United Kingdom would be bewildered. Under the influence of Martin Turner, Sky's rugby producer, Sky have driven on rugby coverage at high pace. They have kicked the backsides of BBC and ITV and woken up the whole televisual field. *Private Eye* runs a column devoted to cringing paeans of praise for Sky written by fellow employees of News International and I made the column once for expressing my admiration for Sky's rugby. Fair cop. The point is that my admiration for Turner's operation is genuine and if I thought that Sky were a disaster I would say so.

Those of us used to Sky's all-seeing battery of cameras were amazed that New Zealand TV could provide not one valid replay of the alleged Grewcock booting. We had to rely on Erickson's say-so. Erickson has never been popular in Europe, among players or officials, not least because some comments he made which were widely reprised in this country appeared clearly to indicate that he was an unabashed Super-12 operator – in other words, that he did not intend to apply any law which he, unilaterally, saw as stopping the precious flow of his game.

Later in the match, Ian Jones of New Zealand stamped on the head of Graham Rowntree, the England prop, with such force that Rowntree was cut – even though he was wearing a heavy headguard. The ball was not adjacent, Rowntree was helpless and prone and Jones came flying in and – so it seemed from every angle – recklessly brought his foot crashing down. Where was Erickson, our fine upholder? Next day when Jones faced a citing panel, Erickson laughably came up with the defence that Jones was merely being positive and engaging in genuine rucking.

Ian Jones is a magnificent character. He is also, beyond doubt, one of the sanest and least vicious players. But Erickson's politically correct defence stuck in the craw, had no moral or legal basis. Shame on England for tamely accepting the disgraceful explanation in public, even though in private they were incensed. Praise the Lord, Erickson's feeble effort constituted the last of the unhappy genre to date, the last time when anyone would condone a boot to the brains of a prone player as in some way a blow for the need for rugby to flow. If kicking to the head is positive then give me negative rugby every time.

It was not – quite – an exclusively bad-news tour. Conspicuous in the resistance throughout the tour were a core of Gloucester forwards: Phil Vickery, creating a fine impression on his first tour, Tony Windo, Phil Greening, Steve Ojomoh and the two locks, David Sims and Rob Fidler. They belied the theory that Glawster men only perform in earshot of the sweet sounds of the Shed. And if there was one moment to elevate the tour, to drag it from the depths of grim weather and grim surroundings and relentless Pom-baiting, then it came four minutes before the end of normal time in the first Test in Dunedin.

Sims had been one of the very finest forwards of his generation in English rugby; he was a superb footballer, to add to his talents as line-out giant and typically boisterous Kingsholm hero. But he had never won a cap, despite playing splendidly in a succession of England A sides for years and then always receding with the tide before he hit the beach itself. It was a travesty. In Dunedin, Sims sat hopefully on the bench, and four minutes from the end Woodward called him on to replace Garath Archer. I freely confess to a tear in the eye as the Gloucester giant sprinted on, so God only knows what the Sims family must have felt. He had crossed the Rubicon, he was in the bed of Red Roses. It was an irony that Sims, one of nature's most frightened aviators, had to fly 12,000 miles for his cap.

Before the match I'd run across Woodward in the team hotel, at a difficult time when he had had to return home mid-tour to attend his father's funeral. 'You've got to get Simsie on,' I said. Next time I saw Woodward, after the match, he smiled. 'Do you know, I almost forgot,' he said. Sims started the final two matches, in Auckland and Cape Town, and it was the least surprising news of the whole rugby season that he looked not like a man out of place but like a hero in his element.

Woodward, meanwhile, had been thrashed, but had escaped to coach another day. A record of three wins from a total of fifteen matches for which he had sent out England sides at Test or tour level would almost surely have got him the elbow. As it was, he won an outpouring of public sympathy (his dignity and refusal to whine won mine), and he touched down with his battered young squad, some of whom were never to be seen again, and carried on.

The build-up to the World Cup began in earnest in the autumn of 1998, and Woodward's next assignment came less than a year from the date of the World Cup final itself. To sort out the issue of qualification for the finals, England had to play Holland and Italy; to the credit of the RFU, they chose the splendid McAlpine Stadium in Huddersfield to stage the matches – even though they then exhibited a complete cluelessness as to how they might market the game.

England duly ran up a century against the hapless Dutch, and they beat Italy by 23–15, though Italy probably had the better of the match, and might well have won had not the scrum-half Alessandro Troncon been denied a perfectly good try when the referee was badly positioned on one side of a ruck of players while the touch-judge, who was supposed to be covering the ref's blindside a few yards away, had apparently gone for a hot dog. Troncon lay around for a little while, pressing the ball over the England line, which seemed to him to conform rather closely to the requirements in rugby law of scoring a try. This was also the game in which the twenty-year-old flanker Mauro Bergamasco first announced himself as one of the kingpins of the European back-row scene. Further announcements have come with increasing frequency.

There was better news in the autumn, for despite a narrow defeat by a mediocre Australia in a match in which both sides played dreadfully, England dragged themselves together and beat South Africa by 13–7, ending a run of seventeen consecutive Springbok victories in thrilling style. Seventeen was the record for successive Test wins so Nick Mallett's

Boks had to share the record with a New Zealand team of 1965–69. They took the lead with a try by Pieter Rossouw but were overhauled by a try from Jeremy Guscott, put over by Dan Luger after a kick ahead by Mike Catt; and some penalties from Matt Dawson. Woodward, quite correctly, pleaded that the result should be seen not in the context of the World Cup but as a wondrous thing in its own right.

Woodward had had his first attempt at a Grand Slam scuppered by a superior French team in Paris. Now, at a time when he was trying to put the final piece of his World Cup jigsaw into place, he needed above all things the equanimity of a Slam, its indication of true hegemony over the rest of Europe. He needed the boost it would give to the country's confidence and to the confidence placed in him by the players.

Yet this second tilt was also to end in brain-numbing disappointment. England saw off a horrendously feeble France at Twickenham; it seemed to me that Pierre Villepreux, the French coach, finally gave away all right to hold the post with his pronouncement that the result did not matter. This was the old puke-making chestnut that coaches somehow glean more satisfaction from performance than result. It was also a vivid demonstration of the nonsensicality into which modern coaches sink and of their collective tendency to be always aiming towards some indeterminate point in the future. Villepreux was to depart his post after the World Cup, and had the brass neck to give a kind of 'my work is done' public utterance on his way through the exit door, like some sheriff who had saved a lawless town. On this occasion, the town had been shot up. France were terrible and had remained so throughout the World Cup, eighty blessed minutes apart.

England beat Ireland by 25–15 at Lansdowne Road, a match famous for the re-emergence of Wilkinson, who was then barely twenty but played in the centre and belied not only his youth but also his size with a thumping epic of an all-round performance. The formality of seeing off Scotland was then completed and England moved on to Wembley, where they were to meet a Wales team which had been revitalised by the arrival of Graham Henry but had nevertheless lost two of their three Five Nations matches and still showed substantial weaknesses.

The match proved to be every bit as devastating and epoch-forming for England as their defeat in the famous Grand Slam match in Scotland in 1990. They played some decent rugby in the first half but always on a weak base, as their scrum was in trouble against the Welsh pack. The captain, Lawrence Dallaglio, passed up a chance of a penalty goal which had it gone over would have taken England ahead by two scores inside the last seven minutes of normal time; and Wales won when they executed a brilliant one-phase attack from a line-out and Scott Gibbs side-stepped his way over. Neil Jenkins kicked what was probably the pressure-goal of his whole career, and once again England had to settle for a position in the pack rather than as its leader.

There was an outpouring of angst and hurt after the match as various England players and coaches tried to come to terms with their defeat. This suggested strongly to me that one of the dangers of England's build-up to the World Cup was that they were overrating themselves, and had therefore assumed that their right to victory over Wales was God-given. A little more humility and they might have concluded, for their future benefit, that they had lost to a team that was superior in the scrum, had a sharper tactical brain, showed greater footballing ability at half-back and was more powerful in the midfield. England, on the run of play, probably should have won. So what?

Instead, in their hearts and minds England saw the result as a freak and carried on their merry way. Woodward made what I consider to be another error in the summer of World Cup year. He and the massed ranks of his backroom boys (England need a back room the size of an aircraft hangar) took a massive squad to Australia. There they spent three weeks working their tracksuits off in a monastic existence at a hotel and leisure complex on South Stradbroke Island, near Brisbane. They stepped up their training and intake of carrot juice to new peaks, grinding on and thus, for those of us uneasy about the time any Test team spend together, running the risk of losing their spark and vitality in both the legs and the head. They emerged to play a tepid and thoroughly disappointing match at Ballymore against a second-string Queensland. Having protested beforehand that they were not really tapered down from their heavy training to play a real Test match (why on earth had they arranged one, then?) since they were aiming for the World Cup, they lost by 22–15 at Stadium Australia. One side was poor, halting and fractured. And England were even worse.

I would have thought that had Woodward taken fewer players, made their time in camp shorter and sharper, come out and played three proper warm-up matches to give the whole squad a run, and honed the training so that the team was fresh and reaching a peak for the Test, then England could quite easily have won and made a powerful statement of intent for the World Cup ahead. Maybe caused a few spasms of anxiety in smug Aussie minds. As it was, we had in memoriam, once again, a tour that proved nothing. I am not saying Woodward's way was wrong or that he planned it with anything but the best of intentions, just that there must be another song to sing than the dirge of endless squad sessions.

It seemed to me that when England returned from that tour their weaknesses were almost precisely the same as they had been when the season began. I never thought that their front-five platform was especially strong or that their scrummage was good. Martin Johnson and Tim Rodber were the only world-class forwards they had in the front five, and Rodber was in one of his infuriating form-troughs. I felt that the back row of Lawrence Dallaglio, Neil Back and Richard Hill sacrificed a really powerful hard-yardage runner in order to include three excellent players. Jonny Wilkinson, the breezy, talented fly-half and wincingly hard tackler, was not yet a fully developed tactical brain, and with Jerry Guscott losing some of the old sharpness, I could not see where England's opposition were to be cut up behind the scrum. Where was the gamebreaker? We were still looking a year later. At the first show of betting, New Zealand had been favourites, with Australia, South Africa and England just behind, and Wales just behind them. Of all those teams, it was in England's value that I had least confidence.

At least the tournament was approaching. Whatever their deficiencies you could never say that England did not try to work them out of the system. They ground on through various tours of (and from) Hell, they sweated their way through tournaments and fitness-testing and Royal Marines assault courses. They nattered endlessly about themselves, not so much because they wanted to but because the English-based media is a voracious beast. It has been augmented by websites by the million, by the proffered microphones of a myriad new radio ventures (if you divide the total number of possible listeners by the number of new stations, you find that each station has around three), plus enough television crews to film the crowd-scenes in *Ben Hur* (and to populate the same). Bless them, and bless all their long lenses poking into your ear when you are trying to ask a sensible question at a press conference.

The build-up period took on a grisly and farcical air as England entered into a sequence of four warm-up matches. I saw not a scrap of merit in any of them. They were just going through the motions. They played the United States, drastically early on in the US squad's preparation (they hardly knew each other's names), and England scored 100. They played a more competitive match against Canada; and then, in two of the biggest wastes of time and space in the history of the modern game, they twice met something called the English Premiership All-Stars. England would really have been better staying at home and watching television. They tried nothing of note, were simply risking injury in half-hearted matches that meant not a whit. The opposition chiefly comprised a bunch of second- and third-teamers from major clubs, who were unpaid and not in the least bit inclined to get injured, and a few real stars who were persuaded to make token, gate-boosting appearances before sneaking off down the tunnel and probably straight to their cars.

Twickenham had decided that three of the four warm-up matches would take place on Saturday evening – in an effort (so they said) to create the ambience of the Super-12. If they were successful then God help the Super-12, because the matches were attended by skeleton audiences, testimony to the staggering fact that the English public would actually rather loll around on beaches with cold drinks or sip cold white wine at barbecues on lawns at warm dusk than go to Twickenham to watch a meaningless charade.

Amazingly, rumours surfaced that the RFU had budgeted for almost a full house for each of the four matches – three at Twickenham and one at Anfield, staged there on the basis that the North should not be allowed to escape either. That would make a total predicted attendance of around 290,000. I suppose the aggregate total was more like 55,000. For the pre-match entertainment, washed-up stars such as Edwin Starr cavorted to backing tracks with a backing group apparently drawn from Equity's 'resting' files rather than the gnarled old blues sweatshops where Edwin learned his trade all those centuries ago. If there were washed-up stars, then there were also still-in-the-sink stars such as Martine McCutcheon. We all suffer decline, but compared to his great days Starr's version of 'War' could not have carried less conviction or authenticity had it been performed by the Bay City Rollers. What was it good for? Absolutely nothing.

The second 'All-Star' match took place at Anfield where, in a spectacular non-promotion for the game, a few thousand hardy souls who had lost their way watched another farce. For me, the event's only redeeming feature was that we stayed at the Adelphi Hotel in Liverpool, star of a recent television series. The genre once known as *cinéma vérité* which then declined to 'fly-on-the-wall' documentary and is now encapsulated by the term 'docusoap' evokes a rage in me that even the threat of imprisonment for my subsequent actions could never assuage.

Take that fat, four-eyed, camp and talent-free prat from Aeroflot who appeared in the *Airport* series and now, in as blistering a reflection on modern television life as you could ever imagine, even has his own shows. I wouldn't fly Aeroflot if they were the last plane out of Hell on a Sunday in the Prohibition era, but I do intend to prowl Heathrow for months to plant one in his chops. I always have a quick look for him whenever travelling out of Terminal Two. Or what about the bearded, obnoxious traffic-clamping warden who was spitefully nasty to offenders behind their backs, splendidly offhand and clever-dick and wonderfully courageous when the camera and crew were recording his activities? I'm waiting for you to clamp me, son. The cameras have gone. The series that someone somewhere felt would rivet a nation has ended. It'll just be you and me. I'm waiting.

And the married blond vets whose elevation to stardom was based on an ability to save a couple of gerbils from well-merited extinction and who demonstrated only an utter lack of charisma and of any talent at all, and of the ability to say or do anything worth hearing or watching. They then got their own travel programme and proved that their display in the vet surgery was no flash in the pan.

Or Titchmarsh, that dreadful boss-eyed sap who does people's gardens while they are out, throwing in a mock cliff-hanger of a race to get it done before his victim has returned from a few days at her grandmother's. And his mate, the girl with the tossed hayrick hair who's short of a bra and a sack for her head and anything telegenic whatsoever. My garden is a mess, Titchmarsh. The hedge is a shambles, the weeds are gaining the upper hand, and Owain the dog makes a mess in it, too.

But if ever I come home and you and your mob have made it over and stuck in a water feature and a crazy-paving path and a gazebo and you're all there smirking, holding a glass of champagne, then I hope that taking a punch is one of the few talents you can prove you have. That and the art of putting my garden back precisely as it was before your false-bonhomie, false-tension bunch pitched up. In terms of the gap between true stardom and radiant goodness, and that conveyed gratuitously (though sadly not posthumously) by low-rent TV programmes, the appearance of Alan Titchmarsh in the same camera shot as Nelson Mandela – on the occasion when Titchmarsh took a few acres of the veld and made it look even more desolate than when he started – takes all the beating in the world.

The worst, however, in my experience (even though I never watch that type of programme, of course, never bother with them) was the schoolmistressy hotel manager in the series on the Adelphi. This drama queen's playing to the camera never quite managed to obscure her sharp-tongued disapproval of anyone requesting something approaching service or the fact that, like Basil Fawlty, she seemed to enjoy running a hotel but didn't like the guests. I would guess that she set back the image of hotels and hotel-keeping by decades.

She checked us into the Adelphi before the England non-match. The cameras had gone. Also gone was the bluster, the sharp remarks behind the staff partition. She'd had her fifteen minutes of fame. She was efficient and pleasant, running a slightly fading old edifice where the taxi drivers were taking the piss out of us for staying. Just shows that it is the camera and the programme-makers that jack up the ordinary people, not the ordinary people who jack up TV programmes. By the end of the rugby match it seemed the whole world was full of bogus stars.

It was not exactly one of the epic days of the season as we attempted to follow the crowd on its way to Anfield and ended up in a nearby McDonald's. Anfield is marvellous when Liverpool FC are playing there, and ridiculous with a token public for rugby. I once reported on Liverpool during their march towards a title; they were inspired by John Barnes, and scored five goals at home. And once again, football's magnificent ability to drag ordinary people out of their normal surroundings, to transport them Heaven-high, was revealed.

We were still making fun of the whole All-Stars thing as we approached the main gate, then stopped dead outside the memorial to the victims of the Hillsborough disaster. I can remember exactly where I was that day (at West Hartlepool reporting on a rugby match); I remember what I felt – the empathy of someone who began as a rugby terrace fan in Newport only because I came from a rugby area (other- wise it would almost certainly have been a football terrace), I remember the sheer joy of transporting myself from the terrace into the dream. The ninety-six Hillsborough victims are all listed, and some of the parents and relations have decided that their loved ones' nicknames and pet names should be inscribed. It is a nice touch, because it conveys some of the humour and effervescence of the football terraces, qualities which are forgotten in diatribes against their banality. Also inscribed are their ages. Some were teenagers, and no doubt their parents subscribe for not one millisecond to that rubbish about them not growing old, even as the rest of us are growing old. Standing there, I was a little ashamed that over the years I have railed against impersonal, almost sterile stadiums with seats too far from the action, whined when the kick-off has been put back because of crowd congestion and our precious deadlines have gone up the creek. These changes are all down to the Safety at Sports Grounds Act. Inconvenient, sometimes. But look at what came before it.

World Cup. Too big. Takes up too much time and energy. England are one of the rugby nations who should live more of their lives, should use the big one as a target only when they can see the whites of its eyes, not when they assume it's round the next corner. England were never going to win, because they weren't good enough. In most positions they had shot their bolt in the sense that they had shown us all they had to offer. Perhaps Phil Vickery, if he developed at Linford-like speed, might become dominant in time. Perhaps Jonny Wilkinson would emerge so rapidly that inside a few months he would jump from talented teenager to boss of the world game. Otherwise, what we saw a year before the finals was what we got during them: fitness, courage, spirit, technical accomplishment. And yet, not enough.

England thrashed Italy by 67–7, presaging a World Cup when far too few of what might be called the second-rank nations showed that they could overcome the privations, the comparisons with the truly moneyed. The pool match against New Zealand was the means for the winning team to escape from a hellish programme in the knock-out stages which lay in wait for the team finishing as pool runners-up. This programme would entail a play-off against Fiji, a quarter-final against South Africa, a semi-final, probably against Australia, and a final against whoever you thought you could beat, conceding that most parts of your body were hanging off. The route for the pool winners was much cleaner and easier.

It must be said that just at the time when England needed to peak, they did. They played splendidly against New Zealand, maximised themselves in most areas, and lost 30–16. Dallaglio played marvellously, so did Phil de Glanville, rejuvenated in the centre; but of game-breakers, of real authority, there was no sign. Not so in the ranks of the Black. Jonah Lomu, battering his way down the left wing, leaving defenders in his wake, won the match with a brilliant score when England had fought back to 16–16.

Throughout the World Cup preamble and even now, in the hour of convincing defeat, Woodward's belief never seemed to waver. 'We are still right in there fighting; we still have as good a chance as anyone left in the competition,' he said. He complained sharply at England's use of the ball, their tactics. It was an implied, and occasionally expressed criticism of Wilkinson. Did we but know it then, both teams had already played their best match of the tournament.

The splendid Fijians were cleared from the path, and then England went to Paris to play South Africa. South Africa had entirely failed to set alight their pool in Scotland, the God's own forsaken country in terms of the tournament. They had beaten the fallible Scots but, like someone trying to shake a yapping terrier off his trouser-leg, even had trouble with Uruguay and Spain. They came with a divided camp. The more racial groups there are represented in the new emancipated South Africa team, the more possible decisions. I remember sharing a taxi once with Nick Mallett, and I hope it would not be breaking a confidence to say that this most impressive man was devastatingly amusing and yet pointedly rueful about the various potential factions in which the mighty Boks can fall. There are more pressure-groups and narrow-interest sections to join than at the Freshers' Fair at a major university. To add to their problems, South Africa were without Brendan Venter, their best centre, who was suspended, and without Henry Honiball, their injured linchpin fly-half. At No. 10 they installed Jannie de Beer, a bread-and-butter operator with limited ability with the ball in hand, as a runner or a conjurer. All he could do, with the greatest respect, was kick. Like a mule.

England's No. 10 had also changed, though not through injury. Here, after years and sweat and talking, Woodward jettisoned the player to whom he had entrusted the pivotal position throughout all the latter stages of the build-up, the man around whom he had (as you do with your fly-half) built the whole effort, all the shape and timing and attacking and defensive systems. He dropped Wilkinson and brought in Paul Grayson, who was not quite as tunnel-visioned as De Beer, and who could bravely try to stand flatter if he wanted, but was essentially an entirely different style of player from Wilkinson. Woodward also brought in the tall full-back Nick Beal on the right wing.

Perhaps there was some excuse to be found in the weather forecast. From the middle of the week the French Met-officers were predicting lashing rains and winds. Evidently that French flair with the rugby ball extends to creative predictions about the weather, because the day of the match was bright, mild, dry and still. And raining – with drop-goals. De Beer stood deep in the pocket, either with first-phase ball or waiting until Robbie Fleck or Pieter Muller had set the ball up midfield to bring him nearer, and kicked devastatingly, beautifully. He kicked England to death. Joost van der Westhuizen and Pieter Rossouw scored tries, and there was not even a hint that South Africa were flattered by the final 44–21 scoreline. As usual, England lacked real authority, their defence lacked real turnover power; their systems were out of synch because Wilkinson, at least till he arrived to replace the harried Grayson after fifty-five minutes, was not even out there.

Next day, as the four teams remaining in the 1999 World Cup travelled to London for the semi-finals, a round which now contained no team from the four home unions, England's players moped around in their civvies. I saw them at Gare du Nord station, shuffling their baggage around, somehow diminished in size as well as in demeanour from the team that had promised themselves, and others, that they would win the World Cup.

Woodward's record was at this stage mediocre, to say the least. Their 1998 victory over South Africa aside, it was arguable that England showed a dramatic lack of tangible progress and few noticeable signs that their standards in any area had improved since he had begun. He was criticised for the style of play he was attempting to impose, because it was harum-scarum stuff, fast and fizzing, but with far too few points of reference. As ever, it seemed that when England were stuck on a course, be it Woodward's wide theory or the old-style attrition approach, they could not switch on the hoof from one style to another as the occasion demanded. England's pack were not called upon to exert enough authority, to lay enough explosive. It was an opinion shared inside the coaching set-up, I can assure you.

It was also bizarre, and a comment on the sheer length of a build-up period, that the fly-half had been changed only days before the crunch-match of England's tournament. It indicated that Woodward's nerve had wavered, that he had therefore changed the script when it should by then have been word-perfect. He had once before faced the looming possibility of being removed from office, after the Tour to Hell, when the results were appalling but the circumstances were beyond his control and so he could not be blamed for them. This time, he had spent £8 million on preparation, had been given all available resources, had no excuses. And had changed his fly-half at the end. Now, he surely needed another stroke of luck to stay for the 2000 Six Nations.

He got it. With the greatest respect (except to the process in which the RFU were supposed to spend millions in order to prime coaching talent for the national post), there was no one else to do his job. There was not a single credible contender who made himself available. Eventually, Woodward appeared at a strained press conference with Fran Cotton, his line-manager in that Cotton was chairman of Club England, the body which runs the affairs of the national teams at all senior levels and which pokes its nose into other areas too.

Cotton was appointed to the post as a conciliatory gesture by Brian Baister, the RFU chairman who had usurped Cliff Brittle – of whom Cotton was for some years a vociferous ally. (The phrase 'backing the wrong horse' did spring to mind on a fairly regular basis. In the years of the Brittle Problem and afterwards, Cotton on numerous occasions either threatened to resign or actually did, proclaiming that he did not need the post and the hassle, that he could go off fishing. However, he always seemed to change his mind.) Arguably, Baister's appointment of Cotton was a strange one, because Cotton's last involvement in the international rugby scene was nearly twenty years previously, and since then his closest formal association with the game had come in an ill-starred reign as coach of Sale – a tenure which, to put it mildly, did not endear him to all the players. His time as a pillar of the sporting world had reached its heady peak when he was a key man on the British Lions tour of South Africa in 1974, but that was twenty-five years before Baister decided that he should head the body which really should have provided an up-to-the-millisecond, cutting-edge lead for the new era.

Cotton and Woodward sat at the press conference at Twickenham and announced that Woodward would carry on as England coach. It was in all respects an odd affair, as several individuals who had been party to the decision to retain him conceded that they had not even seen his World Cup report. Woodward himself admitted, characteristically, that he could have done better. Remember that he was just one of the nineteen coaches in the final stages of the World Cup who failed to win it, and none of the other eighteen publicly took take any blame for doing so. 'I must hit the accelerator,' Woodward said. He admitted that his results as England coach had been unacceptable. Cotton expressed support for Woodward, if in a few rather clipped sentences.

As the new millennium approached it was abundantly clear that certain influential members of the RFU management board did not share Cotton's opinion; it would also be untrue to say that every England player you met was unequivocal in his support. At just about the same time that Woodward was trying to re-define responsibilities in his management structure, assuming he would carry on, some of the grandees were plotting to relieve him of his position. The level of orchestration within the campaign could be judged from the fact that on one Saturday, while covering the Wasps Heineken Cup match in Bourgoin, I took three calls, at half-hourly intervals, from different people informing me that senior management board members were unhappy at the cursory nature of Club England's examination and investigation of the World Cup flop. We were given the name of Dick Best, then coach of London Irish, as a contender to replace Woodward, and Baister himself did not deny that Best was on a shortlist. Cotton acknowledged to Peter Jackson in the *Daily Mail* that a change might even come about in the three weeks or so remaining until the start of the 2000 Six Nations – a ludicrously short time-frame, considering that Best or indeed any other contender would still be under contract elsewhere, and one indicative of a growing momentum.

Best turned England down, no surprise under the circumstances. No one from Club England, a rather blunted cutting-edge throughout the season, could tell him what the job he was being offered actually entailed, and when he asked if it involved being in charge of selection they shifted from foot to foot and looked a little blank. Best would sooner have gone back to his former job as a chef than take a high-profile national job coaching a group of players named on a list which had been written by someone else.

As for the rest of the shortlist, it was not so much short as blank. Here we saw the utter failure of the England game to produce coaches of international potential. Legions of RFU technocrats had always boasted of their 'conveyor belt' system in which not only players but coaches, too, would cut their teeth. Theoretically, coaches would begin with the U21 side, glide on effortlessly to take charge of the A set-up and be champing at the bit at the very moment they reached the throne of England itself. The reality was that various management structures had been formed at those levels but had fallen apart with a mixture of disuse, rank lack of coaching ability and associated failure. And although the RFU never admitted it, the whole thing had become an unedifying shambles with even the leading clubs – themselves in large part disorganised – developing coaches and players at a faster rate. It was more to Cotton's credit that he realised this and has now endeavoured to set up better structures.

So, for all the disquiet at Twickenham, for all the uneasiness of so many people out in the country about England's falling so short of their aspirations, for all the time and money spent to no good effect, the truth was that there was not a single worthy replacement for our Clive. So they didn't replace him. Meanwhile, Club England messed up John Mitchell's re-appointment by making him an offer just as he was disappearing to New Zealand, going home to take up a new post after months waiting for the phone to ring with news of whether Twickers wanted to keep him. The offer came too late, and so off went Mitchell, bewildered as ever by the ways of the English.

So many coaching careers in various sports have been brutally sawn off by poor initial results, by the fact that the media, the public and the board, the hirers and the firers, have such a preposterously low pain-threshold. There can be no doubt that some potentially brilliant sporting careers have been cut off simply because the coach was never able to impose his wider vision and his medium-term plans because his short-term plans, when he may still have been wrestling with a poor legacy, never worked out. It strikes me that so many coaches of any sports could fulfil themselves if, by increased patience or some stroke of Woodwardian-style luck, they managed to keep the job until they grew into it, were able to fulfil their vision and, importantly, learn from their mistakes. Especially the big ones.

Woodward had been given more time than most, since the defeat of his team in Paris in the RWC quarter-finals was his twenty-eighth match in charge. His career had been one filled with the constant pressure of major matches but, as he survived the contender-free scene when his job was on the line, his was also a charmed life.

And so post-World Cup, post-sporting holocaust, Woodward carried on. The 2000 Six Nations, marking Mitchell's last lap as forward coach, approached. So did the wallpapering barrage of publicity which now surrounds the tournament. As someone whose livelihood is dependent on kind sports editors granting me a chunk of their nice white space, I would never, ever say that certain events are over-covered in the media, and I am always fascinated to read items about the groundsmen and coach drivers of the Six Nations competitors. I nonetheless genuinely put the Six Nations high on my list of rugby's Most Enjoyable Bits – second to the runaway leader, Lions tours, and on the evidence of season 1999–2000, at least, with the Heineken Cup now keeping the World Cup out of the medals entirely.

But I have no doubt at all that the sheer torrent of media coverage of England's rugby matters (and doesn't-matters) is a hindrance to them. Let's be fair. Everyone in rugby (or out of rugby) sees the English as arrogant. Even in the years when English arrogance in rugby was clearly the most misplaced stance you could imagine we always thought it of them. There is no question that this perceived arrogance drove Scotland wild, and gave them ten extra points, in the 1990 shoot-out.

Yet Woodward and anyone who comes after him has something of a problem. The pre-international week has maintained the same rhythm (and boredom) for several years. The team gather on Mondays, and there are daily media conferences or handouts. These days, coaches rigorously exclude any reference whatsoever to their chances of winning. Even if England were playing Madagascar or even if the All Blacks were playing Sarawak, the coach would angrily deny that his team were favourites, pointing to the supreme capacity (albeit unrevealed in history) for Madagascar/Sarawak or any other hopeless opposition to spring a surprise. The idea is to leave nothing for the opposition to get their teeth into as a motivational tool.

After delivering a barrage of various newspaper, electronic and battery-driven articles, the media week takes off in earnest on Wednesday, with a keynote conference of team grandees. Thursday is Captain's

Conference, a tradition created in the Will Carling years when Carling bowled up, sat down with the press and said nothing, often for several hours. (Naturally, we were all too polite to ask him the question about his friendship with Princess Diana – you know the one.) Now, Lawrence Dallaglio has been succeeded by Martin Johnson, and then by Matt Dawson and then by Johnson again, in the 101-polite-ways-of-saying-nothing stakes. Poor hacks can thumb through seventeen pages of a notebook after the build-up week and find not a line worth quoting.

Yet despite all the efforts of the tongue-tied, something will always slip out which the opposition can use. You cannot go a whole week, absorbing questions at a rate of, say, sixty a day from various media without saying something that, given suitable topspin, can be presented as English arrogance. Of course, the same goes for the other international teams with their own media; it is simply that the media in England is big to the point of monstrous and the pitfalls much bigger than elsewhere. Now and again you hear teams who have won Six Nations matches expressing thanks for some remark made by the losing team which helped to motivate the victors but was taken clean out of context.

All in all, it would seem that while the number of press conferences mushrooms, so the chance of hearing anything pithy or telling in them is even further decreasing. England have fallen victim more times than other teams, poor chaps. Next question . . .

CHAPTER NINE

Bloemfontein

England II: revival! The march of the massed ranks ♦ Grand tour of the gym ♦ Monastic England find the secrets

England's 2000 Championship was a model of the previous three; burgeoning hopes and a fast-moving style and final crushing disappointment. England had taken on their style to such an extent that arguably the core figure became Austin Healey, the wing who was given free rein to pop up all over the field and whose individual skills, almost un-English in their ability to find space where there appeared to be none, were imperious.

It is less the fault of Woodward and his men and more the fault of weak opposition and law-makers, however, that England's easy home victories over Ireland and Wales showed finally that attempts in the professional era to make rugby more watchable and compelling had failed. The Ireland game especially betrayed all the heroic concepts of what an international match is supposed to be. As well as the usual uncontested scrums and line-outs, we had uncontested phases in the loose, with half-hearted running into a couple of tacklers who immediately disengaged to re-group, conceding possession in the cause of stiffening the defence.

Ireland's defence was still awful as they subsided by 50–18; that of Wales was little better as they went down by 46–12. I remember feeling on the evening following both matches that I had never felt less moved by international rugby; that with the removal of the essential of forward play it has become a de-powered, powder-puff pastime. Granted, some internationals could still summon a little of the old devil, but fewer and fewer of them and for shorter and shorter periods.

England beat a hearty Italy in Rome on an epoch-making day for European rugby, and again they managed to do it without really seeking any confrontation in the forward battle. They did it with three wide tries by Healey and thanks to some awful Italian defending. It finished 59–12.

People still went harping on about the powerful England pack but how did they know? England had not taken part in a forward battle all year. At least Lee Smith, laws and development guru of the International Rugby Board, had the grace to be somewhat embarrassed about it all.

The common factor in many English defeats in the past twenty years has been lack of tactical nous on the hoof. I've said it before and here I go again. English players are not natural tacticians. The ability to make the correct calls to suit the prevailing conditions of match and pitch, opposition style and weather has come naturally to few players – and in that England side in the 2000 Six Nations probably only to Mike Catt. So by extension, whenever they uncover a back who can run the game, England are made.

Chickens came home to roost at Murrayfield on 9 April 2000, in a match to which England came after playing a flighty if successful season and to which Scotland came without having played at all. All Scotland had achieved, with respect, until the fateful Calcutta Cup match was getting four sets of jerseys dirty. They had lost to Italy in Rome to the delight of all neutrals, and then to Wales, Ireland and France. Some fools, including some fool in the *Sunday Times*, predicted a massive England win at Murrayfield; the fool in question was later heard anxiously defending himself by claiming that while the rest of the rugby world predicted the same score, they didn't have to do it for a readership in excess of four million, timed perfectly so everyone read it as they had their brunch before settling down to watch the match. It would be an exaggeration to say that afterwards all of Scotland wrote to the fool via e-mail, fax and personal threat. But only just. It would also be an exaggeration to say that the e-mails were packed with humour, with anything other than a sad hang-up about the English race, and that they included any indication that these past-posting experts had actually backed Scotland before the match, as opposed to telling us what a great side they were when it was over.

The game finished at 19–13, possibly a reflection of the match as a whole but none at all of a final half-hour in which Andy Nicol's marvellous mudlark Scots turned England, harried them like hounds to the fox . . . thrashed them. Duncan Hodge touched down the winning try after waves of pressure, but the territorial domination was equivalent to at least two more tries.

England tactics? Left in the dressing room. In the team they had two of the finest and most hard-headed on-field rugby thinkers of the era in Lawrence Dallaglio and Matt Dawson. The match was played in heavy showers and, eventually, continuous rain which made Murrayfield a bog. In it, Budge Pountney (having a fantastic season) and the Scottish back row and the astonishingly elastic lock Scott Murray wallowed like the happiest of tartan hippos.

So England were called upon to do what they had so rarely done before. Change tactics. A few judicious kicks to turn the screw, some driving at close quarters from Dallaglio and company at the base of the scrum, and England could have turned a few screws of their own. Instead, they blundered horrendously, lost shape and form. Now that the weather had dragged them into a fight – and into an approximation of what rugby should be at Test level – they also found themselves wanting.

Their excuses afterwards were odd. 'The weather was a huge issue,' said Dawson. 'We were thrown into a completely new situation and not at the beginning of the game. If it had been chucking it down at the start, we could have addressed the situation.' The cynics might well suggest that here, in one observation from an honest man, lay the essence of England's failure in its recent history and on its day of dejection at Murrayfield. Dawson was clearly suggesting that England did not change tactics because they had not had time to sit down together to plan. I believe that by those words he was confirming in spades the fears held by so many, myself included, that Test teams, and England especially, spend too long poring over videos, drilling their drills, measuring their fat with callipers and jawing in team rooms. And not enough time nurturing their minds.

This leads to a state of programming and a reliance on the input off the field which cannot cope with the unpredictable. (And even that is accepting the dubious notion that rain and greyness on an April afternoon in Scotland can be described in any way as unpredictable.) No, the England players found that rugby is these days not entirely a game of spiralling basketball in which forwards find the real thrill in gadding around and joining in. Some days, thanks be to God, forward play is something to be performed nose to bleeding nose with the oppo-sition, grimly battering out every inch just as Pountney and Murray and their mates battered. Surely, players in an U12 house match realise that there are suddenly different priorities if it rains; and that if that rain has, inconveniently, decided to fall, you cannot sit in a team room and talk it through. England are the worst country for off-the-cuff rugby.

But there was another aspect to all of this, and the one which got me into *Private Eye*. Early that morning some colleagues and I had flown in from Dublin, where Wales had beaten Ireland and where a group of combative hacks had conducted a vivid and interminable discussion on rugby, during which a strong attack was made on Paul Ackford on the basis of his views, playing history and trousers, an attack which had he been there to defend himself would have been embarrassing for him (which he was, and it was). We had arrived back at our hotel just in time to check out in time to check in for the flight.

Later that morning, by now stretched out with black coffee in an Edinburgh hotel, I watched *Sky News*. I'm not saying that because Rupert Murdoch owns the damn station as well as the *Sunday Times*; I was watching it because it has a weather bulletin every twenty minutes and I was fascinated by what the bulletin said. *Private Eye* thought otherwise and had me down for a hack cringing in front of Murdoch, even though I ring him direct to remonstrate with him whenever his Sky channels dip even one degree from their normal literary greatness.

The weatherman was that faintly campish Francis someone who's been around poking the weather maps since *TVam* began. The first time I caught him that morning, his screen showed an enormous black mass poised above northern and central Scotland. Next time, like underpants with old elastic, it had sunk down a little and its southern edge was hovering just north of Auld Reekie itself. 'The rough stuff will be arriving in Edinburgh around early-to-mid-afternoon,' said Francis. The kick-off was to be at four. Everyone in the hotel foyer had heard the forecast too, and were carrying extra waterproofs to the match.

England's backroom staff that day comprised twelve people. Dawson's post-match reaction sounded as if the rain had come as a shock. Surely there was one person in the party who could have been put i/c weather forecasts and thus reported that something black and wet was arriving and that it would help enormously something dark blue and passionate. England lost; they sulkily failed to show up for Princess Anne's presentation of the trophy marking the fact that they had won the 2000 Six Nations, no small feat. It was intolerable, whatever their spin doctors tried to make out; and good for Jason Leonard for standing out and congratulating the Scots while his mates ran off moodily down the tunnel.

Ian McGeechan sat delighted under the stands afterwards. The old fox had pulled it off again. It was fascinating to dissect how McGeechan had managed to persuade his men, by video and cajoling and underhand means, that they could indeed win. To learn of the tactical ploys, the gambit of cancelling entirely Friday's training session, communicating to the team the calming news that he felt they were ready. Gordon McIlwham, the best-named prop in the game since the heyday of Thumper Dingley of Coventry, suggested that he knew at half-time that England were going, going, gone.

One delirious dressing room. One distraught. A fantastic day in the long and vivid life of the home internationals. England were champions. 'The day had something for everyone,' McGeechan said. 'We won the Calcutta Cup, England won the Six Nations trophy. So everyone's happy.' There was a silence which lasted perhaps a quarter of a second. Then a storm of laughter at McGeechan's choirboy-innocent face.

Before the match there had been a happier presentation. The Princess Royal had honoured a raft of great old Scotland players with some mementos and it had also been decided that Bill McLaren, then in his 146th year of commentary for the BBC, would be honoured for his services to the game. Any present they gave him would be only a token gesture, because nothing could be valuable enough to reflect accurately his contribution. No citation could be long enough. The great man even broke into a decent trot as he came on to the field, then he had a chat with the rugby-loving Princess, took his memento and scuttled back to the commentary box to continue his work.

Not long after the Calcutta Cup triumph, which preceded a magnificent and sorely needed day of joy for Scotland rugby, Bill's daughter Janie died of cancer after a long and brave battle. Both Janie and her sister, Linda, had been the talk of the Borders since their teens. I remember seeing them across the club bar one day when Newport had travelled up to play Hawick, and briefly considering asking either to accept a catastrophic drop in their standards and come for a beer. Only a few others in the room were thinking the same thing: everyone male between the ages of fourteen and seventy-four.

I'd come across the Clan McLaren most recently in a hospitality tent at the 1999 British Open at Carnoustie and, as ever with Bill and Bette and their two daughters, they left me with two impressions – of the charm and warmth they exuded, making you feel that their day had only become worthwhile because they had run into you, and of a family togetherness and love which transcended everything. Janie, at this time in the middle of her fight, looked as glamorous as ever.

'God,' said those a little distant from the Borders when they'd heard of Janie's death. 'I hadn't even realised she was ill.' What they meant was that McLaren's marvellous professionalism had carried him through his major assignments without any indication to the outside world of the pain he was feeling because inside, he confessed to being thunderstruck. 'It's the worst thing I've ever experienced, big lad,' he said to me, as Janie battled on.

Within one year, in what is still a reasonably small community, the rugby-writing fraternity had lost Janie, together with Colin Price, the small giant of the *Daily Mirror*, and Chris Lander, formerly of the rugby circuit but who had moved on, with many a longing backward glance, to report on cricket for the *Sun* and *Mirror*. We almost cried with laughter at Pricey's wake when we recalled the story he'd filed from Durban in the 1995 England World Cup. He had been much taken by reports of the many murders taking place in Natal, and even though these were happening hundreds of miles up country he was clearly concerned with the possibility that the trouble could spread to Durban itself. 'ENGLAND BASED IN THE CITY OF HELL,' said his *Mirror* report.

The article was widely quoted back in South Africa and especially in rather genteel Durban. Pricey was an industrious operator, and in his time off a great sunbather. We used to call him Qasim in deference to his perma-tan. One day he was flat-out on a sunbed at the English team's glamorous beachfront hotel, sipping a cool drink and wearing shades and swimming-trunks. The Indian Ocean crashed in the background. The local paper, loyally miffed by the coverage of their hometown, took a snap of our *Mirror* man which was then plastered across their front page under the heading 'MAKING THE MOST OF LIFE IN THE CITY OF HELL — COLIN PRICE OF THE *MIRROR*'. Pricey happily posed for more pictures.

Rugby's big games now come in droves. As the passing of Colin and Chris and of Janie McLaren reminded us, to get het up over sporting disaster is to miss the whole point of becoming involved in sport in the first place. They were, beyond any doubt, the type of people who made you love sport even more and worry about sporting defeats even less, and made you realise that love and friendships beat anything.

Clive Woodward had been England coach through thick and thin for two-and-a-half years when he announced his touring party to go to South Africa. By now, Woodward had made an important appointment to his coaching staff. Bath's coach, Andy Robinson, had been avidly courted to leave the club he had, judging by their performances in 2000, taken to the verge of new glories, the club from whom he and his heartbeat were indivisible.

He was expected to join the team as forward coach, but his title when it was all sealed and delivered was simply coach. Woodward assumed the position of team manager, being careful to deny that he had lost authority and maintaining that he still picked the team and set overall strategies. I know how much Bath meant to Robinson. 'There is no room for sentiment in international rugby,' he said when asked if it was a fierce wrench to leave Bath and possibly to allow someone else to reap the rewards of his hard work. I gently mocked him afterwards, knowing that it would have been a wrench to take the breath away, and his famous stony face broke into what I interpreted as a rueful grin. But Robinson was quick to assimilate himself into the ranks of the coaches, and appeared as a man who had found himself. He gave England steel nothing less.

The tour of South Africa comprised two Test matches at altitude, in Pretoria and Bloemfontein, and three high provincial matches, none of which was against top-flight teams, in Potchefstroom, Kimberley and Brakpan. It is, for the moment, another story that the itinerary killed off any idea that England's top players might gain something from visiting one of the most spectacular and bewildering places on earth; in the event, they chugged round the highveld from one tour base, a lovely hotel in a dire area of Johannesburg.

For this assignment, Woodward decided that loneliness in all its forms should be banished. He drafted forty players; and there were thirteen back-up staff. These were: Woodward, team manager; Robinson, coach; Brian Ashton, backs coach (and if Mr Guscott tells me that he's the best in the business then who am I to disagree?); Phil Larder, the former rugby league coach invested with the responsibility for England's defence, and a man who holds the art and joy of defending so close to his heart that it is obvious that his ideal sport is one where there is no attacking whatsoever. Just defending. England's defending, mind you, came on in leaps and bounds; Dave Alred, the kicking guru, by all accounts an average player but a man whom most players found helped their kicking enormously and who has been able to overcome a natural reticence to tell us how; Tony Biscombe, a sober, bearded individual whose chief task was to scour videos for helpful hints to shut down the opposition and raise up old England, so he had square eyes; Terry Crystal, the popular team doctor, not averse to letting off steam after all his charges had been put to bed; Kevin Murphy, dogged Northern physio of umpteen tours, tapped up by media for inside scandal for nearly twenty years and still to come up with any; Phil Pask, physio and formerly an outstanding flanker with his beloved Saints, an exceptionally dedicated and exceptionally smashing fellow; Dave Reddin, state-of-the-art fitness adviser, an easier job in this era when players actually revel in your demands; Richard Wegrzyk, the masseur, and just before you think he had it easy, be advised that some players like a massage three times daily; Adrian Firth, the press officer, a new and decent addition and if you think *he* had it easy, then you try dealing with us newshounds; finally, Pete Seward, the baggage master. There was even an ancillary group of Twickers grandees, led by Jeff Addison, then the RFU president. South Africa is no place for the old-style cocktail courtesies and ceremonials, so Addison often appeared to be a function waiting to happen. Also waiting with him were Budge Rogers, the former England flanker and the RFU president for 2000–01; Peter Trunkfield, a former president whom we ribbed with the title 'past-it president' but a wonderful rugby man who did a splendid job in calming the worst excesses of the Bickering Era; Francis Baron, chief executive of the RFU; and Brian Baister, chairman. The other presence you could always sense – though you never actually saw him – was the man who England had made the happiest in the whole of Africa. The chairman of South African Airways.

All right, all right. It is probably too easy to mock all the national squads in the world these days, with their obsession and interminable squad sessions and, of course, the fact that they take themselves so seriously (although they would respond by saying that as international rugby is a deadly serious business, both deadly and a business, then how else are they supposed to be?). I still say that they spend too long together, bless them and their little cotton tracksuits. But I do recognise how much rugby followers want their national teams to win, how much it means to rugby in the winning nations, how high are your head and shoulders on your way to work after your lads have won. And how narrow are the margins.

One night on the tour, the entire management team drove over from the Westcliffe Hotel, the odd and luxurious tour base which reminded me a little of Portmeirion, the North Wales backdrop for *The Prisoner* series (I never missed an episode and never worked out what the sodding hell was going on, even after I read a 340-page book on it). The hotel has excellent facilities and, as usual, it was forbidden to walk out alone, especially at night. A modern-day laager.

The media were staying in the middle of their own encircling wagons, over in Sandton, a supposedly safe area of Johannesburg. But it was now strongly advised that we took cabs around, even to restaurants less than ten minutes' walk away, whereas during the World Cup of 1995 and on the Lions tour of 1997, we had walked without fear. The only time we walked anywhere throughout the whole England tour of 2000 was from the door of the hotel to a sports bar around 250 metres away, to watch one of England's matches on Euro 2000. It was difficult, even then, not to break into a sprint.

Twice in three weeks we were incarcerated in a smashing hotel in the world's murder capital when gunshots rang out nearby. The photographer Dave Rogers had on one of these occasions just walked into his room after photographing training, and still had his cameras on his shoulder; he reacted with commendable quickness and news-sense, taking a couple of quick frames out of his window of a gunman pointing his weapon at some unfortunate on the ground. He had already shot the prone man twice, in the side and the arm. Rogers discovered later that the shot man had tried to mug the man with the gun, but picked the wrong target. All parties hung around expectantly for a while, the police arrived around fifteen minutes later, the wounded mugger was taken to hospital and after a few cursory questions, the man who had shot him walked away. At the time it seemed that South Africa might emerge as host to the Football World Cup in 2006. On the day of this shooting we spent a pensive half-hour over a glass of the fizzy nothing they call South African lager, imagining the consequence of England football fans running round Johannesburg, and the billions and billions of pounds South Africa would have to invest in its police service (per month) in order to avoid some horrendous public-relations disasters as the incoming supporters washed up on waves of crime.

So Woody brought his laager men over. In the old days of touring the media were apparently as much a part of the tour as anyone and were even invited to tour reunions thirty years on. Read the engaging tour accounts by the likes of Bryn Thomas and Vivian Jenkins and you'll see they always went on the trips, were in the lee of the team. These days contact is restricted to fairly stiff and formal press conferences and to the odd snatched conversations as the subjects for grilling are arriving or departing. Woodward is a splendidly engaging and unpompous fellow, as are Graham Henry in Wales, Ian McGeechan in Scotland and Warren Gatland in Ireland. It's just that with so many branches of the media to service there is simply not time for everyone to talk to everyone.

It was therefore splendidly revealing to meet with the England backroom in a different situation. No money changed hands, just a couple of lagers. I found the evening a revelation. I am here to tell you, England fans, that the people in charge of your brave lads are the most dedicated, driven and impressive band imaginable. We'd all attacked Woodward for a little flakiness, for changing his mind and his mood, for losing matches he should have won, for retaining his job when, in other circumstances, he would have walked the plank.

But it was his influence which had, by the time of the tour, welded a group of coaches and specialists and medical men into a formidably tight unit. Management theories meant little when you had a manager, a coach and a local rub-a-dub man. Now, the structure means everything. The individuals were bursting with self-confidence – they all clearly felt themselves to be at the top of their profession in whatever field they were operating and there was, in many cases, evidence to back this up.

Larder, who had coached at high level in Rugby League, was emphatic. 'I can't imagine any job where you could get as much satisfaction as dealing with men of this calibre, both in the management and the team,' he said with feeling. I don't think it's taking advantage of what was a social situation to reveal his view that while he never thought he would ever deal with a player as athletic and dedicated as Ellery Hanley, he has now found one who matches Hanley in both those areas, in Neil Back. Our Backy, the guy who was never going to make it, the fall guy, the small guy. And now, the colossus with scores of caps.

Happily, there was also a keen pastoral affection for the players. I put it to David Reddin, the fitness adviser credited with the latest upturn in sports science and England's physical gleam, that all work and no play would make England's Jacks a bunch of dull boys. I said that less than twenty minutes' drive from the spot on which we were then standing was the Vortrekker Monument, an austere but wonderfully evocative com- memoration of the history of modern-day South Africa, unmissable for anyone wishing to understand the country, even to understand why they couldn't just stroll out of their hotel for a pleasant evening. 'I agree,' Reddin said. 'I really do. But these days they are so selfless, so single- minded. You want them to experience other things. But what happens when you give them a day off? It'll all be a bit quiet and then you'll have a nose around, and find them all in the gym.'

Both Woodward and Robinson were far from myopic taskmasters. 'I worry about them sometimes,' Woodward said of his squad, of the contemporary player. Robinson was even more forceful. 'I hate it when they don't have anything else in their lives, any other string to their bow,' he said. 'Every professional player must make an effort, enrol on a course, find some kind of part-time job that is worthwhile to him, anything.' Robinson had found life with the Bath squad a little too austere. 'We've now issued a kind of edict that we all go out on Saturday evenings for a few drinks, as a squad,' he said. 'We also stay together after training on Tuesday.' It was no surprise that Ben Clarke, at ease with the professional era and yet not enslaved to it, was the ringleader and keyholder. And yet it was a staggering thing that here, in a sport where the drinking culture was once all-pervasive and you had to threaten players in order to keep them out of the bar, there was now a club that demanded its players have a beer, let their hair down, just now and again. The stripling Bath lock Steve Borthwick, who had a fine tour, is almost a complete abstainer. 'I haven't had an alcoholic drink on tour. It is bad for your system and to be in shape is the be-all and end-all,' he said. 'I usually go for a Diet Coke or just plain water.' Briefly, I had this image of Robinson and Clarke kidnapping Borthwick as he tried to escape after training, holding him down on a pub table and pouring a shandy down his throat.

All this, of course, is professionalism of the highest order. Do you really have to know everything there is to know about the operation of the England football and cricket teams to know that in terms of preparation and dedication, the England rugby team leave them light years behind? It is no doubt something to do with the panic factor, because whole rafts of players are anxious for professional contracts and many of them might have two beady eyes on your place in the England team. I suppose it might be difficult for, say, Will Green and Darren Garforth to go out and sample a tourist attraction in South Africa if they had passed their fellow tight-head Julian White on his way to the gym that morning. The margins in international rugby are fine, and I would understand – though not agree with – Woodward and Garforth and Green and White should they decide that the only way to gain that edge is to spend even longer at it. If the major international coaches had their way, the International Board would soon be passing a resolution declaring that there are now thirty hours in every day.

Just think. It is less than seven years ago since there was an official IRB bylaw which forbade international squads from gathering more than forty-eight hours before international matches. England used to have to get round this by pretending that their Wednesday-night sessions were actually individual clinics for which the whole side had happened to turn up. How quaint we all were in those far-off days of 1994. Give them only forty-eight hours to prepare a team these days and the poor lads would only get one sentence out each before kick-off. Bless them all and, despite everything, bless the impressive dedication of Clive Woodward's backroom legions.

England drew the Test series 1–1, a major achievement. Yet the ways in which the 1–1 result was regarded by the two sides respectively was a vivid reflection of their comparative recent standards. In England it was seen as heady old stuff, as a team on the verge of greatness, good old Woody bringing home the Bok bacon, and so on. In South Africa it was viewed as a disaster, a team gone west, Nick Mallett was washed up and woe is us. It seems to me that England really have made it when they all come home after drawing a Test series in the southern hemisphere and the coach gets sacked because of the shocking sense of disappointment. That would be a better barometer of an English advance than winning the 2003 World Cup.

However, for once, I think that their optimism is well-founded. I think (and it was a theory that stood to be shot down in flames in the autumn of 2000 when South Africa and Australia were to come to Twickenham) that finally, finally, England are on the march.

The first Test against the Springboks was played at the Loftus Versfeld in Pretoria. There was a good deal of discussion in local papers of the day in 1994 that Jack Rowell's England had begun their two-Test series on the same ground with a devastating victory over South Africa, brought about partially by Rob Andrew's kicking and generalship but chiefly by a performance of quite staggering power and energy from an England back-row man named Tim Rodber. By 2000 the massive, fast-moving, talented Rodber should have been in his prime. Instead, albeit having given some wonderful cameos in Northampton's Heineken Cup run, Rodber was not even in the England tour party – a victim, it is true, of being meddled and mucked around by generations of selectors, but also and mainly of his own teeth-gnashing inconsistency.

At least we had a true Test match in Pretoria. A marvellous one. South Africa won by 18–13 in what was in many ways a reversion to the days when men were men, tests were tests and basketball was something played by (latterly) rich black Americans over the pond. We had a glorious, thumping contest in which André Venter was almost as supercharged for the Springboks as Rodber had been six years previously. But Johnson's men slugged it out, toe to toe. White, the Saracens tight-head playing his first Test, hung on courageously. Austin Healey, the maverick Leicester man, had been moved inwards from wing to fly-half only when the team arrived at Loftus and they were forced to give up on Wilkinson, who had suffered a bad stomach virus and was sheet-white long after the game. But in the teeth of the storm Healey played better than anyone had a right to expect, making errors, it is true, but toughing it out with the best of them.

Ultimately, they lost for two reasons. First, they started slowly and also scruffily, and gave the explosive boot of Braam van Straaten the chance to kick South Africa into a wonderfully calming 15–3 after only twenty-one minutes' play. In what was not to be a high-scoring match which brought only one try, this was to prove a crippling disadvantage for England.

Second, something that from certain viewpoints might appear as a refereeing decision from the good old days of South Africa home-town alleged cheats (no, it's not your put-in, it's ours) but that was more likely to have been an honestly made and rank bad decision. England had played superbly to peg the Springboks back to 15–10 by the start of the second half, thanks chiefly to a well-sustained movement which swept the field before Dan Luger, the wonderfully committed wing re-emerging after a long injury absence, battered his way over.

A try early in the second half, when South Africa were becoming increasingly frustrated at the England defence, might well have sent England gliding home. As it was, Mike Catt chipped diagonally for Tim Stimpson, the rangy Tiger drafted in on the right wing at lunchtime because Woodward needed his kicking. Stimpson found that the only Springbok at home was André Vos, the captain, and Stimpson was outstripping Vos with almost embarrassing ease as the pair chased Catt's weighted kick. Stimpson reached it first and hacked on as the ball bounced up agonisingly away from him, hopped up again in front of him as his fingers stretched out in anxiety and supplication and, as far as could be judged, was about to fall invitingly and gently into his sweaty grasp over the South African line. At that instant, Vos flattened Stimpson from behind.

Earlier that same day, there had come a highly controversial decision when Australia were playing Argentina in the first Test at Ballymore. A gang of Pumas drove over the line with the ball, and although the referee Jim Fleming could not have actually seen the ball grounded, the circumstantial evidence – four prone Pumas with hardly an Aussie anywhere near, all over the try-line – was enormous. Fleming really should have relied on the instincts he had developed in all his years as one of the finest referees. Instead, and rather lamely, he called upon the video referee. No available camera angle showed the touchdown; the video ref could offer Fleming no help and the Pumas were awarded a scrum. As the four Pumas picked themselves up, you saw the ball lying coyly over the line where they had fallen.

Colin Hawke, the referee in Pretoria, made the same mistake. He should have gone on his instincts and awarded a penalty try. 'My immediate impression was that it was a penalty try,' he admitted. Instead, he handed over the whole thing to one Mark Lawrence, a South African Super-12 referee, who scanned his screens and unfathomably disallowed the penalty try. Vos was not even penalised for his early tackle. Frankly, it was a decision which ensured that in the future video referees would be neutral too, like the referee and his touch-judges.

Afterwards Lawrence (to his credit, but clearly after sorting out his story) faced the music and claimed that Stimpson was deemed fair game

to be tackled, as he had had the ball on his fingertips. This pronouncement caused many people, including those at some English newspapers,
to assume that there is a law stating that if you are juggling the ball on
your fingertips in an attempt to gain possession you are therefore *in*
possession and *can* be tackled. In fact, no such law exists.

Some refereeing groups do deem that you are almost in possession,
and since it's your fault that you can't bring a ball under control after
several attempts they might turn a blind eye to someone who gets tired of
waiting for you to catch the damn thing and therefore hammers you.
Even this weak explanation does not even come close to fitting the facts
of the Stimpson incident, because the ball ballooned up into the air off
his fingers and not even the most hawk-like refereeing society in receipt
of a series of calls from bookmakers and determined to revert to the old
days when they liked to get the home side home, was going to tell us that
Tim Stimpson was in possession of a ball a yard away from him into the
Pretoria evening sky.

Penalty try. It was the only decision. I'd rung and checked the evidence
of my own eyes and my own monitor with the help of two top referees
back in the UK, almost before Lawrence had handed down his pronouncement to Hawke. 'Penalty try, no problem,' said one ref. 'Penalty
try, the cheating South African—,' said the other. Penalty try, Clive
Woodward feels to this day.

The match surged to a conclusion, if anything doubling in seat-edge
fascination. Leon Lloyd, the Leicester back, was brought on in the
final quarter. This is one of the people towards whom Woodward
would point me, I suppose, as evidence of the validity of his programme.
One year before Pretoria, we saw Lloyd play a lively and loose match
on the wing for England against a feeble Queensland selection. He
looked like a guy with some real talent for the sport but without the
necessary bottle, presence and willpower. Now he was back with
England, converted to the centre, hitting hard, playing with fire. A
most impressive transformation and it matters not whether it was down
to the influence of Woodward or to the fact that the splendid Dean
Richards, the Leicester team manager, had thrown Lloyd into the Tiger
centre near the start of the season, told him to shape up and bloody
well get on with it.

However, in Pretoria we found that someone might have gone a little
too far. Lloyd, provoked by some dirty play off the ball, threw a nasty
punch which caught De Wet Barry, and Van Straaten kicked a penalty
to take South Africa ahead by 18–13. This meant that a penalty goal was
no longer any good for England, and it meant that the Springboks, by a

mixture of desperate tackling and infringing, were able to hold out for the victory.

There was one check on the general euphoria on an occasion which restored in many hearts the old passions of the genre. This was the fact that the match almost spilled over into Sunday. It was midnight rugby. Incredibly, there were a total of twenty-nine minutes of injury time played, causing ranting of an unrestrained savagery back at newspaper offices in the UK, I can reveal, but also some frustration even for those who wanted it to go on a bit longer. There were a large number of injuries and blood replacements. Replacements came on and went off at the usual rate (that is, in torrents). There had to be further changes made because both Willie Meyer, the Springbok prop, and Phil Greening, the England hooker, were sent to the sin-bin and so other innocents had to be dumped for ten minutes in order that specialist scrummagers could be drafted. There was the long break as Lawrence took his time with the video replay decision, presumably to ensure that he did not make a mess of it but rather a full-blown cock-up.

What with the hordes of water-carriers and trainers and fourth officials and the like coming and going, no wonder there were so few tries. There was no space on the field in which to swing a cat. There were as many as twenty-four separate movements of replacements or the replaced. It all made for a scruffy, unsatisfying side-show which detracted from the main event. It also showed that if the timekeepers – though on this occasion only semi-official – are off the field operating a stop-clock, the games go on far longer than if the referee simply clicks his wristwatch whenever there is an injury. Most males, and others besides, had developed a decent growth of beard before the final whistle eventually blew.

There was a telling postscript. Players replaced because they need attention to cuts (those in the so-called blood-bin) can be replaced. Others cannot. It seems straightforward. If you are bleeding you can be repaired and return; if not, not. Originally, there was a ten-minute time-limit for the bloodied hero to have attention but this was quite rightly phased out and the length of time became limitless. The alternative was to have some shaking doctor desperately rushing the catgut as he tried to close an enormous wound, leaving the poor devil with an interesting zipper-effect scar to bear for life.

We saw that, as ever, coaches take advantage. Robbie Fleck, the Springbok centre, went off in the early stages with what appeared to be a leg injury – just a wild guess, but the heavy limp and ice-bag strapped to his leg were clues. According to our mates the snappers, strung out with their long lenses along the touch-line, Fleck sat on the sideline for a long chunk of the first half watching the action, and if any doctor was treating him for a cut then it was by faith-healing from a distance of around twenty yards. For the start of the second half Fleck suddenly returned.

I asked Woodward if he felt that coaches were now using the blood-bin excuse for any number of injuries and were withdrawing people to see how a match went before deciding whether or not they were bleeding. 'I asked about Fleck and they told me he had a bleeding nose,' Woodward said. 'I'm not saying they're lying.' He stopped short of claiming that the doctor had punched Fleck in the hooter in the dressing room at half-time. 'Anyway, I'm not whiter than white,' he said, Minds went back to the England–Fiji match at Twickenham when Joe Worsley, withdrawn in the middle of the match, had mysteriously re-appeared; and if his was indeed a blood-bin injury then Dr Terry Crystal stood exposed as the slowest stitcher of wounds in the history of the British Medical Association.

'What it needs,' Woodward said, 'is for a neutral doctor to have a quick look at the player coming off, and say that either he is a blood-bin case, or he isn't. Easy.' Generally, rugby's balance and sense of fair play has held out famously under the supposed onslaught of the bad things about professionalism. But you have to admit that a call for neutral doctors had a ring about it that suggested that sharp practice was not altogether unknown in our fine old sport. Maybe in time we will have a choice in Britain as we fall ill. Private doctor or NHS doctor. Neutral or biased.

Down in the tunnel outside the England dressing room I came across Robinson, who has always been a scowler's scowler – indeed, for a book of *Your 100 Best Scowls* he would unquestionably be asked to contribute a foreword. When it comes to scowling, Robinson proves that southern hemisphere rugby still has an awful lot of scowling to do before they can even begin to catch up.

As I held out my hand, he scowled. 'Er, hard luck Andy; well played,' I said. The scowl deepened before I had even got the words out. 'What the f**k do you mean, well played? We lost, we have got to get the winning mentality into this lot,' he said, pointing angrily towards the silent England dressing room. It was an outward sign of the steel that Robinson hoped to bring – and was already bringing – not only to the team but also to a management group which otherwise lacked someone with his own ferociously competitive edge. By the end of the tour even Woodward was affecting a passable scowl, although he clearly knew he wasn't quite there. The fact that Robinson was granted a profile, a public voice, whereas his predecessor, John Mitchell, was kept in the background also helped enormously. Still, as Robinson said, as yet there was nothing to celebrate.

Nevertheless, even scowlers of some class would have been impressed by England in South Africa. They won all three of the provincial games, and that was a decent achievement. It was not enough to give foundation to the more triumphalist of the celebrations which contended that England, as they had achieved a clean sweep when fielding their non-Test players, now had two international teams and two contenders of international class for each position. It was vital to remember that in midweek England had met none of the Super-12 teams – the Sharks, Stormers, Cats or Bulls – and none of the premier Currie Cup combinations – Gauteng (formerly Transvaal), Western Province, Eastern Province, Natal or Northern Transvaal. In 1994 England had met Transvaal, Eastern Province and Natal and Orange Free State as well as South Africa in the Test series.

In 2000 they met the North-West Leopards, Griqualand West and the Gauteng Falcons and, lowly as they were, the first two of those sides did not even field their top players. However, it must also be remembered that here were alien conditions, alien crowds, thin air – here was rugby out of the comfort-zone in which young Englishmen can sometimes spend their whole career, finding out too late that they can't handle the transition.

Ben Clarke had received his traditional late call-up for the tour after some injuries, and accepted with his traditional good grace when he might easily have told Woodward to stuff it. As befitting a man almost in the division of Pat Lam when it comes to showing rugby in its best light, he played with his usual fine leadership and excellence. The Leopards were downed by 52–22 on a riotously enjoyable evening in good old redneck Potch; the Griquas were thrashed by 55–16 in Kimberley, where the match was refereed by André Watson, the World Cup final referee who showed no better form than he had in Cardiff on final day itself.

England even made a spectacular departure from their new non-touring philosophy by actually deigning to venture out from their Jo'burg hotel to stay a night in a hotel in Kimberley. Good God, they'll all be Phineas Foggs before we know it. They complained about their hotel, of course, but at least they were in it. For a whole night. 'We think that they could and should have seen more of the country and more of what South Africa has to offer,' said Rian Oberholzer, chief executive of the South

African Rugby Football Union. 'We were disappointed that they decided to shut themselves off in a hotel we did not see as a proper tour venue.' Can't disagree.

The non-Test portion of the tour was completed, after the second Test, with a 36–27 victory over Gauteng Falcons. The Falcons also did their level best to recall some of the illustrious history of past tours by putting the boot in and generally pushing and shoving England further out of a comfort-zone. This was like the wild old days when you did not so much face a fixture-list in South Africa as a series of ambushes. Still, the Falcons were but a pale imitation, even when compared to more recent riots such as the Battle of Port Elizabeth in 1994, when both England and Eastern Province discovered well into the second half that they'd started without a ball.

In the three up-country matches, and although they were not playing the provincial cream, England 2000 showed up well enough. Both the sheer intent and common purpose which they displayed throughout the season – Murrayfield apart – and their pride in their own performance was obvious. The good news came in long paragraphs – Will Greenwood, who two seasons ago was the great gangling hope of England centre play, found his best form for ages, after having played little part in Leicester's championship run and then moving to Harlequins in the close season. (God, I know he'd gone off, but surely not by *that* much. Whoops! Sorry. Gratuitous Quins-bashing.)

The second storming back row of Joe Worsley, Paul Volley and Martin Corry played powerfully and it is easy to believe that had Worsley not opted for England, then every other European nation would have been anxiously competing to uncover his grandmother. Borthwick demonstrated one of the drawbacks of being so slightly built when a tackle in the Falcons match almost cut him in two across the midriff; but he was otherwise splendid, able to sneak off with opposition line-out ball and win the restarts almost at will. Must be the lack of alcohol.

Full-back Josh Lewsey played with tremendous dash and verve, and Ali Hepher, the Northampton fly-half whose season had partially disintegrated, came back strongly. There was a decent show from Ben Johnston, the Saracen centre; and enough from the wing Liam Botham to suggest that his dad might one day be known as Liam's father. Mark Regan, the uncompromising Bath hooker, celebrated his return from the wilderness where stroppy old discarded hookers go by showing himself as a hard-edge foil for Phil Greening's outlandish wide game. Lloyd continued his reincarnation as the Midlands' least likely hard-nut. And there was genuine, twenty-four carat class at scrum-half, because Kyran

Bracken was to re-emerge from a desperate period of injury to indicate that his battle with Matt Dawson for the role would be one of the features of the 2000–01 season.

It was important not to get carried away because a fair number of the England squad had proved to be nothing more than bread-and-butter players at home, and if there suddenly appeared to be a red tinge of jam on their games in South Africa then it was only because they were not in contact with the cream. Still, if a tour is only as good as its undercard, and some are only that good, then this was an encouraging one.

It had nothing on Bloemfontein, however. I suppose it is easy to say this in hindsight, but it was a charged, charmed day from the start. Bloemfontein is a true Test venue but not in terms of hotel accommodation or communications, so the press party had to take a charter south to the Free State in the early morning from the Lanseria airfield, a brown-dust establishment miles from anywhere.

South Africa is a country of the most astonishing contrasts, and the clarity of the highveld was shown in all its part-drabness and part-glory as we took off. Such was the sense of excitement in the air that celebrations began even before the match had started. The pilot of the twin-prop gave a quick briefing in which he told us where the sandwiches and soft drinks were. 'There's even a drop of something stronger in this cupboard,' he said, pointing to one of the lockers as he turned towards his seat in the cockpit. 'Help yourself after take-off.' I don't think he meant this to be taken quite as literally as it was by the giant of the media corps who was out of his seatbelt and nosing around in the 'something stronger' cupboard at about fifteen feet high as the wheels were only just retracting into their cowling.

It was a day in which the atmosphere in Bloem was marvellously authentic, with raucous, bearded Afrikaner rugby supporters, together with their menfolk, gathered in massive throng.

And it was, authentically, one of the finest England performances I have ever seen. They won 27–22, levelled the series. South Africa only came remotely so close because André Watson, this time exiled to the video-replay booth (do they do one with bars and a flap to poke his food through?), dredged through various shots of an incident near the end of the match and somehow gained the impression that it was beyond doubt that Joost van der Westhuizen had scored a valid try. It was only through this that South Africa were able to stage a convincing late rally, when it took defensive feats of derring-do by Healey and Ben Cohen to stop certain tries. And to keep England hearts beating.

Wilkinson's tummy was by now sorted. He had only been eating properly for forty-eight hours before the match and had not played a serious game for six weeks. He was also carrying a groin injury which had to be operated on less than three days after the match. But he gave a masterly performance. He kicked all twenty-seven of England's points, with eight penalties from nine attempts and a clever snap drop-goal. He also tackled magnificently.

But it was far more than that. The young, almost baby-faced Newcastle Falcon bossed it like the cruel warder on a chain-gang. His choice of play was immaculate, his tactical nous at least a decade beyond his years. His assurance seeped outwards and inwards. It was the kind of performance England had been awaiting from a fly-half since Doris Day was a virgin and before Dudley Wood was an amateur. In their years of fly-half horror, England had lost countless games simply because this nation of big players, heavy players, fervent players so rarely had anyone to shape it all. Wilkinson promises better, and the landscape of the match – and conceivably that of world rugby – looks blissfully different as a result.

I had always warmed to Wilkinson for his courage in the tackle and his precocious confidence. But I had been reserved because of a lack of evidence that he had the ability to rule a game. Here, in his own image, was Jonny's Test. In contrast, Braam van Straaten in the opposition looked like someone who had entered the World Head-Down Charging heats and got on the wrong plane.

If Wilkinson inspired England's scoring machine and typified the effort, then it was England's outstanding defence, the side-to-side then up-and-down refusal to be drawn out of position or to buckle, that protected Wilkinson's legacy. 'I thought our defence was superb,' Dallaglio said afterwards. 'Even the scrambling defence, when they managed to get behind us. And Jonny? Incredible. Just amazing.'

Phil Larder could celebrate the fact that the Springboks had with a fair share of possession scored just one try against his men in two Test matches, and this at a time when Mallett was trying to expand the Bok style out of the trenches and on to the plains. The only way even Larder could have prevented the one try (Van der Westhuizen's) was by springing up to where Watson was viewing the video replay and pulling out his plugs.

Dallaglio and the back row had once again been mighty and so had Johnson, especially in the sense that he had heeded the pleas to make more runs. Johnson returned to the open fields of his youth, driving and steaming around the place. The Bloem crowd were so quiet that you could hear England shouting orders to each other as they re-positioned their defence for the next onslaught. You could hear them shouting as the great scrum-half Joost van der Westhuizen suddenly ran out of ideas, and stopped.

Afterwards, Dallaglio expressed the hope that this great victory had lifted the spirits of the English nation. In the few days prior to the Test match the football team had lost, abjectly, to Romania and departed Euro 2000. Those of us for whom football began with Newport County and never quite recovered were interested to learn from those who did understand the sport that some England players, on £25,000 per week and more, really did have all the technical accomplishment of a Sunday morning scrambler on the park pitch. England's cricketers had also capitulated miserably, to the West Indies in the first Test match. One week after Bloemfontein, Dallaglio found that he may have started something. England won one of the greatest Test matches ever played, hair-raisingly by two wickets, at a spellbound Lord's.

If Clive Woodward had achieved the same early results in football or cricket – or even in another era in rugby – then he would not have been England's coach by the turn of the millennium, let alone still have been around for their South African tour. As I say, patience, tempers and tolerance for defeat are desperately short in professional sport, as so many have found to their cost.

I have never been particularly struck either way with Woodward as England coach. I did not feel that in terms of winning records or the testimony of people with whom he had worked he was quite in the division of Graham Henry. I liked him as a man and admired his honesty and it seemed to me that, like us all, he was learning from his errors.

And whether or not it was by good fortune, he was still there, and by the time England prepared for their South African tour and especially by the time they flew home, he had found himself. He was no longer flaky, at least on important matters. Who in the outside world really cared if he changed the time of a press conference seventeen times? He no longer changed his fly-half immediately before an important Test – unless, of course, his fly-half was being sick.

He had reined in England's game emphatically from those partly dreadful days against Ireland and Wales when rugby was shown in an airy-fairy light. In South Africa he had the forwards grafting out the hard yards again, making an impact and a dent so that Wilkinson had more time in which to operate. And in that, there was absolutely no doubt that the steely Robinson had helped. But who had asked Robinson join the team? Our Woody. Who had put together, fired up and forged the management group itself, if not our Woody?

It was a fine sight to see Woodward's England fulfil themselves at last, and to genuinely promise better things, even though the excellence of the subsequent 2000 Tri-Nations was just a little sobering. There was Jonny and his precocious new authority; Lawrence and his running; Larder and his defence. There were Vickery and White and Green and Garforth to drive each other onwards on the tight-head. And Clive Woodward and his driven management hordes. As we flew out of Bloemfontein, as the strong-stuff cupboard was breached again at a height of fifteen feet, and all us media cynics chattered with the joy of it all, the future seemed bright, the future seemed Red Rose.

CHAPTER TEN

Bedford Main Line

New club rugby – culture-hopping, culture-changing

i) Ratzo rugby – exit the Goldington saviour

Towards the end of the season 1998–99 Bedford's players, a group who for nearly three seasons had played with such an unfailing pride that they had made a complete nonsense of the idea that club loyalty in the new era meant nothing, faced a match against Northampton at Goldington Road. For various reasons, during those three years the players had often gone months unpaid in a club that was struggling, but, encouraged by coaches of the stature of Paul Turner and then Rudi Straeuli, they fought on.

The idiosyncratic Scott Murray typified their attitude. He was a Scottish international coveted by many clubs, and arguably the best young lock in Europe. 'We had a few meetings and decided that we should all stick together,' he said of one of the frequent occasions when the cheques never appeared and the club teetered. Kathy Leather, an able and ebullient marketing director, was later to tell of debts to the laundry holding up delivery of the jerseys, of bailiffs arriving to take out the floodlight bulbs, the lot. 'There was so much goodwill towards the club in the town, though,' she says. 'You'd go along and ask a sponsor to pay before he was due to and they always would.'

Part of the problem was that Frank Warren, the boxing promoter who had effectively bought the club two years previously, had been engaged in a heavyweight court battle with Don King, he of the electrified hair and insistence that boxing isn't dodgy. Warren's assets were tied up for a long time. Warren was most likely also labouring under misapprehensions as to what professional rugby was going to be when he took over; though to be fair to him he used to rant and chant from his seat in the stand when he was able to attend games and was baffled as to the decisions of the referee, putting him in the excellent company of all the rest of us.

He had bought a struggling club, but Bedford has always been a misunderstood institution. They were able to draw more than 6000 people for a magnificent match in 1998 when they beat Newcastle, then charging away at the top of the Second Division. Their supporters have always been the most loyal and rousing bunch you could ever wish for and in the Warren era, apart from the splendid result against Newcastle, they had their moments in Premiership One, too. Notably when, in what was probably the best Premiership match I have seen to date, they came back from 16–30 down and then, in injury time, 23–33 down against Harlequins. They scored two memorable tries in the last two movements of the match and came home 35–33. Daragh O'Mahony on the wing and Jason Forster on the flank played to international class that day. So did Murray, on any day. One old Bedford fan behind the press box turned to his mate and said: 'This is the best day in sport I've had.' His mate was too excited to speak.

Off the field it was still a battle, so it was with keen interest that the supporters and the players and the media gathered for the Northampton match. As ever, there was a good feeling abroad in the ground, and the financial struggle behind the scenes was hidden just for the day. But better news had broken overnight. Frank Warren, conserving energy and resources for other battles, had sold the club for £1 to new owners, a company called Jefferson Lloyd International.

The representatives of the new owners were due to arrive at the main gate of the ground around fifteen minutes before kick-off, and together with a few curious hacks I stood by the gate to await the entrance of the fairy godfathers. To be perfectly frank, godfathers did not seem far wide of the mark but you wouldn't have called them fairies. All of a sudden, the most astonishing group of geezers you'd ever seen came bustling through. They hadn't been able to park. 'F**k me,' said the lead geezer, 'we've been f**king driving round the f**king ground looking for somewhere to f**king park for f**king ages.' Most appeared to be chain-smoking nervously and one was an absolute ringer for Ratzo Rizzo, the Dustin Hoffman character in *Midnight Cowboy*. You couldn't help but laugh out loud, but when you remained none the wiser by the time they'd spent around an hour outlining their plans for the club after the match, you felt sad for Bedford, because hopes had been raised and were surely about to be dashed. As one insider said, his hopes were dashed before that day was out: 'You never really knew who they were and what they thought they were doing. I suppose they wanted to sell the ground for development, or at least part of it. But there's a covenant on Goldington Road so they couldn't touch it.'

The spokesman for Jefferson Lloyd was one Doug Braddock. A few months after their arrival, Bedford put out a statement from Jefferson Lloyd saying that Braddock had gone, had never had any right to speak for Jefferson Lloyd and would not be returning. The statement attacked him without mercy. One of Bedford's backroom boys actually saw his departure. 'This guy with blue jeans, white tank-top and bulging arms arrived one day and marched upstairs. He left with Braddock and we learned later that he'd taken him to the station, taken away his car and put him on a train.' It appears the ticket was a single to nowhere. Buffet service available and second-class seats towards the rear.

That year, Murray and his men beat Rotherham in a nerve-jangling play-off to retain their status. In the 1999–2000 season, when Jefferson Lloyd disappeared, Bedford could not recover. Murray had already departed with many of the top players. 'It was a tragedy,' Kathy Leather remembers. 'I had a sponsor who was willing to pay half his salary. Scott wanted to stay, so did others. But it was such a shambles behind the scenes with owners changing and people running round not knowing what they were doing. Bedford had a real potential. They still have. It was just unfortunate.' Leather is now at Worcester, where under the enlightened owner Cecil Duckworth life is more orderly.

Bedford are currently in Premiership Two (now called National One), are now owned by a group of people from the town, scaled down. I have not the slightest doubt that their loyal supporters will stay with them. If only in the certain knowledge that one club can have only a finite amount of bad luck. They've had all theirs.

ii) Owners – secrets and salads

They wound up so many people when they came into rugby in 1995 and after. They'd come in, change the club around, demand changes in the season and the whole game, get rid of the old boys who'd stuck on stamps for years, bring in foreigners and chuck out the bloke you worshipped as a player because he nodded to you in Sainsbury's every Tuesday. And what did they ever bring to your club? Yes, well, apart from millions of pounds, OK, OK. Apart from saving the club from a greased pole straight down to Division Six and giving it a professional future . . . Yes, but apart from that.

Some struck unlucky. Bedford, for one. Richmond lost their investor, Ashley Levett, and have plunged back down to amateur ranks with pro dreams dead. There must be other casualties to come, first because rugby is still an uncertain marketplace but also because many of the potential owners and investors are an odd bunch.

But considering that rugby is meant to be such a poor investment, considering that po-faced City men moonlighting as hacks in rugby's trade journals shake their heads warningly, the game has lived a charmed life. Around thirteen clubs have attracted an individual who has invested heavily, and of those no fewer than nine are still in position, shaken but hanging on well – Nigel Wray at Saracens, Keith Barwell at Northampton, Tom Walkinshaw at Gloucester, Paul Caddick at Leeds Tykes, Andrew Brownsword at Bath, Cecil Duckworth at Worcester, Malcolm Pearce at Bristol, Chris Wright at Wasps, Tony Brown at Newport and Peter Thomas at Cardiff. Two other clubs, Sale and Newcastle, were quickly snapped up after their original investors withdrew: Brian Kennedy is now at Sale and Dave Thompson at Newcastle. Only Richmond and Bedford were not quickly bought up again.

It is a stroke of ludicrous fortune to the game that many of the people who departed took the net loss on the chin. Steve Smith, still one of the guiding lights at Sale, said when welcoming Kennedy: 'To be fair to the last bloke (we never knew who he was), he put a few million into the club. We've improved the ground, the clubhouse and some of the infrastructure so the game should thank its lucky stars that these people were around when the transition to the pro game was all up in the air.' Sir John Hall was reckoned to have written off over £7 million when he sold to Thompson.

It is likely that at least one more of the originals will be gone by the summer of 2001, but there is also the sense that the worst may be over, since new proceeds from Twickers will now take care of the players' wage bill for the English clubs, and for the new season the fixture list actually came out more than six minutes before the first matches kicked off – an all-time record. In fact, it came out an incredible five weeks before. My God, next thing you know we'll have a professional game.

They're still an odd lot. Not as odd as the departed Ratzo and his mates. Maybe Barwell, who sipped last season from the European Cup itself (and deservedly, too), can sometimes blurt first and ask questions later when he's roused. Walkinshaw's secrecy does him no good at all, and does his cause no good. Maybe the likes of Nigel Wray are a little difficult to work out, but what you *can* work out, when you look around Saracens and experience the atmosphere in the club, the perfect mix of exotica and English rising talent, their absolutely marvellous community and cashback and education schemes, is that Wray's heart is in the right place and, in what is probably a major feat, bigger than his wallet. That's a compliment, Nigel. I can't see Saracens bringing in a heavy to put *him* on a train at Watford Junction. It is also a compliment to rugby that two men as sharp and impressive as Kennedy and Thompson see it all as worth the risk.

They got it wrong when they started. It's likely that hardly any of them would have bothered if they'd seen the years of hassle which lay ahead. And yet we got them wrong, too. In the regime of Cliff Brittle at Twickenham, he and Fran Cotton and others who followed their line would fulminate away at the club owners, both in private and public. What neither they nor anyone else ever explained was what on the planet the professional game was going to do without new investment, especially this new investment which didn't even demand a return. In how many other businesses would people have stayed so loyal so long and with such a murky balance sheet?

It was the job of all unions, of Vernon Pugh of the IRB and anyone else who grew restive and irked when the owners went public with their grievances, to go to them and sit down with them and give them a path to at least minimise their losses. The shocking failure of the English and Welsh unions to open a proper dialogue with the investors has been a disgrace of the past five years. There has also been rugby's snobbery, the odious notion that someone was unworthy because he was 'not a rugby man' when he arrived, bearing gifts.

I'd say that Sir John Hall wished to shape the game to his own image of football; for the others, the idea that they wanted to take over the game, either the club game or the Test arena, was paranoia. Pure and simple. It was good to hear Francis Baron, chief executive of the RFU, echoing my own views that if people are willing to pay out millions then it is good manners, at least, to listen to what they have to say rather than wrenching off their arms. Yes, an odd lot. I hope that some of you stick around to see the salad days. Or, in your case, the caviar days. You'll never buy me off with your millions, what with my ethics and everything. Though you could give it a try, I suppose.

iii) Newcastle and Richmond – rising together, falling apart

They're hardly Siamese twins, these two institutions. They were born hundreds of miles apart, Richmond into rather a privileged existence and Newcastle into a noble slog. They were raised in different schools of rugby. But recently they have been locked together, miles away. They were bumbling along, both of them, as the middle of the 1990s bumbled. Newcastle Gosforth were gradually fading, living largely on the memories of their back-to-back Cup wins in the 1970s, on their undimmed ability to produce fine forwards who then promptly moved on, and on a club spirit which survived relegation from the First Division and a slide down the Second as well. Richmond, southern slickers, were buoyed as they had always been by a group of dedicated officials and only a small group of supporters. When professionalism was declared they were on the verge of the relative oblivion of Division Three.

They stayed locked, because they were two of the clubs to receive the most outrageous fortune when a raft of benefactors (investors, owners, sugar-daddies, mad fools, call them whatever you like) came hurtling into rugby in 1995–96. Sir John Hall, chairman of Newcastle United FC, hurtled faster than most, because he bought Newcastle Gosforth less than two weeks after the Paris Declaration in August 1995. He added the club to his brainchild, the Newcastle Sporting Club, and although this was an attempt by Hall to ascend to the status of SuperGeordie I always felt that it was a genuine attempt to better the sporting lot of the city. Sorry, Toon. Shortly after him, Ashley Levett, a millionaire businessmen based in Monte Carlo, bought Richmond. No one ever really worked out why, probably not even Levett himself.

They stayed locked. They produced, with the fruits of the invest-ments, a glamorous team apiece for the start of their Division Two campaigns in 1996–97. Hall had already installed as his director of rugby the estimable Rob Andrew, an inspired choice. Andrew signed a gang of marauding and charismatic hard-hitters in the shape of Dean Ryan, Pat Lam, Va'aiga Tuigamala, Doddie Weir, Garath Archer and Gary Armstrong. Richmond, in the foursquare shape of John Kingston, the coach they bravely retained from the amateur years, drafted a rich seam of Celtic glamour with the two mighty Quinns, Scott and Craig Quinnell, the electric Puma Agustin Pichot, the centre's centre in Allan Bateman and the vivid Samoan Earl Va'a. Together, the teams were promoted and in their first seasons returning to the top flight, Richmond finished a creditable fifth and Newcastle, with a team put together more with short-term success in mind, won the Allied Dunbar title, hurried along by the devastating pick-and-drive of their forwards. They had to win against Harlequins at The Stoop to seal the title and, as they did so, Sir John danced and jigged up in the stands.

They then both decided to move, to expand. Richmond headed around forty miles down the M4 to the splendid Madejski Stadium in Reading; Newcastle less far in miles but further in local perceptions, to the Gateshead Stadium.

It was now that divergent paths appeared in front of them, and the only thing they had in common in the next season was that both Hall and Levett pulled the plug. Newcastle, already re-building, struggled in the soulless open spaces of the Gateshead Stadium. It was then that

Gateshead Thunder, a pop-up new rugby league team which played there before falling victim to the King Herod-like processes that always murder fledgling new league clubs, bravely christened the stadium the Thunderdome. It was the least apt re-naming in the history of sport.

Richmond, in fact, did splendidly in Reading. From scratch, they began averaging crowds of near to 7000 and on three occasions, including Boxing Day of 1998 in some of the worst weather in which I have seen rugby played, they pulled 10,000. No one pretended that this meant they were even covering their costs, because these were early days and all investors and all professional clubs were still anxiously awaiting some concert and a structured season to emerge from the disaster surrounding the transition in England to a professional echelon. But they were clearly impacting on the Thames Valley. It was a start.

Hall switched off the lights. I had always found him to be at least in part an impressive man, if hawkish. He was no doubt cheesed off that he would not wield enough authority in the game to advance his investment but he was also not in good health, the final straw. It was a common sight to see Levett's lieutenants taking angry calls from their boss complaining that Richmond hadn't won or hadn't attracted a gate of 25,000 for the visit of West Hartlepool. If no one knew why he had entered the field in the first place, no one knew why he had left it, either.

I recently consulted my notes from a press conference he had given to launch the Madejski transfer in August 1998. He assured Oracle (his major sponsors), his team, local council and potential supporters that he was there for the long stretch. He didn't stretch very far. How harshly should we judge sugar-daddies who quickly go sour? Be understanding because rugby was not living up to their expectations so how could they be blamed for cutting their (millions of pounds' worth of) losses? Or berate them for coming in with their supposed business far-sightedness with their eyes open, raising the hopes and financial expectations of a lot of people then dashing them overnight? I am still not sure what my own answer is to this question.

At least Richmond had always stayed true to their roots. They would bus up their followers from Richmond to Reading; they kept their junior, mini and women's teams running madly at the Athletic Ground. Under Hall, Newcastle rapidly became an exclusive, austere and unloved institution. They ruthlessly cut their lesser teams, their mini-section. They painted over the white lines of their life-members' parking spaces; they abandoned the familiar green-and-white-hooped jerseys of their Gosforth years, re-named themselves Newcastle Falcons and the Gosforth stalwarts stamped off and re-formed the old club, minis and all, a few fields away from the Falcons' Kingston Park. No wonder that Fran Cotton said at the time: 'Newcastle are not a real rugby club any more.' I have never stinted in my admiration for Rob Andrew but there was indeed a hostility abroad in the Hall era, to escape which you needed five tickets of different colours and strong biceps just to be allowed to find a room in the club where you could buy a pint – let alone then emerge to see the match.

Both clubs are alive for the new millennium. But the parting of the ways has been so abrupt that they will almost certainly never play each other again in a competitive match. Newcastle had a resounding, warming stroke of good fortune which is also, I suppose, a vote of confidence in professional rugby (ill-deserved, some would say) and in the spirit of the old club (well deserved). The club was bought from the Hall family by David Thompson, an engagingly blunt millionaire Geordie so well rooted in rugby that he still coaches a junior team and still puts the lot of the youth of Newcastle above the fortunes of the Falcons. I broke bread with him towards the end of season 1999–2000, and behind dry humour and boxer's nose there was the twinkle of a rugby man from way back. He liked Hall as a person, he said. Although he pointedly berated the attempt to take the club over the river to Gateshead. 'Gateshead?' he said. 'We people from Newcastle see Gateshead as the south of England.' I think I liked his parochialism even more than I liked his vision for the Falcons. Club rugby dies without it.

His vision is impressive, however. His first pledge was to restore the rugby-club feeling to Kingston Park. He initiated what amounted to a charm offensive, re-forging the old links with the local schools and the universities and the local clubs. Tentatively, he was hoping for the Gosforth club to return to the mother ship. He has so many plans that one lunch was not enough. And because of the club's thriving academy, he probably has the best crop of young players in the English game, notably the talented young full-back Michael Stephenson. He also had the smallest colossus in the game in one Jonny Wilkinson. It is not fanciful to suggest that the Falcons will be contenders for everything in two years. Thompson quickly became a voice of harsh reason on EFDR and when at the end of the season 1999–2000 another businessman with rugby in his heart, Brian Kennedy, took over at Sale, it seemed that prospects for the top clubs of the North were brighter than for ten years.

Richmond found no Thompson. Just King Herod in the shape of EFDR, the body meant to represent the interests of the top clubs. Not strangle them. When Levett disappeared the club had to go into administration. EFDR were far more interested in Richmond dying, allowing the rest a bigger share of the pot, than giving them either time or resources or help to stay alive. For that and for its trampling of rugby-club ethics, neither the Richmond club nor, I suspect, the game at large will ever forgive EFDR and especially Tom Walkinshaw, the chairman. It was one of the few times when I grew nostalgic for the amateur era. I have not the slightest doubt that Richmond could have been run far better. But that put them in the good company of every single one of their Premiership colleagues, Walkinshaw's Gloucester included.

Then, the Richmond officials who had driven them on for years and adapted eagerly to the Levett era found other knives being plunged between their shoulder-blades. They had a considerable asset in the Athletic Ground and they also had a colossal multi-million-pound offer from Chelsea for the ground, which Chelsea wanted to turn into their training headquarters. Levett, still on the board, was anxious for the sale to go through. So was Tony Tiarks, the investor in London Scottish who was also on the board.

Fine. Sell up and everyone is paid, investors walk away unscathed, the administrator is happy. One problem only. Richmond die. As a professional club they were already dead, swallowed in an asset-stripping farce which some people had the brass neck to call a merger with London Irish – the Irish made the near-fatal error of sharing a ground with the dreaded Harlequins. What they should have done but lacked the guts to do was play at the splendid Madejski, incorporate Richmond properly and call themselves Thames Valley Irish. They did not, and when the Quins jealously kicked them out a year later they had to decamp to the Madejski for 2000–01 anyway, having lost a precious year.

Richmond's loyal group of officials gathered themselves. They were still playing junior and mini and women's rugby in 1999–2000. They even raised a first XV which played against university and services teams. They were given until 31 March 2000 to find £500,000 to save the club. It was what the administrator requested. Otherwise, the old investors pulled out and Ken Bates of Chelsea bought the ground. Long-serving Richmond official Tony Hallett was one of the key figures in the desperate race against time. Why bother, why put up with all the hassle? 'I could not walk away from a club with such a tradition and which has been so special to me. We didn't take no for an answer and we just battled on.'

With so many former friends stabbing them, they needed no enemies. They found the money with what Hallett says was 'almost literally three minutes to spare'. With that splendid understatement which you would expect from a distinguished ex-serviceman, Hallett found the saving of his club 'quite an emotional experience'. Richmond now have more then 700 youngsters playing the game on Sundays in the season. They instituted a third senior team for season 2000–01. The club, reduced from its brief professional glimpse of glory, lives.

There was, however, one further boot in the testicles from alleged friends. They had lost their place in the Premiership and were now, league-less. They asked for an entry point somewhere in the structure. Considering their outstanding service to the game you would have thought that a place in Jewson Two, effectively Division Four, would not have been inappropriate. Adding them to the league would have given the other clubs only one extra match each, and a money-spinning one at that.

The Middlesex County Union, who, judging from some of their dispatches, seem to comprise in part people for whom the Neolithic Age is deemed new-fangled, ordered that Richmond be installed in Middlesex Hertfordshire Division One, effectively Division Eight. 'There might still have been a little jealousy around from our entry into the professional era,' Hallett says. Eight successive promotions and then they might meet Newcastle Falcons once again.

The professional era has been nothing but unpredictable, nothing but harsh. The newly-thriving Newcastle and the post-holocaust Richmond live and breathe. One raised on high, the other diminished in points and playing status but not in spirit. I suppose Richmond will have one advantage. We are in an era when true solvency of the professional club game is still a state to be reached in the future. Now that the tremors of impending extinction have subsided at Richmond, maybe their band of saviours will enjoy a quieter life.

iv) Newport and Cross Keys – big brother is awake

As I stepped down from the train the old home town looked, well, not the same. New pubs and restaurants had appeared around the station. And across the roundabout and over the bridge over the Usk, turning right as I'd turned on winter Saturdays since the age of six, there was a buzz. Long lost, but loud and insistent.

Two seasons before I had been to watch Newport play Caerphilly in a match in one of rugby's most moribund competitions, the Welsh League. It was a Wednesday evening, dank and gloomy. Newport's hopeless floodlights illuminated around half the field to a standard just decent enough not to make it a crime to demand good money from spectators. Newport were terrible. That season, they were to lose to Caerphilly five times. Good on Caerphilly, but it was a horrendous statistic for a team which could once beat Australia, New Zealand and South Africa and complain afterwards that they hadn't rubbed it in.

Amateurism not only meant not paying players, you see. It meant allowing great institutions to atrophy, to slow to a crawl against the brush of conservatism and cobwebs. For the previous twenty years, Newport had not the remotest grasp of rugby's progress, its new marketing theories. Newport stood there, hidebound, and expected top players and companies to come to them – not because they had much to offer, just because they *were* Newport. As for links with the town and the community, Newport merely glared balefully out from behind the walls of Rodney Parade and complained that the town came along not in droves, like in the old days, but in handfuls.

Newport's chairman, David Watkins, had seen professional rugby in action in his days as a rugby league player, and he knew what it took – even if only by default, since rugby league's commercial record is poor. And when it came to what it took, Newport had nothing of it. They did have on their committee Tony Brown, a successful businessman who had arrived in the town because some of his interests were based there and who had been impressed by the warmth of his welcome.

In the summer of 1999 Brown made Newport, the town and the club, sit bolt upright. He invested enough money in the club for them to make such a burst of signings that Newport's followers could hardly believe their eyes. Newport re-signed Allan Lewis, the coach. They signed Peter Rogers, who was to prove the most powerful loose-head in the World Cup; Shane Howarth, the Sale and former All Black back who was already a marvellously inspiring and influential player. They also netted Jason Jones-Hughes, the new Wales centre; Franco Smith, the Springbok back; the splendid Welsh warrior flanker, Jason Forster; and the hard-grafting Fijian, Simon Raiwalui.

It is for the moment another story, but the group demolished, as have other groups, the theory pedalled by so many that foreigners and other outsiders take the money and run. Howarth and the others, whenever I caught them, played as if they'd been raised on a diet of pure Newport and lived in Ringland, Alway, Malpas, Hartridge or Rogerstone all their born days.

Then, as if he had been dared to top that little lot, Brown shelled out for Gary Teichmann, until recently the South African captain, one of the most important figures in world rugby and still loved in his native Natal. On the club's website, long-suffering fans posted pleas for someone to confirm that it was not all a joke. Robin Davey, the rugby writer for the *South Wales Argus*, suddenly had to sift more Newport news in two months that he had sifted in twenty years. 'I can't believe this is happening,' he said. 'Join the club,' I said. 'They are,' he said.

Understandably, the team took time to gel. But even before they did, the town came out. For the first game of the 1999–2000 season Newport faced Cardiff, the oldest and most bitter enemy. The two clubs' World Cup players (and by this time, you were talking of about twenty-two players) were absent. But more than 7000 people came to see the rump of the old giants, and when Newport scraped home it was as if they had won the league and as if the last thirty years of decline had never happened. (Their crowds in the previous season had sunk below 2000.)

Their form dipped, then revived massively towards the end, a revival touched off on a heady wet evening when, with both sides now fielding their top and most glamorous players, Newport knocked Cardiff out of the Cup and more than 10,000 roared and rocked Rodney Parade. As the season reached a climax the crowd support was astounding. Newport had become one of the loudest rugby grounds in Britain – only Leicester and Northampton could dispute the title. They finished second, behind Cardiff, in the Welsh/Scottish League, an event which was still no great shakes but in which the top Welsh sides had, after a desperately long gap, begun to shake themselves awake on and off the field.

For season 2000–01, Newport made the European Cup. Wise heads surveyed their pool – a veritable pool of death which included Bath, Castres and Munster – and realised that they would need to find another twenty points at least in order to finish as high as last but one in the pool. But by participating they also knew that Newport would be at least twenty points better at the end of the season than they were at the start.

The buzz was something to feel in 1999–2000. I sat on the wall behind the dead-ball line, not twenty metres from the spot where I'd watched them beat the Fifth All Blacks in 1963. I witnessed the annihilation of a weakened Llanelli in a match towards the end, saw things on the field, heard things from the crowd, that ranked with anything I'd seen in the hundreds of times I'd been there. I saw friends I had not seen for years, but who had been attracted by the noise from something that had been silent. There were kids there, on free tickets. Watching.

It would be ridiculous to see all this as evidence that professional rugby is thriving. Until the Welsh Rugby Union can enter the new era and show the slightest lead, the competitions which the clubs play in will not be good enough to support the professional game. The WRU are probably the only body who could fail to find a sponsor for a Welsh/Scottish league event that is now crammed full of quality, entertaining international players. They claim that they cannot flog the event to a sponsor because, with so many possible structures around, the future is uncertain. So they are asking us to believe that two of their failures make one excuse. Why not sort out the season then, chaps? It's only taken you five years to date.

But more to the point, Newport's revival is a castle built partly on sand. As David Watkins rightly says: 'If Tony Brown walks away, then we are back to square one.' Brown has done wonders. He is the type of bloke who has been seen selling programmes instead of imbibing in hospitality complexes. Nonetheless it is his money which has given Newport a professional presence. It is a matter of good fortune, not one of hard work or vision on the club's part. One man changing history.

There is also a lesson to be learned here. The arrival of professionalism at Newport came only by default, with a benefactor. But it arrived. Amateurism was seeing the club slowly and yet irrevocably dying on its feet, losing five times in a season to the brave but limited men of Caerphilly. They are now forced to swim furiously for their lives, forced to free themselves from dependency. It is what the sports writer Brough Scott describes as a 'brown-trouser experience'. Partly by the panic factor, it is a club transformed overnight.

Take Newport's plans for the 2000–01 season. This club, whose public relations until recently consisted of announcing the changes to the programme on an inaudible tannoy, now has a teeming family village installed between the clubhouse and the pitch, offering a raft of attractions, coaching facilities, catering, bars and live music. Not for corporate guests – they have a new stand for them. But for people. Newport people.

They also have a community programme which represents the cutting edge of all club rugby's attempts to integrate with their surroundings – and if clubs don't make that effort, they will die. For 2000–01, they instituted Gateway Rugby, a coordinated schools-based programme for children between nine and sixteen. The programme offers the funding and the coaches, including some of Newport's internationals, for an introduction to sport and for improvement which, so the ebullient community programme manager Phil Davies says, 'will point them away from the negative plagues of modern-day society'. They also offer the Sport of Learning, a programme which uses Rodney Parade as an educational resource to allow everyone from infant schools to retired people to pursue various courses. The club are appointing an education officer to run the schemes.

An education officer? Community schemes? My dear old Newport? Are those of us who followed their fortunes through thick and thin going to be made to feel wanted? Probably the last time Newport reached out was when they used to send little packets of blue complimentary tickets to schools; we used to queue for the sports master to sign them, giving us our passport to see David Watkins and the rest.

Compare the two clubs, Newport and Newport, and only one year apart. Chalk and cheese, backward and forward, silence and buzz. Death and life. Dead lucky to have been given the chance, but at last shrewd enough to realise if they want to maintain their heady revival then they have to go out and claim it, earn it from businesses and players and media and the public. Newport are an example to any hidebound club. While tradition does not give you a future, it does give you something to awaken in yourself. Then, you take the future.

Nothing's settled yet, lads. You need concrete in the sand. Square one looms till you find it. But beating Cardiff in front of 10,000, with great international players rating it as one of their most memorable days? Playing Bath in Europe? It's a start. It's a start.

Some days in the old days, there was no game to watch. Newport were playing away and outside the range of your pockets. No way would we go to watch Cardiff unless it was certain that they'd lose and so we'd enjoy the game. Newport County? No thanks. The joke was that if the County were playing in your back garden you'd draw the curtains. Ah well, stay at home, then, or a kickabout in the park.

The final alternative was usually left unspoken because you'd be risking the derision of the lads. Cross Keys. Ostensibly a first-class team, the forgotten brother of Newport who lived over the fence. Earlier in the century they'd been a force, produced internationals and lived higher on the hog. But since they've become a shoestring operation, kept going by efforts of players who never really aspired to the very top level, by a band of good men to run it all. With the evil River Ebbw flowing behind it, Pandy Park's tiny stand could often feel like a freezer, and you'd wonder why the temperature just a few miles up the Ebbw valley from your starting point was six degrees lower. Now and again, they'd rise up and kick Newport's backside, and all the valley fans would come out and unite against the city slickers.

You'd affect a superior air if you went up there, talk among yourselves and watch from the corner of your eye. It was uncool to be too keen. The floodlights were so poor that you'd only know the players were out there from the shrill blast of the whistle. We'd make fun of the shambles as minutes before the kick-off players would run into the ground in their work overalls.

There was a charm. To one side of Pandy Park there is a mountain, and you could climb and climb and look down on two teams of ants, take in the valley and look down with a detachment at the little club and their small and warm band of followers, who'd opted never to leave and watch classy rugby but instead to graft and grind it out, stay with it. Players like Roger Beese and Derrick Morgan and others would choose to stay with the Keys, forgo their chances of top representative rugby, and be content with a spot as travelling reserve when Gwent played a touring side. (Rex Richards, their Wales prop of the 1950s, did leave for wider fame – as Tarzan in one of the Hollywood adaptations.) One day it was so bad that we astounded ourselves by leaving twenty minutes before the end as the Keys and Swansea stood around in a crabbing mass in the mud in the middle of the field.

Last season Cross Keys won Division One of the Welsh League and were promoted to the Premiership Division for season 2000–01. I recently caught a home game with Blackwood and, apart from an extra flash or two on the black and white jerseys, all seemed much the same. This was no mean feat because the division was a tough one, full of local derbies against the faded giants such as Newbridge and Pontypool. There were no really joyful celebrations at the end of the season, simply because the Keys were immediately installed as overwhelmingly odds-on to come straight back down. The nearest giants, Newport and Cardiff, both have millionaire owners; the Keys the same band of loyal local grafters.

One of them is Horace Jefferies, their press officer. The fact that to promote Cross Keys through the media might be considered a testing job has worried Horace not for one second in the decades he has held the post. Rugby heroes? Look no further. Their clubhouse is already excellent, warm with the raised drinks of the community. But they push on. Horace recently had a major press release to put out. As part of their celebrations of 100 years of membership of the Welsh Rugby Union, they are building an indoor training area which will be big enough for their senior team to train and for mini-rugby matches to be played. On the second floor of the building, which will cost a princely £150,000, they will install hospitality suites. Horace's release did not record whether Coke had been on the phone buying one up.

'We will soon celebrate 100 years as members of the WRU and Pandy Park will celebrate 100 years as a rugby ground. This is a wonderful project to mark the occasion. We know that as the professional game develops we will not get back with the likes of your Cardiffs and Newports and Swanseas. But we will make the best of what we have and this project will certainly ensure that Cross Keys will make their mark,'

Horace says. He wants Wales to use the indoor facility. 'Graham Henry has used an equestrian centre for indoor training. But if he wants to train here, he won't find any horse manure at Pandy Park.'

Nor anything bar the heartbeat of rugby in the Welsh valleys, and of rugby anywhere. It is a battle these days in the valley clubs. Alan Francis, one of Pontypool's leading lights, compares the old enthusiasm with the different world of today. 'It's a week-to-week struggle to get people to come and players to join. It's a struggle to get sponsors and the days when the clubs around here were producing players for Wales seem long ago.' There is no doubt that in many clubs the freedom to pay players was taken too literally, bore no relation whatsoever to projected income. There is no doubt that the valleys no longer ring so loudly with the sound of rugby. Pontypool, once a ferocious machine drawing thousands, called in the receiver in the summer of 2000.

Cross Keys proudly announced recently that they are in the black. They announced a few new signings for the Premiership campaign. They denounced, with an understandable anger, what was an alleged attempt by Peter Thomas, millionaire benefactor of Cardiff, to buy off Caerphilly and Cross Keys so that they would not take their place in the top division. The Keys' response, delivered with a fierce relish, was that Mr Thomas was running an operation at a huge loss and they were not, so they did not need his advice.

They may have been a last resort in the old days, but looking back it is remarkable how often we took it – and if we took the piss, then inside we were there partly because of a respect we never even knew we held. They'll still most likely be relegated at the end of season 2000–01, but they'll be back, their sponsors will be proudly raising their glasses in their manure-free hospitality suite and Horace Jefferies will be dreaming up new messages to bash out to the media and the locals. They'll soon be making their dispositions for a new century of rugby at Pandy Park, short of true class and millions but packed with indomitable hope. We should all be filled with that same optimism for them, if only for the dreadful things it says about new rugby if they should ever disappear. My money's on another hundred from Cross Keys, bless their little black-and-white artificial-fibre socks.

v) Hull Ionians, Cardiff HSOB and Esher – imperfect balance

Perhaps the most difficult act of balance lies down the leagues. You are allowed to pay. You sure as hell can't pay very much. But your rivals down the road are paying bigger. Do you join them and keep your players and your accounts flying on a wing and a prayer? Do you let them go, see the team crumble, drop down the leagues like a stone? Cruel choice, cruel world.

Hull Ionians see professionalism as a blessing, not a burden. The East Coasters are up to North Division One, canny and competitive. They reached the NPI final last year at Twickenham; 2000 of them had a day of days and they lost to Dunstablians by 10–6. They have no secretary but do have Paul Danby, a general manager. They pay their players but it is largely only in the form of a bonus when they win, plus a few with bursaries. Their status and their style suit them.

'Our players come from within the Yorkshire area,' Danby says, 'and I believe that they feel a strong affinity to the club. I think that it helps you cope in the professional era if you have that feeling.' Their costs are within bounds, perhaps balanced a little precariously, but you gain the sense of a club that has made the best out of the era rather than either harking back or complaining about it.

Danby is not in favour of the large-scale importing of foreign players – it is often forgotten that there are players available from overseas well below the standards of the most trumpeted arrivals at the top. 'We had a couple of Tongans at the start of last season but the team we played in the NPI final [Dunstablians] had around seven foreign players. I find that slightly absurd.'

Clive Westlake, secretary of Cardiff High School Old Boys, is far from alone in taking a sharply different view. His team, a successful nursery for the senior Cardiff club in the past, has slipped inexorably down the divisions and now play in the equivalent of Division Seven. 'Since professionalism, a great deal has changed in rugby. The number of players here has slowly dwindled and so has the support. The youngsters don't seem to want to play any more and, to be frank, I don't know what will happen to the club.' Bizarrely, CHSOB is the home club of Vernon Pugh, the man who drove the move to a professional sport.

Westlake has no enthusiasm for the new game. 'I'm an old stager. Quite frankly, I don't see why people should be paid to play the game and be paid to practise. Rugby used to be about people who enjoyed playing, who enjoyed each other's company. There was a camaraderie about drinking together. Now, half the players rush off straight after the game's finished. There's no loyalty to the club.'

It would be easy to suggest that perhaps Cardiff HSOB have simply got things wrong, to suggest that the thing to remember about eras is that they end, so all you can do is work to make a success of the next one. But that would be harsh. There are many people who, like Clive Westlake, have toiled against the tide and for whom the professional era has brought nothing but decline and confusion through no fault of the beavers inside.

It can be done. Esher, famous in their Hersham base south-west of London for being essentially a players' club, were merely a London Division One club when rugby went professional, but have enjoyed a marvellous run of success in recent seasons, gaining three promotions and are in what is effectively Division Three for 2000–01. Their domination of Jewson Division Two last season was complete. They have benefited from recruiting top-class players in a fervent rugby area, players who had neither the inclination nor, perhaps, quite the ability to sustain a professional career. Hugh McHardy, a popular and voluble Scot and the former Harlequins and Scotland B scrum-half, is in charge of coaching.

But their recent success has taken them out of their natural habitat of the past decades. Last season, on the way to promotion, they did pay their players something – chiefly, win bonuses. Now, on the verge of the professional elite, they are going to pay nothing. John Inverdale, perhaps slightly less well-known as a fervent rugby fan and Esher official than he is as one of the sporting world's most accomplished broadcasters, typifies what you would hope is a sense of realism now beginning to grip the game far beyond Hersham. 'It just doesn't make any sense for us to pay players. We tried it but we just haven't the income streams to sustain it. We announced for the new season that we would not pay, but we would take the players on a really good tour at the end of the season. Anything else would have come back to haunt us later.'

I asked Inverdale how many players decamped in the close season, miffed because the extra income had dried up. 'None,' he said. 'A few have moved on for other reasons, but I don't believe we will lose anyone because we aren't paying.' You hear of tiny clubs paying large amounts. You hear, occasionally, of plans to re-declare amateurism below a certain level – utterly unworkable plans. It is up to the game, to the clubs, to regulate themselves, to try to be patient so that the prospect of a glorious season does not cloud their sense of financial reality. In many cases, the financial stupidity will continue. It is a happy thought that at Esher, at least, the players recognise those realities, and that it is a prerequisite of the game's future at all levels that the gravy train slows to a stop. Before it crunches into the buffers.

It is also incumbent upon all those of us who tend to hang around with moneyed unions and millionaire benefactors to remember that the new era is not working for sizeable areas of the sport, not working at all. The balance is so difficult to find.

vi) Heroes

'Whatever happened to the heroes?', ran a song by The Stranglers. I know what's happened to one of the heroes. He's been chased from pillar to post for a debt that was not of his making, been threatened with having his possessions removed, including his prized grand piano. His crime was to serve selflessly the cause of Neath rugby club for more than thirty years as their secretary.

Allan Benjamin was one of the trustees of the club when it went bankrupt three years ago, when it was found to be too small and frail financially for the new era. For once, the natural fervency of the Gnoll men had diminished. The Welsh Rugby Union had to save the club and did, effectively buying it up to maintain it as a going concern. Benjamin was one of a group of people liable for the old club. The creditors, including former players, a brewery and other supply companies, have been avidly chasing total debts of more than £600,000. Neath were an unincorporated members' club and creditors were therefore free to go after any official or individual member. This allowed into the dispute, as one observer says, 'an unfortunate personal edge'. Both Benjamin and his wife have been in poor health and inundated with legal bills. One firm of solicitors threatened to send bailiffs to remove his cherished piano. As yet, there is no firm offer of help from the WRU and you might conclude that while they have no legal obligations, their moral obligation is overwhelming.

Steve Bale, my colleague from the *Express*, began working life on the *Neath Guardian* and knows Benjamin well. 'The whole affair makes me sick to the stomach,' Bale says. 'It's one of the worst things I've come across in the professional era.' By all accounts, Benjamin made a hard-working rise from a working-class background, became a revered headmaster at the tough Cymer Afan Comprehensive school in the Afan Valley. To marry that post with the demands of running Neath, unpaid, for more than three decades is dedication bordering on heroism. 'He is a true gentleman,' Bale says. For his reward to be harassment and pressure in retirement is appalling.

Let's hope that the other heroes had, or are still having, a more peaceful and fitting retirement. One of the aspects of the amateur era which has never and will never be in the slightest doubt is that the game at club level was founded squarely on amateur officials, and that the true heroes of rugby are those officials who toiled for nothing, performed administrative heroics, political heroics and acrobatics, got in exchange a few beers and a tie at the end. If there is one body of men who deserve testimonial matches then it is the likes of Allan Benjamin and his peers in rugby clubs both large and small all over the British Isles. It is also important to remember that while the old office of secretary has been swept away in favour of paid chief executives (often, the club immediately then descended into shambles), the heroes are still at their posts in scores of smaller clubs.

They are a mixed bunch in character, perhaps in parts a rum bunch. Perhaps they are either glad to be out, or are unsuited to the new era. Maybe they did run the show as a kind of crusty dictatorship. If that meant they bypassed the committee and its talent for strangling progress, then good on them. Older readers will reel off the names of hundreds, and for them not to appear in my list is only through forgetfulness or because they were from before my time.

But consider the service to Bristol of Tom Mahoney, military-moustached doyen, not unlike Groucho Marx in appearance, a little crusty with strangers but not a man inclined to allow them to be strangers for long. Or to Gloucester of the late Terry Tandy, more easy-going than his mate down the road at Bristol. He once spent ten minutes talking to me about newspapers and then, when I met him in the loo about five minutes later, congratulated me on my performance for Bridgend at Kingsholm that afternoon. John Nelson, late father of my friend Paul, at Cardiff. Bill Everson and Nick Carter at Newport. One evening after watching a Newport match I ran into Nick in the stands. He'd heard I'd played decently that day in a schools' match against Mark McJennett, a likely forward who'd become famous in the local schools loop. 'You know where to come,' he said gravely to me. Short of being invited into bed by the blonde detective in *NYPD Blue*, it was the most arresting summons I had ever had, and a shame that I'd played so far above true form that day.

Or what of the late Durbar Laurie, outer gruffness just a front, a secretary of Bridgend for four decades. We once honoured him at the Rugby Union Writers' Club dinner. It isn't an abstemious bash but you think we'd remember who we'd honoured before. Wouldn't you? Durbar said a few well-chosen words on the subject of how honoured he was to receive the tankard and how well it would sit next to the identical one we'd given him four years previously. He wrote the centenary book on Bridgend, which was as fine, meticulous and warm as Durbar himself. Celebrate your own heroes while I celebrate a few of mine. Maybe, like dinosaurs, their time had come. But there are times when you'd give a cold pasty and a flat beer, their traditional reward, for some of the dedication and organisation they brought. No wonder someone who knows him well feels 'sick to the stomach' at Benjamin's fate.

They kept at it, long into the winter nights, corresponding and organising and fussing and worrying. Although it does say an awful lot for the hold that rugby clubs of any sort can have on people. Tell me now that they are not institutions with a heartbeat. It is to be profoundly hoped that people still will love clubs, at any level, enough to be selfless about them long into the future.

What drove them on? Dedication? A sense of duty and propriety? The feeling that they wanted a gang of young lads to go out and represent the club with honour and decent admin back-up? It could be all of these things and, taking a wild stab at the motivation of the old buggers, I'd guess at another incentive. Pure, irrational, love.

CHAPTER ELEVEN

Melbourne – Indoors

Pitfalls of the professional era, and rugby losing balance

i) Easy life for Rod Macqueen and the national coaches

In early July 2000, just before the Tri-Nations of 2000 began, Australia and South Africa played an extra Test, in Melbourne. It was dubbed the Nelson Mandela match, far less a tribute to arguably the greatest man that civilisation has ever produced than a desperate excuse to breathe life into a wholly superfluous exercise and not even officials of the Australian Rugby Union appeared to demur when one of the Australian writers dubbed the affair a 'cash cow'. No doubt Mandela was overwhelmed at this new diamond in his life's crown. About as overwhelmed as he must have been when, with about ten years of his incarceration remaining, the politically correct and politically ludicrous city council in Leicester re-named a perfectly ordinary piece of dog-mess meadow where the Tigers played a few junior games Nelson Mandela Park.

There was something remarkable about the match, however. It was to be played indoors. The Colonial Stadium, Melbourne had enjoyed a rather chequered infancy, with bits of its sliding roof crashing to the ground and its playing surface churning up like a cow pasture. But it was here, perhaps at the personal behest of Nelson Mandela (and then again, perhaps not), that the ARU decided to stage the match.

The subsequent outpourings in the days before the match unquestionably represented the most grim and depressing reflection of modern day rugby I can imagine. It was also in many ways the most despairing low point of my fourteen years (oh, all right, twenty-four years) covering the brilliant sport we used to know and love as rugby. Not just because of what was said but because of the violation of rugby which the views represented and, therefore, the indication of the way in which some influential people wish to push the game – into a coffin.

Listen to Rod Macqueen, the coach of Australia, defend the playing of a serious rugby match indoors, under a closed roof. And shudder as he tears up rugby in two Aussie hands and in a few Aussie sentences. 'It makes the coach's job easier,' he said. 'There is no rain or mud and you see good, open football.' No. Let him finish. We can remind him another time that the most heart-stirring match of 2000, the most shockingly surprising, was that between Scotland and England at Murrayfield and was played on a storm-lashed afternoon mitigating against flow – but not against a magnificent occasion. But let him finish.

'The roof means that we don't have some of the uncertainties you have in other Tests, when you're worrying about the weather, and if there's going to be a wind factor, and if there going to be a change in the weather half-way through the game.'

Rugby is an outdoor sport. Full stop. It was never meant to be anything else. What it was never, ever, in a million years, meant to be was predictable. Easy to coach. If it was ever, in a million years, meant to be predictable, then why on earth did it ever saddle itself with the capricious, wicked leather-egg thing? Snooker? Now there's an indoor game. A game full of precision and exact angles and perfect run of the balls. I tell you what rugby it not. It isn't snooker.

Is it not overwhelmingly one of rugby's arts to adapt to weather? Is it not one of rugby's unpredictabilities? Is it not the true test of the excellence of a rugby team that they should adapt to all the myriad changing circumstances of match and margin, pitch and weather, on the hoof? England revealed themselves short of greatness as a rugby team in the 2000 Six Nations when they cruised easily through on dry pitches and then failed the test of adaptability on a wet Edinburgh afternoon. So they would have won in an indoor rugby match. So what?

Macqueen had whined and griped in the week before the World Cup final because the authorities at the Millennium Stadium refused to have the roof shut for the match. They shut it in the days and hours before the game. They opened it only at kick-off time, when it wasn't even raining. But Macqueen wanted it shut throughout. Before the Nelson Mandela non-event, Macqueen unctuously offered to send a video of the match to the Welsh Rugby Union so that they would know 'how to use the roof of the Millennium Stadium a little better next time'. And fair enough. Send them your video, Rod. I'll ask them to send you one in return – of a real rugby match.

Daniel Herbert, the Australia centre, chirruped into the chorus. He said that to keep the roof closed would have 'added to the spectacle and grown the game'. Lessons on growing the game would be better directed to the ARU, who despite a massive campaign, could find only 30,000 Melbourne suckers to watch a non-rugby match, than to the Welsh

Rugby Union, who can fill a 72,500 capacity stadium six times per year. The great bowl stadiums these days already keep out seventy per cent of the weather. What else do they want?

If you could ignore the thoroughly bogus nature of proceedings and were enamoured of the endless pap continuity of events, then the match was up your street. It ended in a win for Australia by 44–23, the kind of scoreline beloved by people who market rugby these days, especially those people brought in from other sports who assume that vast barrages of scoring are the be-all and end-all of a rattling good time. One day, a statistician will find a way of calculating exactly how many people leave their seat for a hot dog or a beer while the match is still going on, and how many are actually taking much interests in proceedings. Still, at least the citizens of Melbourne who did turn up could leave their coats at home. Let's not knock such epoch-making benefits.

So playing indoors makes it easier for a coach? It begs the question as to why anyone should expect the job of a national rugby coach to be easy, but it also begs the question as to how much easier Macqueen would like it to be. Compare his lot with that of a predecessor in the job from only a decade ago. Macqueen, instead of doing the whole thing himself, is now merely overseeing a mighty raft of backroom staff attending to every department of the team.

He has his players together for month after month, and they are contracted to do what he says, whereas in only the recent past they could tell him, if they wished, to stuff it. He is part of an Australian system which, by a complete accident of geography and a complete accident of structure, is made for the development of a national team. Rugby in Britain is far more vibrant, multi-faceted, interesting, commercially successful, exotic, outgoing, sociable and unpompous than rugby in Australia but nothing like as well set up for the bettering of the national teams.

More yet. The video age has given Macqueen a slow-mo insight into every team and individual he meets; he no longer even has to get his selection right because he can bring on hordes of alternatives under rugby's ludicrous replacement laws. He can even bring on people outside rugby's ludicrous replacements laws – either that, or Jim Williams, the back-row man who left the field against New Zealand in Wellington in August and returned around half an hour later, really was having attention all that time in the blood-bin. And kangaroos fly.

Rugby is already so numbingly predictable that we already know who will win the ball at the line-out, the scrum, and in the pathetic little huddles that pass, these days, for mauls and rucks. Do none of these fine

Aussies realise that predictable sport is the most boring sport of all?

More even yet. He can even get his tactics wrong because at half-time, he now gets ten minutes for another chance to address his troops, a luxury denied to his predecessors. He can send on messages, new tactics, bollockings, orders, with any number of water-carriers, physios and miked-up doctors. No doubt he'd love to install a receiver in the headguard of Steve Larkham so he can call the action play by play. Makes it easier for the coach? How much easier, how many more advantages, does Macqueen want? Poor Bob Dwyer, the man who really put Australia on the rugby map, the man who really grasps the wider picture, had to hack out his coaching tenure mostly on his own, living on his wits.

But here's a funny thing about Macqueen, indoor rugby or not. He might well be one of the better coaches around at the moment. His team which won the World Cup were no great shakes, because they had only second division standards to better. But since that tournament, Australia have improved out of sight. In the 2000 Tri-Nations, they showed a happy new facility to dispense with the endless sideways recycling drift of rugby and attack up the middle, finding space with power of running but also with skills of runners either side acting in concert with the ball carrier. By the end of the Tri-Nations they were a better team by around eighteen points than they were at the World Cup.

It suggests that Macqueen is indeed one of the better coaches around. Is it not a better test of Macqueen's coaching that his team should be exposed to, whisper it very quietly (as if it was a mass murderer), unpredictability? Evidence suggests that if he trusted himself to live on his wits, rather than demand all kinds of advantages that lesser coaches could then also enjoy, he might come out even further ahead. Good luck to him if he does, but let us never again hear serious rugby people in senior positions spouting garbage about taking the unpredictability out of rugby, taking the weather out of rugby. Taking rugby out of rugby. It makes you realise why Rolf Harris stayed in England. Out in his homeland, he's wasted. Wasted.

Herbert pointed out after the non-rugby Test that it had been a huge advantage because of 'the lack of dew on the ball'. God, a narrow escape. How are today's highly paid stars expected to function with dew on the ball, even brilliant centres like Herbert? 'Both teams seemed to enjoy throwing caution to the wind,' he said. Now what wind would that be, Daniel?

Rugby is now, effectively, run by the leading national team coaches. Their influence is all-pervasive. They are given the chief role in law-making, even though they will always tend to pass laws for the good of the strengths of their own team rather than for the good of rugby. Do not expect any movement towards genuine forward confrontation returning to the game, for example, because none of the three Tri-Nations teams has a single tight forward – John Eales apart, and now that Richard Harry has retired – worth a light compared to their illustrious past.

They run, and ruin, the timetable, dispensing with proper rugby tours to worship at their altar of Test matches. The 2000 Wallaby tour of the United Kingdom contains only international matches, no midweek epics so that the British public can see the Wallabies play locally, maybe even get to know them and like them. Just the indigestion and boring familiarity of the sterile, Tests-only fixture list.

And international rugby is throttling the game. Still, there is no move to cut down the number of international matches that are played, so no move to preserve the essential health of the goose that lays rugby's golden eggs. Still, so much of domestic rugby in the major countries is meant to be in thrall to the supposed needs of the national coach and the national side.

Take Scotland. There, they have shoved away, disenfranchised and disillusioned a whole paying public, ham-fistedly jacking up the two Super-Districts teams, Edinburgh Reivers and Glasgow Caledonians, rather than allowing their wonderful traditional strengths to breathe. To focus only on your international team is to lose your rugby heart and soul, and therefore, to lose your national team. Last season I went to the Scottish Borders, the heartland, the world's most fertile growing territory, bar absolutely none, for international rugby players. You should try it. Go and find the true Borders greats, players and officials and spectators, and ask them if they are going to watch Edinburgh Reivers' next match. I did. They aren't.

And why should the game be so much in thrall to these coaches, and their unions? Take the example of England and Wales. At present, the technical accomplishment in both countries resides among the rugby clubs. Why shouldn't the clubs be allowed to proceed with producing a thriving domestic game and a conveyer belt of players for national duty? What is it in the knowledge, recent achievements (lack of) and influence of the national unions which causes them to believe themselves better qualified than the clubs and so able to demand power over the clubs?

It is not that the national coaches are ogres, or malevolent to the greater good of the game. They are probably decent guys, all of them. I can speak for Woodward, Mallett, Henry, McGeechan and, by reputation, Macqueen. They seem to be good blokes. It isn't just that their influence has become too all-pervasive. It is just that the greater good of the game is not, strictly speaking, their field, just the hacking-out of the next Test victory. The two are often incompatible. Praise be, that Clive Woodward should be brave enough to state, at the end of his successful tour to South Africa, that he originally had his attitudes wrong, that he now believed in encouragement of England's clubs, and their burgeoning academies, to thrive and to do his work without a kind of Kremlin-like central control.

It is time for the fever of national coaches to be cooled, for their influence to be restricted simply to their national task in hand, for spokesmen to raise their voices for a less narrow goal. It is time for other voices to be raised in the fields of laws and scheduling and development and touring. It is time to shut big traps, not sliding roofs. You shut your roof, Rod. And we'll draw the curtains.

ii) Wapping – popular front for real rugby

Well, it wasn't often that Wapping was the centre of the rugby world last season. In fact, it was never the centre of the rugby world last season. Nor in any previous season. In fact, it isn't the centre of anything. Unless you count the fact that it was the base for a couple of rugby fans who'd seen enough – or, to be precise, not enough.

Our gang – well, my colleague Nick Cain and myself – were mulling over the previous Saturday's match, when England defeated Wales at Twickenham in early March 2000. It was a fine win for England but it was also one of the least gladiatorial, least crunching rugby matches I had ever seen. The primary phases of rugby were already long established in a hateful phase where the scrum had been depowered and the line-out reduced to a farce by the well-worded charter to make inferior line-out teams win a stream of possession (called the laws relating to lifting). The traditional confrontational nature of forward play had been further diminished by the nonsensical use-it or lose-it laws passed in the early 1990s, which, although later partially repealed, took forwards away from forward play and allowed them to hang around in midfield.

In England's two home games in the 2000 Championship against Ireland and Wales, the forward confrontation had declined so far as to be almost unopposed. No fault of England, as teams are victims of the laws, their effect, their development and the way they impinge on every coach's imperative to use them to the best advantage of his team. But England's game, and those of many other teams, were with every moment looking more like rugby league and less like the rugby we know and love.

We decided to expose the new pansy rugby in an article in the *Sunday Times*, and one night, driven by specially selected lorry drivers out of Wapping (specially selected because it was their shift), the revelations sped throughout the game.

Sorry for the repetition if you memorised it word for word from the paper at the time. But here goes:

Rugby is now a game for wimps. From the ludicrous spectacle of unopposed line outs to the shameful absence of grinding confrontation, it has renounced that which made it great.

The chaps laid on their best and most apposite heading. 'GOING SOFT', it said.

Rucking has never been done better – with more quick ball produced with such a scientific brutality and, frankly, more danger to life and limb to those killing the ball on the floor – than by the Otago provincial team in the 1960s. Victor Cavanagh, the foremost professor of rucking, refined the phase so that at least seven forwards, bound and bent low with beautiful body-positions, would thunder over the top of the ball to leave perfect second-phase possession for the scrum-half.

It was a wonderful ball with which to attack, because the opposition pack had been driven backwards and were temporarily out of the game. New Zealand were masters of the ruck and usually gave themselves space in which to attack after only two phases of play. Done well, rucking is one of the most compelling sights in the game. 'A bit like being rampaged on by multi-Adidas-ed centipede,' says Peter FitzSimons, the former Australia lock and one of rugby's hard men. Remember them?

There was something vaguely resembling a ruck in the recent match between England and Ireland at Twickenham, as long as you believe that a striped domestic cat resembles a tiger. After sixty-four minutes of play, Mike Catt of England brought off a tackle and four Irish players converged, scraped around, fought among themselves for a few seconds and won the ball. There was not one England player involved in the ruck. The unopposed ruck is with us, and another nail is driven into the coffin of true forward confrontation. With no England players committed, all fifteen were lined up ready to snuff out the next Irish attack.

It is not a criticism of England, who are playing the new laws and new rhythm of rugby, and who have talented players wide out, but the

England–Ireland Six Nations match was one of the softest Tests ever played – until the next one, because rugby is fast retreating from its roots and ethos. The elements of thunder and confrontation are disappearing without trace. The element of attrition has disappeared too, with hordes of fresh players reinforcing inferior teams that deserve to be picked off in the final quarter. The one-on-one confrontations, where hard men would rigorously search for flaws in the technique and character of their opposite numbers, is another aspect of the game confined to the past.

There is much talk these days of the athleticism and commitment of the top players. But it is a lung-bursting, running commitment. It is not an examination of heart and soul. Today's players have more skills, but they have fewer dimensions.

As the mountainous French bruiser of the 1970s and 1980s Gerard Cholley says with deep regret: 'There is no fear in rugby any more.' For me, the most compelling sporting events I have ever witnessed were rugby internationals in the Parc des Princes in Paris. They were the supreme physical examination available in any sport, any time. Even a player as fierce as Mike Burton, one of Cholley's old adversaries, used to offer up a prayer at the end of the game, for mere survival.

When you left the stadium, you found the thunder of the confrontation reverberating in your stomach and your soul, long into the evening. These days, to be frank, you feel like popping off and having a beer and talking about something else.

For a start, from where has rugby's new rhythm come? No mystery. In 1992 the International Rugby Board brought in the appalling ruck/maul turnover law. Previously, you had to commit your forwards to these phases because if they ended without the ball emerging, the team going forward was given possession. It was a fundamental dynamic of the whole sport.

The new law, disastrously, gave the next scrum to the team which had not taken in the ball. At a stroke, you found that you no longer had to commit forwards, but could merely string them out in a long line across the field.

So much of rugby union these days – and this is increasingly the case – is like two bad rugby league teams having an off-day, and doing so without pace or devil. To tie in all those massed ranks of fringes you have to bash-bash your way upfield, with no great pace or conviction, and hope that after recycling the ball about twenty times, you might find some space in which to work. While teams dutifully trot through these phases, people in the crowd tend to chat among themselves. One of the most wounding aspects of the new feebleness in rugby is the catastrophic decline in crowd noise and atmosphere.

And the marvellous element of confrontation is lost not only from full-scale rucks. Because of the sanitisation of the scrum, even convincingly superior scrummages are not allowed to stick it to the opposition and drain the life from their legs. The line-out is well established as the most ludicrous sight on any sporting field, as inferior jumpers are hoisted way above people who deserve to win the ball. But the essential blast of rugby has also declined because of the establishment of the nanny state in the game, which has seen the crack-down on foul play go to ridiculous lengths.

What should rugby really be looking for? A few weeks ago another law was passed taking power from the scrum. It is now by law impossible for teams to drive, and then restart the drive if they are held. This allows all kinds of inadequate scrummaging teams to escape scot-free. When the batch of laws including this measure was announced, there was a reaction from Chris White, one of the best referees in the game. He was clearly taken in by rugby's obsession that continuity of play should be placed above all else. 'The new laws will speed up the game,' he said. 'Do people really want the ball to remain on the same spot on the field in a succession of scrums?' White assumed he was asking a rhetorical question, but the answer as far as I am concerned is a resounding yes.

The truth is that rugby's richest and most compelling moments often come during those heaving, seething goal-line stands, with four or five or six scrums in succession. This is unquestionably when crowd-noise is at its highest, when excitement as the home team edges forward by a few inches reaches a crescendo. For me and many others, one of the fondest memories of last year's World Cup was the heroic stand mounted by Fiji against France. It was almost unbearably exciting and the ball never moved more than one yard in any direction for around ten minutes. The crowd were beside themselves. Compare that with the negligible reaction as the teams in this year's Six Nations have recycled the ball, bashing it up left, right and centre to no apparent effect. It's rubbish, it's interminable and it is closer to basketball than it is to rugby as we once knew it.

So, drastically little confrontation, fewer blasting runs, fewer searching questions asked and a bastardisation of rugby's rhythm. The answer is not to simply repeal some of the laws which have landed rugby in this bog. The answer is to realise that rugby is a sport apart, that if you like your basketball and your rugby league with the ball endlessly in play, then you are welcome to it. But if you like true rugby, then you love it in all its arcane forms, in all its explosive forms and in all its faster forms. You have only to consider the spread of rugby union relative to the spread of rugby league to conclude that perhaps continuity of action is not after all what the world of sport really wishes for.

There was one item of good news last week. The former All Black captain David Kirk wrote an article heralding some major forward confrontations in the early rounds of the Super-12 tournament. But since it was the Super-12 that sent rugby off in its wimpish state, it is still very much in the red to the rest of the game.

The performance of the England hooker Phil Greening against Wales last weekend justifiably took many plaudits. He was popping up in the centre as often as the centres. No blame to Greening, because all he can do is play the rugby of the era. But the truth is that hundreds of players do it better than Phil. He is a hooker guesting in the position and not remotely as good as a specialist centre.

It is time to return to specialisation. It is time to restart rugby's engine – not to return to the days of the fat boys but to commit forwards to a newly empowered forward battle, and to free the field for the people who are better in space. It is time to stop throwing up hands in horror if rugby occasionally wears a snarling expression. It is time for rugby to stop this utter betrayal of itself. Rugby, is currently as hard as melting butter.

Talk about striking a chord. We received nearly 300 e-mails within three days of publication, a forest of faxes and phone calls and letters. At the time of writing, four months after the article and some back-up panels appeared, I am still replying to people in all parts of the world. Mike Teague, Iron Mike, was scathing. 'The game I used to play has gone. In certain phases the game seems easier, particularly in the tight forward play. It's all a bit robotic. Take the Ireland game at Twickenham this season [1999–2000]. We won by fifty points but ... there was no atmosphere at Twickenham, no nip-and-tuck, no edge, no "Swing Low". It's sad when the atmosphere is so flat. Now it's almost like "And now it's try-time" every five minutes.' Willie-John McBride was another to respond to the end of confrontation. 'The aggression has gone. People talk about big hits but they've all got body armour. The line-out has gone because there is no competition between jumpers. There is something wrong with the scrum when you are ninety-nine per cent certain of winning the ball.'

And Charlie Faulkner, the left-hand side of the Pontypool front row and no mean forward coach, said of the end of the scrum confrontations: 'The new law about the wheeling scrum was introduced, so they say, because no one wants to watch five scrums in a row. Rubbish. A goal-line stand of five five-metre scrums is one of the most compelling sights in rugby.'

We had to follow up the article a week later, together with an article by Lee Smith, then the laws supremo of the IRB who had at least tried to maintain a modicum of forward-clash in rugby. He was not as pessimistic as we were but, to his credit, nor did he deny that there was massive disquiet in IRB circles that the game was moving far too far away from its roots. Smith has been a marvellous influence on the game since his arrival as game development manager and it will be a disaster of seismic proportions should he leave the IRB. In his response, he expressed relief that the debate was being taken up generally in the game because of his view that the roost was being ruled by people who had a vested interest in a narrow area. 'It is better that the wider views of the game are being discussed rather than the parochial interest of one coach or team.' This is an absolutely vital point and one which the game ignores at its peril. For too long, leading national coaches had no say in law-making, which was a nonsense. But as with so many things in modern-day rugby, the pendulum has swung dramatically too far.

A raft of law changes introduced early in 2000 sprang almost entirely from an ad hoc gathering of the top coaches. These are men under so much pressure that all they are going to do is press for laws which either emphasise the strengths or mask the weaknesses of their own team at the exact time of the meeting. Rugby needs a more global view. It needs to wrest itself from the grip of the (understandably) self-serving. 'I fully accept,' Smith concluded, 'that we have to ensure that the essential principles are not eroded.'

The communications we received were in agreement by a ratio of roughly eight to one. Those who took us to task did so on the basis that we were calling for a return to the old days of muddy forward slogs and 6–3 scorelines. In fact, we were calling for a return to the days when forwards made space for backs, instead of closing that space down.

The truth of the matter is obvious. As the professional era dawned the game realised it had to sell itself as never before. It jumped from the high board immediately by instituting the Super-12 as an event with endless action, torrents and tries and (as they admitted themselves by their u-turns of later seasons) left an after-taste that lingered for milliseconds. You watched, you clapped and, un-moved in the heart of your rugby soul, you went home.

The evidence of 1999–2000, of the uncontested phases, of the drive above all to stop people defending, to aid recycling, was that the game was still suffering from the same total misapprehension – that fast-moving matches with one team retaining the ball were the best. They are not. Goal-line stands create crowd noise like nothing else in the game. So do tight finishes, low-scoring and lung-bursting confrontations. When the game accepted massive cheques from News Corporation in the southern hemisphere and News International up here, we were all anxious that television moguls and producers would push us into blind alleys chasing false concepts of entertainment. They didn't have to. We rushed down those alleys without being asked.

The first and only lesson that rugby needs to learn about its pursuit of box-office is that to pursue the concept of rugby as an entertainment is to make the game less entertaining. The most memorable matches of 2000 – the Heineken European final, the Calcutta Cup, the Tri-Nations extravaganza between Australia and New Zealand, were great matches because they had movement but also light and shade, close-quarter battling and hard-hitting power-driving. And this because it was usually the backs who were given the ball in space. Not the other lot.

I was delighted that we had touched a nerve in rugby. We were spoiled for choice as we tried to choose extracts from passionate letters from all points, bemoaning what rugby had often become. I was even more delighted to hear, at the IRB's press conference in April 2000, that not only Lee Smith but also Steve Griffiths, referees' controller, and none other than Syd Millar, the game's premier laws grandee and grey eminence of play, broadly agreed. I detected the first signs of a move to reverse the sorriest of recent trends. Good on you, chaps.

Don't chase entertainment. Rugby must have been entertaining already because if it was not, no one would want to play it or ref it or watch it in some burgeoning numbers, nor pay so many millions to screen it. The less we see of forwards in the next decade, the more we should applaud them.

We are not alone, among newspapers, not by a long chalk. The thunder of the biggest gun of the *Guardian* was even heard in support, and the mighty Frank Keating took aim. And destroyed the target. 'There goes rugby in a witless search for empty spectacle,' he said. 'Any day now, rugby is going to wake up and realise that it is no more than a blood brother to the weird and singularly unwonderful game of basketball, where two or three scores a minute are chalked up in metronomic, empty, end-to-end non-significance.' Keating lamented the 'headlong search for spectacle' and the 'casting off of [rugby's] basic and founding fundamentals in its five years of professionalism'.

He was discussing reaction to the astonishing Australia–New Zealand Tri-Nations match at Stadium Australia, a surging epic of thrills and spills. He took slight issue with me for calling it the 'greatest ever' on the grounds that these days, great games are judged on how big the hatful of tries and how long the ball is in play, and other non sequiturs to true rugby appeal. Actually, though I took Frank's point, I did think that the Sydney feast was a genuine diamond, because both teams appeared to have taken the game out of its dire, recycling rhythm and showed genuine ability to take the ball forward and break the defensive lines – although I have to admit that it was rugby in Australia in 2000, more so than in any other part of the world, where the importance of the forward battle was most diminished, so that teams would merely make scores without the need to win consistent possession, to wear down the opposing defences.

However, Keating's core philosophy, his core anger as he blasted the stupid pursuit of the false gods of thrill, was marvellous.

The truth is that rugby survives as a pro activity despite the prophets of doom. The truth is that players are wonderfully dedicated and fit and intent. The disaster, the biggest disaster of the era, is that the age-old framework and wondrous rhythm of the game has shattered. The chase of entertainment has shattered it.

So the world did not change because of anything that came out of Wapping. The best we did was put something urgent near the top of some agendas. However, when the game re-establishes itself as a proper contact sport, never fear. We'll still claim all the credit.

iii) Cloud-cuckoo-land: the unstoppable rise of the rugby guru

Guru. This is what the *Collins English Dictionary* says. '*n. often derogatory*; leader or chief theoretician of a movement.' It doesn't say that they have infested rugby, but my dictionary was printed in 1996, and they'd hardly started to then. At this moment, the new edition will be chiselling out an enhanced definition of the word. Something like: 'a person who turns up claiming almost mystically deep knowledge of something we all thought was simple, and who requests big wedge for passing on these inner secrets'.

The key unit in rugby at present is the international or professional club management team – there is nothing so important, so agenda-setting.

And so paranoid. Many people in many fields – medical and quasi-medical, conditioning, psychological, motivational, or a technical specialist, a statistical analyst of such depth that he'll tell you how often your men sneeze during each half, or a transparent loony masquerading in any of the aforementioned fields – have set out to obtain a position in the management set-up of big rugby teams around the world.

In other sports they have the same phenomenon, in individual sports it's called an entourage, and it reaches its spectacular height with the clear evidence in major boxing promotions that around 100 people have generally convinced the champ that they are indispensable. Sometimes it all grieves me, because the more of a player's time you fill with babbling experts the less he becomes used to thinking for himself.

The great Australian golfer Peter Thomson complained a few years ago about the number of 'fringe-dwellers' who'd arrived on the scene and scoffed at the so-called Team Norman entourage of Greg Norman, who needed a 737 just to cart them all to the tournaments. 'I'm sorry to see somebody using someone else's brain,' Thomson said.

Considering that coaches panic at the idea that someone else might be stealing the tiniest march (Nick Mallett's got a specialist testicle-squeezer in his team; we've got to get one) or that they should be shown not to be up with the latest trends, then the fringe-dweller's path to a paid post is often an easy one. And this is quite apart from the fact that some of the specialists pressing themselves on the game are direct from Cloud-cuckoo-land.

The whole question as to whether they are any good and whether they earn their money rests on another question. Did David Leadbetter make Nick Faldo, or did Nick Faldo make David Leadbetter? Faldo went to Leadbetter, a reasonably well-known sultan of the golf swing, when he became obsessed with the idea that his swing would not survive the pressure of the big finishes in which he expected to be involved during his career. Leadbetter came in, Faldo began to work with him with a grinding concentration. Effectively, while the swing was re-cast, he lost two years of his golfing life. Golf writers became cringingly bored with his summary after any round that had gone wrong by as much as one shot – 'I'm off to do some work with Lead.' But Faldo began to win majors and currently has six. That, almost certainly, is that. Leadbetter is now gone, dismissed in a letter by the man whom he served, but that is another story.

What was the root of his triumph? In *Beyond the Fairways* by David and Patricia Davies, the authors ask whether Faldo's success is 'due to the constant care he got from Leadbetter, or is it a consequence of natural talent allied to immense hard work'. Other golfing teachers claim that Faldo's swing has hardly changed from that of his younger days. Leadbetter seems certainly to have changed – he has a string of golf academies, has produced enough books and videos to sink a medium-sized island (Britain, say). It seems to me, while not pronouncing in any way on the mysteries of the golf swing, that Leadbetter's *raison d'être* lay in isolating around 2,000 moving parts in the golf swing, body and club, and thereby giving himself an unlimited number of things to teach. Sometimes, you just wanted to tell Faldo to go out and swing and hit the bloody ball. Sometimes, it appears to be the case that rugby gurus – kicking gurus and scrummaging gurus and throw-in gurus and the rest – have a vested interest in proving to their charges that an essentially simple, even rhythmic activity is in fact a large number of linked jerks which, taken together, give the impression of being smooth.

All right, all right. You just cannot take anything away from the contribution of someone like Phil Larder, guru of defence and allied trades to the England squad. I have never seen a home-country rugby team defend anything like as well as did England on their two-Test tour of South Africa in June 2000. They conceded one try, and that only because that video referee was obviously watching the cowboy film on the other channel when they came over to him. Larder's success may, or indeed may not, be a proper excuse for the sudden urge in the game to regard anyone with any association with rugby league as the finest defensive guru to emerge since the architect of Hadrian's Wall, usually without any proof. Ellery Hanley is at Bristol, Cardiff's pre-season build-up involved a visit to a rugby league club, and if I were anyone from Alex Murphy to Andrew Farrell I'd stand by for a whole new career (and read up on defence).

Kickers also swear by (and at, by all accounts) Dave Alred, England's guru of the boot, who had a rather in-and-out early career with England before being drafted by the 1997 Lions. While I would imagine that some natural kickers would be better off being left to swing smoothly and in peace, he has quite obviously done a good job with others, even manufactured kickers from a standing start, which is a decent feat.

I'm still suspicious of the breed, however. The stats gurus can be fascinating. The former international referee Corris Thomas has produced some telling stuff, not least that referees sometimes give penalties against teams not because they have infringed but because they are leading the match. There was also a spiteful flying-handbags spat between two sets of stats men recently. After the second Test between New Zealand and Scotland in Auckland in June 2000, the statisticians working for Sky

Television in New Zealand revealed that despite their heavy victory, New Zealand had won only thirty per cent of possession and Scotland the other seventy per cent. It was a perfectly – believable statistic, because instances of losing teams recycling the ball more than three times as often as the winners are no longer rare.

But the official All Blacks statisticians got all stroppy and stamped their feet, the poor dears. George Serrallach and a team of four from Massey University (bet they're all swots with glasses and white coats) took until the Tuesday to complete their own figures. George the Fact claimed that the stats on television were 'totally incorrect'.

'It's not true,' he said. 'New Zealand touched the ball eight per cent more times than Scotland, so the statistics the public get are rubbish. They have no meaning.' Serrallach claims his system is accurate to 0.01 per cent. I trust he's working on that final 100th of a percentage point, the fly devil. His analysis revealed that the time in possession was virtually even 49.4 per cent to the All Blacks, 50.6 per cent to Scotland. The territory was 43.8 per cent to New Zealand, 56.2 to Scotland. Serrallach told a news agency that 'the only effective way to analyse a match is to do it frame by frame, as was done at the Institute of Rugby'. How marvellous. Gurus gone mad? Yes. Anyway, I haven't heard that either team wants to replay the match.

It is a tribute to the pull of rugby and the money available for back-room staff (even if some of it is fool's gold) that someone should come up from as far afield as Australia to pitch for a place in a back-up team. Last year *Rugby World* magazine featured a gun for hire in Mark Zanotti, formerly a top Aussie Rules player, who was in London, touting. He had, so Chris Jones wrote, 'travelled across the equator armed with kicking and catching skills he believes could provide an edge at the World Cup'. It immediately made you suspicious that if this was so, then why had Australia not snapped him up?

His philosophy was substantially based on the idea that an end-over-end kick as used in Aussie Rules was more effective that the torpedo kick. He reckoned that there were about twelve key kicking tips which he could pass on. He got that completely wrong. He had no chance of extended employment unless he promised around 2000 kicking tips. He was betraying the fact that sometimes 'hoof it and think about it after' is every bit as effective as 'think about it, *guru* it, and kick it to the sounds of hordes of moving parts merrily clanking in your brain'.

Recently, Lewine Mair, one of the most telling of golf writers, discussed a revival in Faldo's form. Faldo had consulted Kjell Enghager, a Swedish golf psychologist. The effect was interesting. 'From the start,' Mair wrote, 'he saw that his student [Faldo] was hopelessly embedded in thoughts and theories. He stopped all the double-checking at address and in doing so, cut Faldo's pre-shot routine in half. At the same time, he started to peel away long years of negative thinking.' She spoke of Faldo as a man 'emerged from the wrapping'. There are more than a few black marks there for gurus. Though it took a guru to find that out, I suppose.

I'm going to put myself up to a rugby team as a media guide. Indispensable. Take the keyboard. Now there's something with 121 moving parts. I've just counted.

iv) Dublin – death to the invading hordes of replacements

How many matches do you see these days that don't so much come to a conclusion as peter out? End as an unholy shambles so that you're glad when the ref blows up? Until quite recently, you lived through the first hour drooling for the last quarter. This was that period of the match, you see, when your team made its killing. If it was superior at all points and especially if it had more powerful forwards, this was the time when you'd have that deliciously satisfying sensation of seeing the other lot go, crumble, leave gaps for your brave lads to cruise through. And that was so stunningly, perfectly right. You'd worn them down, you'd sapped them. Then you reaped your reward.

Two things make today's climaxes not worth waiting for. First, tight-forward play is now so emasculated that the wearing-down process is more difficult to achieve – and I am considering putting up my auntie as a forward guru. Second, and in the most pathetic, unwanted and crass visitation of the professional era, you can take nearly half your team off and send on a fresh lot. There is no earthly point in wearing a team down. There is hardly any point in bettering your opposite number. There is no dividend for being superior for the first hour.

You've stuffed me for sixty-five minutes. Why do I deserve to bring on a fresh man?

In top matches you can bring on up to seven replacements. It used to be six but at a seminar of the top coaches last year, John Hart of New Zealand wanted seven. Why not thirty-odd, Harty? Give them ten minutes each. You wouldn't even have to get them doing endurance training. The sense of drama is gone and into the bargain the fact that it is now easier to score high numbers means that late-score, match-turning drama comes along every blue moon. That was why Jonah's try in the magnificent Bledisloe Cup match in July 2000 was such a lovely throwback.

It is not just in the declined drama of the exchanges that the matches fizzle out. It's in the interminable and frequent stoppages and hordes running on and off and while the harassed fourth official tries to light up the right number on his board so that Jason Leonard doesn't suddenly run on to replace Dan Luger. The nadir, and the kick in the backside for the game (on second thoughts, don't kick it in the backside – it'll replace itself), came in the first Test in Pretoria between South Africa and England in June.

There were, altogether, around twenty-four separate player movements when you took into account the temporary blood-bin replacements; the replacements made so that teams had specialist front-row players because both Willie Meyer and Phil Greening had been sin-binned; plus the usual Gadarene rush of replacement swine in which coaches, depending on your point of view, make strategic and knowing touches on the tiller or think to themselves in desperation that they'd better bung on so-and-so. There was also the tactical use of the blood-bin – hence Clive Woodward's suggestion for a neutral medical team. The end of the match was, like so many others, disfigured and devalued and depowered, and what was otherwise a splendid affair lost its final dramas.

So all in all, I enjoyed listening to the powers that be on the International Rugby Board when they held a press conference in Dublin in April of 2000. It isn't often I can say it, but when I left them it was with a kind of glow. The granite slab called Syd Millar; the old Lion, was there as chairman of the influential technical committee. So were laws, and refereeing, grandees Lee Smith and Steve Griffiths. They were quick off the mark, complaining and threatening to ban the ludicrous amount of padding which is now worn by players. Some matches appear to be a face-off between two families of Michelin men. Millar pointed out, quite correctly, that it helped the defenders' hold on the game if tacklers were able to launch themselves like armoured human torpedoes. 'My personal opinion is that padding should only be allowed if it is protecting specific injuries,' he said. Let's hope the legislation comes in soon.

The lads were only warming up. They agreed with my view that one of the blights on the game is the quick-tap penalty by the scrum-half in which he intends only to draw a penalty from the opposition. A quick-tap penalty is not a skill, especially if referees are never going to enforce the correct mechanics of the act. Again, bring in the banishing measures.

Then they turned to replacements, and brought out the cannonballs. All the IRB's top table felt that replacements had gone too far, raving mad. That they were disfiguring the game, ruining the final quarter and offending one of the great tenets of a contact sport by mitigating against domination by force and experience and iron will. 'Again, this is only my personal view, but I'd like to go back to allowing subs only due to injury,' Millar said. This would need Woodward's Dr Neutral, because free replacements were only allowed in the first place because of the sharp practice when players ran happily off, grievously injured. Good old Syd. A man with rugby's heartbeat as his own. Griffiths suggested that he would put up with two replacements being allowed, apart from those for medical and safety reasons. I'd love Millar's hard line, but would settle, at a push, for the Griffiths plan. Please, gentlemen, retain your zeal for the next laws meeting, don't regard biased national coaches as the only fount of rugby law.

Whatever, bring back the climax of rugby. Stop bailing out the losers and the failing. Stop fracturing the action. It's time to chop to matchwood the replacements' bench, lock the lot of them in the dressing room and throw away the key. So that back out on the field, just as the superior team is preparing to prove it, some inadequate prop is having his nose rubbed in it.

v) Land of nod – players' columns, ghost-writers in the sky

One of the burgeoning features of the new game, given that you can play and be paid, is the number of players and agents keen to play and be paid to write about it. So attention, players. I'm here to tell you, wherever you are in the rugby world, that however badly you think we journalists would do if we tried to play international rugby, it isn't half as badly as we think most of you do when you try to do our job, and write about it.

Yes, our readers *know* that you're very pleased to have been selected for England. They've probably already *guessed* that you are very disappointed to have lost by forty points in the World Cup. Yes, we *understand* that the spirit among the lads is good. But couldn't you just once, from your insider's position, tell us something, anything, that we didn't already know? For God's sake, even after you retire most of you prattle on stating the bloody obvious, desperate not to offend anyone, though those of you who always whined about the media never seem to be particularly averse to popping in and joining our despised ranks when the prospect of a few pounds and an agreeable hotel near the Test venue rears its attractive head.

Some of you are fine to work with, and if you want a crack at doing it yourself then we admire you. Around half the contracted players (and let's emphasise the word 'contract', you aren't doing it for fun and often receive a vanload of money) are meticulously reliable in being available to give the actual writer the basis of what they want to say. When he was still playing, Paul Ackford was brave enough and good enough to ring the copytakers of the newspaper for whom he wrote (for those who regard the *Observer* as a newspaper, that is) to dictate his own material. Lawrence Dallaglio, who signed a contract to contribute to the *Sunday Times* in May 2000, fancies a crack at writing it himself, therefore at least ensuring authenticity. Tony Underwood wrote a fine column at the time of the 1995 World Cup. Jonathan Davies is an absolute revelation in his newspaper column, splendid in commentating on both codes of rugby, impish and interesting and yet playing only at being himself. There are a few other column gems too, but not many.

Dallaglio, Jeremy Guscott and Brian Moore, three players I have worked with, may not always have had the newspaper lawyers poring anxiously over their words, but they are meticulously reliable and professional. Moore was a gem. He was always forthright, not to mention cunning. If England had a bad game, and some of the senior players were at risk of being discarded, he would always open his column with an exhortation to the selectors not to panic, keep faith with this team, just about to turn the corner, I'll be dazzling next week, and so on.

Other players are reliable but so tuned into mediaspeak that you couldn't even get them to admit they were pleased if they'd just scored seven tries and beat the All Blacks by 100–0 and gone to bed with Sharon Stone. You sense just as they open their mouths that they have flicked a switch so that their mouths work but that the words which emerge have been sifted rigorously to remove any trace of controversy and interest.

A sizeable chunk of player-columnists, however, simply take the piss. Money for old rope. You'll meet colleagues who've just come from meeting their 'player' and are settling down to ghost the column. This is a typical response from a poor hack who'd returned from the England team hotel in South Africa with what was supposed to be the bones of a riveting column. 'He said f***k all; absolutely f ***k all. I waited for him for two hours and when he came he said he could give me only five minutes.' One former England star was signed up by a big Sunday paper. The ghost-writer, realising he was stuck for the duration of the contract with the job of sprinkling stardust on to dry bread, decided to make the best of a bad job, to give the new player-writer a ring to congratulate him on what was a highly lucrative deal, and arrange for the first piece to be done.

'Who gave you my number?' our would-be literary giant asked, huffily.

CHAPTER TWELVE

Rome

The new polish of professional rugby, and perfect peace

i) The entry of the sixth gladiator, and the Six Nations

Giampiero De Carli, a Roman pillar of the front row, took the ball only a yard or two from the Scotland line, briefly braced himself and thundered forward. There were two minutes of normal time remaining. All around the Stadio Flaminio, people stood up. All around me, people stood up too – and I was watching on television in the media box at Twickenham, bored as were those people around me by the powder-puff action trying to masquerade as an international rugby match between England and Ireland. The action from Rome was so much harder, paraded so much more of a thump. For anyone with a wider vision and affection for rugby, it also tugged harder on the heart, profoundly so. It was something different.

De Carli crossed the line and scored. People went wild because it was the score that put Italy clean out of sight. It was the score that gave sheer relief, because international rugby had become predictable, had become the haunt of the old guard, the moneyed teams. Wild. Not only the Italian team on the field, many of them veterans of the long march towards recognition and towards this triumphant entry into the new Six Nations tournament. Not only Italian rugby fans but, as it turned out, newspapers and citizens who had always ignored rugby for the mighty god of football. Romans, who now realised why men in skirts were happily drinking in the sights and sounds and beers and wines of their city and, on learning that they were British, were astonished that they did not bring with them knives and ill-intent and damage and fighting or anything much but *lire* and bonhomie. Took back with them only their clothes and mementos and breakfasts. Most of them.

De Carli marked his feat in a strange way. He took the rest of the season off, missing out on the chance of more glories. He and his wife had decided to adopt a Romanian orphan, so spent weeks in eastern

Europe going through the rigmarole of the process before returning with their new daughter.

'The Eternal City took its place at the heart of European rugby,' ran one account of the Italians' 34–20 victory. Italy had spent years aspiring to the Five Nations, had beaten France, Scotland and Ireland in one-off matches, been to Australia and competed superbly in a two-Test series, had fought against the dreadful prejudice, the dull myopia, of the other competing unions, including a notorious occasion when the Irish Rugby Union came out against Italy's inclusion only a few weeks after Italy had soundly thumped them on the field, thereby robbing Ireland of any moral right to oppose Italy's entry. The IRFU's smugness has discovered few bounds, then or since.

Here they were, the Azzurri, making six from five. The dispassionate prayed for them as they ran out to face Scotland. As an absolute minimum they were adding another edge and another magnificent backdrop to the heady culture of the international series, but those of us who had admired the courage and skill of their run into prominence were deeply anxious – their ageing team had been audibly creaking for more than a year, they had been thrashed by England in the World Cup, and had conceded a century to New Zealand. It would have been intolerable, and petrol for the flames of those who did not want them crashing the smug old party, if they had collapsed at precisely the wrong instant.

They had, admittedly, brought in Brad Johnstone, the fine Kiwi coach, whose performance in forging a team from the disparate elements and attitudes of Fijian rugby had made him, as I have already recorded, easily the coach of the 1999 World Cup. Why should it always be Kiwis who have this facility to identify priorities, to take a scythe to bullshit?

Johnstone's long hop from his office in Suva to his office in the Olympic Stadium, represented the most dizzying move in terms of culture, resources and surroundings in the history of sport. 'I left part of me there with those marvellous people,' the vastly impressive Johnstone said of the wrench, of the civic and national honours and church services and simple warmth that greeted his departure. Johnstone quickly moved to short-circuit the normal procedures, to shore up some of the edifice and to bring morale and discipline into the demoralised Azzurri. He instituted a system of fines for various disciplinary transgressions, and became the first to pay up when he left his mobile phone in a restaurant.

The Midas touch had not deserted him when Italy met Scotland, but it was not to the new man that tributes were paid, but to the old guard. Diego Dominguez, the slight fly-half, scored twenty-nine points against Scotland, which was an individual record for a Five or Six Nations match, a wonderful effort by the little master at his first attempt.

But both the Italian team and also the Italian television producer knew where the main tributes and the most fervent hugs of congratulation were to be bestowed on the final whistle. By the time the cameras panned around to find the real focal point of the Italian celebrations, I had almost entirely forgotten the England match I was supposed to be reporting on, and can only hope it didn't show.

The team, fittingly, crowded around the battle-scarred figure of Massimo Giovanelli, the flanker. Giovanelli had been the driving force behind the Italian rise, had been one of the true giants of world rugby for almost five years. When I wrote that he was fit to be compared with Sean Fitzpatrick, John Eales and François Pienaar among world leaders, I received not a murmur of protest. By 2000, he was no longer captain. Both Johnstone and Giovanelli realised that his days were numbered. The old pace had declined, both his knees were shot to pieces, the scars of the warrior, nobly borne, were starting to take their toll on the thirty-three-year-old. 'There is a price to pay for rugby,' he once told me. There was also a price to be paid for a car crash in Parma in 1995, which shattered his leg. They said it was unlikely that he would walk properly again. Eighteen months after the crash, with one leg a centimetre shorter than the other, Giovanelli returned to the Italian side, carrying just a few extra pounds and the weight of the six metal pins in his leg.

Yet there was enough left in the tank, and Johnstone knew that his experience was vital. Giovanelli played a wonderful match against Scotland, inspirational as ever. As ever, the piratical air of the man took the eye. Giovanelli was a firebrand from way back; he has more nightclub incidents against his name than John Travolta's character in *Saturday Night Fever*. He was made captain of Italy by Bertrand Fourcade, his first national coach, because, so he says: 'The best policeman might come from the ranks of the former criminals.'

He and his team calmed the wasteful passions over the years, but never the sporting ones. 'When the Azzurri were at the start of the adventure that brought us to the Six Nations, we were playing rugby with the heart but not with the proper preparation. We did not live the life of the professional rugby player. It was a social life, with sport added.' You could trace the wounds in him from the ride, and also share his pride at the outcome. There was no more stirring sight in rugby in season 1999–2000 than the battered countenance of Massimo Giovanelli breaking into the familiar fierce grin of deep satisfaction. The contrast between the ephemeral joys of his younger team-mates and the knowing demeanour of Giovanelli was telling.

Against Scotland, Giovanelli suffered an eye injury which was to end his rugby career. He knew he was not long for the active sporting world, however, and he must, surely, be retained near the national team for the crumpled but explosive example he sets. But if to miss out on the remainder of the first season's Six Nations was inappropriate, then at least the great Giovanelli played the first Six Nations match, and received the tributes of the men he, by his own example, had put out there. It would have caused the fates to stand accused of the most extreme malevolence had he not played for Italy in the Six Nations.

Neither Giovanelli nor Johnstone was under any illusion even in the immediate aftermath of the win over Scotland. The city and the country took notice of the rugby team and most accounts of the match were at pains to point out that it was not a victory based solely on passion, newness and the boot of Dominguez, but that Italy had played some good stuff. Yet they were still callow, poor in defence, still relied too much on Dominguez for their points.

They played bravely in Cardiff against Wales but went down by 47–16, gave their one abysmal performance in abject defeat against Ireland, when they lost 60–13. They played well with the ball in hand, and yet badly in defence, in a 59–17 defeat against England in Rome, on a warm day for weather and atmosphere and when thousands of England supporters marked their first Six Nations match in Rome in fine style. As the tournament wore on, some of the early optimism began to fade.

Elsewhere, this inaugural Six Nations was unsatisfactory. It was packed, fast-moving and it ended with the killing, chilling climax for England in defeat against the turbulent Scots at Murrayfield. England did see off both Ireland and Wales at Twickenham, albeit in matches which attracted such little crowd fervour that it was plain that dear old Twickers shared the reservations about the style of modern rugby and its lack of reference points and explosions and battle.

It was unsatisfactory for Ireland, because they were thrashed by England at Twickenham and gave a painfully stilted performance, they were well beaten by Wales in Dublin when a Welsh team in the grip of the eligibility scandal should have been at the mercy of the supposed Irish revival. And in a way, what we thought might be a harbinger of that revival – the amazing victory over France in Paris, the first Irish win there for twenty-eight years – only became part of the frustration because it flattered Ireland to deceive themselves. There was no mistaking the merit of Ireland's 27–25 victory and no mistaking the most vivid contributor – Brian O'Driscoll, the young centre, ran with dazzling wit and pace.

But steadier Irish heads would have pointed to the fact that France were injury-ravaged and that Bernard Laporte, the much-heralded new coach, used his replacements so abysmally badly that in the crucial closing stages, with the match in the balance, France had only one experienced forward on the field in Fabien Pelous – the others, for some reason, had been dragged off by Laporte.

It was also telling that as an occasion, the whole thing and this afternoon of Irish glory was devalued by the devil of Sunday play. For once, Paris was immune to the traditional passions and riot of the international weekend. When Keith Wood and his emerald heroes did a lap of honour, richly deserved, they found only one bunch of Irish fans to wave to. The defeat by Wales at the end of the Six Nations dashed, yet again, the risen hopes. The progress of O'Driscoll in 2000–01 will be fascinating. Second season blues await him, because he will be dogged by the defence, worked out on video, will no longer be the new meteor. By the end of season 2000–01, we will know about O'Driscoll, and let us pray that what we know will confirm our sensational early impressions.

It was unsatisfactory for France, especially after the heady start of a 36–3 win in Cardiff against Wales. Injuries did cripple the French as the season wore on, but this was hardly an excuse for the lame effort they put up against England in Paris, when England were good value for the 15–9 victory. Laporte showed few signs of selectorial inconsistency, too many signs of random shafts of speculation in most of the moves he made.

It was unsatisfactory for Wales, in that they were embroiled in the eligibility issue which was to show that neither Brett Sinkinson, the workaday flanker, nor Shane Howarth, the inspirational full-back, was properly qualified to play for Wales. It was never proved, nor can it ever be, that the Welsh team hierarchy had drafted ineligible men deliberately. Instead, the impression was that they had merely cashed in on the prevalent mood in the rugby world that nationality had gone by the board, even for national teams. The pious interventions in the debate of New Zealand and Australia, who have systematically denuded other national teams of their players for nearly twenty years, struck me as equally depressing and culpable and two-faced as the actions of the men who had failed to check birth certificates.

While he was embroiled in this issue, I felt that Graham Henry also made his first mistakes as Wales coach, allowing better players to trickle out of the squad. All in all, for Wales to win their last two matches, both after the scandal had broken, spoke volumes. The advance of Geraint Lewis, the ball-playing No. 8 from Pontypridd, was just one sign of a growing depth in the team; it is for Henry to re-motivate the likes of Robert Howley, Neil Jenkins and Chris Wyatt, all of whom were out of the team at the end of the season but all of whom, when they are firing, are among the best in their positions in world rugby.

Non-vintage Euro fare? As a showcase for rugby class it did not compare with the 2000 Tri-Nations, which was patchy but reached greater heights. But as ever, it was something for rugby to revel in. It might have been non-vintage but we had England's defensive heroics in Paris, we had the brightness of their play; we had Ireland's new cutting edges, the evidence of Welsh back-line talent from Shane Williams and Stephen Jones; we had the final, devastating Scotland riposte to all England's hopes of a Grand Slam and, still, the English came up well short. We had the endless panoply, tragedy, soap opera and comedy that is French rugby and the affairs of the team.

Ultimately, despite Scotland's late heroics, the 2000 Championship will be remembered for its new arrival. And ultimately, too, not just for the wonderful baptism of fire. Italy struggled after the initial success. Johnstone simply did not have the time or the deep well of true Test class to stick his bucket into. Italy's defensive frailty against England, when they conceded five tries to Austin Healey and Ben Cohen alone, was painful.

But there was more to them. There is hope. When they controlled the ball, some of the driving was excellent. Luca Martin and Christian Stoica found a way through the England defensive wall for tries and even in the 59–12 scoreline there was no sense of a side out of its place. These days, in the era when possession is so easy to retain, teams can concede four quick tries without being particularly at fault. 'Italy are a credit to the Six Nations,' Clive Woodward said afterwards.

And in their final match, when they ran France close in Paris, drew a crowd of over 70,000 and played some superb rugby, there were signs that Italy were finding their feet. They lost 42–31 but the match was tighter than the score suggests, Italy suffering from the sending-off of Valter Cristofoletto and France led at half-time only because the officials awarded Thomas Castaignède a try when the touchdown was clearly made out of play. It was the latest hurry-up for the arrival of video refereeing.

In Paris we saw signs of the new generation, the men to follow in the relentless footsteps of Giovanelli and the fighters of his era. Mauro Bergamasco was already arguably the finest young forward in Europe. He had played sensationally on the flank as a nineteen-year-old when England met Italy at Huddersfield in 1998 and in Paris, he was everywhere, making surging runs and heavy tackles.

Yet it was the new foundation of the team which struck me. Against England and France, Johnstone had drafted two young props, wound them up and – not without a prayer for their youth and inexperience, no doubt – sent them out to try to anchor Italy. Tino Paoletti, a twenty-two-year-old from Livorno, and especially Andrea Lo Cicero, a twenty-three-year-old Sicilian, looked the part. Shaven-headed, grim, big, square, carrying themselves like two wielders of the false violin cases in Lo Cicero's native Sicily. They held on well against the experienced England and France forwards; you could see them finding their footballing feet as their crash courses flooded them with new knowledge. You could see a pack developing around them, and around the flying Bergamasco, Giovanelli's true successor.

Even in this selfish age, it is incumbent upon supporters of every one of Italy's fellow teams in the Six Nations to celebrate wildly when Italy gain their first victory over their own darlings in Six Nations play. Rugby's world is too small as yet, too predictable, not to require earth-moving victories from the so-called lesser teams. People felt that Italy would let the whole thing down. I have the feeling that as their team grows in stature, and as our friends Tino and Andrea mature, then the earth will move sooner than the unsuspecting old guard would believe. Ask Scotland: Italy's entry galvanised the scene on the field as well as off, earned them respect.

The great old tournament, justly our pride and joy, now stands, more securely than ever, on six columns.

ii) Peace! How money bought calm, not catastrophe

The great bulk of John Fidler blocked out the moon as he approached. A hard-fought Bristol–Gloucester league match had finished an hour before at the Memorial Stadium with Gloucester taking the prized scalp. There had been a few kerfuffles on the field, a few punches thrown and a bit of a fuss afterwards as Bob Dwyer, the Bristol coach, complained that a Gloucester player or two had not been cited. People bustled about talking about the bruising match and its aftermath.

The looming Fidler, then Gloucester's team manager, was openly disparaging. 'Call that 'arrd?' he said. 'Call that 'arrd? Bloody soft as anything. I've been out there playing against the Greek [Mike Fry, the old Bristol prop of ferocious memory] and he took my eye out. Gave it back to me after the game. I've seen worse things than that out there today in moi missus' kindergarten.'

Violence and the professional game were once deemed to walk clenched

At the gates of the tour to hell. England take the field in Suncorp Stadium, Brisbane, in 1998, for their greatest thrashing of all time (*Colorsport*)

ohn Eales, holding the Cook Cup, tries to pretend that he has played in a serious nternational match, a point of view dynamited on the scoreboard in the distance *Dave Rogers/Allsport*)

Andy Nicol playing wet-ball rugby as the rain lashes down on unsuspecting and inflexible England in the 2000 Six Nations climax at Murrayfield (*Colorsport*)

Breyton Paulse, great news for those anxious about token selection, because he has given them a non-white wearing the Springbok jersey on merit alone (*Andy Redington/Allsport*)

Somewhere underneath a pile of Springbok beef, Dan Luger has resuscitated England's challenge and his own injury-riddled career with a try in the first Test in Pretoria (*Colorsport*)

Understandably, Clive Woodward takes it out on the nearest South African official (Tappie Henning) after the video referee has ruled out an overwhelming case for an England penalty try, first Test in Pretoria 2000 (*Colorsport*)

By the end of England's 2000 trip to South Africa, their aspirations to the top of the world rugby tree were taking off in earnest. Matt Perry, left, wins the communal high-jump in Bloemfontein (*Colorsport*)

Sporting heroine. Gill Burns in action against Wales in the 2000 Five Nations Championship, celebrating her 50th cap (*Dave Rogers/Allsport*)

Jason Robinson. A splendid man and a splendid rugby player. But worth £750,000 of union's money? One of the season's gambles in the offing (*Alex Livesey/Allsport*)

They waited for so long their form collapsed when they were finally allowed in. But on the first day of their Six Nations lives, Italy, wonderfully, won. Giampiero de Carli, the replacement prop, crashes over for their inaugural Six Nations try in the 34-20 victory over Scotland (*Dave Rogers/Allsport*)

The supercharger is turned on, as Pat Lam takes on the rugby world he saved (*Dave Rogers/Allsport*)

Budge Pountney, Northampton and Scotland, apparently playing a season powered by everlasting batteries, not to mention indomitable courage (*Jamie McDonald/Allsport*)

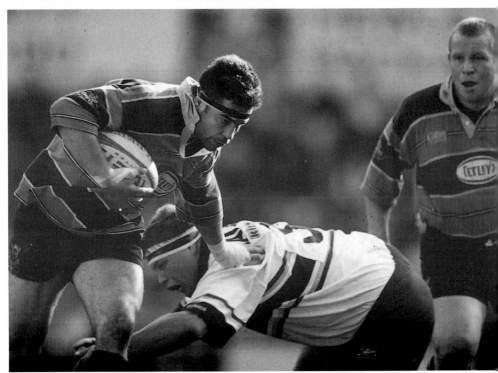

Safely escorted home by the old contemptibles in Peter Clohessy and Mick Galwey, John Hayes strikes a blow for Munster's emerging generation with a crucial try on a brilliant day in the Stade Lescure, Bordeaux. Toulouse were put to the sword and knocked out of Europe (*Jamie McDonald/Allsport*)

Keith Barwell, Northampton's owner, drinks from the well of potential new prosperity in the dressing room after Northampton's European triumph (*Dave Rogers/Allsport*)

Graham Henry, contemplating an ascension to hero status in Wales, interrupted rather by revelations on the ineligibility of some of his draft choices (*Laurence Griffiths/Allsport*)

Shane Howarth. We later discovered that he was not yet eligible to wear the red jersey. Eligible or not, he wore it with tremendous pride and skill (*Colorsport*)

Action from the match with no soul and, practically, no contest. From the side, England's 50-18 victory over Ireland in the 2000 Six Nations represented one of the softest confrontations in rugby's history, a sure sign of a sport that has lost its crunch (*Alex Livesey/Allsport*)

fist in clenched fist. In Paris, when they buried amateurism, there had been an aftershock to the main shaker. Open-mouthed in the now-famous Parisian hotel conference room, trying to take in the enormity of the idea that rugby had, seconds earlier, been declared an open game, we asked what restrictions were still in place. Surely you haven't gone as far as allowing win bonuses, we asked. Yes, we jolly well have, they replied. Anything.

If old amateurs were revolving in their graves at the news that you could now get paid, then the news that you could get paid even more for winning had them spinning faster than an old Hank Williams record at seventy-eight revs. It was, even for the die-softs among us, the shortest route to World War Three you could imagine, short of hiding the keys to Yeltsin's drinks cabinet. It was the overriding fear of all the fears of the old guard. 'Players who may be on a win-bonus and devoid of the spirit of the game may resort to violence to win,' former RFU president Ian Beer had preached in the 1990s.

The remarkable news here, after five years of long outbreaks of peace shot though with pulled punches, is that it didn't. It had the opposite effect. Since Paris, since win bonuses of full-wedge size in top rugby, violence in the sport has declined dramatically. Perhaps even more remarkably, the advent of win bonuses has seen violence in the lower levels drop. Here in rugby's heartlands, a win bonus is often the only money being played for. It is often £50 or £100 for a win, or nothing. Zip. If professionalism and pay-to-win were ever to affect rugby then it would be down here in the third and fourth and fifth divisions.

Why the end of the day of the loonies? First, one of the great flashpoints is gone. Many of the highest-profile injuries and the most nasty incidents came with boots on prone heads and bodies at ruck time. Consider the horrendous head-injuries suffered by Phil de Glanville and Jon Callard in matches against New Zealand and Eastern Province respectively. All kinds of violence bore the stamp, often literally, of rucking. For years, players had to put up with grievous gashes just because trendy coach-speak had it that those lying on the floor were fair game – even if, as in the case of de Glanville, they were not near the ball and were in fact trying to get clear of it. Rugby is lucky that no one suffered either loss of sight of an eye or brain damage because of the juddering boots. However, the ruck has now gone, disappeared. A museum piece. The swarming, fly-booted rat-a-tat of studs is finished, succeeded by an apologetic two- or three-man effort to which the good name of rucking can only be demeaned by its application. Fewer rucks, fewer stitches.

Also contrary to Beer's fears, the monetary value when it comes to violence turned out to lie in biting the bullet, not the opponent. The win bonus is at stake if either the referee, or the touch-judges with their talking-flag communications system, spot you being naughty. I remember England B being called back in a match in 1991 after touching down for what would have been the winning score against Ireland B at Donnybrook, because one of the touch-judges had seen Graham Dawe, one of rugby's true hard men (by that I mean uncomplainingly tough, not gratuitously violent) hitting someone off the ball. These days, Dawesie would have been even deeper in the doghouse with his team than he was then, because he would have cost them a lot of money as well as the match, especially as Ireland scored at the other end immediately after his scrubbed-out England try – though you'd have to pay someone else to go and complain to him. Or send him an e-mail.

If you add to the match officials the beady-eyed citing commissioners and the all-seeing eyes of the television cameras (and these days there are few angles uncovered, save that angle which gives you insight into the players via what might be termed the rear exit) then it is no longer worth it. Someone will see you, and your win bonus will be gone. If they see you and cite you and suspend you, then your next month's wages will be gone with it. Foul play is no longer worth the effort. Professional rugby players would prefer to concentrate on their profession.

It would also be nice to think that violence has declined because of professional respect. Ian Beer's words suggested that the essentially fine characters of rugby gladiators over the years would be adversely affected by money. But if a sport does produce men of inner stature as well as physical stature, then surely it is an insult to them to suggest that their goodness simply disappears in a puff of smoke once you pay them.

The upshot of rugby's transition is that we have had five of the cleanest seasons in the history of the game; that the last game of real vintage brutality came more than six years ago with the Battle of Boet Erasmus between Eastern Province and England. We have had a World Cup of such cleanliness that the citing commissioner was reduced to ridiculous over-reaction, such as when Colin Charvis of Wales lost two matches from his World Cup campaign for a punch which, in the days of big John Fidler, would not have alarmed a fly. For goodness' sake, something you'd *like* to see is a bit of an old-fashioned war. We didn't sign on for vicar rugby, that's for sure. No wonder the old hard men scoff.

The bygone angry match, such as the final Allied Dunbar match of the season between Leicester and Bath, had its moments, in that instance mostly centred around Richard Cockerill and John Mallett, the two front-row men. Cockerill's antics, all the barking and shouting and posturing, have always been an acquired taste, but as rugby moves further towards respect and simply getting on with the game, so our Cockie is beginning to stick out like some kind of ludicrous sore thumb. Elsewhere, through the Six Nations and the domestic events in all the main rugby countries, it is difficult to remember much mayhem at all. Even the Heineken Cup, traditionally the arena for throwbacks to the old angry era, was a reasonably quiet affair.

Until fairly recently we all clustered admiringly round the retired old bruisers on their barstools, like bean-eating cowpokes round the campfire as the gunslingers reminisced. These days the modern player would just let them gibber in the corner. There'll just be the two of us left, I suppose. We used to put them all on a pedestal, compete for their attention.

The gargantuan Gerard Cholley was arguably the finest exponent of what might be called the post-whistle arts. He once went through a Scotland team out on the Parc des Princes, perhaps the spiritual home of the angry years, felling them in turn like a quick-working lumberjack. In the Parc one year, in that concrete bear-pit, we watched the Worst Match Ever, when Racing Club played Agen in the French Champion-ship final of 1990 when Patrick Serrière, the Racing captain, laid out an opponent who was chasing the kick-off, and the referee, Claude Debat, lacked the bottle to send off a player after less than five seconds of play. We saw eighty minutes of a *Clockwork Orange*-type violence and since the teams were level on points at the end (on the scoreboard and on the cards of all three judges) we had extra violence too, ten minutes each round. Sorry, each way.

Those of us present have at a later occasion dined out on the story, but Cholley was once holding court behind a mountainous plate post-retirement in a Basque restaurant in Paris, the night before a France–England match. Suddenly, the door swung open and crashed against the back wall, rebounding like the doors of Wild West saloon.

It was Fran Cotton, one of Cholley's major adversaries, a man who, like Cholley, was massive as a player and who had managed to conquer anorexia since he'd given up active service. There was a crash as Cholley stood up and the two men faced each other at opposite ends of the restaurant. People shrank back to give them a corridor and they clump-clumped their way towards each other. When they met, they collided in massive embrace. Cholley traced with his finger a old scar above Cotton's eye. 'It healed up well,' he growled.

Cholley sees much of the softer rugby today as a *fumisterie*, a hoax. He weighs in at around 150 kilos these days, and that excludes his trademark log-like cigar. 'The major difference today is in the way the game has become sanitised. In my time, we didn't need a referee to police things, we sorted problems out ourselves and in our own way. There was a real *combat ∂e chef∂*, a lot of intimidation and staring down your opponent.

'Players today do not know fear any more. Everything is strictly controlled and surveyed from every angle. They can insult the opposition, provoke them, call them all sorts of names, because they know that no one will risk retaliation. In my day, retribution was not always instantaneous. You had to learn to be patient. But sooner or later it would come. It would come.'

All right, I know it's a recipe for a game in flames. Only France could have produced a character like Cholley. Ask poor old Mike Burton about him. He had to play Cholley four times out in Paris and never once at home. But Cholley does have a point that there was once a forbidding climate of fear in matches in Paris which had to be overcome and that these days, as the Stade de France falls often to visiting teams, it has gone. It is worth telling young forwards from England and Wales who talk about tough matches against the French in the Stade de France that they are playing rose-petal rugby compared to the challenge of facing Cholley and his jaw and his mates out in the dire and glorious days of the Parc.

Still, we can't have it all ways. We can't secretly long for an old-style game once in a while and then preach about the end of the game and a sad day for the sport if it all goes off with a bang. The money bought peace and respect for rugby, not the advent of a kind of professionalised kick-boxing and other mayhem. Out on the fields, it's all quiet.

iii) Quotas – hard roads and high principle in new South Africa
Nick Mallett endured a fiendishly difficult season in 2000, as his Springboks struggled against England and through the Tri-Nations. Mallett did not suddenly became a bad coach and is most certainly one of rugby's premier statesmen, a man who had been around, coached around, and can see further than the end of his national nose. It was just that things were going badly, as he tried to re-design his team in a different style, and cope, as ever, with the factions and the factions within factions in every Springbok, well, faction.

He did have one stroke of luck. Or streak of luck. Breyton Paulse, the deadly-sharp coloured wing from the Western Cape, did Mallett the enormous favour of being good enough to be chosen on merit for the Springboks in 2000. He proved it with some deadly running after beginning the season by carving Canada up in a Test at East London.

Affirmative action is the latest twist in the tortuous metamorphosis of South African life and sport. There is no formal compulsion on Mallett to pick what are now called 'quota' players, previously 'players from the formerly disadvantaged communities', before that, non-whites. But by government spokesman or government whisper he has to make some recognition of the need, as Mallett says himself, 'to make our national team representative of our nation'.

But to follow that principle can often cause the coach to transgress the first principle of selection for a country's team – that it should comprise the best fifteen players. Paulse was such a blessed relief because Mallett could put his hand on heart and tell everyone, and more pertinently, tell himself, that he would have picked Paulse if he had been white. It is even more difficult when there is no formal quota system, but only a kind of informal but powerful pressure from on high. It is then that, unless you have a Paulse, you have to live with transgressing at least your sporting principles.

Lower down the scales in South Africa, the quotas are imposed. In the various competitions, each representative team must field a certain number of non-whites. In the Currie Cup itself in 2000, each coach had to choose three 'quota' players in the match twenty-two, of which two had to be on the field at all times. No excuses were to be accepted. Rian Oberholzer, chief executive of SARFU, said that 'so-called injuries could not be used as excuses', and that any union found guilty of bending the rules could be fined up to R100,000 (£10,000) or have points deducted in the Currie Cup table. The rules were taken so seriously that for an early round of the Currie Cup, Western Province left out Pieter Rossouw, the celebrated Springbok left wing, in favour of Jeffrey Stevens, a 'quota' player. The Blue Bulls chose Norman Jordaan, the national U21 scrum-half, in place of the great Joost van der Westhuizen. Once, in the days of apartheid, such selections were called token, which they were. Now, still token after a fashion, they are deemed progressive.

No doubt they cause problems, no doubt the white players left out are miffed to furious. No doubt non-white players can be found wanting, as was, for example, Owen Nkumane, the hooker Mallett brought to the UK on tour in 1998 and who struggled desperately. Chester Williams, the highest-profile non-white Springbok, while he supports whole-heartedly the drive to elevate more non-white players, also gives a warning. 'It is important that there should be black and coloured players in the sides, but they mustn't be there because they have to be there. They should be there on merit. Otherwise, they might not feel welcome, and the whole game might drop down.'

Two points here. First, since there is a generation of highly promising young non-whites emerging, an inevitable consequence of greater equality of opportunity and resourcing, then the whole, fiendish problem is mercifully a temporary one. It takes years for a promising youngster to become a Springbok, someone able to breathe the most rarefied sporting air. But they are gradually bearing down on that green jersey.

Second, you simply cannot hound SARFU and South African rugby. They are trying. Barely a month seems to pass without some new edict, without the adoption of some new charter to fight discrimination. It is high time for those of us who were deeply unhappy that the rugby community wanted to keep playing with apartheid South Africa to acknowledge the attempts to make the best out of a bad job.

It is not as if we had everything right. I still wince when I realise some of the fallibilities of our own arguments. After the first week of the 1987 World Cup, the *Sunday Times* carried a ludicrous mish-mash of a story under my name, datelined from Wellington, New Zealand. It had started as a heartfelt hymn of praise to the first and thrilling seat-of-the-pants week of the first World Cup. I'd filed the story, downed a Kiwi beer or two and gone to bed. Back in London, my colleagues were still working.

In the early hours, I was woken by a call from the then sports editor, John Lovesey. From his tone, it seemed that the world had ended, and I immediately assumed that one of the teams had been wiped out in a plane crash or as an absolute minimum, a top player had tested positive for steroids. What had happened was that a gang of young England players under some banner or another had announced they were going to make a rugby tour of South Africa. It was not a national or representative grouping of any sort. Just a tour. Bad lads. Goodnight, John.

I soon gathered that Lovesey saw it all as some modern-day revisitation of Nazi Germany, felt that to condemn these evil young lads was a bigger priority than bringing to our readers the story of what was the greatest week in the history of rugby. In the end, cringingly, we cobbled together a dire story which hailed the new World Cup and decried the tourists in the same piece, almost in alternate paragraphs. I resented Lovesey's tendency to build this up into something it was not, but had to find a way of preserving some kind of element of the real story of the week. Just a tiny example of the way rugby had to thrash around battling with itself, as well as with South Africa.

Breyton Paulse's dazzling skills illuminated the South Africa season, provided a perfect role model in that here was a great player wearing the famous jersey, and wearing it because he deserved to wear it for rugby ability. It is incumbent upon everyone, the dropped white players, the impatient government hawks, the national and Currie Cup coaches, to be patient until that blessed day when a whole line of young non-white South Africans comes streaking by in the wake of Paulse. Until then, South African rugby can hold up its head. It's trying.

iv) The steaming ether of rugby's new Web world

It would be harsh to call them rugby's new underclass, but they are nonetheless something of a class apart. They seem to sit glued not to rugby on television or video but to websites, rugby of the ether. They are rugby's newest important constituency and the rugby websites are the sport's newest meeting place, repository of love and affection and bitterness and disrespect; and its newest marketplace, because the sites make some of their money from direct sales.

But the lifeblood of the sites is not in the e-commerce adverts or the news sections or the guest columnists (and here in the register of author's interests I should lodge my fortnightly column in planet-rugby.co.uk and, in the interests of fairness and posing, also mention gwl@d.com, who named me their rugby writer of the year). The lifeblood flows in the message boards, where the Web-ites gather to chew the rugby fat, chew each other, post their best ever teams, pick over the bones of matches in the past and the recent past (ending five seconds ago) and rant and rave at Planet Rugby's guest columnist.

I am not, by nature, a surfer – be it at Fistral Bay or on the Internet – although on rugby's Web you find sites of a real, fighting excellence. Notably those of the USA Rugby Union, the IRB, and the Newport, Royal Navy, Northampton, Gloucester and Newcastle Falcons clubs – not by any means an exhaustive list, since there is a limit to the time my son can spend pressing the keys for me. And on most, you can access the raging, ranting, spiky and loving fans of rugby. It is not the worst way for the sport's various hierarchies to learn of the views of the rugby man and woman on the terrace or in the armchair. Gwl@d's message board, satisfyingly anti-English, is streets ahead for a kind of street-smart rugby erudition.

The heaps of mush and the occasional four legs good, two legs bad myopia whingeing its way on to the screen from, say, 12,000 miles away can also be balanced by the odd sharply insightful contribution. Look back through the log of a night's postings and you'll find some sleepless anoraks have gone on all night, posting their views to the great unseen. Some are excellent and, as ever, it is the sad inadequates who post anonymously – an anonymity now denied to me after my bright office spark decreed that *Sunday Times* articles should appear bearing the writers' e-mail addresses. You have only to mention Pontypridd Rugby Club, rugby league, the drop-off of players from rugby (well over 300 e-mails on that topic), the move away from physical confrontation in rugby (almost as many), and how absolutely two-eyed and unmyopic are the fine men and women of Welford Road, and the 'new messages pending' light blows its gasket. Powerful medium.

Or if you mention the All Blacks. There is no topic so guaranteed to fire up the feverish 'posters' on the message boards of rugby's air highways. Once, just gently, in a shortish Web article on Planet Rugby, I made a little fun of the All Blacks. I had the gall to suggest that the midfield players they brought to Rugby World Cup 1999 could have removed the skin from rice pudding only with a lot of help. The message boards hummed with a savage derision.

Later, spotting not so much a gap in the market as a gap in the psyche, we tried just a little apologetic pop at the fact that the old Kiwi rugby stadium is not of a palatial quality. From the reaction to this and to the efforts of several other Web columnists, it seemed that no Kiwi posted on the Planet Rugby message board would ever grasp that if you removed the blatant areas of irony then what was left was an almost total respect. They knew their rugby. They wrote at length. But they never grasped the irony.

Eventually, to gently reveal that we were extracting that stuff which Sarah Miles drinks, we decided to lay it on with a trowel. Planet Rugby ran my grand list of:

THE TEN NATIONALITIES EASIEST TO WIND UP
(Incorporating: The Utter Failure to Get Irony Championships)
We gave as the current standings:

1) New Zealanders (North Island).
2) New Zealanders (South Island).
3) New Zealanders (Stewart Island).
4) Anyone in a scruffy combi with a chunky pullover.
5) The boring barman in my local who claims he once played for Counties.
6) Aussie-based Kiwi armchair-based 'rugby writers' who get into a right old tizzy when someone gives them some stick back, the poor old dears.
7) Kiwi contributors to Planet Rugby's message board who courageously sign themselves 'Anonymous'.

8) Descendants of New Zealanders.
9) New Zealanders in exile anywhere in the world, Welsh caps excluded.
10) Everyone else Kiwi, except John Hart, Dame Kiri, and all my Kiwi mates.

Utter failure. Not one New Zealander who responded on the message board even appeared to realise that our affectionate Failure to Get Irony awards might be ironic in itself. Long diatribes were received as to why they were not the slowest to grasp irony (ironic, that). There were threats, po-faced opinions that there were at least eleven other nationalities who were easier to wind up, and why. Demands that I be banned from New Zealand which, considering I love the place almost without reservation, would be a blow. Ah well. On that note we gave up. Months later, I was still being introduced on New Zealand radio shows, up the phone-line from Auckland, as 'the man who hates New Zealand'.

I even had my own little war of the websites. I never declared it or gave a flying fish about it, but I was told that I was in it after it had started. While breakfasting in a Sydney hotel just prior to England's tour match against Australia in 1999, I was thrown a local newspaper by a colleague with an invitation to 'have a look at that load of old toss'. The article in question bore the byline Spiro Zavos, of whom I had never heard, or if I had heard, had forgotten. It was a striking piece because in an attack on aspects of rugby in Europe it pandered lovingly to every known anti-Brit rugby prejudice, trotted out a cringing raft of theories and so-called perceived knowledge of our rugby that in no case was less than fifteen years out of date. At first, until a colleague confirmed that Zavos did exist, I genuinely could not work out whether the whole thing was some kind of crass and failed send-up, like the Kiwi cartoon terrace-rugby hero Loose Head Len, who blathered about all his prejudices in New Zealand papers. Maybe I'd become Kiwi-like in my failure to get irony.

In an answering column in Planet Rugby I posed the question as to whether someone so out of date, so convinced that European rugby was one entity with one style, was a real person or a cartoon character or other creation. I attacked Zavos, if it was he, for perceived prejudices, and perhaps an underlying message was contained therein that Kiwi arrogance has always tended to be what came before a Kiwi defeat and, sometimes, caused it. OK, OK. Waste of good ether time, but it was a slow week.

Suddenly, it wasn't. The Webs started spinning. On Planet Rugby and on at least three other websites I read, the whole thing was portrayed as a major battle between major writers. 'Jones v. Zavos', the message thread said, and supporters of both articles came zinging their way on to the screens. I was astounded. 'Why did you give publicity to that prat?' asked a Kiwi colleague. I was asked to take part in the Grand Debate on a large number of Down Under television and radio shows. I patiently tried to disabuse all the producers of the nation that this was in any way a significant issue, but it seemed that once it was on the Web, then it was big stuff.

I did appear, by the miracles of modern telephone, on one radio show broadcast in New Zealand. Zavos himself had appeared the night before, apparently considerably agitated, upset that I had attacked him and, as one of the amused presenters told me, so irate that eventually 'he almost started squeaking'. Apparently he was accusing me of racism; but since I had no idea what race he belonged to I could hardly be said to have insulted it. If he let me know which one, I could have considered it.

The debate raged on on the websites, and gave me some idea of the power of this new medium, though I never quite got over the fact that I had given someone a platform on which, from what I had read, he was not qualified to stand. He even approached me, still squeaking, at a World Cup match somewhere in Europe, still flustered and agitated. A ringer for Ted Glen in *Postman Pat*. He considerably ruffled Chris Jones, the *Standard* sportswriter who was sitting next to him in one press box, by screeching 'yeeeessss' whenever New Zealand scored a try, and if Jones had not been so busy he would have looked for a marshal to dispose of our man on the grounds that he appeared to be a fan.

Websites. The highly significant new, teeming conduit for rugby fans everywhere. A beast of the professional era. A medium also for those who, it appears, enjoy dishing it out but are not so partial to taking it back. Now there's irony.

CHAPTER THIRTEEN

Popocatapetl

The death of the rugby tour – sport's last great adventure ♦ No anthems for Rotorua ♦ Dusty diamond day in Potch

Early morning of a southern hemisphere winter's day, clear and cold and promising one of those crystal Kiwi skies, with the blue not degraded by such manifestations of the real world as pollution. A grandeur transcending the cutting rasp of any rugby-obsessed native. The hotel is stirring and the party making up the 1983 British Lions touring team, some nursing aching heads because this was still an era when even the Lions used to drink of an evening, blearily prepares for breakfast.

It is a travel day, when the party packs its kit and its memories of another stop-over on a long touring road, packs up memories of the last match, of new acquaintances and experiences, and checks them all in as baggage for the next stop. And the head-up tourists, those who attempt to get under the skin of the country as well as the skin of its rugby players, leave enriched.

At midday, they will fly from Christchurch's airport, on the South Island's east coast, over to Hokitika on its west coast, a town which sprung up in the gold fever of the 1860s, the location of the nearest airport to Greymouth, where the Lions will play their next match against the west coast provincial team. In Greymouth, youngsters will already be in an excited flap that these sleek giants of the world game, this latest party bearing the Lions' name and springing from rugby's history, old newsreels, tour books and the vivid memories of their parents, will descend on their tiny rugby community and demonstrate yet again the pulling-power, the fine social interaction, the enriching vigour of sporting travel for the party itself and, yes, the essential magic of the real rugby tour.

That tour party was disastrously selected and disastrously led, because neither Ciaran Fitzgerald, the Irish army officer who was (ridiculously) made captain, nor Willie-John McBride, the long-maned old Lion who was manager, even began to measure up to their allocated tasks. Fitzgerald was never remotely good enough as a player and McBride, one of the sport's all-time heroes, was exposed in a kind of no-man's-land between eras. The Lions lost the Test series by 4–0 to a non-vintage New Zealand. But that is another story.

Some of us travelling hacks were already checking out and slamming car boots as the Lions awoke. Two carloads had decided to drive over to the west coast, across Arthur's Pass through the Southern Alps, the raised spine of the South Island. It was only my second-ever day out of the northern hemisphere, on my first tour as a journalist. New Zealand, for me, was still the grim and black place it had always been in the mind's eye of my youth; I associated the blackness of the jersey and the grimness of the demeanour of the All Blacks with the appearance of the country itself.

Revelation day. We drove out of Christchurch to the west, left the flatlands of the suburbs and were soon climbing up into the Southern Alps past Sheffield and Springfield and into the Arthur's Pass National Park itself. You felt your breath begin to catch, first with the altitude and then with the spectacle and the colours. It was a stunning journey, spent winding up and across dizzying gorges, waterfalls, white-water rivers and scenic look-out points and tarns; past habitats of the tui and the Alpine parrot; past snow-capped peaks. We begged the driver to take it slowly as the road suddenly emerged on the edge of the fenceless drop and called for a measured left- or right-hander to continue the winding progress. Later, we sighed with relief when we heard that big Clem Thomas, our rumbustious colleague in another car, took the route as a challenge to his warrior instincts, spun and slid around the mountains millimetres from the drop. Apparently he gave his trademark Clem-laugh, the fruity 'hur, hur, hur' known throughout rugby, in the frightened silences as the car teetered on the verge like the coach at the end of The Italian Job.

At the top of the pass, in a small settlement, we ate smorgasbord – then the new culinary cutting-edge of New Zealand – in a mock-Alpine restaurant, lashings of salads and hogget, the Kiwi label for a sheep caught and slaughtered in between the lamb of its youth and the mutton of its maturity. We were pursued by hogget at tables throughout the tour. At the end, we exited, pursued by hogget.

Lunch over, swilled down with the gaseous Steinlager, it was on down past waterfalls and rivers of the Otira Gorge, twisting and turning and wow!-ing. On the road map, New Zealand's Route 73 looked a substantial thing. When you take it, you realise that no one defeated the

Southern Alps to build it, no one breached the country. They merely laid tarmac wherever the geography, wherever elemental Mother Earth, grudgingly ordained it could be laid.

Eventually we came out of the mountains, hit the Tasman coast at Kumara Junction and ran north a few kilometres into Greymouth, nodded to the one horse of the town, found the one hotel which, in turn, contained the one restaurant. I remember sitting on the edge of a shabby bed in a motel-style cabin, heated by an electric fire, which opened direct on to a freezing outside corridor, and realising that New Zealand was already growing fast on me. The players wore black. The country didn't. Wonderful place. I had an affection for New Zealand which has ever since grown only stronger.

The focus on the Lions was total. Hundreds came to watch them train, the hotel pulled out all the stops, with special menus and promotions and above all a warmth which made up for the petty privations. I recall that tour, with its one-horse stops, a tour on which the inherent warmth of a cold Kiwi winter and a raft of new experiences diffused the disappointments of the rugby, with a vast fondness. It opened my eyes to rugby's goodness and opportunities. The Lions beat West Coast by 52–16. Dusty Hare kicked beautifully, landing ten out of ten. We packed, and flew to Invercargill. It was Sunday. It was shut. It was great.

Nothing has been remotely so evocative in my rugby life (nor in the lives of most of my rugby-loving friends and colleagues, nor especially in the lives of the great players of old) as British Lions tours, and other major rugby odysseys. The tours I read about as a youngster, or followed on the radio in the early hours – I once danced with Roger the milkman in the Saturday dawn in 1971 when J.P.R. Williams dropped a goal, tied the fourth Test, and John Dawes' Lions beat the All Blacks. Or those which I have had the preposterous good fortune to watch at first hand.

W. J. Turner's 'Romance' tells of his transportation into exotic places via school atlases and school lessons. I remember only bits of it.

> When I was but thirteen or so
> I went into a golden land.
> Chimborazo, Cotopaxi
> Took me by the hand.
>
> I walked in a great golden dream
> To and fro from school –

Shining Popocatapetl
The dusty streets did rule.

The houses, people, traffic seemed
Thin fading dreams by day;
Chimborazo, Cotopaxi,
They had stolen my soul away.

Well, volcanoes in the Andes were all very well for Turner. But it was
bits of New Zealand which did it for me. In schoolrooms I was
transported to Pukekohe and Timaru, Coromandel and Te Kuiti and
Gisborne and Masterton and King Country; and perhaps oddly, was
thrilled by the evocative names of the combined teams the tourists would
meet – Manawatu–Horowhenua, Wairarapa–Bush, West Coast–Buller,
Marlborough–Nelson Bays–Golden Bay–Motueka. I'd be transported
at high velocity to those places where tours touched and, later in life, no
longer youthful, I'd be transported away from the newspaper terminal at
similar speed.

The best tour tales could involve Test-match glories, but equally the
provincial matches in which the Lions would take on the locals and local
people could touch them – and not only those in New Zealand but also
in Australia: Dubbo or Cobar against New South Wales Country; or
South Africa against Southwest Districts or against Eastern Transvaal in
Springs or the Leopards in Mdantsane or wherever the caravan stopped.

Two years ago I caught a train from London to Cardiff for the funeral
of Bryn Thomas, the kindly and prolific rugby writer from the *Western
Mail*, one of the journalistic pioneers whose tour books first pulled back
the curtain on the panoply. Cliff Morgan and Jeff Butterfield were on
board. Both had played on the 1955 tour of South Africa, an impossibly
glamorous experience. The Lions were revered as wonderful sportsmen,
and held the status of Hollywood film stars. They made heroic flights in
Dakotas, long journeys hauled by steam trains, relaxed on beaches and
in game parks, played on light-brown and baked highveld pitches with
eight-panelled leather balls, fell foul of home-town referees. Absorbed
experiences and cultures and new friendships like giant sponges. They
even drew the series 2–2.

When the tour ended, reported the great Vivian Jenkins in *Lions
Rampant*, every South African newspaper fêted the Lions. 'Thousands
fought for the privilege of seeing them play,' said the Johannesburg *Star*.

The two old greats must have reminisced on that tour 500 times since,
but they were flowing beautifully before we were out of Paddington – we

were on our third bottle before Bristol Parkway; it was not yet 10.30 a.m. Apart from setting them off, I spoke not a word till the tunnel outside Newport. I remember the late and lamented Dewi Bebb, wing poacher supreme, telling me about the 1966 Lions tour of New Zealand when the party had been away for two months and not arrived in New Zealand at all, what with the long journey and the preliminary bits in Australia. If we humble rugby fans can treasure all our memories, if they translate with a vividness on to newsreels and more modern media, then imagine the sensations available to those gladiators who actually went out to play.

This is not to demean the attitudes of the international players of the day, whose form and fitness are their livelihood. You are a prisoner of your era, I suppose, whichever one it is. Anyone with the committed yet relatively gentle mentality of the 1955 Lions would quite possibly have been sent home from a 2000 tour on the first day. Say Lawrence Dallaglio had toured with the 1955 Lions, then his supremely professional attitudes, his dedication and hard-nosed aura would have seen him stand out like a sore thumb, even a freak, someone not quite right and proper. An alien force. These days, of course, he is seen as the epitome of the professional rugby player.

Cliff Morgan and Jeff Butterfield had their culture, and their era. So did Fergus Slattery, the superb Irish flanker who toured with the Lions in 1971 and 1974, and who was famous for not passing up any chance to make a trip, to take advantage of some local hospitality, to see a sight. What a marvellous attitude. I'm sure that Slattery firmly believes that his rugby-playing life was all part of his education, was the richest tapestry.

For all the Lions and all players who toured with their own national teams throughout rugby history, to play in the amateur era was still to be fabulously enriched. Perhaps because you'd toured under apartheid and understood politics and inhumanity better; whether you'd seen Table Mountain or Arthur's Pass or the Sydney Opera House or Rorke's Drift; or whether you'd been adopted by a school and met some wide-eyed kids or just gone to the pub and argued the toss with some annoying local. And all that is quite apart from the magical (and still unmatchable) experience of representing the British Lions on the rugby field.

In which other sport would the great teams drop into the outposts? Imagine the Dallas Cowboys appearing on a redneck village dustbowl; imagine Real Madrid playing football in Redruth; or Pete Sampras on the municipal courts of Hunslet. But the parallels are exact. It would be the same as the British Lions flying 1200 miles to play in Greymouth, a tiny town at the far west of the end of the world. (Greymouth recently reappeared on the rugby map. Waikato, holders of the Ranfurly Shield, took it on the road and defended it against West Coast at Greymouth and North Otago at Oamaru. Good for the Mooloo men, and good for West Coast in keeping the score below 100 – admittedly by only one point – and North Otago, too – by a princely five points.)

John Hopkins, a rugby writer of note and now golf correspondent of *The Times*, put it brilliantly in his book *Life with the Lions* about the Lions tour of New Zealand in 1977. He estimated that the tour, which lasted a total of fourteen weeks, involved thirty different flights, ten major coach trips and a myriad other journeys. The team played twenty-six games, were watched by 718,000 spectators, and made over NZ$2 million for the home union. 'A major rugby tour by the British Lions is a cross between a medieval crusade and a prep-school outing,' Hopkins wrote. Inch-perfect, Hoppy, old son. A tenner for every time I've quoted you, and you can retire.

But who cares which tour you are on? It is a privilege to have a mighty rugby team come to your town, a privilege for the tourist and the toured. But you don't have to be a Test-class tourist. Hardly a rugby player at any level and hardly a schoolboy in the increasingly wide world of school tours has not made a rugby tour, been battered at Easter in Cornwall or in Munster or South Wales, or, frankly, everywhere.

It still seems incredible to me that I once toured Cornwall with a team drawn from old pupils of my school at Bassaleg and played in all five tour matches in five consecutive days against the rough men of Falmouth, Redruth Albany, Illogan Park, Camborne and Newton Abbot; incredible that we stupidly drew the fire of the opposition by sending them a tour programme revealing that at least ten of our team were playing top-class rugby in Wales, even though their clubs let them play for us only sporadically and so left the rest of us to battle on against sides expecting ferocious opposition. I dined, so far as I can remember, on curry and bitter each evening, stayed up most nights so that we clashed with the breakfast of other guests. I lay on my back with arms and legs waving in the air along with thirty others in a Redruth street brought to a standstill by the call of dead ants, watched as Blackie urinated through the open passenger's window of a Rolls-Royce, felt suicidally depressed each time we lost and on top of the world when we didn't.

And experienced nothing more or less than millions of other players following rugby's longest established and finest tradition, who have taken their senior team or colts team or women's team out on the road, have experienced the wondrous cross-pollination of sport, and the cross-cultural experience that is the rugby tour – the weekend jaunt or the crusade. No other sport has a tradition to rival it, not even to come closer than a Kiwi bull's roar. We might have learned as much about Asian cuisine as that of Cornwall, but that tour gave me a respect for Cornish rugby people and also a love of touring which has never wavered, not even when it meant cruelly missing my children. And as far as the love of touring is concerned, the experience helped me to feel ever more strongly the privilege that it is usually someone else who now pays for me to go. Touring has simply made rugby lives worth living.

It has also set rugby apart, done so much to perpetuate that old smugness we held that our sport was, in the heart, more global and yet more family-like than any other. It has been where we score over football every time. Touring has also kept a balance. To meet other cultures is to understand them, to stop them clashing. That is the reason why I have always felt the Lions should make a twelve-match tour of France. It has kept a balance, too, because there have always been other benefits to be gained if the results did not work out, British Lion or humble Easter rabbit. I wouldn't have swapped any minute of any tour I've made or followed from afar for all the curry in India or all the tea in China or all the spectacle of Arthur's Pass. Nor would you.

How desperately sad, therefore, when you consider now what touring has become. So the game is now professional. So what? You would think that with the pressure on family and business life removed by the fact that players earn their living from the sport, tours would be more numerous, not less so. But even at the amateur levels club tours are in decline. Clubs in all the touring hotspots are stuck with league fixtures over the holiday periods, and because of the pressures of modern life, it is more difficult for people to be away. Certainly, not even the most honeyed optimist could expect a reprise of the Dewi Bebb-type tour where you'd miss most of the year.

But the fate of international rugby tours, the lifeblood of the game and its culture, is far worse. The crusade is reduced to a flat, cultureless, colourless, boring grind, the most sterile, hermetically sealed experience imaginable. Tours to Hell leaving every year. Sure, the players get paid these days. They need to be. There is nothing else to gain from the experience bar a boarding pass, a registration card and a gallon of isotonic syrup on a training paddock. The only way you meet someone from the host country other than those paid to perform some service for you, flying or feeding you or driving you, is if you accidentally turn left instead of right and thus enter the street outside the hotel instead of the team room. (Don't worry, you can scuttle back soon enough.) The only way they meet you, ditto. Unless the tour sponsor has bunged you to glad-hand your way round a business dinner, wearing not the No. 1 rig of old but your dress tracksuit and cleanest daps.

One of the most jarring aspects of major touring is the ludicrous pomposity in the bearing of the teams, padding and posing in self-important fashion round foyers as if the country should stop to gaze in awe at someone who has lost the sense of awe they once had. Sure, you'll meet up with your opposite number – but only on the field. It is usually only a few rounded heroes, the Jason Leonards or Dan Crowleys, who will down a beer in each other's company after the match. The fact that it might better your own rugby career to gain a perspective of rugby from someone whose vantage point is thousands of miles from your own is now deemed irrelevant. The magic conveyed by incoming touring teams is also sharply devalued by the fact that they come so often not on tours as we would know them, but on almost annual one-Test trips, so that players like Joost van der Westhuizen and John Eales are as familiar as your brother.

Professionalism is not in itself to blame. Just the sense of paranoia that it has created. The true rugby tour was already in decline. Stuart Barnes, the former England fly-half and now Sky's highly-rated rugby man, had toured enough by 1994, when he bowed out of top rugby with England in South Africa. The team had played in Kimberley but not gone to the Big Hole, the extraordinary excavation reaching to the bowels of the planet where human hands had been torn in the search for diamonds during the nineteenth century. They had been to Durban but no one had even considered visiting Rorke's Drift. 'If I had my time again,' Barnes said at the time, 'I'd have played soccer. I chose rugby because it gave better opportunities for socialising. Sport must give you a wider dimension, but that dimension is disappearing. We are becoming dull cabbages, obsessed with rugby.'

The culprits are easy to find. They are the technocrats and the national coaches of the major unions who simply cannot countenance the fact that any of their charges should spend as much as a second in what (in their blinkered opinion) is an extraneous activity. Look at the recent history of the rugby tour and see what you can list under extraneous. Let's see: meaningful provincial games, anything cultural, anything rendering you likely to meet a normal inhabitant of the hosting country, anything which might interfere in even the most roundabout and irrelevant way with the worship of the god of training, especially since the penny is yet to drop in the minds of any serious coach that time spent on the training field could just as well rob the team of its verve and appetite and spontaneity as improve that team. Overdone cabbage.

Is there any hope? The Lions tours still retain a semblance of the old magic, even if they too are now duller of sight. The outline itinerary for the 2001 tour to Australia contained ten matches, at one time was even sidling up towards a semi-epic of twelve. The ten-match tour would hardly have been long enough to get Morgan and Butterfield into their stride, of course. And with Graham Henry installed as coach, lacking the historical perspective, there was always the chance that the tour would be sucked dry of more of its sweet juices, become something closer to the now traditional dour slog.

South Africa's tour in the autumn of 2000 was due to take in Argentina and three of the four home countries, with non-Test matches in midweek, although it remained to be seen if these would simply be day-trips for the second string, final whistle and shower and hightail it back to base. But good on them for at least shaping up as tourists. John O'Neill, chief executive of the Australian Rugby Union, even said at a press conference in Sydney in 1999 that he strongly wished for a reversion to real touring. 'They are what sets rugby apart and I feel that the IRB should make the re-institution of touring a priority. They are a tremendous promotion for the game and we have ignored them recently while paying attention to other aspects of rugby.' Quite beautifully put, I felt at the time. I hope that O'Neill is able to carry enough people along with him, that he ignores some of the views of Rod Macqueen, his own national coach, who is so inextricably welded to the needs of his national squad and his national squad only that his vision for the rest of the sport outside, the other ninety-nine per cent, is as dry as dust and dull as ditchwater. It was O'Neill's wish that the 2001 Lions should play twelve games, and good on him, too. But on the Australian tour of France and Britain in autumn 2000 they were to begin against the French Barbarians, and after that to play just Test matches. Sterility.

It is the individual country tours which so violate the game's finest traditions. Who remembers who wins the myriad Test series on non-tours? It was on an England tour of South Africa that I asked one of the players for his off-field tour highlight. 'Paint-balling,' he said. I did not want to be too harsh – most of his colleagues would have opted for golf or swimming at Sun City. 'But you can go paint-balling at home,' I said. I could have added that he was in the most evocative, vivid, frightening and glorious place on rugby's planet, so why waste his spare time paint-balling?

'Ah,' he said. 'But at home, the guns are shite. Here, they're much better.'

❀ ❀ ❀

The blame must be shared, though England must bear a heavy responsibility. I commend elsewhere in this book the fact that Clive Woodward and his management team are fully aware of the pitfalls of modern rugby and the deadening effect it can have on their lives. Their sympathy is obvious. It is also important to point out that Woodward and other national coaches are not responsible for setting fixture-lists but are prisoners (as in international cricket) of contra-deals. Has there ever been a more ludicrous example of fixture-making than that which called for England to play Australia in the (bogus) Cook Cup in 1997, one week after the Lions tour had ended in triumph but with most of the party shattered by the fierce season? Some of the Lions' braves had to pack their bags and fly from Johannesburg to Sydney. Do you know what? They lost.

But it was England who pioneered the nonsense that brought all three southern hemisphere giants up to the old country in the same autumn, for four Tests at weekly intervals. How we were supposed to get to know and love each touring team, how tourists were supposed to get to love our green and pleasant lands, has never been clear. Even worse, England's national set-up has pioneered the concept of hogging the whole tour itinerary for themselves. The itinerary they set for the incoming New Zealand tour in 1997, in which all three of the non-Test matches they were granted were filled by England A combinations, was a disgrace on the face of rugby. If they had regionalised the teams a little it would have been marginally better.

Then there was Hell. As I've said, I was there, in 1998, and still shudder. Hell wore the label of a real rugby tour, and mocked it. England's tour of the southern hemisphere (most of it) brutalised the touring squad and also rugby's tradition so violently that it still offends me to this day. It was instructive, as the media are so often accused of being wise after the event, to see in the cuttings library that the 'Tour to Hell' was so dubbed well before it ever took off.

Even when your men are being paid, what lasting benefits can be derived from arranging two Tests against New Zealand, one against Australia and one against South Africa, and three fierce non-Test matches, on the same five-week tour? What is the point even if you are not in the least bit interested in fixing a tour that your players can enjoy? No wonder nineteen players, all the cream, found reasons not to attend, decided not to aggravate further the injuries they were carrying. What eventuated was an embarrassing shambles in which England, their team and reputation, were murdered. What is now so wrong with the concept of, say, a seven-match tour to one country where you have two Saturday matches in which your Test team works up and acclimatises, three provincial games for the second-string players to test themselves (not against the Combined Yokel Second XV, but against good provinces) and then the two-Test series? And to break camp at least every week, so that the tour moves on and absorbs more of the sporting and other cultures? What is so wrong with that concept?

The Tour to Hell brought barely any recompense. The team flew into Brisbane, had a few days' recovery, were smashed by Australia, flew out. The itinerary in New Zealand defied belief. They spent ten interminable days in Rotorua, a long journey by road south of Auckland through some of the least arresting countryside in New Zealand. It was not as if Rotorua provided a training base of particular majesty. The hotel was reasonable, its gym minuscule, and the training pitch was a training pitch. It was rectangular in shape, and had posts and grass.

It was not as if they were building for a match. They did not even play a match there in that whole ten days, but travelled from their base half-way back to Auckland for a dire game on a filthy night in Hamilton against New Zealand A, then back again after midnight to Nowhere Base, Rotorua. Meaning that they had effectively and needlessly retraced their steps three times.

Fair enough to Rotorua. The Whakarewarewa, the venue of the boiling mud-pools and geysers, is fine for a half-day visit, even for those of us who'd seen it and smelled it before. But each day, the party of earnest England no-hopers would go out and train. And then mooch. There were a few activities, some of which were cancelled because of the foul weather. The aroma from the emissions of hydrogen sulphide was ghastly.

'The pungent odour is highly noticeable when you first arrive,' one guide book said. 'Strangely, you soon get used to it.' No you bloody well don't, Mr Guidebook Author. I remember Eddie Butler's fervent heart-cry, uttered as he walked the same dark and lengthy corridor to his room for the 100th time in ten days, listened to the same horrific muzak bellowing through the speakers, reached his room, which featured an emissions outlet outside the window, and swore that this was his last tour.

We'd exhausted the possibilities of the two decent restaurants early in the stay-over, moodily mooched around as the team mooched. There was one memorable night, when the assembled hacks, staring at fizzy lager in practically the only bar with a light to illuminate the drizzling dark, decamped to a Chinese restaurant, begged them to stay open longer than the traditional nine o'clock, clicked into some kind of gear and cleaned them out of all their alcohol. We decided on a sing-song. Having no common repertoire barring the national anthems we had listened to before kick-off in a variety of countries around the world, we sang all those, or hummed if we didn't know the words. The only rule was respect for the anthems of other countries.

When I went to the loo, I realised that the bellowing waves of noise were breaking over an otherwise deserted, shut and silent town. In tribute to South Africa, we toyi-toyied our way back to the hotel, reflecting that it must be bloody awful for the players because they couldn't even have a drink to break the monotony. We ran into Ben Clarke, that great man dedicated to the realities of the era of prohibition and austerity and yet with a foot and a heart in the great days. 'Clarkie, you must be hating all this,' we said. 'Well,' said the genial Clarke. 'It can be a bit of a trial.' The mood had dissipated half-way down the corridor to our rooms.

Colleagues who had never toured New Zealand before wondered aloud at the heady testimonies I had given the place. I had to explain, as the tour rambled on and moved interminably towards South Africa, that the planners had set out to show New Zealand in the most grisly possible light, had dragged us to all the worst bits in a wet winter and let down not only the history of rugby tours but also the image of the Land of the Long White Cloud.

The final provincial match was something of a puzzle. Having already stayed in Rotorua for ten days for no apparent reason, for the last provincial outing the team had to fly down from their base in Auckland. To Rotorua. By that time, many of us had become immune to the rape of the touring concept and therefore did not have the heart to ask why England did not play a match in Rotorua during the pointless time we had stayed there. Matt Dawson and his team remained loyal, worked hard. It was difficult to believe that Cliff Morgan or Jeff Butterfield or Fergus Slattery would not have retired on day two of a tour like this, such was the drastic paucity of things to do, people to meet, culture to dive into. It would hardly have been a surprise if Big Ben had chucked it in too, since he was old enough to remember when touring had been a privilege and a joy and to be offended by the lack of either.

When in June of 2000 England ventured out again, this time only to South Africa, the tour-planners were miffed when the *Sunday Times* revealed that the party had chosen austere surroundings and itinerary. The South African Rugby Football Union were so cheesed off that the party intended to see so little of their country and rugby population that they even refused to pay England's hotel bill. In exchange for touring finery, we had the converse. A splendidly dedicated group, eschewing frippery and tourism and culture in favour of rugby. To the point where Woodward and his chiefs worried about them. You cannot mock such dedication, you cannot try to impose the values of an earlier era. You can, however, theorise that there is a balance that can be struck. A real tour does *not* imply lack of professionalism.

It was partly found in the first full week of the tour when England had to emerge from their hotel grounds to play a provincial match. My account of the day never appeared in the *Sunday Times* that week, and quite rightly, because if we had not run the report of the Southern Counties Underwater Bowls Championships then readers would have been up in arms. This is what the paper would have carried had the bowls been rained off.

South Africa's N12 is a dusty highveld road which snakes southwest out of Johannesburg, bypassing Soweto without you ever realising that the teeming urban sprawl is even there, because the rulers in the apartheid years wished this reservoir of labour for Johannesburg to be out of sight as well as out of mind. The road passes nothing in the way of creature comforts, nothing bar dry veld and flywheels drawing up water; nothing to interrupt the ribbon of tarmac except for the occasional four-way crossroads here and there where no one, especially the visitor, is really clear as to the right of way. You either get four vehicles stationary, waiting for another to move, or four vehicles crashing in a heap in the middle.

They told us that the journey back to Johannesburg after dark should be made only in convoys, because the road is the haunt of car-jackers. We took their advice, and there were no good Samaritans to stop for cars we found broken down at the side of the road, kilometres from anywhere, and no roadside phones.

Emerging last Tuesday morning from a modern-day laager, taking the N12 from Johannesburg in their air-conditioned coach, was the England rugby team. They drove out from their hotel in the northern suburbs of Johannesburg, from which they are warned not to emerge at night on foot – not that there is anywhere or anything to walk to in any case. But for one day they were more than a cocooned, scientific-ally prepared group. They were a travelling band. They will stay in the same hotel for every night bar one of their trip, but last Tuesday they were forced out to meet the locals, and to play the Northwest Leopards down the N12 in Potchefstroom.

It is to be sincerely hoped that at least some of the party knew, or took the trouble to learn, about the hosting town, orderly in its residential blocks but scruffy and functional and unlovely. It was my fifth visit to the place, and on each visit it has been possible to trace the development of South Africa itself, the steady, halting and yet in some cases determined plod towards a different society. Potchefstroom was, and at heart still is, redneck country. A large proportion of the crowd at the match were conservative Afrikaner men of the land. And not rich arriviste owners, but people born and bred in the district and with the veld in every pore. Apartheid died hard here.

At the time of transition in 1992, when South Africa were allowed back to international rugby and the African National Congress were preparing for election, there was a major clash in rugby between the old and new cultures. It was always in Potchefstroom that the biggest majority of the crowd would still be flying the old South African flag. It was always in Potchefstroom that the biggest majority would want to sing 'Die Stem', the old Afrikaner anthem. It was always in Potchefstroom that you felt the non-white players in the home team were there not on merit, not even as a token, but as a sop.

This time, we could see only one old flag, and a decent number of non-white rugby followers among hordes of stolid locals stolidly taking in their beer and the curtain-raisers. Curtain-raisers are usually impossible in wet old Britain, but here on the dry grounds and on the tough grasses we saw no fewer than eight. They ranged upwards in ages and abilities culminating in a storming match between Rand Afrikaans University, the famous RAU, and Potchefstroom Gymnasium – two U21 teams, but for this country typically massive.

The whole scene was culture-shocking for the English, and especially for the younger players on their first major trip – the likes of Liam Botham, David Flatman and Steve Borthwick. It must have seemed like they had stepped on to another planet. The Olen Park Stadium has a gaunt stand on one side and on the other a giant, rusting scaffold contraption holding thousands of spectators, which any inspector from the Safety at Sports Grounds Act in Britain would have condemned without even having to leave the car park to begin his inspection.

Indeed, a few of the England team almost left the planet. The pitch was circled with the most mean and vicious band of police dogs you've ever seen, including one giant Rottweiler which snapped and slobbered as the English replacements were trying to warm up down the touchline. You got the impression, not to be too British about it, that South African police dogs are trained up until the point when they are let loose, so that while British police dogs are taught merely to restrain, their South African counterparts simply make their own arrangements once off-leash.

And England could easily have lost a few more personnel in one of the most memorably dishevelled pre-game shows imaginable. Half an hour before kick-off, the pitch was absolutely packed with people. In one half, around eighty old players from the Northwest team paraded. They were led by Johann Claassen, the former Springbok great. It should have been a wonderful occasion, except that because of the predilection of the Potch spectators for drinking beer and talking among themselves, hardly anyone acknowledged the poor old dears. The other half of the pitch was filled by the England squad warming up.

Then, in the middle of it all, a posse of sky-divers hurtled down, with every man desperately trying to adjust as he approached terra firma so as not to flatten someone on the ground. One parachutist missed Simon Shaw by only a few feet, and another almost wiped out half a generation of former Northwest greats, then landed a few feet from the snapping jaws of the Rottweiler.

Even the match programme was uniquely African. It revealed that the name of the home manager was Arthur Breakfast. Also, in what was either a printing mistake or a deliberate mickey-take of events surrounding the arrival of Andy Robinson as coach and speculation that this was a down-grade for Clive Woodward, it stated that Robinson was head coach and Woodward his assistant. The score-board recorded a match between Luiperd and Engeland, so we suddenly realised that when England's football supporters chant their boring chant, they are merely speaking in Afrikaans.

The scoreboard also recorded a very fine 52–22 victory for England. And at the end, the travelling party scuttled off in convoy for the security-patrolled high walls of the Johannesburg hotels, leaving scruffy Potchefstroom behind. What a day. I loved every moment, and sincerely hope that some of the players did too. 'All that lot want to do,' one of the coaching hierarchy told me, 'is get back to the hotel and start their active recovery programmes, and then go to bed.' I hope that at least some of the English team realised that they had had a day straight from the grand old days of rugby lore. Despite the frustrations and the privations and the dangers, they had seen another culture. They had met not abnormal people but normal people. It might have been just for one day, but last week in Potchefstroom, England's rugby trip became a rugby tour.

❊   ❊   ❊

When Martin Johnson returned to England he penned his usual column for Planet Rugby. It was a good read. He revealed that as the England team waited at Johannesburg International, they ran into the Springboks, who were waiting for their flight to Australia. 'We bumped into the Boks . . . and André Venter gave us his card and offered to put any of us up at his place if we wanted a holiday. Nice guy!' No doubt he is, Martin. And I'd bet that some of the other Boks are nice guys – and shame you didn't get the chance to find out.

It was, perhaps, ironic that concurrent with England's non-tour of South Africa, the RFU's splendid museum back at Twickenham was showing a special exhibition devoted to touring's grand history, which they called 'Distant Shores'. There was an exhibit on the 1888 tour of this country by the New Zealand Natives team, when they played a ludicrously heroic seventy-four matches. There was a pre-Subbuteo 'tactics board', a beautifully made small table in the shape of a rugby pitch, with beautifully made small figures, so that the 1950 British Lions party could talk tactics on their sea voyage to New Zealand, Australia and Ceylon. There were away from home for six months.

There was also recorded a complaint from the Scottish lock, Gordon Brown, from a previous tour on which Brown had been unimpressed by the hotel. 'I said to the hotel manager that this was supposed to be a five-star hotel and there was bloody hole in the roof.' He turned round and said to me: "That's so you can see the five stars." '

And there was a quote from Lawrence Dallaglio. 'If touring ever goes, rugby will have lost part of its soul.'

I do not blame the players of today, because they – Dallaglio and John Eales and David Young and Todd Blackadder and young Steve Borthwick and the others – are men of their time. Mostly they are spending their time in the way that they choose. I do blame, in part, the prevalent near-paranoia which so affects the affairs of national-team squads and their management teams. And I do not think that it was simply inevitable that the pendulum should have swung so abruptly and so completely away from vivid experience and fun and towards austerity. Towards a situation where Clive Woodward, who made some of the great tours as a player, can now say: 'The old-style tours are dead. Gone.'

From grand adventure and crusade to sterile sport. No, I do not blame the modern player. But I do deeply mourn for him for what he is missing. And I mourn for rugby, and the end of the great adventures.

CHAPTER FOURTEEN

Waterloo

Fast women: Gill's girls find fame ♦ The black shadow of New Zealand, playing on the edge of arrogance

The assembled company were more than a little surprised. It was late and that day's international was finally chewed up, and the restaurant table resembled a mini-Manhattan skyline of empty bottles – and I felt like I'd drunk the Empire State Building. Right. Before we go, we all have to name our ultimate rugby hero. Waiter, another skyscraper . . .

I mulled over my contenders – David Watkins, Keith Jarrett, John Rutherford, Jeremy Guscott, Ben Clarke, Al Charron, Dave Sims, Frank Bunce, Shane Howarth, Sean Fitzpatrick, Wade Dooley, Martin Johnson, Newport's captain in any season, hordes of unsung greats and all-time greats and Dragons and Lions. And I realised that it was none of these, that my rugby hero was from the relatively humble Waterloo club; and that it was not a hero, but a heroine.

She once approached Mick Cleary, now rugby correspondent of the *Daily Telegraph*, at a sports writers' dinner and asked for his autograph. Cleary almost fell over. 'I think this should be the other way round,' he said. We haven't let her forget it.

Gillian Burns is still a teacher of physical education at Range High School, north of Liverpool. She is no longer England's rugby captain, having been superseded for the Five Nations Championship 2000 season, in which England won a resounding Grand Slam, by the Wasps full-back, Paula George. Burns moved downwards to the England A team, was agonisingly stuck on forty-nine caps for her country, as the coaches went for a new approach – and, frankly, as they began to plan rather nervously for the era in which England could no longer rely on the dominating presence of either of their world-class players of the past decade, Burns and the scrum-half, Emma Mitchell.

Burns, typically, was refusing to let that era dawn. 'I still think I have something to offer,' she wrote in her own website column at the turn of the millennium, perhaps aiming the words at the England selectors as well as at the Web-ites. The selectors appeared to have read it. Clare Frost, the Saracen who had taken Burns's place at No. 8, was injured for the match against Wales in March. Burns stepped up, led the team on to the pitch at Newbury to mark her fiftieth cap and played as well, as far as I could see, as she must have done in the other forty-nine matches. 'She was the first of us who ran and played like a player, not just like a woman,' said one of the veterans of the early years.

The first time I met her was about five years ago on the playing fields of her school, in a free period between lessons, on a bitter morning of white frost. The great photographer Chris Smith, the only journalistic colleague of whom I am in permanent awe, was clicking away with his camera. He came up with a delightful photograph for the *Sunday Times* that weekend, with Burns framed by powder-blue winter sky and white frosty pitch, her shoulder leading and the ball tucked under her arm as if she were making a driving burst. It demonstrated her power and athleticism and yet retained, if in her guise as international rugby player she cared, her femininity. Thanks, Smithy. How am I supposed to accompany that in words when your camera has already written them? I looked in the back-issue department the other day to see if I'd done Chris and Gill justice. I hadn't.

The interview was back at the start of 1996, but by this time Burns had already been captain for three years and was already the most recognisable, erudite and best woman player. She'd started by accident. 'I met some hockey players at a tournament who were wearing rugby-club sweaters. I went with them to Waterloo, where they trained. In my first match I was crawling around on the floor conceding penalties because I didn't know the laws. But afterwards there was this incredible buzz. I had played many other sports, but I thought to myself: "I love this." '

She was also years before her time. The England squad in 2000 comprises a group of outstanding athletes, whereas in the early years the squad were the best fruits of a motley band who'd decided to give the sport a lash. But Gill Burns had always been ahead of the pack. She had represented British colleges at swimming, athletics, basketball and hockey, was still competing in hammer, shot and sprints. In the summer this strong-running, hammer-throwing, shot-putting No. 8 would revert to a family love – ballet. Her mum taught it. 'After the season is over,' she told me, 'I dance like mad to be ready for shows in June and July.' This amounts to a quite staggering array of talents, way above that displayed by the most talented all-rounder in the men's national team.

Burns has always had to range far from the field of play. Her car and its mileage became a standing joke in the game. The clock was up to 150,000 those five years ago – from chugging to away matches on Sundays, packed to bursting; to the daily training sessions; and also to workshops and coaching sessions and newly formed clubs and any-where else where she and her England-team colleagues could promote the game to youngsters. She was obviously a sportswoman of the most fierce dedication, whether on the field or off. And her belief in rugby as a recreation and even as a career for women was and is implacable.

These days, with Sport England providing the life-blood of funding under its World-Class Performance lottery grant (and unlucky lottery players can be assured that in fewer places is their money better spent), the top women players have assistance towards training and living expenses, can even eke out a living if they combine their onerous training regimes with part-time jobs. It may not be much, but it is not so long ago that being England's captain cost Gill Burns a fortune.

It is appropriate that she should still have been playing well and at the top when funding arrived and profile expanded. She has been through all the phases in the women's game. Not just the dawn of international-class athleticism; not just the era in which the International Rugby Board brought the women's game under its wing and staged a proper World Cup; not just the era in which players at the top level had to make sacrifices; but even the era before that. Players new to the England squad should remember that Gill Burns also had to negotiate – with profound patience and with teeth gritted, and yet also with true missionary zeal – in the era when all kinds of people were snide and even abusive about a woman's right to be on a rugby field in the first place. That is something for the new women stars to ponder, left as they are to concentrate on their world-class performance in a sporting world that entirely accepts them. If I were Gill's agent (well, if she had one) I'd demand ten per cent from them all for what she did for them in laying the foundations.

That endearing and misplaced diffidence she demonstrated when she asked for Mick Cleary's autograph remains. There is a shyness about her which evokes profoundly different emotions from those you feel when you see her play. She was distraught at having to miss the crunch game of all England's women's rugby history, against the brilliant New Zealanders in the World Cup semi-final in 1998. England lost to the Kiwis, battling magnificently, missing the teak-tough attitude of their captain. I met her hobbling around the stadium in Amsterdam before the match, visibly fighting back the tears because the tendon injury she had sustained in the pool games wasn't responding. It was all I could do not to give her the biggest hug I could muster; something in me wanted to do it but something else warned me that she might deem it patronising.

She seemed to be vaguely mystified when in 1999 the Rugby Writers' Club honoured her for her services to the game at their annual dinner, whereas anyone in our organisation who had ever come across her was well aware that the gesture was the very least we could do. And no one would have felt in the least bit uncomfortable – or, indeed, would have deemed it inappropriate – had she arrived at the Café Royal in a chariot and dressed as Boadicea. Instead, she arrived armed with only a soft Scouse accent. It is a wholly remarkable feat to reach the top of women's rugby and compromise neither your sex nor your sport.

Still, maybe we shouldn't feel too endeared. You cannot achieve what she has achieved unless you have a profound sporting self-belief and talent. Forgive for the moment the narcissistic quote-back, because I did concede that the article did justice to neither Gill Burns or Chris Smith, but I wrote after that first interview: 'It is a long time since I was so impressed by someone in sport. It is not so much that she is a fine player and athlete, such a selfless ambassador for women's rugby . . . it is that Burns came across, in every respect, as a genuine, twenty-four-carat English sporting heroine.'

Even under the influence at the Manhattan-style table four years later, I found no reason to change those words. Especially not the last one.

They keep escaping you, these women. Getting away. They are always on the far horizon, especially if you are too ensnared in the men's game to follow them closely enough. By the time you catch up with them they've moved their game on, in terms of numbers and standards. They've moved on so long ago that the dust has settled. Women's rugby in the current era is one of the marvels of any period in any sport.

I had never seen a women's match prior to the 1991 Women's World Cup, which was held in Cardiff in a pioneer spirit. If one of the visiting teams had no money for food, the others would give them some or cajole someone to put them up. I did know that the explosion in the numbers taking up the game had seen scores of new clubs formed, and while hundreds of sports always claim to be the fastest-growing, it was statistically proven by official measurers that women's rugby was by miles the fastest-growing sport in Britain.

At the time of that tournament, too, the initial rush of abuse that women players suffered was losing momentum – whether this abuse came from the fogies and other helpless defectives who told the women that they had no business on a rugby field; from the feature-writers (of both sexes) who always concentrated almost exclusively on irrelevancies, in the manner of the Monty Python interview with the leading composer Arthur Two Sheds Jackson, in which they kept referring to his two sheds and not to his genius; from the drunks and phwoaarmongers who imagined that a women's rugby match would be played by two teams of models in their underwear and therefore, when a match took place between two teams, even those at the top level, who had decided for some unfathomable reason not to play in heavy make-up and stockings, called them butch or lesbian or other terms they imagined were either offensive or hilarious . . . By 1991 a few profile-writers were even going along and asking the girls about their rugby, their sporting lives and their sporting pride. Respect.

England reached that 1991 final and were to play the United States on the Cardiff RFC ground one Sunday. To preview the match (and being clueless) I needed some kind of reaction from one of the England team as they prepared. I rang the England centre, Samantha Robson, because they told me she spoke well. They were right. In the back of my mind, I suppose I had thought she'd come up with some kind of endearingly naïve look at the final and about how nice it all was, that she was learning lots of rugby's rudiments every day and that her boyfriend was managing to put up with her playing, and so on.

It was in around the second minute of Robson's charming and yet supremely hard-headed and wise assessment of what England had to do to win and fulfil their goals that I realised that it was me, not she, who was naïve, and that it was highly probable I had seriously underestimated the progress that the women's game had made. This was proven in a splendid final in which two well-organised teams battled it out and England lost by 19–6. There were two major weaknesses. No one could kick the ball very far, either at goal or out of hand, and therefore infringements were not punished with the requisite severity. Second, the girls had obviously put much time into the arcana of set-piece and ruck and maul, and had not concentrated sufficiently on what they should have been better at – running and handling.

However, they were extremely impressive; and the excellence of the United States backs was quite startling. The sharpness and assured running lines of Candy Orsini, the American full-back, were outstanding and the overall standards and application left me feeling shamefaced. It was not as if I'd ever felt women shouldn't play rugby. Not that I felt that they were out of place in any way whatsoever. It was nice that rugby's family was expanding so rapidly. It was simply that I couldn't believe how far they had come.

And just when you thought you'd caught up, there was another quantum leap for the next World Cup. In the inaugural tournament there was still a feeling abroad that it had to be an entertaining match for the good of the sport. By 1994 the top teams wanted to win, take the title – stuff the spectacle. It was another sign of a fast-growing maturity. When the United States and England once again battled through to the final, at Raeburn Place, Edinburgh, England dynamited any notion that the women's game would follow different precepts and have a different engine to that of the men's; in other words, that their game would not be based on power but would find some other basis. England won by 38–23, completing a vengeful mission by crushing the life out of the USA with a ferocious display of scrummaging that gave them the title in a welter of pushover tries, one from Gill Burns, and penalty tries. I was impressed by the entirely single-minded way in which they set their targets. There was no talk of running the ball to give the match the air of a festival. That would have played into the hands of the Americans, who had scored 364 points in their four matches. The women's World Cup was established as something worth winning at any reasonable cost. England were the World Champions.

By now, the exploits of the England team and the gradual shaking down and improvement in teams in Wales, Scotland and Ireland had seen the advent of home internationals; the sheer numbers had seen a little more shape in the anxious efforts of overworked amateur administrators like Rosie Golby and Susan Eakers. I had come to know Gill Burns and Emma Mitchell, and realised the formidable and selfless dedication with which they went about their rugby lives. It was a time when it cost the players hundreds and even thousands a year to play at the top level. There was once almost a wild celebration when an England–Wales match at Sale actually made a profit on gate-takings.

It was an era when sheer love and application shone through. Maxine Edwards, England prop and a single parent and qualified electrician, had to marshal the demands of Sean (then five), of revising for important exams, and of personal and team training, and all that in the week of an international in France.

Next quantum leap. By the time the 1998 World Cup was staged, in the National Rugby Stadium in Amsterdam, the women's game had been brought under the aegis of the IRB and the World Cup had become an official IRB tournament. My original feeling was sadness that the verve and burgeoning power of the women's game would be suppressed by a load of conservative men in suits who secretly shared Ron Atkinson's view that the little ladies belonged in the kitchen, bedroom and boutique.

I was profoundly mistaken. The IRB helped with finance, promotion and organisation and IRB council members such as Vernon Pugh and Rob Fisher did such a marvellous job in liaising with the leaders of the women's game that they helped to produce an absolutely first-class tournament. From the first match I saw, I realised that again there had been almost a geometric progression from the previous tournament. Just when you thought you knew where you were with them, they'd ploughed on some more.

However, a black shadow had already fallen on the sunrise of women's international rugby in the northern hemisphere. It was another sign that the improvement in standards was actually increasing in pace, but this was something else again. Embossed on the blackness was a silver fern. The grip first squeezed in earnest when England, the reigning World Champions, made a tour of New Zealand in March 1997. New Zealand had lost in the semi-final of the first World Cup and had not competed at all in the second, but in the intervening time – in a kind of parallel with the puppies taken away at birth and raised in *Animal Farm* – they had grown up unheralded and unseen and were then released on an unsuspecting world for a reign of terror. England, admittedly hampered by unavailability and a fractured period of preparation, went down by a shattering 67–0. It was for some of the girls a traumatic match which savaged their self-confidence. It was a sign that, in the rush towards new standards, one country had hit a point of critical mass at which the leap forward was devastating.

The New Zealand team at the 1998 World Cup were one of the most remarkable sporting teams I have seen. In attitude and demeanour, and in their existence on that razor-blade edge of arrogance, there was no difference between them and the men's All Black team. They walked the same walk. They felt the honour of the Black jersey every bit as keenly. Their captain was Farah Palmer, a hooker with precisely the same clipped charm, steely eyes and unnerving cool as Sean Fitzpatrick himself. She was asked why she felt that her team would beat England when the two fought through to the semi-final. She said simply: 'Because we are All Blacks.' As the tournament progressed, as usually happens with the many great New Zealand teams, the desperation for someone, anyone, to beat them and shut them up was overshadowed by an admiration for their supreme pride and application and technical ability. They won their first match, against Germany, by 130–6 and typically – or arrogantly – they announced that they were extremely unhappy about the fact that they had been so disastrously lax as to concede the six. There, there, dears.

For God's sake, even their names were delightfully world-class –

Annaleah Rush, Monalisa Codling, Melodie Robinson, Sayonara Su'a, Kellie Kiwi. Their marketing was also sublime, sometimes by accident and sometimes by design. They had their own Jonah in the strapping left wing Louisa Wall; they had their own *haka*, which Maori elders had allowed them to perform. Wall led it in Amsterdam. 'It is a challenge to the opposition. We imagine that we have them around their throats and are strangling them,' she said. There was a few seconds' pause as we waited for her to burst into the grin that said she was only joking. Took a long time in coming, that grin.

They had their squad beauty-queen in Melodie Robinson, a former Miss Canterbury – and shame on those who have visited that great province in the South Island and joked that she couldn't have had much to beat, because she was an incredibly striking girl. It was announced that Melodie, obviously a handful on and off the field, had tired of the regulation shapeless blazer-and-skirt uniform and the lumpy tracksuit alternative, and designed, herself, a new team uniform. The squad paraded in sharp charcoal-grey suits which made them look like a group of focused, attractive and impressive business people. (Robinson herself was unblinking as a nasty cut on her forehead was stitched, leaving, at least initially, an ugly wound. Her modelling career evidently came second to her sporting career.) It was certainly a profound change for the world-weary ranks of rugby photographers to be able to complete an assignment where the subject did not have to be pushed and pulled into some kind of snappable position and told to wipe at least some of the scowl off his or her face, but instead posed photogenically, suggested new ideas herself. Happy snappers.

How had the Kiwi women's squad convinced New Zealand's some-times unemancipated rugby men that they meant business, were worthy of support and worthy to wear the New Zealand fern? Not by crying into the isotonic drinks that rotten old males were putting them down, that's for sure. 'We told them that they had to go out and earn respect,' their coach, Daryl Suasua, told me. 'They had to put in the work, to play attractive football. Then people started appreciating them as the athletes they are. And we all live for rugby. The girls' fathers and brothers have all played, so they understand the game. Most of them have reached the top in other sports too. They bring with them values about quality of performance and motivation.'

The authorities were convinced. The New Zealand Rugby Union gave excellent moral and practical support, and have extended their package for 2000. The support given for the 1998 World Cup was outstanding and left other teams a vivid green with envy and frustration.

The girls were paid expenses, they were given a daily allowance and any loss of earnings was made up. By previous standards it was a grand and noble gesture; by modern standards, and because of the good that the girls did for the name of New Zealand and for women's rugby, it was the very least the Union could do. But at a time when funding to alleviate hardships was only just beginning to trickle into the other leading squads, particularly England's, and when most of the participating sixteen teams were suffering huge financial losses, it gave the Kiwis an overwhelming advantage. On the England men's Tour to Hell and New Zealand in 1998, the All Black girls were produced at most of the games and other gatherings, celebs to the letter.

The support enabled Suasua to achieve a supreme level of planning and organisation. A year before the World Cup he had written a game-plan and set down the qualities required in each position in order for it to be fulfilled. Then he went round New Zealand and found the players to fit his bill. 'I asked the selectors to find one to play and one as back-up in every position. For example, I wanted two different styles on the wing, one big and strong player to set up play; the other with blistering pace who is expected to play on both sides.' So with the powerful Wall on one wing, he added Vanessa Cootes, an explosively fast player who scored a sensational thirty tries in her first six international matches.

Throughout the tournament New Zealand played with a marvellous mixture of athleticism and rugby nous. Their tight forwards were only so-so, but Robinson and her back row were exceptional and their backs were dazzling by any standards. Their passion was enormous. 'We get so much from our sense of history and everything that the All Blacks jersey means,' Suasua said. 'We heard Michael Jones saying that every All Black jersey he has won meant as much as the first. That makes you well up inside. We give out match jerseys individually. Before the opening game, I'd say that ninety per cent of the squad had tears in their eyes.'

This taught us all lessons, not just on the New Zealand women's team but on the All Blacks of either sex; on that mystical bond, that brotherhood or sisterhood of the Silver Fern, that unbreakable attachment to history which dictates that when you wear your All Black jersey you join all those who have worn its number in the past. It is a belief in their history and destiny that the players of no other nation, with the possible exception of the Springboks, have to anything remotely like the same extent. They say rugby is a technical exercise, but if you watched Suasua's All Blacks you would realise that New Zealand greatness goes far deeper than something you can chalk on a blackboard in a team room. It goes to the depth of the Black sporting hearts.

❊ ❊ ❊

The wider tournament. It was a particular delight that the ability of the women's team often bore no relation to that of the men's team in the same country. Kazakhstan beat Wales, guided beautifully by Altiya Tamaeva, a fly-half with a stunning natural talent for the game. Spain, probably the smallest team in the tournament, played with great courage to finish fourth, fighting all the way in defeat in their pool match against the All Blacks.

England had been given the shock of their lives when they had crashed so heavily in New Zealand, and they had only a few short months before they faced the same challenge in the World Cup. By this time, the years of heroic privation in which Gill Burns had begun her England career had given way to an new era of proper preparation and back-up, and even some funding from the Sports Council's World-Class Performance grants. They were able to employ Carol Isherwood, a former flanker who had become probably the most rugby-wise woman in the sport, to oversee the application of the grant and to account for the fact that it was well spent. They appointed from Loughborough Rex Hazeldine, one of the most famous fitness and conditioning experts, to augment their usual coaches.

Throughout the preparations the team was splendidly defiant. I put it to Emma Mitchell, who had become every bit as outstanding a player and as fine a spokeswoman as Burns, that England's real problem in the World Cup lay in the fact that they must be expecting defeat at the hands of New Zealand, and so would suffer one. Defeat, it seemed, had never even entered her head. 'We have been working extremely hard; we have been honest about the defeat in New Zealand and we firmly believe we can beat them in the World Cup. They are good, but they are not invincible.'

These were brave words, even though I had a feeling that the Kiwis had simply stolen the kind of march on the rest of the sport that Bob Beamon had stolen on the long-jump in 1968 in Mexico. So it was to prove. England had to meet New Zealand in the semi-final. They also had to do so without Burns, beaten by injury on the very day of her whole career when she most wanted to be fit. It was still a remarkable match, played in temperatures in the nineties, on a hard, harsh field. England fought the Kiwis, all their preparation and *haka*-ing and funding and arrogance, as if possessed. The No. 8, Clare Frost, had a magnificent game, and the England forwards gained the upper hand in the first half. Near to half-time the New Zealanders, clearly shaken, led by only 6–0.

England were eventually overwhelmed and lost by 44–11 to a team that was outstanding at every point. The satisfaction for England is that for long periods the ice-calmness of the Kiwis disappeared. I have no real measuring rod because I had seen relatively few England international women's matches, but I strongly suspected that the first half, because it pitted two teams which (with the greatest possible respect) were ill-matched, represented the finest half-hour or so in their history. New Zealand then went on to beat USA by 44–12 in the final.

The cloud is still hanging. It seemed to me highly unlikely that the All Blacks would lose a match in the next five years, possibly even ten. They have such support, of both practical and moral kinds. It seemed it would take the other fine teams in the world, the likes of England, Scotland, Australia and the United States, a long time to narrow the gap to a point where results against New Zealand are not foregone conclusions. All the players and back-up people involved in those teams will have to redouble their efforts; funding will have to be increased. The whole national rugby scene will have to reset its sights.

And the drawback may well be that the current players in all those squads will not be there to savour the fruits of their labour, that the uplift they create will reap rewards only for their successors. There is no doubt that women's international rugby is still enjoying a phase of heady improvement. But it also seems to me that New Zealand's extraordinary advance has thrown the sport at the top level out of kilter.

Or will England, and others, confound predictions yet again? I met one of those who has inherited Gill Burns's legacy just before the 2000 Five Nations, an event which for the first time included Spain. Nicola Jupp, the Richmond and England centre, six feet tall with a career as an international heptathlete behind her, personified the current state of the game, state of the art, even. The squad for 2000 contained hardly a single member who did not have behind her a major achievement in another sport. They also had a further upwards revision of their preparation culture, which now involved a host of medical, psychological, nutritional and technical back-up, with Isherwood as performance director and a high-powered Australian, Rob Drinkwater, as individual player development manager. As ever, the sense of purpose was fierce. It seemed that England were chasing the All Blacks at a high pace.

The presence of Jupp and others in the squad confirmed an important truth – that high-class athletes were now seeing rugby as a natural outlet for their talents instead of opting for other sports. And with the lottery money they could even go full-time; if they could not earn enough to buy a house, then it was at least enough to keep the wolf from their door.

Jupp still worked for Carlsberg-Tetley in Northampton but maintained a blistering schedule of team, unit and individual training and retained her own track coach outside the squad loop.

Her application was formidable. She keenly felt the pressure of representing her country and of having to live up to the World-Class Performance tag. 'The goals are so high, it is hard to get there and harder to stay there. When you are out on the field, internationals are just a job. You can enjoy them afterwards but it ain't nice out on the pitch.' The last of the wide-eyed wonder of the top women players seemed well in the past. Jupp's vitality, her appetite for the sport and the goals she had set seemed thoroughly modern.

Some of the pressure is unnecessary. The only silly aspect of the grant system is that it can be taken away on the grounds of the odd sporting defeat. The Scotland team were given similar funding and yet were assured of retaining it only if they won the Five Nations in 2000 – the fact that they could have improved six times over and used every penny wisely was apparently not taken into consideration, which is ridiculous. England won a Grand Slam, with the key victory coming in France. There, the commitment was thunderous, and Jupp helped set up an England score with such a clattering tackle on her opposite number that it must have seemed as if an unholy combination of a tank and the angel of death had arrived at once. However, they were beaten by France in the European Championships at the end of the season, a defeat which caused a wave of anxiety, and redoubled commitment.

Nicky Jupp has no intention whatsoever of allowing New Zealand to lord it over anyone a second longer than is necessary. 'I played against them in the Hong Kong Sevens and I found them a great set of girls and a great set of athletes. But so are we. Our coaches have analysed the tapes over and over again to find what makes them tick; our preparation now is brilliant, we feel we are improving all the time. Of course we can catch up with them. Of course we can.' So I could even be wrong again; and some time in the near future England, or another top team, could yet complete the most difficult advance of all and down the Blacks – muddy those charcoal suits, throw the *haka* back and get their own hands round Kiwi throats. See how they like it.

There was a final sign of well-founded self-confidence earlier this year when one of the sport's sponsors, Bread for Life, and the Women's RFU initiated a survey among the top players which unashamedly pushed sex-appeal. It is a fact proven beyond all doubt by men's teams that not everyone in a side can be sold on the way they look, and so it is in women's teams. But after years during which the girls were anxious about exploiting their own advantages, so anxious about pushing the wrong image that they hardly had one, they came out and (tongue-in-cheek) began to tease their way into greater consciousness. We learned which heart-throbs the top players most wanted to snog. We learned about the favourite parts of their own bodies, about their lifestyles. It was fun, harmless, it caught the attention and it did them good to flex different muscles. It was a supremely well-judged manoeuvre. It seemed there was an enormous difference between selling yourself in a certain fashion because you craved attention, and doing so because you'd received it as your due.

By the turn of the millennium women of all playing standards had asserted themselves in numbers. They had become, because they had earned the right to be nothing else, entirely unapologetic on the rugby field. At international level, in terms of commitment and driving for excellence, they had earned the right to be ranked alongside any sportsperson of either sex, the England men's rugby team included.

I suppose, therefore, that it was with the cares of a father that I hoped little Rosanna Angharad Jones would never have to stand out there while the Kiwis' *haka* menaced her team. Still, I've been wrong about the women's game before. Maybe there is an international player in the family after all. Not the worst way to gain due respect for her sex.

CHAPTER FIFTEEN

Canary Wharf

**Re-fuelling – gracious rugby life in the services ◆
Eavesdropping on the Russians ◆ The good news that the
Navy's *still* here**

As a means of reaching the heart of the City of London, it was unbeatable.
HMS *Marlborough*, a Royal Navy Type-23 frigate, glided inch-perfect into
a narrow dock near Canary Wharf, touched the sides to tie up with
hardly a nudge of the dock wall, the fenders hardly crunching. There
was nothing to jolt the multi-million-pound array of weapons systems
and other space age technology, nor the Lynx helicopter (at present
without its Sea Skua missiles) sitting inoffensively on its pad at the back
and unremarkable until its pilot explained to us some of its capability –
and then we were grateful not to have been in Iraqi patrol boats in the
Gulf War as this hornet from Hell flashed towards them.

And nothing to disturb the drinks of the guests on board, a party of
non-combatant chickens for whom the best form of defence has always
been retreat – from the rugby media. We were being entertained with a
view not only to showing the senior service in a good light but also to
encouraging a few words of preview for the forthcoming inter-services
tournament. The majesty of the ship and the calm ultra-professionalism
about the people who sailed in it, not to mention the awe in the faces of
those down below on the dock gazing up at this sleek wonder, left an
indelible impression.

It had picked us up from a naval tender out in the Thames, had come
out of a mist, surging along towards London. 'God, are you sure it's
going to stop for us?' we asked one of the naval coves as the bow wave
rose higher. 'No, it isn't,' he said. The tender came alongside as the
Marlborough slowed slightly, a rope ladder came flying over the side,
flung by unseen hands into our bucking boat. The sides of the warship
above bevelled outwards, so as to hinder radar detection, they told us.
And also to hinder boarding parties of queasy hacks who'd been fêted at

the Royal Naval College the night before by Captain Chris Tuffley of the Royal Navy and the Rugby Football Union, a man who has always been disappointingly and entirely reticent when we asked for all the scandal from his time as captain of the royal yacht *Britannia*. The first marauding hack up the ladder swung away from the ship, then cannoned back into it and fell off back into the tender. Bravely, we pressed home our assault and, green-faced and quivering, were hauled on board by laughing sailors, and later told seafaring yarns about sailing on the tempestuous high seas of the, er, Thames.

Press days laid on by the services have been one of the joys of a hack's life, speaking for this hack. So many memories from the pre-pro days. There was a magnificent evening in Aldershot when the Combined Services played, then entertained the touring Soviet Union rugby team, themselves featuring a large contingent of servicemen, including front-line pilots. To get over the language problem they stationed interpreters from the signal corps between each Brit and each Russian, and everyone chatted happily. The signals people had spent their working lives listening into transmissions from the Russian military. None of them let on if they recognised any of the voices around the rugby tables. Someone played the Post Horn Galop on an upturned rifle. We bought Russian tour T-shirts from them at £5 a time.

Once they took us on board HMS *Amazon* off Plymouth, in high seas. One of our hosts, Commander Tony Hallett, was reckoned by foul rumour-mongers not to have joined us after all because it was too rough for him. After firing off its guns, *Amazon* demonstrated its turbo engines, as opposed to those it used for normal running. The ship appeared to rise out of the water and became some kind of giant, blistering speedboat. Its helicopter flew off and gave a hair-raising flying display, seemingly standing, poised, on its end in the sky.

There was an adventure in a glorious, cloudless sky over Britain when they took us up in the RAF VC10 tanker, and we flew high above northern Britain making rendezvous with Harriers and Tornadoes, which would materialise out of thin air and slide alongside, edging forward on to the snaking full lines. Then we sat in the cockpit and the giant tanker flew up a few yards behind a sister plane, itself trailing a fuel line for us to lock on to.

Even Flight Lieutenant Rory Underwood came alongside us in an aircraft to give us a promotional wave. He was sitting in the back, being piloted. 'Don't strain yourself, Rory,' shouted someone as Underwood waved in a Queen Motherly fashion. The level of professionalism about the whole thing was preposterous. Don't set sporting professionalism alongside what these guys do, even in peacetime, we all concluded back on the ground at RAF Brize Norton.

They even laid on a jump by the RAF Falcons for us and for service grandees. We were used to sky-divers by now, as we had watched various ragged-backsided troupes delivering the match ball before kick-off at a variety of rugby grounds around the world, including a diver who landed in the next stadium after bouncing off the roof at Lancaster Park, Christchurch; not to mention the diver who missed Simon Shaw by a foot in Potchefstroom. Not much of a comparison, in fact. The Falcons gave a staggering display. You could see them stacked perfectly after they had left the aircraft, see them arcing down in a variety of close formations, then landing one after another on an area not the size of a rugby pitch but of a pinhead.

On these occasions, servicemen of stratospheric rank had to rub shoulders, in the cause of PR, with dishevelled rugby writers. Once at Twickenham a face I vaguely recognised nodded to me as we both bustled in opposite directions. 'All right, matey?' I called out. It was only later that I realised with a devastating horror that my old matey was Air Chief Marshall Sir Michael (Matey) Knight, a man of such military and educational distinction that using only the letters after his name you could keep a whole family absorbed in Scrabble for months. I avoided him successfully for the next twelve years. The thin smile he gave me when next we met indicated that it wasn't long enough.

These days it's almost impossible to find a slot for promotion of services rugby, to go along and watch a match. Everyone is away listening to Clive Woodward's 546th press conference of the season, following up the news story that Scott Quinnell has a hamstring injury, fielding the latest background information call from one intriguing faction or another. Like so many other sectors of rugby, the new era has simply shoved it to the side, not quite rudely but firmly, with an air of inevitability.

At one time, and indeed until fairly recently, the services were one of the doyen areas of the rugby scene. The inter-services tournament at Twickenham was always widely reported, so were inter-unit matches. The influence of services people on the administration of rugby in England has always been monumental. Hordes of past presidents of the RFU have been high-ranking servicemen and so too, a long list of former secretaries, those often forbidding custodians of the conscience of the game, its amateurism and its paper-clips – including the famous Air Commodore Bob Weighill. And if it was occasionally possible to detect in Weighill an underlying trend of bufferism, then it was always easier still to see that any drawbacks were effortlessly outshone by the grace and integrity of the man.

Weighill was succeeded as RFU secretary by plain Dudley Wood, in an interregnum before order was restored by Hallett (albeit with Hallett finding himself trying to run not so much the governing body of the game but a nest of scorpions). I always patiently explained to Wood that lack of military high rank obviously left him denuded for the tasks he had to achieve as secretary. He once confessed to me that he had never shot anyone down in his life.

To this day, the match between the Army and the Royal Navy attracts a crowd of more than 30,000. Yet the old influence has waned, and more rapidly of late. The two other two rounds of the event have been moved away from Twickenham, for the moment down to Kingsholm, Gloucester and Plymouth. The Army are reigning champions for 2000, having beaten the Royal Navy by 32–14 in an entertaining match at Twickenham. The Army only just saw off the RAF, by 13–11, and the Navy beat the RAF by 23–5. Perhaps standards had dipped, but not devil and endeavour.

Each of the services retain their representation on the RFU, but far from controlling events they now hold a rather peripheral role. They allow their best players to go off and earn a sporting living in clubs and international squads. Great rugby players are still attached – Tim Rodber to the Army, for one. Rodber is still, ostensibly, a lieutenant in the Green Howards. Spencer Brown, the England wing, is a Royal Marine bandsman. Players like Dean Ryan, now the Bristol coach, were given their start by services rugby, in his case by the Royal Engineers. Major John Quin, formerly the services rugby media man, discovered the rough-hewn young Ryan and kept a fatherly eye on him, in between assuming the secretaryship of Bath and defusing gigantic bombs, as he did in several of the world's trouble spots. But these days, professional rugby comes first, and services players tend to gravitate into public-relations roles. They don't even turn out in the inter-services tournament itself.

Services teams cannot take on even Division Four clubs any more. The Combined Services have lost their place on the fixture list for incoming tours and where once there was a well-merited swagger about military people in rugby, now there is an uneasiness, even an apologetic air. Times change and in the professional era, they change at pace.

Even the existing influence is under threat. People are calling for the end of the services' representation on the RFU council, for further phasing out of their interests. The Reform Group – a body of dire and supreme irrelevancy who promote themselves as a ginger collective for action on the RFU's supposed weaknesses, but whose actions reveal them as the last revenge of jealousy and amateurism – have campaigned for the disenfranchisement of individual naval ships, which have always been regarded as properly constituted rugby clubs. The Reform Group say that this enables the Navy to wield a block of votes, and naturally their stance is based on the highest of principles, not simply that they think those block votes have been used against the interests of the likes of Cliff Brittle and Fran Cotton, whom they support.

I wonder if they have ever stopped for a second to consider the contribution of services people, and more particularly the contribution of individual naval ships, in the spreading of rugby. There is absolutely no doubt whatsoever that for most of the last 125 years, rugby was pushed far more effectively by the arrival of Royal Navy ships in outlying areas and countries, nurtured by repeat visits and ceremonial rugby matches, than by any contribution of the International Board. The Royal Navy RU's mission statement is to 'promote, develop, foster and finance rugby in the Royal Navy throughout the world, in support of the RFU'. This is a statement to foster in itself, and I would take the vote and the power from not one of the British ships enrolled at Twickenham.

When it comes to military matters and the ethics of employing military might, I suppose that most of us inhabit a kind of middle ground between pacifism and the bridge of a gunboat. But it is surely entirely possible to be wholly pacific and still admire the military excellence of British forces when they are employed in those roles for which they exist, not in ancillary doodles such as rugby. And not just their military excellence but a humility and humanity, too. Is it my imagination, or are United Nations missions always useless unless there is a British contingent?

There is nothing for which people involved in services rugby should apologise. The old influence has waned, and may never recover. But they are asking, in rugby, for nothing more than the respect due for their achievements both on and off the sporting field and for their role in the future, promoting the game wherever their assignments and their time allow. They still do it better than anyone. There is still, even in the time of swingeing cutbacks, a marvellous style about services sport. They seem to be adjusting to the new era better than another institution, the Varsity match. The 1999 affair was incredibly poor in standard, and there was another example of its proponents claiming it as the last great amateur occasion. Silly rituals are one thing, but for God's sake, let's not see an amateur tag as anything to celebrate.

Perhaps the old services empire is even striking back. Last season the Army announced a three-year sponsorship of the Rosslyn Park Schools

Sevens, a splendid move for all concerned – especially now that the faintly pompous past of the sevens has been replaced by a marvellous egalitarian attitude. Strong links have been forged between the Royal Marines and Clive Woodward's England squad. The England squad have spent two team-building periods with the Marines. 'Those guys are amazing. We talk about professionalism but we have nothing on them. The guys were almost in awe of them,' the hard-to-impress Martin Johnson said of the Marines they met. And more modernisation – the Royal Navy RU website is one of the best and most uplifting on the rugby scene.

Then, in May, the talented Wasps wing or full-back Josh Lewsey announced that he was leaving the full-time rugby scene to become a trainee officer at Sandhurst. 'I felt that I wanted to experience other things in life,' he said. Of course, he was given time off by the Army to make the tour of South Africa, and has to report back to barracks at Wasps now and again. Can't have these people having too much of a life outside the game. But good luck to Lewsey for articulating the fears of many of us anxious about the futures of young men after their rugby careers, and about the stultifying possibilities of a life watching daytime television wearing a tracksuit. It's too early to say whether it is the start of a major services recruitment drive in the big rugby clubs.

I know how Martin Johnson felt when he praised the servicemen he had come across. On the privileged days on which we attended their promo days aboard ships and planes, I always felt that no one really needed to sell the services. Long may they thrive.

CHAPTER SIXTEEN

Blackwall Tunnel

The trumpeters of Rugby League ♦ The undiscovered outpost of the Broncos ♦ The sound of the retreat

I'll tell you why no one goes to the Millennium Dome. It's not that it's a mediocre thing, because although it *is* a mediocre thing, you don't realise that until you get there, do you? My mate Spanner's reflective assessment of the Dome and its attractions ('It's shite') means he won't be making a repeat visit, but at least he paid one. The problem with the Dome lies in getting close enough to make an assessment. If they'd bunged it in Brum near the motorway network, they'd have opened the box-office and doubled their money. But south of the Thames on the small Greenwich peninsula? London brutally seals off its own southeast corner – and the southeast of the country itself – just by being there, big, smoky and impassable. Keeps out the hordes from the North and West and Midlands. The cross-town transport routes are still fairly poor, the South Circular road just a collection of signposts and traffic lights which make you weep for the poor old Yanks and other visitors who take the so-called circular route in their hire-cars, expecting to glide around a six-lane freeway.

Once you've striven heroically and get into the rough locality of the Dome (I mean by that the approximate locality, not rough in the sense of fierce and scruffy and naughty; at least, I think I do), maybe past the City of London itself or down through the clogged north–south routes, and if you are any personage other than a resident of the East End, me old china, or from the southeastern corner of the country, you have to cross the river on the old Woolwich ferry or make the gloomy dive under the well-named Blackwall Tunnel. Then you pop up among retail warehouses and drive-in burger chains and confusing roundabouts, and the first thing any visitor must want to do when they get to the Dome is not so much feast upon its attractions as sit down and have a nice cup of tea with the same kind of exhausted but triumphant air that must have surrounded Sir Edmund Hillary and Sherpa Tenzing Norgay when they accomplished a journey of similar length, discomfort and confusion to the top of Everest.

I'll tell you, too, why no one goes to watch rugby league at London Broncos. Not just because they're shocking. At least, why no one watches them in their current home at the Valley, home of Charlton Athletic, near the Millennium Dome through the Blackwall Tunnel. It's for the same reason. By positioning themselves in the London hinterland, in the London cut-off area, they are inaccessible. Charlton Athletic, now in the Premiership, can draw a crowd because their local roots are deep, because football is massive. People leave their front doors and walk to the Valley. Whether town or wider conurbation, no single locality outside the M62 corridor has enough rugby league fans to breathe life into a professional rugby league club. Not one, no matter how hard rugby league expansionists would try to convince us otherwise. The only solution is to stick the London club at some point which is reasonably convenient, so that the catchment area becomes a big chunk of the country. In Charlton the catchment area, for all bar rabid League fans, is Charlton. Charlton, whatever it is and is not, has in this context the considerable drawback that it is not Wigan.

On the subject of rabid rugby league fans, I took Duncan Jones, then aged six, to the Valley in the spring of 2000 to see the Broncos play his team, St Helens. Duncan had already been one of the Saints' most fervent fans for around a year. Newspaper speculation that his favourite player, Fereti Tuilagi (Freddie Two Lagers, we *cognoscenti* call him), might be signing for Leicester and rugby union went down hard, and Tuilagi duly signed in June. It was bad enough when Apollo Perelini went to Sale for the 2000–01 season. But Duncan and I were up for the Saints' trip to London.

So here's a puzzle for any anorak route-spotter. How to get from my home, thirty miles west of central London, to a place well east of London and across the Thames, in the teeth of the rush hour? The answer was a great circle around London, taking the M4 and M25 clockwise and then the M11, the motorway that ends at nowhere, dumping hopeful travellers somewhere near the East End. Then, with Duncan on his fourth packet of crisps, the rat-run towards the City and (three hours after setting off on a journey which, as the crow flies, was around forty-two miles) the Blackwall Tunnel and the Valley. Saints fans in the car park, seeing Duncan wearing the replica jersey and assuming we'd come from the deepest, northest North, clustered round, anxious to compare routing notes. We soon discovered it had taken us as long as it had taken them. London. Bless it.

Was it worth it? Yes, a good night's entertainment. Traditionally mediocre fast food and an excruciating programme article by Richard Branson, the Broncos' chief investor and major follower of rugby league – even if the technical tone of his piece appeared to indicate that he'd never watched a match in all his born days – in which he brought all the rugby league fans up to date with the current trading positions and new management structures of some of his companies. Riveting. There was also his apology (no doubt standard issue) that he couldn't be there at the Valley with us tonight. Maybe he was stuck in a jam; maybe he should have taken one of his 767s from Heathrow to London City Airport, from which it's only a few miles (i.e. an hour) to The Valley. Not much time to reach the cruise altitude, though.

The Valley had a weird air. There were barely 3000 spectators, of whom a good few were travelling Saints, and everyone was forced into one stand. Obviously the BSkyB producer wanted hordes of excited fans as a backdrop to the action on the understandable basis that if the TV viewer sat down and saw something that was being played to empty rows, he might well subliminally decide not to bother watching either. Three sides of the ground were completely closed so that opposite the main cameras were all the paying public. I'd always wondered why I'd watched this excited and packed house on Sky's Friday night rugby league but next day the official attendance figure was often tiny. Now I knew.

We had a splendid night, though. The pre-entertainment was not quite excruciating, a major advance for either code of rugby at present. The crowd was good-humoured and was kept well informed; before the match there was a short seminar on the laws. The refereeing of rugby league matches, the unpompous authority which the referees wield, the clarity and uniformity which accompanies their decisions, is an object lesson to any other sport and a massive tribute to Greg McCallum, the Australian who is the Rugby Football League's referees' controller. The video-referee system, with a giant screen of far sharper resolution than those you sometimes see at union grounds, showed the same pictures as the video ref was seeing, adding to the excitement and providing the excuse for the whole crowd to give their decision. For a disputed London try, the whole of the Broncos' contingent held up placards that Sky had distributed saying 'Try'. Duncan held up one saying 'No Try'. In union, you merely see a ref babbling into his microphone, eventually making a decision on the say-so of some disembodied voice which, on the evidence of England's tour of South Africa, gets it wrong. Hardly drama.

The game was excellent, for the Broncos made up in commitment (stirring) for what they lacked in finesse (you name it). Their team, as it has been for years, was predominantly a bunch of Australians unwanted by the National Rugby League in Australia and over to hack out a living in the UK. St Helens, who overhauled a large deficit and won 26–20, keeping themselves at the top of the Super League, had the extra class. Kevin Iro was powerful in their centres but the most compelling figures, for those with an eye to rugby class, were Tommy Martyn and Sean Long, the half-backs. They had splendid skills under pressure and a tremendous vision. I could happily have paid the money and watched only those two. Duncan loved it because Freddie Two Lagers played a good match. He loved it because it was all far simpler than rugby union, the code more beloved by his elder brother and sister. League is far more immediate for young kids and other newcomers to rugby. He loved it more than anything, however, because the Saints won. At least, with the rush hour past and with central London now reclaimed from its own gridlock, we were home, from this home match, just before midnight.

London Broncos – under that name and in various other guises, under various other ownerships and in various other grounds, showing such a wanderlust that if they'd signed a gipsy he'd have asked for a transfer because of the continually changing locations – have been operating on the fringes of London sport since the 1970s. Since they began, on 14 September 1980 at Craven Cottage, Fulham, my friends and I used to emerge from suburban bedsit land on Sundays and go along. We were there for their first ever game, when they thrashed some team called Wigan before the princely total of 9954 people; also when they beat Leeds in the Challenge Cup. And Mal Aspey and Derek Noonan, I thought, were two of the best centres I'd seen. We did not then fully understand the concept of a sporting flash in the pan, or the theory which has never been disproved that it is impossible to transplant a sport on any significant permanent basis into a country or even an area where it does not have a culture. We enjoyed it. And, like Fulham RLFC, we moved on.

They went to play at Crystal Palace National Sports Centre; to Chiswick Polytechnic, never to be confused with the Maracana; back to Crystal Palace; they became the London Crusaders and played at Barnet Copthall; became the London Broncos after a (short-lived) take-over by Brisbane Broncos; they moved to The Valley; to The Stoop Memorial Ground; and, now, back to The Valley. Every time they moved or changed names, they announced that they were about to take London by storm. We caught them, years later, playing a Cup match at the Chiswick ground. We counted 220 spectators, including both benches. The newspaper report gave the crowd as 1,500. The pre-match entertainment, billed as the 'world-champion fire-eater', burned his mouth.

The only constant has been their role in providing employment for a gang of Aussies fancying a crack in the UK, the devotion of a small group of dogged devotees to keeping them going, and the noise from a lineage of owners and investors who have proclaimed annually that London was desperate for a rugby league club, that league was about to take over from union as the capital's fancy, and who barked their way along all the way to the departure lounge at Heathrow or wherever they left from after a journey of such hope. There have been better days, as witnessed since the advent of Super League, when the Broncos, buoyed up with News International's funding and by a special stipulation that they could field more foreign players than the northern-based clubs, reached the 1999 Challenge Cup final at Wembley, losing heavily to Leeds Rhinos. It increased their core support by hardly a single fan, and it provided an absolutely devastating comment on English rugby league that a group of travelling Aussies, augmented by Shaun Edwards so far into the twilight of his career that it was almost the early hours of the next day, should beat off the top established clubs *en route* to Wembley. But there they were, and they did not disgrace themselves.

By the end of the Super League 2000, as the grand final played 'Auld Lang Syne' to another season, London Broncos, the old nomads currently hitching their wagons to God-forsaken Charlton, after play-offs for which they had not qualified were still drawing small crowds through the Blackwall Tunnel, reaching 3,000 only if the other lot brought a thousand or more down with them. They still had no well-known player who was not an Australian; they sacked John Monie, their coach, and London still cared not a fig for them. But by way of Fulham, Chiswick, Crystal Palace and Barnet and everywhere else they had paused, they had found destiny of a sort. By 2000 they were by a vast distance the most important institution in the world of rugby league. They were the only excuse to call league other than a sporting catflap.

I humbly suggested in *Endless Winter*, which appeared in 1993, that rugby league was in danger of disintegrating as a serious professional sport – and in that was a given that you could rank any activity as a serious professional sport were it played within such minuscule boundaries. The statistics of the decline were at issue only to those native to the habitats of the cloud cuckoo. Television audiences and interest had reduced dramatically, the average attendance in the top division in Britain had then declined to 5683 and was to decline further so that by season 1995–96 it was only 5515. The numbers had decreased for the fourth consecutive season, and without any significant international or representative numbers to boost the figures this meant that the entire professional game was founded on a shockingly small base. However, as I pointed out, administrators and followers were at the time too engrossed to notice that their backyard was crumbling. After decades in which the two codes touched at certain points and rugby union took an interest in league affairs, if only to keep track of what players they might next lose, rugby league these days touches, affects and fascinates union less than it ever did. Unless a major union wishes to make some ready cash by hiring out its stadium – and therefore wishes to portray the subsequent match as an historic coming-together, an end-of-centuries-of-warfare, blah-blah-blah – there is little contact made.

I also explained that rugby league was too busy using its crumbling backyard for a supremely misguided assault on the world outside. Rugby league's history in the past twenty years is packed full to the gunwales of earnest lumps of bullshit expended in the cause of promulgating the code. Matches were staged in the United States, Russia, Ireland, Scotland, Wales and other parts; wasting time and money which was so sorely needed internally, the marketeers and apologists issued excited press releases (I still have them, by the score) because, for example, Warrington once played Wigan in Milwaukee and this meant – for some reason they never explained – that America was on the point of abandoning American football, baseball and ice hockey and converting to rugby league. I have a press release from the original owner of the Auckland Warriors rugby league team stating that rugby league would overcome union by the end of the 1990s; another release of a more recent vintage claims that rugby league in South Africa 'is gaining ground hand over fist in its battle with the established union code'. I have been to South Africa on eleven separate occasions and have never seen a rugby league match on television (and this in a country which has such over-capacity that it heavily features skateboarding from the United States), I have never read about one solitary South African rugby league match in the newspapers, and I have never heard one South African discussing rugby league, whether at home or abroad. A slightly less than successful assault on the monster that is rugby union in the Republic of South Africa, some might say.

As I wrote in 1993, the virulence with which rugby union was attacked and blamed for most of the ills of rugby league – just because union realised it was a rival code and a rival business and had the most perfect right to act like it (and still does) – wasted even more time than the code would have spent in putting things right. The trend for this most odious inverted snobbery continues still. Someone even recently produced a book purporting to show that it was dastardly rugby union men in cahoots with the Nazi occupiers of France that crushed the league code in that country. A weakly spun web of circumstantial evidence is given a decent airing; less well aired is the suspicion that France has never given two centimes for league – before the war, during the war and after the war – and that the league code has been spectacularly outdone for appeal at every stage. No, can't be that. Must be few moustached old collaborators. No doubt it was rugby union men who piloted the German bombers in the Blitz.

The point I was trying to make was this: you cannot promote a sport into existence; only by a gradual, grass-roots approach lasting decades could you begin to say that a sport is bedding down even at the most elementary and amateur level. I suggested that rugby league's sole criterion of greatness as a technical activity – that the ball was in play for long periods of time – seduced no one. I suggested that if the sport was brave enough, if it was for one moment prepared to acknowledge that no one was interested in its silly one-off stunts, its feeble-bully bravado in insisting that its club-based activity was somehow harder or inherently superior as a skill than other codes of football, if it was to douse itself in gallons of cold reality, then it might just have a future.

At the time, it was not prepared to do these things. It gave me my finest moment in journalism (especially since my sideboard full of awards so justly handed on by various groups of meticulous judges has never contained one with a cash alternative). A rugby league writer described me as 'the most hated man in rugby league'. It was not that I wanted to be hated, particularly in rugby league, it was just that a journalist who is loved is on the wrong tracks. It gave me my second-favourite moment when Neil Tunnicliffe, a former chief executive of the RFL and described to me by one of his predecessors as 'not dynamic, in fact rather weak' (and that was before I turned off my tape-recorder), reported the *Sunday Times* and myself to the Press Complaints Commission after we ran a perfectly valid and meticulous attack on a part of his crumbling empire (and while we treated all PCC complaints very seriously it would be an exaggeration to say that we tossed and turned all night over that one). When I mentioned this complaint to Dudley Wood, former secretary of the Rugby Football Union, he said: 'Good God. If we'd gone to them every time you'd attacked me they'd have had to take on extra staff. Mind you, I'm still considering it.' In a sport perhaps well accustomed to swallowing media releases, rugby league people apparently do not take kindly to having home truths placed under their noses.

And especially not by me. It was easy to respond when they were attacked by the true-blue conservative rugby union officialdom. They trotted out the card-carrying reverse snobbery, spoke of English gin-swilling dodderers and a game of the middle classes trying to kill them. In my case, not being a dodderer (not then, anyway), not being gin-swilling (except on Tuesdays) or English (ever) they struggled. My coming from a working-class Welsh background didn't help them at all. As one of my rugby heroes from both codes once told me: 'You've stuffed them. They don't like criticism and they don't know where you're coming from.' When *Endless Winter* came out – and, indeed, whenever the *Sunday Times* has made criticism of some aspect of rugby league – the letters have flooded in, and when people in the North finally mastered e-mail they put their pigeons out to seed and reacted electronically, too. Bless them all: the bloke from Leeds who writes six letters in the same handwriting and changes the names; the sad guy from Wimbledon with the scrawled bitterness; and all the real rugby league followers who, deep down and if truth be told, were slightly miffed because they fully believed their code to be vastly superior and, when confronted by the evidence that no one south of Manchester agreed with them, tended to react with a real hurt and bitterness. Who is this idiot, making all these stupid comments about our thriving game?

The pigeons all came home to roost in 1996. So many did so all at once, proving almost every point I had made, that it was like a scene from *The Birds*. Maurice Lindsay, chief executive of the RFL and a man for whom I have enormous respect even though we have crossed swords so often, suddenly had something else to sell. He had to sell the impending death of rugby league. Rupert Murdoch's parent companies, News Corporation in Australia and News International in the United Kingdom, moved boldly and massively into rugby league. They saw it as a reasonably cheap (by global standards) and cheerful means of filling what were then long silences in the schedules of their massed ranks of sporting channels around the world. The upshot in Australia was a brutal war between television magnates. This was settled only last year and its aftershocks still rumble, with great old league clubs forced to merge with each other, thereby sacrificing two great names.

In Britain, the upshot was the Super League. This was unveiled in 1995 and, unlike the previous and almost annual new plans to revise rugby league, all the working-party documents and 'Framing the Future' (which shuffled a pack with no aces), sent the sport giddily reeling to three divisions, back to two, then to three. This was a real break. News International invested £87 million in a deal lasting five years. Lindsay had to sell it hard because of the resistance he knew there would be. 'The sport is haemorrhaging alarmingly; this could be our last chance,' he said. This was the man who had told us that the sport was in fantastic health and about to conquer the world, but who knew in his heart that it was no such thing – far from taking on the world, rugby league hardly had the strength to do something nasty on its own doorstep. The BSkyB television people had spent a long time exulting about how marvellous everything was: how Olympic decathlete gold-medal winners really never touched the league players for athleticism; how even the most dreadful 2–0 mudbath was a wonderful advertisement for rugby league – the crowd were really packed to the rafters, with thousands outside clamouring to get in, it wasn't just that they'd shut most of the ground to make them look like sardines for the main camera . . . These same men were suddenly forced to concede that it all was, in fact, a sorry mess, and so the News International plan had to be shoved through. The shiny-bonced Sky summariser Mike Stephenson, who had had hardly a bad sentence to say about the state of the game on television for what seemed like decades, was now saying, 'The game's going down the gurgler,' prompting many of us to wonder why he had never mentioned this before.

Ah well. What also had to be sold were two revolutionary concepts. The Super League would run in the summer, at least partly to avoid the winter ball-sports counter-attractions but also to allow the advent of one of the 'big ideas' of the whole new shooting match: the end-of-season play-offs. These were to pit the champion clubs of Australia with the championship clubs of, er, Europe in a thundering cross-hemisphere, even-more-wonderful-advertisement-for-the-code spectacular, and all that stuff. The other rather significant point was that, to leave room for the gleaming new clubs which would bust the game out of old borders and enable the title Super League Europe to be something other than a crashing misnomer, a good few of the existing clubs would be disbanded, or merged, often in the most ham-fisted way. Teams called, non-evocatively, Calder, Cumbria, Humberside, Cheshire and South Yorkshire were to be created.

No wonder the big schmoozing battalions had to be brought out. This stuff took some selling. As Lindsay once told me, sitting in his fine house full of Wigan memorabilia (and in the very seat where this small but charismatic man had persuaded Martin Offiah to sign for Wigan): 'There's an element in rugby league that can't see past the end of their noses, an element that is more comfortable complaining about a game that is fading away, rather than trying to do anything about it. It can be an extremely inward-looking arena.' It was well said and, as I told

Maurice, I could think of another code to which that could apply too.

As is now history, the amalgamation was a non-starter. Rugby clubs, excuse me if you've read this before from me (and count yourself lucky if it is less than a hundred times), are living and breathing beasts; their followers, and the affection they derive, cannot simply be tossed away, meshed and amalgamated. The switch to a non-winter season did come about, and the Super League completed its fifth season in the sun in summer 2000. There has been a little harking back here and there – the big clubs, chiefly St Helens and Wigan, missed their major Christmas-holiday battles and resumed them with friendlies, earned a decent wedge from the gate – and no, Duncan, I'm not taking you to Knowsley Road on Boxing Day. The Northern Ford Premiership, its second division comprising a bunch of smaller outfits in a desperate battle for points and survival, switched back to part of the winter. This was sensible only because they picked up a few fans whose main teams didn't emerge till the summer and who could therefore be persuaded to revive the days of cold hands, warm clashes and pies warm on the outside and cold in the middle, if only by watching lesser teams. Otherwise, give or take a few matches in which the players could easily have been in a sauna, the balmy seasons have gone down well inside the game.

But what about the highest promise of all, the Holy Grail which seemed only a step away when Mr Murdoch offered the cheque and Mr Lindsay and others bravely battered their way through ingrained custom and practice so they could bank it; when a game that was slowly winding up, on the fields and in the banks, could breathe again? What of the heady talk of expansion? 'This will enable rugby league,' said Lindsay at the time that the Super League offer was revealed, 'to make ourselves a genuinely national sport in Britain at last.'

Phew, £87 million could pay for a few missionaries after all. And today Britain, tomorrow the world. I recently pulled up a raft of newspaper cuttings greeting the investment of News International and the theories and heady speculation of officials and paid observers as to the rugby league explosion. Culling the gist from the raft, and mixing metaphors a bit too, we were promised teams in Manchester and Birmingham, in Paris and Toulouse, and the possible 'annexation of the Milan union team'. We were promised a true pan-European effort with the greatest clubs advancing to meet their Aussie counterparts in the cherry on the icing on the marzipan on the top of the new cake.

Off we went. Paris St-Germain were unveiled on 23 March 1996, playing their first match in the new Super League at the Stade Charléty, watched by a splendid 17,873 – and if no one could find in that happy and rather bewildered throng anyone who had actually paid to get in, then so what? Paris St-Germain beat the Sheffield Eagles by 30–24, and the stately *L'Equipe* even professed itself mildly interested. And every rugby league follower who mistook the trappings of marketing and development for the real thing, all those who forgot that it was the first five matches Paris lost that would be the true test, not the first one that they won, hoped for great things. Eighty-seven million smackers was what it cost for the boundaries to be crossed.

Today, the invading army is wiped out and decomposing. The £87 million has gone. So have Paris St-Germain, buried with few mourners less than two years after. They followed the long lists of clubs that are no more because they overestimated the appeal, and so league was born and then died in Cardiff and Carlisle and Mansfield and Scarborough and Bridgend and Maidstone and, now, Gateshead. No other new teams were ever formed in Europe, making the Super League Europe, still the handle for the League's governing body, a nonsense. The original sponsor, Stones Bitter, has gone. So has the next sponsor, JJB Sports. Neither exercised its option to renew. Gone, after one season, is the Gateshead Thunder Club, born at the atmosphere-free Gateshead Athletics Stadium, who played for the 1999 season by giving even more employment to itinerant Aussies. With wondrous optimism they had called the wide open spaces and empty seats of the stadium 'The Thunderdome', but its only rumblings came from a small group of diehard supporters when Shane Richardson, the club's Australian chief executive, abandoned all promise of endless summers of rugby in Newcastle and district. 'We overestimated the amount of support the club would attract, and the loss sustained was even more dramatic than we envisaged,' he said. The fact that he was articulating the core mistake of so many others who tried to start professional rugby clubs could not obscure the fact that he'd chucked it in after one season.

If ever rugby league lunacy in presuming that to establish a serious club was anything other than a decade-long process as a minimum, then it was in the departing Richardson's words. Still, there was a fantastic compensation for Gateshead fans. As part of a policy among the major clubs that the fewer clubs there were, the bigger their bung, they encouraged mergers, so Gateshead, way up in the Northeast, 'amalgamated' with Hull, that handily placed town way, way down the east coast, a culture away. At least you could break your journey at somewhere bracing like Scarborough if you wanted to stay overnight *en route* to a home match. The Aussies went home, Gateshead shut up shop. Gone.

To be fair to Richardson, the game at large put him under fierce pressure, because without Gateshead's input the famous Hull club would have sunk down out of the Super League, proving once again the desperate fact that heartland clubs were weakening too.

So there was to be no expansion. No nationwide game. More recently, the Sheffield club, one of the newer pro outfits, demonstrated alarmingly that even on the fringe of the heartland it was all a hard life. They effectively collapsed and merged with Huddersfield, predictably harnessing none of the remaining strength of the two old clubs, and subsiding to the bottom of the 2000 Super League. Hull and Sheffield had therefore shown themselves to be incapable of sustaining a separate existence, and the Super League continued to shrink. Shockingly, it was less than two years since Sheffield had reached the Wembley final. One of the heroes of that Wembley day, Mark Aston, wanted to re-start the original Sheffield club in the Northern Ford Premiership. The RFL wouldn't let him. Wembley to oblivion. Wakefield found financial disaster in September 2000. 'They talk about expansion, then shoot themselves in the foot,' he said. 'LEAGUE IN RETREAT OVER EXPANSION', said one headline. The average attendance at top-division matches last season, compared to the last year before the Super League, was up by 321 people per club. It cost £87 million to bring in 321 people to each club.

At least Sheffield lived longer than the vaunted World Club Championship play-offs. They lasted one year, having been heralded as the panacea for half the game's ills for three times as long. Frankly, while they brought in decent crowds in England, they were a grievous embarrassment for anyone connected with English rugby league. The awful truth was revealed for the top English clubs. They had been playing with each other for decades, had nothing in their vacuum with which to measure themselves. When they found a measuring rod in the shape of the big Australian sides they found that they were hopeless.

Given that to play one of their counterparts from Australia at home required the visiting team to make a 10,000-mile journey, and considering that it normally takes two weeks to fully recover from the effects of circadian disrhythmia (jet lag), you might at least think that our brave boys would beat the Aussies at home. Humiliatingly, England clubs won only seven of the thirty matches in the doomed event played in England, and only Wigan, who won at Canterbury Bulldogs, won a match in Australia. Bradford Bulls and St Helens were practically wiped out, St Helens going down by 70–6 to the mediocre Auckland Warriors and Bradford entering the knock-out stages having lost all their games, their presence being required to maintain some semblance of an inter-hemisphere contest. The English clubs had suffered a brutal savaging, and Australian rugby league had run out of means with which to market the matches (not to mention run out of ways to patronise the English), so the plug was pulled and, like so many rugby league initiatives, high hopes turned to shambles in an alarmingly short time. Saviour to devil inside three months.

The problem with hope, I guess, is that it springs eternal. Warrington and London Broncos played a match at Rodney Parade, Newport, recently as part of Super League's strategy to take it on the road. A mild amount of interest was drummed up, and a crowd of roughly half Newport's average saw an average match. My mate Wendy, a Rodney regular, reckoned that if you take away the travelling fans of the two teams then there were around 2000 people present. Yet again, people started talking of a Newport-based Super League side, even though for a one-off you would surely want to see 10,000 coming in before you'd even dream of a such a move. People looked to the great David Watkins, the Newport chairman, to give a lead. Super League spokesmen made appeals to local businessmen to wield their cheque books. You'd have to say that if they find one, he will have (as we used to say of the flash and the profligate in the old days in Newport) more money than sense.

An independent report that emerged early in 2000 from Sheffield University tore away the last remnants of the notion pedalled by rugby league authorities that their sport was buoyant and galvanised by the summer Super League. It claims that the sport had 'largely wasted' its £87 million windfall; it showed that the sport's aggregate television audience had almost halved inside five years and that the BBC's figures for the Challenge Cup final, once the precious jewel in the crown, had suffered another catastrophic drop. Chris Caisley, chairman of Super League, was rather muted in his attack on the survey and on a BBC radio programme which featured it. 'I certainly agree we have not much to show for it in terms of what's been produced. If you're telling me that the balance sheets might not be any better, then I might agree.' He did go on to point out that clubs were better run, had massive staffs compared to the old days, and that ground improvements had ensured that some of the Sky money was soaked up in a good cause. But compare the heady talk when Murdoch arrived as Father Christmas to the bald facts in the survey, and you find a cavernous gap between hope and reality.

CHAPTER SEVENTEEN

Beirut

How international rugby league went East, and West ◆ The super hot-house ◆ The long, long march to Leicester

Walid Jumblat. Crazy name, crazy inside-centre? Once that celebrated rugby league nation Lebanon qualified for the 2000 Rugby League World Cup, to be held in the autumn, my colleagues and I were quick to assess the composition of their team. Walid was one of key players in that bewildering era in Middle East politics of the 1970s and 1980s when no one except the most dire dinner-party bore had any idea whose side anyone was supposed to be on – and Walid, judging by the sudden and drastic decline in his TV appearances from his rather unkempt heyday, appeared to have backed the wrong one. He'd be too old, I guess, to consider representing his country at rugby. But will Lebanon's team for England 2000 be based more on Druze elements, or would the passions of Hezbollah lead to a strong militant contingent? Or would no one faction dominate? Would Michel Aoun's followers bury the hatchets with Walid and form a joint front? Would the squad be based in Beirut for their training camps?

Or will Lebanon prove to be something of a bogus outfit? Sixteen teams will contest the main event, and of those sixteen a good few will be representative not of rugby league in the countries they are representing (because there *is* no rugby league in some of the countries they are representing) but of the ability of the Australian league game in particular, and also the English league game, to produce from their ranks enough players of various descent to form 'national' teams. Happily, some of the eligibility criteria are stronger than they were at the Rugby World Cup in 1999, when you could play for a country if you, your parents or your grandparents were born there – and if not, well you could just play anyway. Yet some aspects of the League World Cup are preposterous – notably the admission of New Zealand Maoris as a separate team, and the Lebanon phenomenon, whereby a gang of Aussies of Eastern descent have decided that they feel a World Cup adventure coming on. All the squad they announced were Australians.

Obviously we are in for some decent matches as the established nations square off, and some charming matches, inferior in standards but outstanding in appeal, as the lesser teams battle it out (provided they can all find twenty-odd players who have some qualifications). There is even an Emerging Nations' side-event, with the United States and Italy among the contenders. The Italian captain rather spoiled the effect at the launch party in May, when he confessed he'd neither worn the jersey ever before nor even seen one. No one was unkind enough to ask him if he could name another Italian player.

But rather than trying to parade the illusion that there really are sixteen bona fide Test-playing nations in rugby league, the organisers really should have cut their losses. The crucial thing in a real World Cup is to maximise the pulling-power of the bigger nations. Splitting the Great Britain team into four drastically reduces the prospects of a home win. Instead of pretending that Wales, Ireland and Scotland are genuine Test teams they should have entered Great Britain, given them pick of all the players, and put up the three other countries in the Emerging Nations' event. Russia, Lebanon, the Cook Islands, South Africa and the New Zealand Maori team should also have been restricted to the EN competition.

A concentrated eight-team event comprising Great Britain, Australia, New Zealand, Fiji, Tonga, Samoa, France and Papua New Guinea would have had a more authentic ring, and given the EN event more glamour and less chance of horrendous one-sided beatings. As RWC '99 showed, the least attractive matches are those in which the lesser teams are pulverised. And in the final analysis, do we want a home win or not? Someone has to shut up those Aussies, and a Great Britain team, properly prepared and raucously supported, might have been the team to do it. As the event approached, hordes of the England potentials de-camped to other teams.

But if you take a wider view, it is vital that rugby league recreates the old marvellous electricity and ferocity of international rugby at the top level, instead of mucking about parading a falsehood. The proud history of Test-series clashes between Great Britain and the Kangaroos measures up to the finest of sporting confrontation and sporting glory. The absence of that kind of satisfying crunch has cost rugby league more than it will ever understand. International profile is everything. At present, rugby league does not have one. Good luck to World Cup 2000.

❊ ❊ ❊

Consider the recent carnage in the concept of international rugby league. I used to gently remind all my league-loving mates who proclaimed that to play in a top league match was to be gladiator-like in your sheer toughness that international rugby is always five steps up in terms of brutal intensity, and that they should consider, before making such sad judgements, the true clash of the steel. A club match in any code could never compare in the realms of sheer physicality with playing for England away in South Africa or New Zealand, or going to Apia to play Samoa, or to France to try to exist in the old Parc des Princes and keep enough wits about you to do a quick testicle-count as you stagger off at the end to see if the normal complement is present.

The chances of top British players finding the serrated-jaw bite of true international competition are becoming fewer and fewer because the serious international game is close to complete collapse. Seeing nothing of true meaning in the activity, the National Rugby League in Australia now prefer to concentrate on their domestic event and State of Origin series. The New Zealand team are vastly declined, beleaguered by competing demands of the clubs in Australia and England for whom most of their internationals play. Great Britain, rampagingly unsuccessful since the mid-1980s in any case, are now further denuded for the 2000 Rugby League World Cup. Iestyn Harris, for example, will be playing for a Wales team scraping for a squad now that all the gems from their last campaign have scuttled back to the union fold, whereas his talent would have been one key to unlock Australia, given good players around him. He now faces being obliterated on the world stage, a fate which his splendid talents do not deserve (although in his turning down of a Welsh Rugby Union contract it was possible to detect a desire to stay in the comfortable zone with which he is familiar, rather than trying to absorb the fiendishly complicated role of a union fly-half).

Great Britain no longer have European opposition, a warm-up, because France are now of a standard too dire to bother with. The decline has gathered momentum. In 1998 Great Britain narrowly avoided their first home-series whitewash against New Zealand. Because of the disputes in Australia, the true clash of the Ashes Test series has not been heard of in these shores since 1994. Rugby league has spectacularly missed the obvious fact that the only true international promotion of the game will come when they have Australia over for a three-Test tour, give them massive guarantees to keep them interested and offer major prize-money to give the Super League clubs the incentive to rip the tourists' guts out along the way and deliver them to the Test series – as brutal provincial teams have delivered so many British Lions teams over the decades – as gibbering wrecks. Play a Test at the Millennium Stadium in Cardiff (where you get 72,500 these days for a skittles match), because if you are fielding a Great Britain side then they are genuinely the home team for the fans.

The most chilling match I have ever seen as an indication of the future of rugby league came in April 2000, when New Zealand played the ANZAC Test match in Stadium Australia in front of a derisory crowd. The two giants of the international rugby league scene faced off with a fair amount of razzmatazz. Australia, who would still have won had they almost literally played with one hand tied behind their backs, scored fifty at a canter, found an opposition so poor and so lacking in commitment they defiled the black jersey. It was by all accounts a poor Aussie team.

In that New Zealand team were Henry and Robbie Paul, the brothers who both now play for the Bradford Bulls. When, two years ago, I invited Maurice Lindsay to give me the name of the next generation of household rugby league names to replace Ellery Hanley, Martin Offiah and, to a lesser extent, Shaun Edwards, he had a long think and came up with the names of the two Pauls. I found it odd that no list of young Englishmen had tripped off his tongue, but the pair do seem to be the glamour lads of the Super League.

When the Pauls arrived back in Britain from Sydney they faced a Bulls game. Robbie was quickly quoted in the paper expressing total confidence in the Bulls' chances, pointing out how good this team were, how threatening they felt against any opposition, generally talking a magnificent match. I would hope that his employers in New Zealand and Bradford found his words just a little distasteful. Even were I his biggest fan, my temptation would be to tell Mr Paul to keep extremely quiet until the memory of New Zealand's abject surrender subsided; and to remember that the true measure of sporting greatness comes only when they take you out of the familiar comfort-zone of your club and throw you to the lions and devils of international rugby – where, on this occasion at least, the Pauls had so utterly failed to measure up. No wonder that Ray French, a dyed-in-the-pies rugby league man from way back and formerly a BBC commentator, took a decidedly anxious tone in a column he wrote soon after the non-Test non-match. 'What price international rugby now?' said a man who was old enough to remember the magnificent history of Ashes clashes. Now, just clashes to ashes.

When Super League Five ran down its curtain in 2000, and the game looked nervously around to see which of the famous old names of club rugby would be the next to be erased from the game's map, attention certainly turned to the deep Southeast and to London Broncos, and to their struggle to survive and our struggle to go and watch them. They are already treated as a special case but no case can be considered more special than theirs. They just have to survive. It is overwhelmingly vital to attract national sponsors, to give a tint, a semblance of a national profile, to have a team called London, for God's sake, to have just a fingertip hold – if these things are lost, then rugby league retreats, both literally and figuratively, into a tiny parish and plays with itself, never to re-emerge. London must be made a flagship, even if the other clubs have to chip in from their own coffers, and they must be re-located where those other than the citizens of Charlton can find easy access. They also need Englishmen, lots of them. There are too many Australian accents being heard at present all over the sporting world, let alone in one Rugby League club. Local kids do not identify with unknown Aussies. You have to ask, however, how many people would put hand on heart and swear that a London rugby league team will exist in three years.

If the game shrinks even further, if London once again becomes a league-free zone, then more rugby league players will be picked off by rugby union, because now that professionalism in union has given a level playing-field all the code-switches are one way – with the exception of the Wasps back Paul Sampson's transfer to Wakefield. (He soon returned.) International rugby union especially is a moneyed monster desperate for success. (Though whether league converts would ever contribute to that success is open to the most monumental doubts. There really is small use in union for the trademark post-tackle league action of lying on the floor, kicking your legs in the air and nodding your head vigorously up and down.) Yet pride, passion and pursuit of excellence will always be welcome. Rugby league has all those qualities, but not the wit and wherewithal, and not enough appeal in its game, to spread them. They are spread thickly in the northern corridor; elsewhere, the bread never even made the pop-up toaster. The cross-code passage claimed Joe Lydon recently and that fine man became manager of the England U19 union team. More will follow.

One of my colleagues on another newspaper, domiciled in Leeds and with an encyclopaedic knowledge of rugby league, believes that the game's heart has never really been in expansion. 'What they really want to do is cut down the teams, cut out anyone from outside the Yorkshire and Lancashire corridor, share out all the Murdoch money, make the game the best they can, push it among the locals, take the boost given by the fact that all the games will be local derbies and so will get decent crowds, and plug along like that for ever.'

Those who do not share such a down-home view will hopefully prevail.

Chris Caisley, Super League chairman, was recently bravely insisting that expansion was still the way forward. 'Our plans are not at an end, not at all,' he said as Gateshead collapsed, Hull merged, Sheffield died. 'Now, we have a very strong twelve-team competition. Sometimes you have to take a step back and rationalise before you can go forward.' The trouble with all this reduction, downsizing, whatever you wish to call it, is that it never ends. Super League Five had a twelve-team league. In every league there is always one team which has a nightmare, finishes bottom, collapses financially. What then? An eleven-team league, so that the bottom club at Super League Six crashes out too? The domestic game no longer has the desperately needed glamour of rugby union converts, who drew the crowds and the fascination even if they were clueless. It no longer has the glamorous Aussies (as opposed to the mediocre and also the deadbeat Aussies) because the seasons are concurrent. It has turned in on itself in the most dramatic and complete way. Partly through bitter experience and burned fingers, it is the most inward-looking, iconoclastic pursuit it is possible to imagine. Apart from Belgian stilt-walking.

So why would I agree with the television pundits who claim that each Super League has been better than the one before? Duncan and I watched some matches in season 1999 which were indeed a marvellous advertisement for the code, although you'd rather not be reminded of it every four seconds by Eddie and Stevo. Yet this pair also make the simple and obvious error of decrying low-scoring matches, especially those played in rain. The Castleford–Halifax match in 1999 was a ferocious and flawed battle, made more compelling, not less, by the mistakes caused by the wet ball and raw passions.

The narrowing of rugby league horizons has had one beneficial effect. Thank goodness, it seems that fewer people are relying on ludicrous stunts and hopes and pie-in-the-sky. Rugby league's retreat behind its old walls has had the effect of a hothouse, focusing and nurturing. They may be playing without union stars and Aussie greats, but by God, are they playing. The marketing of the Super League appears to be concentrating on the art of the possible, not the art of shovelling something nasty that the bull left behind. In this off-pitch regard, the return to the league fold of Peter Deakin, formerly a brilliant marketing director of Saracens and then chief executive of Warrington Wildcats, rubbed off all over. Deakin later returned to union with Sale. The staging of matches, the replica kit, the accessibility to the supporters and the local community, the recognition of the prime importance of establishing

282

academies, the cheery websites, the almost-not-excruciating pre-match entertainment . . . these are life-giving matters. The splendid use of the video replay to inform and entertain as well as to get the right decision is masterly and must be followed by rugby union's authorities. The refereeing, as I have said, is outstandingly good and sympathetic.

On the field, better yet. The battle for the top places in Super League Five, for the right to a place in the play-offs, produced some splendid and high-class rugby. It was, indeed, the best seen for years. It was, indeed, played with great skill. It was, as ever, played by some of the finest characters in sport. I had the good fortune to meet Phil Clarke in May at the Professional Rugby Players' Association dinner. Clarke, the former Wigan and Great Britain hooker who retired after a nasty neck injury in Australia, was about to expand his interests to include a website. Cliff Morgan introduced us. Cliff's marvellous Saturday sports slot on Radio Four is, sadly, no more. But he told me that he reckoned that Clarke was one of the finest men he had interviewed on his show and, bless him, he got through a few.

Such characters, and also the intensity created by the financial panic factors, by the need to retain the interest of News International and to extend the pool of top players that English rugby league is now called upon to produce, have probably made English rugby league better than it ever was. Duncan can't see past the Saints, but I'm less biased. I've been fascinated by odd individuals – Chris Joynt of Saints seems to be a player for all roles; Adrian Vowles, the Australian loose-forward at Castleford, seems to have an amazing armoury of inspiration. Of course, it can get samey, because with Sky concentrating on the top few you can become cheesed off with Jason Robinson's post-tackle writhing and Stuart Raper's thunderstruck expressions when Castleford concede a try. It's forced me out and around some of the smaller grounds. As ever, there is no lack of appetite for the battle, whether for points or survival.

Whether or not rugby league advocates admit it to themselves, the intention has been to draw in horns and maximise what is already in being. The crust is still wafer-thin, but the base to push off from is then, eventually, stronger. This new-found strength will ensure that the prospect of union swallowing it up completely – already a tiny one, since league is so locally strong and since amalgamation would take place under union rules – would recede completely. There will be no such thing as a hybrid game, because union law-makers and marketeers will not be inclined to forsake any of the characteristics which have made the game take root and prosper in most parts of the world in favour of playing concepts imported from a code which never exported them. So by its recent polishing up of itself, rugby league has ensured that it will always be.

Long live Super League. It now has a new sponsor in Tetley's, and News International have re-signed, showing faith and hope. It needs hope and also it needs an international profile and a Great Britain team, not four washed-out individual countries – and I say that in spite of my respect for Clive Griffiths, the coach of Wales and yet a man good enough to coach splendidly in both codes. Even more than that it needs Great Britain; rugby league needs Great Britain to stuff Australia. Oh, and it needs a London club side, somewhere where Duncan can go to watch the Saints and still get home to bed on the same day.

What of what Ian Millward, coach of St Helens, describes as 'the threat from the big union clubs'? He was speaking as a man who had just lost Tuilagi and Perelini to union. Will there now be a mass buying up of rugby league talent as rugby union slowly and surely gets its own back for the years when its great players, young and old, were preyed upon? It must first be said that if the threat is real then it is not well founded. The professional arm of club rugby union has weathered the worst but is still in parts built on shifting financial sands. There is ample scope for a union club to do a Widnes – buy and pay more than you can afford, and then downsize so rapidly that it can hardly be seen through a microscope.

Some former union players can be successfully re-converted to their old code, but out-and-out league men would be a high-risk investment. It is a matter of both public record and perceived opinion in the sport that the raft of league players who have appeared on short-term contracts – the Pauls, Jason Robinson and Gary Connolly – all struggled desperately. Jason Robinson is obviously one of the best characters in British sport, and one of the best rugby league wings. But it was a lunacy for the RFU, festooned with ready-made class wings, to offer him a package totalling £750,000 to switch, and the stroppy RFU reaction when I expressed this opinion in the *Sunday Times* may have had something to do with their own unease.

The situation in Australia is even less clear. The bitter battles between rival leagues have given way to one league and yet more bitter battles as great old names disappear in forced mergers and as some of the remaining teams fight for life. Even though the best of Australian rugby league is still marvellous, a little of the old swagger has gone. Australian rugby union has three things to offer to the country's rugby league men. Contracts (and fat contracts, too), which it could not do in the amateur days; a thriving domestic structure with the three Super-12 teams, New South Wales Waratahs, Queensland Reds and ACT Brumbies, who failed to win the 2000 Super-12 only because of some bone-headed tactics and some poor refereeing. And finally, a true, global profile. This has always been union's trump card, but is more so now that true Kangaroo challenges are so few and far between and the Wallabies are the glamorous World Champions.

And add to all this the fact that rugby union, especially in Australia, resembles league so closely these days that only the two flankers give the clue to which is which. The first raft of ex-league players are already in the Super-12 and the Brumbies full-back, Andrew Walker, was one of the stars of the whole tournament. John O'Neill, chief executive of the ARU and not the least excitable man in sport, recently promised major raids to steal away league giants, as if to back up his boast that one day, 'Union will destroy league.' This led to a memorable handbags-at-dawn spat between O'Neill and David Moffett, the NRL's chief executive, who upheld what he saw as the superiority of league and announced moves to exempt from its salary cap players who converted from union.

O'Neill gleefully seized his chance. Until recently Moffett was chief executive of the New Zealand Rugby Union, and while there had apparently described league as 'five tackles and a kick' and described the Super-12 as a 'sexy, one-stop entertainment shop'. O'Neill suggested to Moffett that he 'make up his mind'. Steady, dears, steady.

What is true is that the Super League in England has begun an entertainment shop. Who knows, now that ludicrous talk of expansion is over, now that people realise that a one-off missionary match doesn't mean the country's conquered, and now that the home fires are burning, maybe the expansion will actually begin. Rugby league's amateur arms are embracing a few parts of the country that professional bullshit could not reach, with various conference and student competitions growing steadily. It is as if, contrary to its own belief, there is, after all, no law against rugby league in Bristol and Hemel Hempstead and Birmingham.

It will take twenty years for a new rugby league club in say, Leicester, to infect enough people in the locality to consider creating a professional team (unless a magnate dips in his toe and no one bites it off). Even then it will need twenty years of fierce application – by amateurs. That, you see, is precisely how Leicester Tigers came to establish themselves in the city, not because some fool with a few borrowed quid came by and tried to convert people to something alien, and had only a day or two to do it before he got bored. But the roots will be well founded when the day comes, the day when you have to take a route to rugby league which does not include the M62, or the Blackwall Tunnel.

CHAPTER EIGHTEEN

Samoa

How professional rugby was rescued from disaster – by the men who play it ◆ Free at last and for ever – the great escape of the greatest sport

Pat Lam held the Heineken Trophy above his head. Tim Rodber had to take one of the handles because Lam suddenly remembered, in those moments of joy, that his shoulder was so badly damaged that he should never have started the game, nor many others in Northampton's fierce and emotional late-season run. Typically, the first time the ball had come to Lam in the 2000 European final he had deliberately driven hard into Munster tacklers with the damaged shoulder dropped and leading, as if to impart what was for Northampton the glad news and for Munster the frightening thought that he was to be at his supercharged best. Agony or not, one writer recalled that 'he was to make spectacular yardage on every carry'.

Lam is one of the smallest giants in sport. He can be a volcanic presence on the field. I always find it difficult to think of a better word than 'supercharged' as he blasts around, punching with the ball and in the tackle way above his weight. So I've given up trying. He is probably the most galvanising leader in the game. But his essential humility and his religious faith have given him a marvellous serenity and balance, a sense of sporting goodness. 'How bad was Pat's shoulder?' I asked Phil Pask, Northampton's physiotherapist, a month after the final. 'Bad,' Pask said. I also asked Pask for his opinion on Lam the man, the character. 'Is he *really* everything that he appears to be?' I asked. 'No,' Pask said. 'He's even more than that.'

What if rugby decided to have its own flag? There would be a fierce debate as to which colours should be included to reflect the sport's global spread, and which designs or motifs to reflect culture and ethos. Ultimately, the process would probably be too much of a hassle, given that the sport's leading administrators are currently unable to agree on anything and each would flounce out if his country's colour was passed over. The alternative would be to adopt the flag of one country, but a country which portrays in its own rugby all that is fine about the sport and little of what is petty and selfish. In which case we would hoist on all our flagpoles, wherever rugby is played, the red and blue flag of Samoa.

For goodness' sake, Mr Supercharged is only one of many. Consider the vivacious crowd-pulling appeal, the influence rubbing off on the players around them and the sheer technical ability of the Samoan players who have arrived to play professionally in Britain. Va'aiga Tuigamala is probably grandfather of the extended family. He has been wonderfully influential at Wigan and is so now at Newcastle Falcons. Junior Paramore was revered at Bedford and is so now at Gloucester. Trevor Leota is the crowd hero at Wasps, his bobbing pineapple-style haircut and battering running as much their trademark as Lawrence Dallaglio. George Leaupepe, one of the few centres I have seen I would place in the same division as Frank Bunce, came over to usher Bristol back into the top flight; Terry Fanolua is loved as fiercely at Gloucester as if he had been born in Longlevens. Fereti Tuilagi has just re-joined rugby union and Leicester from St Helens rugby league club; likewise, Apollo Perelini has joined Sale. Mike Umaga is Rotherham's full-back in their ascension to the Premiership One for 2000–01. And there are so many more. Take them away, and much of the colour drains from the sport in Britain.

And yet apart from some tackles on the northern borders of the shoulders and the southern borders of the head, have you seen a Samoan player take a real cheap shot, give anything other than his best shot, whine about something afterwards, behave with anything other than rugby's proper decorum? Nor me.

It is likely that the heroic Lam is the most famous living Samoan. He was born in Auckland of Samoan parents and is quite ferociously proud of his country's traditions and culture – as are all the Samoans who play their rugby everywhere in the world. The week of the Heineken final was momentous even by Lam's standards. Stephanie, his wife, had given birth to Josiah, his third child, a brother to Michigan and Bryson. No doubt the first message of congratulation, referring particularly to Stephanie's speed of delivery, came from Northampton's coach, John Steele. His players had been dropping like flies all season and Lam, bound by the powerful Samoan sense of duty to family, would not have played had the birth still been imminent by the Saturday. Broken shoulder, fine. Broken leg, let's get on with it. Family? Priority.

Two days later Lam went to a function at Lord's Cricket Ground to receive arguably the most coveted award in any sport – the players' Player of the Season. He had the grace to attend even though he was a new dad and faced vanishing point of the season two days later. The Professional Rugby Players' Association had made him their man. 'I am a little embarrassed and I accept it on behalf of my team-mates. I came here, to this country, to represent my wife and family and the Samoan people. This week I saw my wife give birth without painkillers, and I realise that what I have to go through is insignificant.'

Lam arrived at Newcastle Falcons at the start of the professional era in Britain. He was a galvanising force then, just as he had been in any team he played for as a boy in Auckland, just as he had been when he chose to play for the country which was in his soul, not the one in which he lived. Had other South Sea Islanders made the same choice, not been (understandably) beguiled by the salaries and prospects in New Zealand and Australia, then the World Cup every four years would be a complicated exercise to see who could win the fourth semi-final place alongside Samoa, Fiji and Tonga – and it would most likely never be New Zealand who succeeded. Just a thought.

It hardly goes without saying that Newcastle Falcons won the Allied Dunbar Premiership with Lam installed. It is barely worth remarking that he now captains Northampton even though the club has natural leaders such as Matt Dawson and Tim Rodber in their ranks. Lam is not surprised that Samoa produces more great rugby players per head of population than any other country. For God's sake, Samoa produces more great players than any other nation, full stop. No need to speak of relative size and population.

'We are born to be rugby players,' he told David Walsh in an interview in March 2000. 'We have innate skills and a love of physical contact. But more than those natural advantages, the emphasis on family in Samoan culture means that they fit comfortably into a great team game. You won't see too many Samoans excel at individual sports; they just love to have people around them, love to be able to do things for other people. Wherever I have been, Newcastle or Northampton, I have tried to bring this philosophy. You play for each other, you are part of a family.'

After the European Cup final, Lam pulled his team, coaches and medical staff into a tight circle, still out on the pitch at Twickenham. He is a born-again Christian, after originally losing his faith because he tired of repetitive formal worship and being forced to attend church. He asked the whooping and hollering Saints to give him a Christian minute. 'I said to them that maybe we should just say thanks. They were very good about it.' Listening to the great man afterwards, watching the eyes burn in a relaxed frame, you suddenly knew why Northampton had won against all the odds. 'I said to the guys on Friday that I had already received my prize, with Josiah's birth. I made a commitment to them that I would go out and play for them, so that they could experience something of what I felt with the arrival of my son.' Blimey, I thought. Given Pat in charge, I felt I could have gone out myself and seen off Munster.

But it was a heady day from every angle. As the trophy was held aloft, Lam turned to his left, to where 20,000 supporters of Northampton were experiencing the highest emotions of sporting ecstasy and relief. This is a club which, around ten years previously, had had an average home crowd of 1000. Their team had at one time in 1999–2000 been strongly in contention for all three major trophies. They were beyond any doubt the best non-international team in the British Isles and France. But they had been drained so badly by the growing pressure and savagery of the fixtures programme that they had come up short in the Premiership and the Tetley's Bitter Cup and had not even qualified for the life-giving European event for 2000–01. Now, they had the biggest trophy of all, the first major cup in the history of the rejuvenated Midland giant, and they would qualify because they were holders. Owners.

The Northampton fans went bananas when Lam showed them the cup. But there was also noise from elsewhere. Around 25,000 Munster men and women had come to Twickenham bedecked in fighting Munster red, bellowing 'The Fields of Athenry', the rugby hit of the new millennium. In defeat, they gave Lam and Northampton a warm ovation. Shortly afterwards both teams did a lap of honour, Munster anti-clockwise and Northampton clockwise. When the two teams met, there were hugs and handshakes which to me spoke volumes for the mutual respect of professional rugby players. Keith Wood, Munster's talismanic hooker on their fantastic run to the final, said later: 'We're shattered, absolutely shattered. But I have to say that Northampton deserved it; they've been the best team in England for nine months and it would have been hard for them to finish with nothing. I'm pleased for them.'

When the teams reached those parts of the stadium containing the rival fans, both were applauded long and loud. Hardly a Munsterman left his place. It set the seal on a marvellous competition. This was practically the finest day that Twickenham had seen since it was rebuilt; it was the first time it had appeared to work as a genuinely raucous, atmospheric arena.

It represented a sea change in the fortunes of professional rugby clubs in the home unions because the Heineken Cup gave them, in effect, a life of their own. Club affairs had always been an add-on, a few extra quid, when rugby unions negotiated with the major television companies for the rights to international rugby. Here, in the testimony of the BBC, for a start, was evidence that there was now a club event that broadcasters wanted in its own right. That professional club record was catching on.

Mike Hales, head of BBC sports publicity, examined the evidence of the viewing figures which had seen up to six million taking in the final in Britain. 'It has been a success story for us ever since the opening Bath–Toulouse match in the pool attracted nearly four million viewers. If you are up around three or four million on a Saturday afternoon then you are talking about a serious figure. The Heineken Cup represents a quantum leap, and one which is lifting standards and the perception of club rugby among viewers. With the game turning pro, it represents the change from a game for enthusiasts to a serious professional sport.'

This was all fine and dandy. It ensured that the season went out on a surge of new optimism. I was pleased for Northampton and their fans, pleased for the image and prosperity of the club game and delighted with old Twickers coming alive. The spirit of the followers on the terraces was wonderful. In all these matters, it seemed that many of the dire predictions of people who said that club rugby could not work in a professional era, who said that *rugby* could not work in a professional era, were being proved wrong. On this evidence, it was thriving, bubbling. On this evidence, with Keith Wood's noble views, with a mighty attendance in such high sporting humour, it seemed that rugby's goodness, that aspect reckoned to be most at stake, was still high and mighty.

The truth is, of course, that it was a heady day, but still just one day. Since rugby went professional, many of the warnings of the true blues who fervently wished the game to stay amateur have been revealed as paranoia. Perhaps not all of them, however. My impressions when season 2000–01 started were that the game was in a few areas still struggling badly, agonisingly, to find its pro feet; and always, there has been the chilling howl of the wolf at the door. Many structures were based on sand.

The ill feeling caused by the shortcomings of officialdom was pervasive in 1995, and it remains so. At least part of the cherished idea of a universal game in which major unions fought for a common goal had clearly gone. In favour of self-interest. It seemed that international rugby was being played far too often and that the authority wielded in the game by national-team coaches of the top countries was becoming ruinous, even running amok. That the game at all levels on the field was diminished in the search for a bogus concept of entertainment by the removal of its points of confrontation.

Whether or not professional rugby as a concept and pastime has a long-term future, it has not yet quite secured that future. While it has waited to decide and to claim its own salvation it has been at the mercy of the unforgiving marketplace, of short tempers and short attention-spans of new investors and agents and officials. It has been at the mercy of hopeless officialdom. There is absolutely no doubt that large parts of rugby's fledgling professional empire could easily have come crashing down in ruins at any stage of the past five years.

And there is no doubt who saved it. Pat Lam. And his wonderful Samoan family of players. But not only them. We are talking about a bigger family here. Lam's domination of events before and during the Heineken European Cup was eloquent testimony that the game is still being played by men of the highest calibre – whatever the fears of the old guard that a better class of chap was drifting out of the sport. It has been saved, been granted more precious time to sort itself out, by Lam and also by Martin Johnson, Robert Howley, Keith Wood, Gregor Townsend, Abdel Benazzi, Taine Randell, Agustin Pichot, Steve Larkham, André Venter, Alessandro Troncón, Marika Vunibaka, Rod Snow, by the peers of these players in all countries where professional rugby is possible (and those where it is not, but where they're trying anyway).

They have saved the game by their patience, of course. Players all over the world have had to struggle through as contracts were found to be worth less than the value of the paper on which they were, or were not, written. But it is far more than contracts. After what was probably a slow start, the echelon of professional players has become as dedicated a group of sportsmen as there is. For me, as I say, the selfless, driving and almost ruthless application of the current England international rugby squad is light years and oceans of sweat in advance of that of the football and cricket squads.

It is silly to be too sweeping, because in any team, professional or amateur, there are fakers, short-cutters. Once they could hang on and primp and pose for a season or so. Now, in the new culture, they don't last a month. The drive for excellence in rugby at the moment – as far as it is possible to judge for those of us who have seen a bit of action here and there, who have come across the players at work – is a wonder of the sporting world. There was always a work ethic, but under amateurism there was always an excuse, too. That blessed man Andy Ripley used to say that to be an amateur at least gave you a divine right to be hopeless.

These days, just as those who were once starving can better appreciate a sudden sustenance, those who were once left unpaid for their commitment to rugby realise more than other athletes the heavy responsibility conveyed by the salaries. Team still lose. It is highly likely that at least one team in every match will always fail to win it. It is by no means always true that all the paymasters at all the professional levels can really afford what they are paying. But it is certainly true that the players are earning their money.

It is not so much in their play, or in their dedication, but rather in the ethics of their approach to rugby that they have come through so strongly. Respect for opposition is at an all-time high. It varies inversely with the amount of actual social contact with opposition players, but that, for the moment, is another story. Violence is way, way down. The game has never been so clean. One in every two players who played in the 1999 World Cup was tested for drugs, and of the whole lot of them, all under pressure to perform, there was only Anton Oliver's positive test, and that because he had inadvertently taken a prescribed drug containing a banned element.

Perhaps there is more sledging on the field, more unhelpful advice and winding-up at close quarters. But it strikes me that if respect has diminished, then violence would not have done so. Perhaps there is now more backchat directed at the referee, more raised eyebrows and shoulders and voices. The looming Johnson is happiest when fixing the ref with his cold gaze. Yet referees themselves seem happier with more of a relationship, with more of a discussion so that their preventative refereeing can thrive.

They still have the weapons of the sin-bin and the extra ten metres, after all. Still have the option exercised by Les Peard, the fine referee of the turn of the previous decade who gave the formidable Wayne Shelford a fearful verbal roasting for his continual attempts to referee the match.

And in any case, with what are you comparing these things? With Paolo Di Canio pushing a referee off his feet? With Roy Keane and Jaap Stam of Manchester United chasing Andy D'Urso, the referee who had just awarded a penalty against them? The pictures the next day as the two berated the referee were the ugliest I have seen in sport, because the players' faces were grotesquely twisted, almost mutated in fury. I don't think that Johnson suggesting to the ref that he might consider getting a grip is enough evidence that rugby is on that route.

For what it is worth, I would suggest to anyone complaining about backchat and discussion today that the current processes are far more healthy than in the days when the referee was effectively a sergeant-major and you could not only not say a word to him but also had to bring his boots up to a shine between scrums. Then you had to thank him for giving up his afternoon even if he'd been a nightmare. The best British refs (and they are still easily the best in the world) now set out to have a working relationship with the players, and the likes of Brian Campsall and Chris White, in particular, appear to have succeeded. Referees are less precious, more consistent and better than they have ever been. The rubbish that because we couldn't have a game without them meant that they were above reproach is in the dustbin. They are now, correctly, subject to onerous performance criteria. No mutant response needed from the players.

What of the warnings about greed, demands for money? This was another of the cesspools into which rugby, we were told, would sink. Players would hold clubs and countries to ransom. Again, I think that professional players have acquitted themselves well. You can read stories of athletes holding event-promoters to ransom; of footballers refusing to fulfil contracts which bring them obscene rewards. I cannot recall a single serious monetary dispute involving an international rugby squad. I can recall only a handful of disputes at clubs, and very little flouncing off.

Of course, agents start the bidding with ridiculous requests. Of course, rugby players try to drive the hardest bargain they can with a prospective employer. Why, in this sphere, should rugby be any different from any other business – journalism, architecture, factory work, company directing? I have heard far fewer players whining about money (even when their contracts have been dishonoured) than I have heard players claiming, with a stamp of authenticity, that the money is not an issue in their pursuit of excellence.

You hear old clubhouse doyens, those in the bastions of amateurism, drinkers at the bar in small clubs, claiming that the pro players are greedy, aloof, don't pitch in and buy their rounds any more. You do hear the odd story that so-and-so wouldn't do up his laces for less than £100,000, as if rugby really should be egalitarian, with every player receiving a few pounds whatever the standards. Again, the best practitioners in any field are paid more. Rugby is not outside that market force.

The modern-era professional player has indeed changed. Usually, he simply does not want to drink. He wants to keep the edge over people after his place in the team. He is inside his team laager so often that he can appear aloof and detached when he is outside it. Elsewhere in this book I humbly suggest that the players sink a few and go out and damage a few deserving hotels, down some aftershave, take up the chase and try for what Bruce Springsteen once called a close inter-personal relationship with a member of the opposite sex. For a night. Or two. But however a professional player behaves he is not preventing the rest of the game behaving precisely as it always did. I have no evidence to suggest that in his heart, off the field and even when thrashing out his new deal, the pro player of today is an unattractive beast.

A honeyed view of the new breed? I think not. I have seen rugby sights, heard rugby bickerings and misjudgements which in the past year have sickened me to the core, shaken my faith. There is still so much work to do and so much ground to make up. But none of this has been the fault of players. The supreme pride and dedication of top rugby players have not so much survived the arrival of professionalism as thrived on it, driven it along. And by pride and dedication and inner balance, saved it. It was easy to forget, watching Pat Lam surge around the rugby season and hold up the Heineken Cup, that it could easily have gone the other way. It did not.

Today, with such a fine culture established in the game, and as they wait for the other aspects of top rugby to catch up with them, the players can claim with justification and pride that wherever they play, whichever national emblem they wear on their jersey, they are all Samoan.

So let's summarise, not so much what I saw on fields in the past year or so, but sensed in hearts and minds. People said our fine old game would die if it went pro. Rugby lives and breathes and is bigger than ever, and growing. People said it would become dishonest. At present, rugby is a more honest sport than at any time in its history and all the shabby shamateurism is gone.

Honesty. Just before the World Cup of 1999 I wrote an article in praise of the bold stance of the International Rugby Board in drug-testing as many as half of all competitors in the event. I received a disparaging letter from a colleague who reported on athletics. The cynicism associated with athletics these days was ingrained in every sentence. I was being naïve, he said. What about all the masking agents around? How many players would simply not show up for the tournament because they feared testing? He said that anyone who had withdrawn injured should be under suspicion. How could rugby have had a drive for improvement and no drug problem? he asked.

I had neither the heart nor the time to ask him why he felt that rugby players were chemically and medically sophisticated enough to be able to mask their endemic drug-taking (and don't forget that rugby's clean sheet extends far and wide, out to tiny World Cup qualifying matches and all levels of club play) while athletics, where drug-taking and masking have been going on for decades, still produces positive after positive.

Maybe I am naïve, but I do not believe that rugby has a drugs problem and I know the reason why. Not because of fear of testing. It is because rugby's culture has always been to have fair competition, man to man (or woman to woman). No ducking. No diving. Despise the cheats. Fair enough, maybe the odd elbow in the ribs at a line-out; maybe the odd nonsensicality such as Andy Haden diving out of a line-out to earn a penalty. Otherwise, the sport's culture was, and is, completely intolerant of anything that smacks of taking unfair advantage.

Let's summarise also by grasping that amateurism may have meant ambience and affection but it also meant indolence, smugness and under-achievement. People could sit on their backsides because there was nothing to get up for; rugby chugged along. Only now is rugby even beginning to explore its own possibilities.

The commercial imperatives, even panic, have brought about revolutions. They have forced a smile on to rugby's outer face for its paying public. Facilities at the gate-taking grounds and international stadiums are profoundly improved. Crowd noise is down because the new rhythm of rugby is less exciting, but at least the sense of welcome is now warmer. The little receiver system called Ref-Link, introduced to England in 2000, enables spectators to listen in to the ref, to participate more in the game. Little receiver, but significant gesture.

Yes, it costs more to watch professional rugby. Yes, if you want the replica shirt you'll have to shell out. But I believe firmly that the value has actually increased. Which is better? A fiver for a slow match and a cold pie on a wet terrace, or £20 for a fast match, a warm welcome, a decent dish and an environment to which you can bring your family? Keith Grainger, chief executive of Newport, recently showed me around the place. Family village, family stand, food outlets, transformed programme, jazz band, community programme, education programme, a target that every school in Gwent would be visited by the players. 'And I'm determined that no one will have to wait two minutes for a beer,' he said. 'So we've taken on lots of extra bar staff.' And that's at Newport. Until recently, they gave you the impression that they were doing you a favour by allowing you in.

But rugby has changed for the better not just because it had to, so that more people and more TV moguls would pay for it. It has changed because of a professional pride – not only in Pat Lam and the uppermost echelon of players, but also in every other section in the top levels of the game. In referees and their leaders – refereeing around the world has improved dramatically. I spent an instructive morning in September 2000 listening to Clive Norling and the Welsh referees fervently explaining their drive for a better game and for uniformity. God, I almost started liking them. But everyone from coaches to groundsmen has picked up the same pro pace.

The players have been rewarded, and not just by salary. They have their home lives back. They come home from work and join the family or their friends instead of coming home from work and rushing out to rugby. It is to be hoped that their employers are giving them balance, suggesting or even demanding that they retain other interests, even plan for other careers; that even national coaches will grant them richness of experience as well as miles of training trudge.

I asked every last player I interviewed in the past year if they loved pro rugby but also whether they had something else in their lives. Happily, almost all did. As the splendid Victor Ubogu said, after an appearance on the rather dire *Through The Keyhole* programme, 'The players all took the piss when they saw it. But at least I was earning a few pounds. They were the sad ones, all sitting around watching daytime TV.' It is vital that characters are allowed to thrive and that the old dazzling flash of a Victor Ubogu waistcoat should shine through what is potentially grey and conforming.

There is so much left to do, chiefly because rugby's administrators are lagging behind. Rugby desperately needs new blood in all its various unions and other institutions around the world. It still cannot fix up a decent World Cup, chiefly because too many old-style blitherers have held on to the reins. I do not believe that any of the four home unions are anything like up with the pace, and I think that all three of the southern hemisphere unions are setting the wrong pace.

It will be particularly fascinating to see how quickly the feel-bad factor in British rugby dissipates when the structures for the pro game are finally laid down in concrete – if they ever are. Certainly, there was public resistance around at the start of the 2000-01 season when the crowds at Zurich Premiership matches were disappointing. Rugby, I repeat, has lost millions because of bad publicity. Pat Lam's example is still not being taken to heart.

What else is left to do? Reduce financial dependence on playing vast numbers of international matches; reduce the length of the season; and, in Europe, begin it on 1 September, not before. Reduce the stupid chase after airy-fairy rugby in the cause of entertainment, and realise that thud and crunch and even blunder, that goal-line stands and passion and biff and bosh can be as compelling as all the continuity in the world. And while we are at it, act decisively on the recent southern hemisphere initiative for a single, global season which ties Europe into the same event windows and drags us to a summer season. Let us act decisively by shoving the southern hemisphere initiative somewhere where the sun shines neither in the summer nor the winter, and let us lock ourselves into winter rugby now and forever and throw away the key.

And now, more than ever, we need the International Rugby Board to grow and grow and grow in power. We need it to solve what I consider to be the one genuinely nasty upshot of professional rugby – that success now depends more on money than on essential rugby goodness. It means that fine clubs have declined and, on a global level, it has had the horrendous result of cementing in the old and moneyed guard and savaging the aspirations of potentially wonderful rugby countries such as Canada, Samoa, Fiji, Tonga, Romania, Argentina and many others.

The cavernous gap in resources, preparation time and culture means that thrashings, and not marvellous, world-stunning shocks, have become the norm. The IRB have recognised the fact by instituting a fast-track funding plan for the second rank of countries but it is a profound sadness to me that matches between the old elite and other countries are played on a field with a severe slope, and in both halves of the match the other teams are playing up the steep hill.

Indeed, the sadness does in part mask what is essentially the runaway triumph of the IRB in the global development programme. The way in which the likes of Vernon Pugh, Lee Smith and many others have devoted their energies and the IRB's purse to global development, regional development, regional events, to bringing balls and boots and rugby brains and videos and victories to the have-nots, is quite magnificent. One hundred years overdue, but still magnificent.

It must continue. China, buoyed by IRB support, announced their intention recently to win the World Cup in the foreseeable future. New Zealand v China in Peking? Far-fetched. But three years ago, no native Chinese had ever played the game in China. Last season, China won two international rugby matches. Rugby is spreading like fire on dry tinder. It is only to be hoped that soon the fire engulfs the top countries and gives us fifteen genuine contenders at the very top.

But more important still is that the IRB respond to the death of inter-nationalism in their members. This is now a more selfish age. Whereas the major unions would propose measures for the good of the sport, now they propose only measures for their own short-term good. With the age of selfishness comes contemplation of the backyard and not the neighbourhood. It is critical to the game's progress that the IRB is made bigger, given more staff, more executive power, so that it can fill the vacuum. There is probably nothing more important for international rugby.

There are no rose-coloured spectacles here. I have grieved for rugby more often than I have celebrated it in the past five years, as the uncontrolled explosions I always predicted have duly come about. Yes, there is less of a warmth around. Yes, I have friends I respect who have been turned away. But we have struggled because amateurism gave us no quarter, no transition period, not because professionalism succeeded it. In the final analysis, the transition to paid play was inevitable. But it was also for the good of rugby. That's it. Full stop.

We are always reminded, of course, that more than 95 per cent of the sport remains amateur, and officials welded into the old era and those trying to account for the drop in the numbers of people who actually play the game have never stopped blaming the transition for all the ills. There is much talk that the elite swan around in big cars while the fifth-teamer still pays his subs; that somehow, money which is the due of the minnows has been stolen. That ambience has gone, that the top men scuttle away after the Diet Coke.

I do not buy it. I never will. The jealousies say more about the die-hards and the whiners than they do about the professional elite. It is incumbent upon all sections of the game to hack out their own existence, for grass roots to be nurtured but also to grasp that they can be nurtured from above, by the shining example of the show windows of rugby. Of all the theories as to why fewer people play, as to why the clubs no longer field fifth and sixth teams, none beguiles me quite as much as the theory that in the age of improvement, fewer people are keen to celebrate and advertise the fact that they are not very good at the sport. Long live rugby of all standards, but it does not mean that rugby's appeal is shrinking if every park pitch is not packed every Saturday. The game has changed; the best deserve to be paid, their lifestyles cannot absorb both professionalism and gibbering around the bar. It's life. For everyone, rugby life is still there to be lived. No one died.

Ultimately, the doctrine of amateurism removed the rights of young people. If you had a rich talent, if there was some potential post or profession for which you had a marvellous aptitude and/or loved to do, then you could earn your living from it. Be it a sport, one of the arts, one of the professions, anything. The only people who could not earn their living from that which they could do best of all in their lives were those with an outstanding aptitude for rugby union. Over the decades, so many young people from all social classes in all the big rugby countries had what should have been their living denied to them just because of a hopeless, pompous doctrine imposed by history and grandees.

Very few people can choose from two or more fields of their own genius in which to earn a living (and those of us who are so blessed do feel privileged). But take two players who are arguably the most dazzling talents to span the two eras – Jeremy Guscott and Jonathan Davies. Guscott's brilliance was always obvious but because rugby was amateur he had to hack his way around a mixed bag of jobs – bus-driving, forestry, bricklaying – which did not begin to satisfy him or extend him. Davies's most memorable job in a chequered career involved twelve-hour shifts cleaning the mud from bulldozers. He understandably decided to exploit his own sporting brilliance by leaving to play rugby league.

So it was fortunate for both men that their talents did extend further. Here you have two of the sharpest men the streets of the sport have ever seen, two men with a wit and all-seeing experience to dwarf the reactions and even the intellect of someone with three degrees. One was a bus driver. The other cleaned bulldozers. And they are clever enough to savage you with their lacerating and mickey-taking tongues before you can squeeze out a retaliatory expletive. They were also wise enough to get around the privations of the old era.

And yet even when I've had the pair chipping away at me, I'm somehow warmed by the realisation that rugby has given me some knowledge of and even friendship with two of the best and most well-balanced blokes I've come across, and that even rugby's old attempts to crush genuine aspirations of young men with its ham-fisted dogma failed completely. Here are two brilliant escapees. The point is, though, that not every talented young player was so lucky.

Now, their successors, those who possess their genius for rugby are blissfully free. They are free to choose rugby, or not to choose rugby. They are free, if they so decide, to maximise their rugby talents, to earn their livings and fulfil their sporting dreams. They are lucky in one sense, but in another are taking no more than their due.

On the backs of Jeremy and Jiffy and on the injured shoulder of the marvellous Pat Lam, rugby has finally gained – and earned – its freedom.

CHAPTER NINETEEN

Andes

Postscript: rugby's team spirit; victory and defeat, life and death

Many claims are made for rugby. Builds the character, good for the soul, imparts the value of hard work. You know, the same kind of benefits attributed to the application of cold showers, fagging, birching and many other kinds of high-Tory and old-school suffering. Rugby is meant to convey more of these benefits than other activities because it is a contact sport, apparently teaching you to accept physical pain with stoicism; and it is a team sport, teaching interaction and trust and selflessness. Good theory, anyway.

Not everyone subscribes to it. I remember a long and tetchy conversation I held with Dudley Doust, the American-born sports journalist once with the *Sunday Times*. Dudley was and is a friend, a singular operator and, when he hits his stride, a fine writer. He is no fan of rugby for various reasons, chiefly because he was always inclined to buy in too readily to the more hackneyed theories on its supposed weaknesses. Over dinner at one of the British Opens we were both covering, he totally dismissed the concept of team spirit in sport. He did not believe that such a phenomenon existed.

I found this dismissal staggering coming from a man familiar with many sports, and suspected it stemmed from his excellence in profiling individual sportsmen – he was superb on Botham, Ballesteros and others – and not the collective; and because American team sports are anally retentive backyard rubbish compared with the global games played in the outside world. I believe passionately and irrevocably in the notion of team spirit and the power that a team can generate. I can find no evidence that in rugby this is doing anything other than thriving in the professional era, especially with most teams running an egalitarian wage structure; especially with high stakes requiring as much courage and togetherness as ever. I played from the age of eleven until I gave up regular participation at twenty-two to become a hack, and so had to don the working overall on Saturdays. To me, the concept of team spirit and the game's goodness is rugby's engine. Still. But Doust certainly made me realise that there are people who flatly reject the game's ability to do good things for the body and mind, and for life.

Rugby-loving parents will obviously wish their offspring to have a crack at the sport that served them so well. But if you go to clubs running mini-sections, you'll find hordes and hordes of parents who never played rugby and know nothing about it (not that it ever stops them barking useless advice), but who enrol their children because of what rugby can supposedly do for them. I suppose I like to believe it. I even have evidence. Andrew, my elder son, was a diffident character until he took up rugby at nine. His confidence appeared to improve rapidly as he took to the game, and it seems to me far too much of a coincidence not to attribute some of that improvement to rugby.

Team spirit. His mini-mates' team lacked it. They grew up together over the years, on dozens of frozen or windswept Sunday mornings, but they were always a group with cliques. Some came from private prep schools, and some of them clearly because parental egos were put before the good of the children; others were from the local state junior schools, a few from broken marriages. The group feeling in this fractured bunch was never high, hardly existed.

But on their last two days ever as a mini-rugby team, in April 2000, they finally, belatedly pulled together. They played in a big mini-rugby tournament in Somerset. Perhaps it was the adversity of good opposition, perhaps it was the closeness conveyed by the touring environment, but they battled on, becoming ever closer as a group as the opposition grew harsher. By the end, a reticent and scattered bunch had become purposeful and homogenous, and they won the tournament, taking the trophy from Matt Perry, the presenting celeb. In the presentation picture they looked like something they had never been over the previous four years – a unit, a gang of mates who'd come through together.

That was in Burnham-on-Sea. There was another gang of rugby mates who pulled through together and to whom their shared sporting experiences may have meant something. They were high in the Southern Andes, in one of the most wildly beautiful and murderously remote spots on earth, between the Sosneado and Tinguirrica mountains between Argentina and Chile, twenty-eight years ago.

They came from the Old Christians Rugby Club, the former pupils of the Christian Brothers School in Montevideo. And you'd have to say that their second tour of Chile was less successful than the first. On the first, they'd had a marvellous time and had underlined their reputation as one of Uruguay's best clubs. On the second, in 1972, they never even arrived. For anyone who has forgotten the astonished press reports of the time, or if you missed the film *Alive!* based on Piers Paul Read's book of the same name, a Fairchild F-227 aircraft hired by the team from the Uruguayan Air Force (it's difficult not to rank that body with the Gobi Desert Canoe Club and the Russian cricket team) crashed in the Andes because the pilots lost their bearings in cloud and descended, thinking they were clear of the highest mountains. The tail and the wings were chopped off by different impacts on jagged mountains, and total destruction was averted only because the wingless tube of fuselage found a snow field and came to a halt after shooting across it like some enclosed toboggan – although the stopping in itself killed some and injured others.

The team had to absorb a succession of thunderous blows – the death of twelve of the forty-five passengers and crew in or immediately after the accident, and of so many others due to untreatable injury or, later, to an avalanche that consumed the wrecked plane that had become their refuge. There was also the despair of listening to a radio programme they managed to tune into which said that the search for them had been called off (the plane, lost in the vastness of the snowbound Andes, had a white roof); of the desperate cold and other privations.

And, above all, the fact that to stay alive they eventually had to eat, usually raw, hacked-off chunks of their friends' dead bodies – lungs and testicles and all. One of the painful ironies that the surviving team-members had to contend with was the discovery after their rescue that only five miles away from their crash position was a hotel, closed for the winter but stocked with tinned food aplenty.

Ten weeks after the crash, after several expeditions by small groups had failed – essentially, the survivors had no idea which way to head and which of the encircling mountains to scale in search of green civilisation – Robert Canessa and Nando Parrado succeeded in making an heroic trek out of the Andes. Filthy, bearded and emaciated, and wearing random layers of clothing and rugby boots, carrying raw human flesh in rugby socks as food for their journey, they came across some startled Chilean peasants who fed them and alerted the authorities. The remaining fourteen survivors were rescued by helicopter and the full story of the Miracle of the Andes emerged.

Some of the parents had refused to believe their sons were dead, had continued to search long after the official rescue services had given up. Now, more than half of the parents, relatives and friends of the party were to have their hopes raised with the staggering news that there were survivors, then cruelly dashed when their own loved ones were not among them. Those who experienced the unutterable joy of having their sons return had one final hurdle to negotiate: they feared both public and religious outrage at the cannibalism that had saved them, not to mention the possible reactions of the distraught families of those whose bodies had been consumed. As it turned out, almost all opinion was understanding.

The film *Alive!* imparts some of the horror and heroism of the story but is in general very poor, very Hollywood. It glosses over far too many glories of the story – the trek by the saviour heroes, the charged meeting with the peasants, the unquenchable faith of some the parents back in Montevideo. Piers Paul Read's book I found monstrous in parts. It certainly conveys the vividness of the story, some of the heroism, the despair and shafts of hope – although with such subject matter, how could he fail to do so? It would be bloody difficult to write a bad book about it. It is decently researched and in parts it strikes a chord.

But it has a dire tendency to concentrate heavily on the petty arguments, odd vicissitudes and tiffs among the survivors and blow them up into vast character defects. Meanwhile very little is said about the obvious quiet and dogged comradeship and selflessness and the pervading courage of the men, as if someone exhibiting a little self-centredness, lack of decision or indolence among dead friends – and despair, snow-blindness and the weakening effects of altitude and anticipated death – must in real life also be sorely deficient. I was not in the least surprised, after setting Read's book against other material I had read, to see in his own foreword to the paperback edition: 'Some of the survivors were disappointed by my presentation of their story. They felt that the faith and friendship which inspired them in the *cordillera* do not emerge from these pages.'

Read's excuse is pathetic. 'Perhaps,' he says, 'it would be beyond the skill of any writer to express his own appreciation of what they lived through.' Well, it shouldn't be, Piers old son, for anyone with any talent whatsoever, considering you were given a huge wedge for taking on the job that you'd applied to do; given almost total cooperation and *carte blanche* by the survivors, help from the families of the dead and scores of other sources, and had a squad of researchers and other helpers. Shakespeare did a decent job with *Julius Caesar*, and he didn't have any access whatsoever to the people involved.

Read also says, 'At times, I was tempted to fictionalise certain parts of the story because this might have added to the dramatic impact.' Bloody right, too. Next time anyone crashes and is pitched into savage conditions, bleeding and starving and shocked, and has to eat his dead friends, for goodness' sake think about the poor old writer's problem and add some drama; don't just lie around all day suffering and dying. It seems that fate had a final kick in the teeth even for the survivors, in the shape of the man who told their story.

I went to Uruguay in some spare time when covering the 1999 Wales tour of Argentina. A boat will take you across the muddy River Plate from Buenos Aires to Colonia, a small port with the only disused bull-ring I have ever seen and a farm with the world's second-largest collections of key-rings. A tourist combie took us round a loop of the farm on, er, safari. In some fields stood an old goat, a donkey, some scruffy sheep, some large birds and a small antelope-type beast. 'At last,' cried out Mark Souster of *The Times*. 'I've seen the Uruguayan Big Five!' A long drive from Colonia is Montevideo, Uruguay's capital; and there is the Old Christians clubhouse, paid for from the royalties from the Read book. It is in the suburb of Carrasco, where also stands the Carrasco Polo Club, where the Uruguayan national rugby team play most of their games.

Because the story of the Andes Miracle involved a rugby team, it always fascinated me. Would it be ludicrous to regard the players' team spirit as a factor in their survival? Could the selflessness and together-ness they had developed as a group on the rugby field be said to have aided the miracle? Dudley Doust would never think so.

Gustavo Zerbino does. Zerbino was one of those rescued from the mountain and he went on to play for Uruguay and to become a senior union official. 'After we were rescued, we were told that it was impossible to survive in those conditions. Perhaps the fact that we were naïve was a bonus,' he told rugby writer Chris Thau. Perhaps, just as people inexperi-enced in fights go limp as a blow arrives instead of tensing themselves, the Old Christians' naïvety was better than confronting the problems of the high Andes head on. Zerbino also makes enormous play of the fact that all the party were deeply religious. 'It was God's will,' he says.

But he also has another theory. 'There is very little doubt that the fact that we had played rugby together helped. Rugby played a significant part in our survival.' Others among the survivors are on record as taking the same line. Despite their shortcomings, even the film and the book illustrate a togetherness and unselfish pursuit of the collective which is characteristic of the best rugby teams.

Who was the strongest survivor of the initial crash? Marcelo Perez came through the crash itself intact. He rallied the shocked troops straight away, and in the time immediately after the crash became a heroic figure to the other survivors, an optimist, a man of practical ideas, a leader. He was to die in the avalanche. Perez was the captain of Old Christians, the man the club had chosen as its leader for the minor tragedies and the buffeting fortunes of sport. He proved a fine choice when the leadership and goodness and courage shown in his rugby surfaced in tragedy. Rugby's spirit was boosted into the spirit of life.

'After the tragedy and the miraculous escape, rugby then helped us regain our sanity and sense of purpose,' Zerbino says. 'It was a therapy for life.' The survivors decided to put the crash and their inner disquiet at the cannibalism behind them and, with the exception of those too badly injured, all resumed playing within three months of rescue and such was the near fury in the play, the way in which they tried to honour the memory of their colleagues by training hard and playing well, that Old Christians were Uruguayan champions in twelve of the next fourteen seasons. 'We were desperately short of players,' says Zerbino. 'My brother George came out of retirement to give us a hand. Another brother, Raphael, was a soccer player but he turned to rugby to help us, and eventually played for Uruguay. There was incredible passion. We played as if our lives depended on it, we had on the field a team of fifteen friends and we played in the memory of our lost friends.'

Alejandro Nicolich, another Uruguay international, is brother of Gustavo, who did not survive the ordeal, and therefore a member of one of the families that had their hopes raised so dramatically when the news broke that there were survivors. 'The closely knit rugby family and the strong Christian message of our rugby mission helped us to absorb the pain,' he says.

It is, of course, perfectly valid for anyone to dispute the contention that rugby is character-forming, to accuse us rugby lot of exaggerating the game's goodness. It is valid to dispute my belief that the ordeal would have been markedly more vicious had it not been for the natural cohesion of a close rugby community. It is valid to dispute my conviction that fewer would have been brought down from the Andes had they merely been individuals brought together only because they happened to have booked on the same flight.

But you can't argue with those who were up there. It is impossible to dispute the fervently held view of those who themselves went through the ordeal – and found sporting spirit to sustain them in high adversity – that they lived to play rugby again partly because they were rugby players.

❊   ❊   ❊

Twenty-seven years after the events which scarred Uruguayan rugby, the national team – impossibly callow in world terms – appeared on the world stage for the first time. Los Teros had battled their way through their qualifying group and competed with great fortitude, beating Spain and losing with honour to Scotland and South Africa.

Gustavo Zerbino always had faith in his nation's rugby men. 'There is a steel in Uruguayan players which only becomes apparent when they are under pressure. This is expressed in our ability to challenge Argentina when, given the resources of Argentine rugby and the shortages of Uruguay, there should be no contest. But we have always given them a good game. Although our kids grow up in the comparative comfort of middle- and upper-class families, they have retained a primaeval capacity to adapt to difficult circumstances.' They were never disgraced. 'A primaeval capacity to adapt to difficult circumstances.' Perhaps the resistance of the Uruguayans in Scotland contained just a little distilled spirit of the Andes.

Rugby's spirit. It is a well from which we have all drunk. The people who so vigorously defended the amateur principle always said that rugby's spirit could never survive if the players were paid. But the players up in the mountains stayed alive in part because they were a rugby team, had a togetherness forged in sporting battle. So if you believe that rugby's power cannot survive the advent of professionalism then you must believe that if the Old Christians had been a professional team, they would all have died. It is a nonsense. Rugby's spirit and goodness rests elsewhere, in areas far removed from monetary reward, cheap cash transference. Events have proved that it springs from far deeper.

Rugby's spirit survives.

James, Carwyn 10
James, Dafydd 48, 111, 113
Japan 53, 85, 107, 114
Jeavons-Fellows, John 29–30, 72
Jefferies, Horace 185–6
Jenkins, Garin 47, 50
Jenkins, Neil 23, 48, 50, 109, 113, 116, 117,
    137, 217
Jenkins, Vivian 157, 232
Johannesburg 241–2; Ellis Park 26, 27; Sandton
    26, 156–7
Johnson, Martin 132, 138, 148, 168, 244, 263,
    292
Johnstone, Brad 91, 95–6, 213–15, 217–18
Jones, Andrew 123, 301
Jones, Chris 207, 228
Jones, Duncan 265–7, 273, 282, 283
Jones, Ian 134
Jones, Omri 111
Jones, Rosanna Angharad 257
Jones, Tom 104
Jupp, Nicola 255–6

Katalau, Emori 92
Kayser, Deon 86
Keating, Frank 203–4
Kefu, Toutai 115, 122
Kendall-Carpenter, John 10
Kennedy, Brian 40, 174, 175, 178
Kiernan, Tom 67–8
Kingston, John 176
Kirk, David 10, 201
Knight, Sir Michael 260

La Plata, Argentina 42, 44
Lam, Pat 1, 4, 53, 109, 114, 117, 165, 176,
    286–9, 291, 294–7, 299
Lamaison, Christophe 123–4
Lander, Chris 154
Lansdowne Road, Dublin 100–1
Lapasset, Bernard 73
Laporte, Bernard 216
Larder, Phil 115, 155, 158, 168, 170, 206
Larkham, Steve 115, 116, 122, 126, 291
Laurie, Durbar 190
Lawrence, Mark 161–3, 170
Leadbetter, David 205–6
Leather, Kathy 171, 173
Leaupepe, George 53, 114, 287
Lebanon rugby league team 277–8
Ledesma, Mario 53, 102
Leicester Tigers 16, 23, 35, 162, 166, 192, 220,
    265
Lens stadium 97, 101
Leonard, Jason 152, 236
Leota, Trevor 53, 287
Leslie, John 86–7
Levett, Ashley 40, 173, 176–8
Lewis, Geraint 216
Lewsey, Josh 166, 263
Limerick stadium 99–101
Lindsay, Maurice 271, 273, 280
Liverpool FC 141
Lloyd, Leon 162, 166
Lo Cicero, Andrea 218
Loftus Versveldt, Pretoria 160
Lomu, Jonah 23, 24, 26, 27, 62, 83, 90, 121,
    124, 142, 206

London Broncos 265–8, 276, 280–1
London Irish 179
London Scottish 40, 179
Long, Andy 130
Long, Sean 267
Longo, Gonzalo 54
Lovesey, John 225–6
Luger, Dan 136, 161
Luyt, Louis 18, 26, 27
Lydon, Joe 281
Lyle, Dan 99
Lynagh, Michael 100

McAlpine Stadium, Huddersfield 73, 135
McBride, Willie-John 201–2, 229–30
McCallum, Greg 266
McGeechan, Ian 86, 130, 152, 157, 196
McGruther, Dick 131, 132
McHardy, Hugh 188
McIlwham, Gordon 152–3
McJennett, Mark 190–1
McKibbin, Harry 6–7, 11–12
McLaren, Bill 86, 153–4
McLaren, Janie 153–4
MacLaurin, Lord 32
Macqueen, Rod 193–5, 197, 237
Madejski Stadium, Reading 40, 176, 177, 179
Maggs, Kevin 54
Magne, Olivier 123, 124
Mahoney, Tom 190
Mair, Lewine 207–8
Mallett, John 220
Mallett, Nick 87–8, 122–3, 135, 142, 159, 168,
    197, 205, 222–4
Malo, Albert 82
Mandela, Nelson 62, 140, 192
Manic Street Preachers 103, 127
Maradona, Diego 42
marketing 40; of World Cup 65–7, 71–2, 75, 85
Marlborough, HMS 258–9
Marlow 22
Martin, Luca 217
Martin, Marcel 64, 70
Martin, Rolando 53, 54
Martyn, Tommy 267
Matthews, Cerys 52, 103
Mayfair Agreement 38–9
media: RFU briefings 14, 22; and tours 157;
    World Cup facilities for 69–72
Mehrtens, Andrew 125
Mendez, Fréderico 47, 50, 52, 58
Mendez, Hector 52
Menem, Carlos 43, 45, 56
Meyer, Willie 163, 209
middle-class image 17–18
Middlesex County Union 180
'midnight rugby' 163
Millar, Syd 203, 209, 210
Millennium Dome 264–5
Millennium Stadium, Cardiff 62, 69, 75, 96, 115,
    125, 279–80; compared to Arms Park 46, 79,
    105; non-rugby events 107, 127; roof 193–4;
    World Cup opening ceremony 52–3, 103–8
Millward, Ian 284
Mina, Ramiro 78–9, 82, 102
mini-rugby 301
Mitchell, Emma 245, 250, 254
Mitchell, John 133, 146, 165

Moffett, David 285
Mola, Ugo 93
Moorcroft, Dave 31, 32
Moore, Brian 13, 16, 210
Morgan, Cliff 11, 232–3, 240, 283
Muller, Pieter 143
Munster 87, 286, 289
Murdoch, Rupert 16, 26–7, 99, 152, 271, 273, 276, 281
Murphy, Kevin 155
Murray, Cammie 120
Murray, Scott 151, 171–3
Murrayfield 150–1

Namibia 92, 93
Neath 189–90
Nero, Durtis 79, 82
New Zealand (All Blacks) 26, 91, 100, 106, 112, 207, 238; and eligibility of players 216; epic Tri-Nations match 204; and 1987 World Cup 113–14, 126; and 1999 World Cup 60–1, 83, 84, 86, 88–90, 120–1, 123–6, 142; and professionalism 27; rebel tour of South Africa (Cavaliers) 12; use of Islands players 89; women's team 247, 251–5, 256–7
New Zealand (country) 232, 239; British Lions tours of 229–31, 233–4; England tour of (1998) 133–5, 239–41; websites controversies 226–8
New Zealand rugby league 277, 279, 280
New Zealand Rugby Union 252–3
Newcastle Falcons (formerly Newcastle Gosforth) 35, 41, 86–7, 118, 172, 174–8, 180, 287–8
Newport (town) 103, 108, 141, 180–1, 276
Newport rugby club 4, 23, 85, 87–8, 111, 153, 174, 180–4
News Corporation 26–7, 203, 271
News International 133, 203, 268, 271–3, 283–4
Nicol, Andy 150
Nicolich, Alejandro 305
Nkumane, Owen 223
North-west Leopards 165
Northampton Saints 86, 120, 160, 171, 172, 174, 286, 288–9
Ntamack, Emile 91

Oberholzer, Rian 165, 223
O'Brien, Paddy 23–5
Observer 211
O'Connor, Michael 27
O'Cuinneagain, Dion 101–2
O'Driscoll, Brian 215
Offiah, Martin 276, 280
Old Christians Rugby Club, Montevideo 301–6
Oliver, Anton 82, 292
O'Neill, John 72, 131, 132, 237, 285
Ormaechea, Diego 80–2
Orrell 20
Orsini, Candy 249
Osborne, Glen 88

Packer, Kerry 27
Palmer, Farah 251
Paoletti, Tino 218
Paraguay (Yacares) 80
Paramore, Junior 53, 287
Paris: 1995 professionalism decision 16, 26–7,

34–41, 43, 219; Parc des Princes 199, 221, 222; rugby league club 273–4; Stade de France 120, 222
Pask, Phil 155, 286
Paul, Henry 280, 284
Paul, Robbie 280, 284
Paulse, Breyton 125, 128, 222–3, 224–5
Peard, Les 292
Pelous, Fabien 124, 216
Perelini, Apollo 265, 284, 287
Perez, Marcelo 304
Perón, Juan 43
Perry, Matt 301
Pichot, Agustin 50, 53–6, 58, 59, 102, 176, 291
Pickering, David 48, 109
Pienaar, François 62, 214
Planet Rugby 225–8, 244
political correctness 95
Pontypool 186, 202
Portugal 81
Potchefstroom, South Africa 242–4
Pountney, Budge 120, 151
Price, Colin 154
Prisoner (TV series) 156
Private Eye 133, 151, 152
Professional Rugby Players' Association 288
professionalism 290–4; benefits and drawbacks 19–25; Paris decision (1995) 16, 26–7, 34–41, 43, 219; *see also* amateurism
Pugh, Vernon 16, 62, 64–5, 68–70, 72, 105, 131–2, 175, 188, 251, 297
Pumas *see* Argentina

Quesada, Gonzalo 47, 52–3, 58, 59, 101
Quin, John 261
Quinnell, Craig 48, 109, 118, 176
Quinnell, Scott 48, 109, 113, 114, 118, 176, 260

Racing Club 221
RAF 259–61
Raiwalui, Simon 92, 181
Randell, Taine 89, 124, 125, 291
Raper, Stuart 283
Reddin, Dave 155, 158
Redruth 73, 234
Rees, Gareth 92–3
referees 100, 117, 162, 295–6; rugby league 266
Regan, Mark 166
Reggiardo, Mauricio 47, 50, 53, 58, 59, 102, 112
replacement system 208–10
RFU *see* Rugby Football Union
Richards, Dean 162
Richards, Rex 185
Richardson, Shane 274, 275
Richmond 35, 40, 173–80
Ringer, Paul 111–13
Ripley, Andy 291
Robinson, Andy 154–5, 158–9, 164–5, 169–70, 242
Robinson, Jason 283, 284
Robinson, Melodie 252, 253
Robson, Samantha 249
Rodber, Tim 138, 160, 261, 286, 288
Roff, Joe 115
Rogers, Budge 156
Rogers, Dave 157
Rogers, Peter 47, 50, 110, 111, 113, 181
Romania 84, 97–9